TRANSITIONAL JUSTICE IN POST-COMMUNIST ROMANIA

A close examination of an understudied European Union member state such as Romania reveals that since 1989, post-communist state and non-state actors have adopted a wide range of methods, processes, and practices of working through the communist past. Both the timing and the sequencing of these transitional justice methods prove to be significant in determining the efficacy of addressing and redressing the crimes of 1945–1989. In addition, there is evidence that some of these methods have directly facilitated the democratization process, while the absence of other methods has undermined the rule of law. This is the first volume to overview the complex Romanian transitional justice effort by accessing secret archives and investigating court trials of former communist perpetrators, lustration, compensation and rehabilitation, property restitution, the truth commission, the rewriting of history books, and unofficial truth projects. It details the political negotiations that have led to the adoption of relevant legislation and assesses these processes in terms of their timing, sequencing, and impact on democratization.

Lavinia Stan is an Associate Professor of Political Science at St. Francis Xavier University, Canada. She is a regional editor for Europe for the peer-reviewed *Women's Studies International Forum* and a member of the Scientific Council of the Institute for the Investigation of Communist Crimes and the Memory of Romanian Exile, the Social Science Adjudicating Commission of the Romanian Ministry of Education, and the editorial boards of eleven scholarly journals in North America and Europe. Her books include *Church, State, and Democracy in Expanding Europe* and *Religion and Politics in Post-Communist Romania* (both coauthored with Lucian Turcescu); *Transitional Justice in Eastern Europe and the Former Soviet Union: Reckoning with the Communist Past; 1989–2009: Incredibila aventura a democratiei dupa comunism* (coedited with Lucian Turcescu); *Leaders and Laggards: Governance, Civicness and Ethnicity in Post-Communist Romania*; *Romania in Transition*; and *Encyclopedia of Transitional Justice* (coedited with Nadya Nedelsky).

Transitional Justice in Post-Communist Romania

THE POLITICS OF MEMORY

LAVINIA STAN
St. Francis Xavier University

CAMBRIDGE
UNIVERSITY PRESS

CAMBRIDGE UNIVERSITY PRESS
Cambridge, New York, Melbourne, Madrid, Cape Town,
Singapore, São Paulo, Delhi, Mexico City

Cambridge University Press
32 Avenue of the Americas, New York, NY 10013-2473, USA

www.cambridge.org
Information on this title: www.cambridge.org/9781107020535

First published 2013

Printed in the United States of America

A catalog record for this publication is available from the British Library.

Library of Congress Cataloging in Publication data
Stan, Lavinia.
Transitional justice in post-communist Romania : the politics of memory / Lavinia Stan.
p. cm.
Includes bibliographical references and index.
ISBN 978-1-107-02053-5 (hardback)
1. Transitional justice – Romania. 2. Law reform – Romania. 3. Justice, Administration of – Romania. I. Title.
KKR471.S73 2012
949.803–dc23 2012023655

ISBN 978-1-107-02053-5 Hardback

To my family

Contents

Foreword

Mark Kramer
Harvard University

Coming to terms with mass atrocities is a difficult task for any country. Even now, nearly 150 years after the American Civil War ended, the United States has not made a full reckoning with the abomination of slavery and the century of violent racial segregation that followed. In countries that were ruled by repressive dictatorships in recent decades, notably the communist regimes of Central and Eastern Europe and the former Soviet Union, the process of reckoning with the past has been slow and erratic. A few of these countries have done essentially nothing to account for past crimes; most of the others have made at least a nominal effort; but not a single one has come fully to grips with questions of individual and collective responsibility and complicity.

This new book by Lavinia Stan illuminates why the process of facing up to the communist past has been so difficult in Romania, a country that was subjected to extreme tyranny during the Stalinist era (1944–1953) and that remained under dictatorial rule throughout the communist period, even after the worst of the Stalinist abuses were over.[1] Although Nicolae Ceauşescu briefly pursued a course of relative liberalization after he came to power in 1965, he soon abandoned it and plunged the country back under increasingly harsh rule.[2] Ceauşescu's nearly quarter-century as First Secretary of the Romanian Communist Party (RCP) came to an ignominious end in 1989 when he and his wife were forced to flee Bucharest on December 22 amid widening popular unrest and violent instability. The two of them were quickly captured in Târgovişte and then executed by firing squad on Christmas Day after a perfunctory trial.

[1] For an overview of the Stalinist period in Romania and the early years after, see Dennis Deletant, *Communist Terror in Romania: Gheorghiu-Dej and the Police State, 1948–1965* (New York: St. Martin's Press, 2000).

[2] Vladimir Tismaneanu, *Stalinism for All Seasons: A Political History of Romanian Communism* (Berkeley: University of California Press, 2003), ch. 7. See also Dennis Deletant, *Romania under Communist Rule*, rev. ed. (Bucharest: Centrul de Studii Româneşti, 1999), pp. 114–172.

The violent upheavals that led to the Ceauşescus' downfall resulted in extensive bloodshed, but the large majority of casualties in Romania in December 1989 and early January 1990 – a total of more than 1,100 deaths and 3,350 injuries – occurred *after* Ceauşescu and his wife had fled and were no longer in a position to control any of the forces engaging in armed clashes.[3] Precisely who ordered the use of deadly force on such a massive scale has never been clarified.

Lavinia Stan is an ideal person to undertake a comprehensive assessment of the official and unofficial efforts in post-1989 Romania to come to grips with the crimes and abuses of the communist era. Not only has she published several excellent books about political and social changes in Romania since 1989; she has also been at the cutting edge of scholarship exploring the conceptual and practical dimensions of transitional justice (the diverse set of measures intended to achieve redress for egregious human rights abuses) in the former communist world. Stan's in-depth research on this topic led to the publication in 2009 of *Transitional Justice in Eastern Europe and the Former Soviet Union: Reckoning with the Communist Past* (of which she was editor and chief author) and will also be the basis for the forthcoming publication by Cambridge University Press of the *Encyclopedia of Transitional Justice*, a landmark three-volume compendium that Stan coedited with Nadya Nedelsky. In these groundbreaking studies, Stan combines social science methods with extensive fieldwork to address questions that not only are of great scholarly importance but also affect the everyday lives of people residing in the former communist states. The combination of methodological rigor with empirical richness makes Stan's work on transitional justice in former Warsaw Pact countries, especially Romania, stand out.

In the current book, Stan brings together her major areas of expertise – the political and social dynamics of post-1989 Romania, and the theoretical and empirical aspects of transitional justice in former authoritarian states – to produce a splendid analysis of the challenges of transitional justice in a country that has only sporadically shed its authoritarian past. After Ceauşescu's ouster at the end of 1989, many observers both inside and outside Romania were hopeful that democratization would take hold in Romania and that the country might, for the first time in its history, have a chance of moving toward Western standards of openness, accountability, and democratic governance. Despite the damage inflicted by some forty-five years of communist rule, the idea was that, with the Ceauşescus finally gone, Romanian pro-democracy activists and nongovernmental organizations (NGOs) would grow in numbers and influence. In due course, they would gain sufficient strength to pull Romania firmly away from its dictatorial past.

3 Peter Siani-Davies, *The Romanian Revolution of 1989* (Ithaca, NY: Cornell University Press, 2007), pp. 97–143.

Some individuals and groups in Romania did seek to promote liberal democracy after 1989, but the basic obstacle they confronted was that the political leaders who removed Ceauşescu and who gained control of Romania's polity were former high-ranking communist officials, most of whom had worked loyally under the Ceauşescu regime. The new leader of the country, Ion Iliescu, had been one of Ceauşescu's closest aides until the early 1970s, when the two men had a falling-out. Iliescu thereafter was gradually deprived of his posts in the RCP's ruling organs and was assigned to relatively obscure ministerial posts. As the head of the ruling National Salvation Front (Frontul Salvării Naţionale, or FSN) that took over in the wake of Ceauşescu's departure, Iliescu pledged to reform Romania's communist system, but not to dismantle it.[4] He and other leading FSN officials called for the near-term adoption of "original democracy" in Romania that would keep most of the basic elements of the communist system in place.

Subsequently, after consolidating his power via the FSN in the May 1990 parliamentary elections, Iliescu formed his own National Salvation Democratic Front, which he later renamed the Party of Social Democracy and then the Social Democratic Party. In keeping with practices of the communist era, Iliescu used thuggish, extralegal violence in June 1990 to bolster his power in the face of popular unrest, and he continued to rely on unaccountable security organs to silence and intimidate opponents. Iliescu gained easy reelection as president in late 1992, enabling him to extend his domination of Romania's polity, including its treatment of the past. Hopes of meaningful democratization were stymied during the seven years that Romania languished under his rule in the 1990s.[5] After he lost his bid for a third presidential term in November 1996, Romania did make significant progress toward greater openness and accountability under Emil Constantinescu, but renewed political turmoil facilitated Iliescu's return to power in the December 2000 presidential election, giving him another four-year term. Romania managed to gain admission into the North Atlantic Treaty Organization (NATO) in 2002–2004, even though NATO officials were well aware of Iliescu's unsavory past. In 2007, a few years after Iliescu left office for good, Romania was granted entry into the European Union (EU).

Nevertheless, despite having gained membership in both NATO and the EU, Romania (along with Bulgaria) remained an outlier in the former Soviet bloc, a

4 For useful background information on Iliescu, see the lengthy two-part U.S. embassy cable, "Romanian President Ion Iliescu – A Political Biography," No. 006434, 23 June 1995, classified Secret, posted on numerous Web sites through Wikileaks.

5 Steven D. Roper, *Romania: The Unfinished Revolution* (Amsterdam: Harwood Academic Publishers, 2000), pp. 65–86. See also Frank Sellin, "Democratization in the Shadows: Post-Communist Patrimonialism," in Henry F. Carey, ed., *Romania Since 1989: Politics, Economics, and Society* (Lanham, MD: Lexington Books, 2004), esp. pp. 120–125.

country plagued by the lingering residue of the communist era. In these circumstances, attempts by the Romanian government to make a reckoning with the crimes of the communist regime were mostly stillborn, especially during Iliescu's presidency in the 1990s. Prominent holdovers from the Ceauşescu era, who were present at all levels of the political, judicial, and security structures, had no interest in embarking on a thorough, no-holds-barred investigation of past misdeeds or in pursuing redress and justice for victims of the communist regime. Nor were the authorities inclined to disclose the identities of Securitate officers or the names of the hundreds of thousands of informants (*informatori*) and collaborators (*colaboratori*) who secretly aided the Securitate's repressive apparatus. To the extent that the Romanian government took any punitive action against those responsible for communist-era atrocities, this was done mostly as a way of settling political scores or deflecting pressure "from below" (i.e., from NGOs and activists) for far more sweeping action. Much the same was true about attempts to provide compensation to some of the victims of communist repression. Such measures had to be pushed forward by activists outside the government, often over the objections of senior officials, members of parliament, and judges.

In a series of fascinating thematic chapters, Stan explores every dimension of transitional justice in post-Ceauşescu Romania – judicial and nonjudicial, official and unofficial, local and countrywide, national and international. She shows that in one or two areas, notably the removal of symbols of the communist regime (e.g., the ubiquitous portraits of Ceauşescu, the statues of leading communist figures, sundry objects adorned with the hammer-and-sickle or with the RCP's insignia and flags) and the renaming of streets, bridges, and buildings, the Romanian government did act relatively swiftly to make a break with the past. But in almost all other areas, such as the proposed overhaul of the state security sector, the rewriting of history books for public schools, the establishment of a truth and reconciliation commission, the construction of new public symbols (including statues, memorials, and museums dedicated to the victims of communism), lustration, the initiation of judicial proceedings against the worst perpetrators of abuses and in support of victims, and the granting of access to secret police files, the Romanian authorities either were very slow to act or declined to do anything at all. Even when they did act, the steps they took rarely had much lasting effect. The impact was negligible in many cases because the resources allocated for the specific activities were too meager; in other cases the proclaimed measures were never actually put into effect. Programs initiated by NGOs and other groups outside the government made up part of the gap, but some of these programs (e.g., an unofficial trial of the RCP, the scattered naming of Securitate officers) had very little impact and were never sufficient to make up for the woeful lag in transitional justice in the first half of the 1990s.

Moreover, as Stan shows, the task was complicated because Romania after 1989 had three distinct periods for which transitional justice was needed: (1) the wartime years (1940–1944) when Romania was ruled by a brutal, pro-Nazi regime; (2) the period from 1944 to 1989 when Romania was ruled by a communist dictatorship; and (3) the revolution and bloodshed of December 1989. For various reasons the third period commanded highest priority for the Romanian authorities, many of whom stood to benefit personally from their participation (real or otherwise) on the side of the revolution. Because the violence was clearly etched in people's memories, and because the victims were active in seeking redress, the 1989 revolution tended to dominate the agenda for official transitional justice programs (especially during Iliescu's initial two terms), often at the expense of attempts to remedy injustices that occurred during the earlier periods.

Stan's wide-ranging survey of the different elements of transitional justice in Romania underscores the large number of actors who have been involved. Political leaders, bureaucrats, legislators, and judges have been supplemented (and often outdone) by NGOs, victims' groups, religious denominations, and international organizations such as the EU, NATO, the European Council, and the European Court of Human Rights. The presidential truth commission that was set up in 2006 under Vladimir Tismaneanu played an important and salutary role in the process, compiling a detailed report about the atrocities perpetrated by the communist regime.[6] The impact of the report may have been ephemeral, but it amassed evidence that could not easily be glossed over. Institutes that were established to investigate communist crimes and to study the Romanian exile (the institutes were merged in 2009–2010) also were centrally involved in transitional justice efforts, including exhumations and forensic investigations as well as historical research.[7]

Stan captures these diverse efforts in all their complexity and detail without losing sight of the larger picture. Although the book focuses on transitional justice in Romania, it offers illuminating comparisons with experiences elsewhere. The book

6 *Comisia Prezidenţială pentru Analiza Dictaturii Comuniste din România: Raport Final*, Bucharest, 2006. On the report and its impact, see, in addition to Stan's discussion here, Charles King, "Remembering Romanian Communism," *Slavic Review*, Vol. 66, No. 4 (Winter 2007), pp. 718–723; Vladimir Tismaneanu, "Confronting Romania's Communist Past: A Response to Charles King," *Slavic Review*, Vol. 66, No. 4 (Winter 2007), pp. 724–727; Cosmina Tanasoiu, "The Tismaneanu Report: Romania Revisits Its Past," *Problems of Post-Communism*, Vol. 54, No. 4 (July–August 2007), pp. 60–69; and Alina Hogea, "Coming to Terms with the Communist Past in Romania: An Analysis of the Political and Media Discourse Concerning the Tismăneanu Report," *Studies of Transition States and Societies*, Vol. 2, No. 1 (June 2010), pp. 16–30.

7 Stan and I served on the academic advisory board of the unified Institute for the Investigation of Communist Crimes and Memory of the Romanian Exile from 2010 to 2012. Both she and I stepped down from the board in mid-2012 after the change of government in Romania led to political interference in the institute's complexion and work.

allows readers to ponder key questions about the reciprocal connection between democratization and transitional justice and the means by which former authoritarian countries can remedy past abuses and overcome the baleful legacy they have inherited. Stan's discussion of fundamental issues, including whether democratization is likely to facilitate transitional justice (and vice versa), whether some methods of transitional justice are more conducive than others to democratization, and whether some instruments of transitional justice may actually stymie democratization, will be of broad interest to political scientists in several fields: comparative politics, political theory, and international relations.

A sizable literature has emerged over the past two decades about specific elements of transitional justice in Romania and other former communist countries, but Stan's book is the first attempt to bring these far-flung strands together into a coherent whole. It is an ambitious task, but Stan passes with flying colors. She has produced a comprehensive, in-depth analysis of the obstacles, tribulations, setbacks, and occasional successes in the pursuit of transitional justice in Romania. Her book is a model for all future studies of transitional justice in Eastern Europe and elsewhere.

Acknowledgments

I have studied the transitional justice methods discussed in this book for more than a decade, ever since a chance re-encounter with Nadya Nedelsky convinced me that the "politics of the past" was worthy of close examination. A grant from the Social Sciences and Humanities Research Council of Canada helped me study transitional justice in Romania, and Eastern Europe more generally, and ponder over the theoretical and empirical questions raised in this book. The generosity of the Council, which also funded my work on religion and politics, facilitated yearly field trips to Eastern Europe, participation in international conferences, and frequent meetings with colleagues from other universities, research institutes, and civil society organizations working on similar topics.

Over the years, a number of close friends and collaborators have assisted me in bringing this project to completion. Nadya Nedelsky of Macalester College has supported me in this and other projects, with patience, many good words, and timely expert advice. Helga Welsh agreed to share her unpublished work with me and guide me through important lines of inquiry and literature that I might have otherwise overlooked. Eva-Clarita Onken Pettai of the University of Tartu, Estonia, clarified the differences separating truth commissions from historical commissions in terms of their organization, membership, and transitional justice role. Laurence Whitehead of Oxford University; Elazar Barkan, John Micgiel, and David L. Phillips of Columbia University; A. James McAdams of the University of Notre Dame; Tom Gallagher of the University of Bradford; Vladimir Tismaneanu of the University of Maryland at College Park; Vesselin Popovski of the United Nations University in Tokyo; Joan DeBardeleben of Carleton University; Louis Bickford of the International Center for Transitional Justice in New York; Dennis Deletant of University College of London; Gary Bruce of the University of Waterloo; Roman David of Newcastle University; Peter Solomon and Alexei Trochev of the University of Toronto; Klaus Bachmann of the University of Wroclaw; Monica Ciobanu of the State University of New York at Plattsburgh; F. Peter Wagner of the University of

Wisconsin at Whitewater; and some of my colleagues at St. Francis Xavier University have all raised questions or provided suggestions on various book chapters, articles, or reports that I wrote on Romania's efforts to work through its communist past. Carlos Closa Montero coordinated the monumental project on "How the memory of crimes committed by totalitarian regimes is dealt with in the member states," commissioned by the Direction D: Fundamental Rights and Citizenship of the Directorate-General for Justice, Freedom and Security of the European Commission in 2009, and then organized a wonderful conference in Spain in 2010. My participation in that project spearheaded the present volume, whose publication owes much to the generosity, patience, and support of John Berger, my editor at Cambridge University Press. My copy editor, Susan Kauffman of PETT Fox, Inc., was instrumental in revisiting the volume's accuracy and improving its quality, as was Bindu Vinod. The students in my classes on transitional justice and intelligence services at both Concordia University and St. Francis Xavier University, especially Philip Jones, Thomas Lattimer, Alyssa MacDonald, Maureen McEwan, Justin Rafton, and Ross Watt, have challenged me to explain more fully the need to reckon with the recent past during transitions to democracy.

In Romania, Florin Abraham, Gabriel Bădescu, Romulus Brâncoveanu, Cosmin Budeanca, Gabriel Catalan, Bogdan and Cristina Cazacu, Adrian Cioflâncă, Bogdan Din, Sabin Drăgulin, Constantin Ticu Dumitrescu, George Dobrescu, John Gledhill, Ema Grama, Alexandru Gussi, Bogdan Iacob, Gabriel Marin, Mihaela Miroiu, Silviu Moldovan, Iulia Motoc, Daniel Neacşu, Viorel Neamţu, Stejărel Olaru, Damiana Oţoiu, Mircea Stănescu, Justina Sora and Iulian Tudorică, Ioan Stanomir, Raluca Ursachi, Diane Vancea, Adellaine Voicu, Larry Watts, Rodica Milena Zaharia, and Răzvan Zaharia have assisted me in obtaining valuable data or simply navigating my visits to that country. Claudiu Secăreş, Margareta Drăghici, and Dragoş Petrescu from the National Council for the Study of Securitate Archives released data I used in Chapters 3 and 4. Carmen Lascu, a lawyer with the Constanta Bar Association, generously agreed to explain the pluses and minuses of the legislation on compensation and rehabilitation, reading several drafts of Chapter 7. Gabriel, Daniela, and Liviu Andreescu have been a constant support, sharing their opinions with me and helping me gain access to valuable publications. Levente Salat patiently assisted me in rewriting key sections of Chapter 1. Raluca Grosescu, Bogdan Murgescu, and his wife, historian Luminiţa Mirela Murgescu, have been instrumental in bringing Chapter 8 to completion. In his apartment in Paris, close to a decade ago, writer Paul Goma agreed to show me photographs from Lăteşti and to talk about his experience in Romanian communist prisons. In London, longtime friends Mura and Gautam Ghosh showed us the wonderful book collections housed with the University of London library.

Above all, my family has provided me with invaluable endorsement in everything I ever attempted. This book was no exception. I thank my husband, Lucian Turcescu, for keeping an eye on relevant news, reading the manuscript with a critical eye, and standing by me for close to thirty years, especially the months during which the Securitate decided to make me their target. Our work on the property restitution conflict that has divided the Romanian Orthodox Church and the Greek Catholic Church is reflected in Chapter 6, while that on the collaboration of priests with the Securitate informs Chapters 3 and 4. Our son, Luc, and my mother, Sabina, a former scientist, have always enthusiastically supported all my efforts and ambitions. My thanks to all, especially to Mark Kramer of Harvard University, for taking the time to write the foreword to the present volume.

Romanian Institutions, Initiatives, and Names

Appeal for Romania (Apelul pentru România)
Association 21 December 1989 (Asociaţia 21 Decembrie 1989)
Association for Private Property (Asociaţia pentru Proprietate Privată)
Association of Former Political Prisoners and Anticommunist Fighters (Asociaţia Foştilor Deţinuţi Politici şi Luptători Anticomunişti)
Association of Former Political Prisoners in Romania (Asociaţia Foştilor Deţinuţi Politici din România)
Association of Owners Abusively Deprived of Their Property, Former Deportees and Refugees (Asociaţia Persoanelor Deposedate Abuziv, Foştilor Deportaţi Refugiaţi din România)
Association of Owners of Property Abusively Confiscated by the State (Asociaţia Proprietarilor Deposedaţi Abuziv de Stat)
Association of Publishers in Romania (Asociaţia Editorilor din România)
Association of Tenants Living in Nationalized Dwellings (Asociaţia Chiriaşilor din Casele Naţionalizate)
Association of Tenants Who Acquired Ownership through Law 112/1995 (Asociaţia Proprietarilor pe Legea 112/1995)
Association of Victims of Magistrates (Asociaţia Victimelor Magistraţilor din România)
Association of Victims of the Bolshevik Communist System and Its Legacy (Asociaţia Victimelor Sistemului Comunist Bolşevic şi a Sechelelor Sale)
Braila Big Island (Insula Mare a Brăilei)
Bus Trial (Procesul Autobuzul)
Carol Foundation (Fundaţia Carol)
Civic Academy (Academia Civică)
Civic Alliance (Alianţa Civică)
Coalition for a Clean Government (Coaliţia pentru un Guvern Curat)
Coalition for a Clean Parliament (Coaliţia pentru un Parlament Curat)

Coalition for Clean Universities (Coaliţia pentru Universităţi Curate)
Community of Legitimate Owners and Descendants in Romania (Comunitatea Moştenitorilor şi Proprietarilor Legitimi din România)
Conservative Party (Partidul Conservator)
Contract with Romania (Contractul cu România)
December 1989 Commission (Comisia Decembrie 1989)
Declaration for National Reconciliation (Declaraţia de Reconciliere Naţională)
Declaration for Romania (Proclamaţia pentru România)
Democratic Convention of Romania (Convenţia Democrată din România)
Democratic Party (Partidul Democrat)
Domestic Red (Roşu domestic)
External Information Service (Serviciul Extern de Informaţii)
Fagarasi Fortress (Cetatea Făgăraş)
Free Press House (Casa Presei Libere)
French Association for Defending Property Rights in Romania (Asociaţia Franceză pentru Apărarea Drepturilor de Proprietate în România)
Gheorghe Ursu Foundation (Fundaţia Gheorghe Ursu)
Greater Romania Party (Partidul România Mare)
Group for Social Dialogue (Grupul pentru Dialog Social)
House of the People (Casa Poporului)
Institute for Military History (Institutul de Istorie Militară)
Institute for Research in Pedagogy and Psychology (Institutul de Cercetări Pedagogice şi Psihologice)
Institute for the Investigation of Communist Crimes and the Memory of Romanian Exile (Institutul de Investigare a Crimelor Comuniste şi Memoriei Exilului Românesc)
Institute for the Investigation of Communist Crimes in Romania (Institutul de Investigare a Crimelor Comunismului în România)
International Centre for the Study of Communism (Centrul Internaţional de Studii asupra Comunismului)
International Commission on the Holocaust in Romania (Comisia Internaţională pentru Studierea Holocaustului în România)
Ion Gavrila Ogoranu Foundation (Fundaţia Ion Gavrilă Ogoranu)
Justice and Truth Alliance (Alianţa Dreptate şi Adevăr)
Memorial Museum of Anticommunist Resistance Fagarasi (Muzeul Memorial Rezistenţa Anticomunistă Făgăraşi)
Memorial of Victims of Communism and of the Resistance (Memorialul Victimelor Comunismului şi al Rezistenţei)
Miners' Street (Strada Minerilor)

Motherland and Honor Solidarity Foundation (Fundaţia Solidaritatea Patrie şi Onoare)
National Anticorruption Department (Departamentul National Anticorupţie)
National Archives of Romania (Arhivele Naţionale ale României)
National Council for Textbook Approval (Consiliului Naţional pentru Aprobarea Manualelor)
National Council for the Study of Securitate Archives (Consiliul Naţional pentru Studiul Arhivelor Securităţii)
National Salvation Front (Frontul Salvării Naţionale)
Negru Voda Cultural Foundation (Fundaţia Culturală Negru Vodă)
Ombudsman (Avocatul Poporului)
Party of Social Democracy (Partidul Social Democrat)
Peasants' Street (Strada Agricultorilor)
Presidential Advisory Commission for the Analysis of the Communist Dictatorship in Romania (Comisia Prezidenţială Consultativă pentru Analiza Dictaturii Comuniste din România)
Presidential Commission for Analysis and Policy-Making in Education and Research in Romania (Comisia Prezidenţială pentru Analiza şi Elaborarea Politicilor din Domeniile Educaţiei şi Cercetării din România)
Presidential Commission for Analysis and Policy-Making in Health Care in Romania (Comisia Prezidenţială pentru Analiza şi Elaborarea Politicilor din Domeniul Sănătăţii Publice din România)
Presidential Commission for the Analysis of the Communist Dictatorship in Romania (Comisia Prezidenţială pentru Analiza Dictaturii Comuniste în România)
Presidential Commission for the Analysis of the Romanian Political and Constitutional Regime (Comisia Prezidenţială de Analiză a Regimului Politic şi Constituţional din România)
Property Fund (Fondul Proprietatea)
Red Flag (Steagul Roşu) factory
Restitution in Romania (Interessenvertretung Restitution in Rumanien)
Revolution Square (Piaţa Revoluţiei)
Romanian Academic Society (Societatea Academică Română)
Romanian Communist Party (Partidul Comunist Român)
Romanian Information Service (Serviciul Român de Informaţii)
Royal Palace (Palatul Regal)
Social Democrat Party (Partidul Social Democrat)
State Secretary for Religious Affairs (Secretariatul de Stat pentru Culte)
The Plague (Plaga)
The Spark (*Scînteia*)

Timisoara Society (Societatea Timişoara)
Union of War Veterans of Cluj (Uniunea Veteranilor de Război Cluj)
University Library (Biblioteca Universitară)
Victory of Socialism Boulevard (Victoria Socialismului)
Work Street (Strada Muncii)
Worker's Street (Strada Muncitorului)

1

Introduction: Memory, Democracy, and Justice in Post-Communism

Transitional justice has attracted increased attention since the term was first used during the 1970s to describe state and society efforts to come to terms with past human rights abuses. After the collapse of the communist regimes in 1989, Eastern Europe joined the growing number of regions interested in reckoning with their recent dictatorial past in judicial and nonjudicial ways, adopting methods tested in other corners of the world (such as court trials, reforms of the state security sector, the rewriting of history books, and the construction of new public symbols, including statues and memorials) and expanding the repertoire of solutions by devising new methods (most importantly, lustration, the governmental ban on communist decision makers from holding positions of power and responsibility in the new democracy, and access for ordinary citizens to the secret files compiled on them by the political police). When it comes to Eastern Europe, specific transitional justice methods (lustration and court proceedings), countries (especially Germany, Poland, Hungary, and the Czech and Slovak Republics, which have engaged in more sustained efforts to reckon with the past), and themes (e.g., the reasons why some post-dictatorial governments opted for "forgiving and forgetting," whereas others "prosecuted and punished") have been closely examined.[1] This fine literature serves as a good starting point for any research on transitional justice in the

1 For example, the Transitional Justice Data Base, which lists English-language references, includes fourteen titles for Czechoslovakia, eleven for Hungary, and twelve for Poland, but only five for Romania, one on Albania, and one for Bulgaria. Fourteen of these titles deal with lustration. The International Internet Bibliography on Transitional Justice, which mentions both English and German sources, lists nineteen titles for the Czech Republic, eighteen for Poland, nine for Hungary, and three for Bulgaria. It includes no references for Albania, Romania, and Slovakia. Although incomplete, these databases illustrate the quantitative, if not qualitative, disparity within the literature. See *Transitional Justice Data Base*, available at: https://sites.google.com/site/transitionaljusticedatabase/transitional-justice-bibliography/europe-and-the-former-soviet-union (accessed on 24 August 2011), and Gunnar Theissen, *International Internet Bibliography on Transitional Justice* (27 January 2000), available at: http://userpage.fu-berlin.de/theissen/biblio/ (accessed on 24 August 2011).

region. Nevertheless, additional important theoretically driven questions remain unanswered.

These questions can be divided into two distinct sets. The first relates to the relationship between transitional justice and post-communist democratization, especially in countries where the process has paralleled European Union (EU) accession, as was the case in Central and Eastern Europe. Do transitional justice projects impede or promote post-totalitarian democratization? Do some transitional justice methods contribute to trust, the rule of law, and the break with the dictatorial past more than others? Did EU accession help or stifle the politics of memory in post-communist times? Does accession explain why transitional justice unexpectedly took center stage a decade after the region underwent a radical regime change? Does late reckoning with the past signal democratic consolidation or democratic malaise? As Ruti Teitel contended, punishment of former perpetrators is often justified as a democratic requirement, because trials provide victims with legal redress, unveil the truth about the past, may reconcile victims and victimizers, and restore trust in the judiciary.[2] Transitional justice can facilitate democracy, but the effects are delayed, appearing only a decade after the regime change takes place.[3] The dominant assumption is that trust – a core democratic feature – is positively correlated to transitional justice, as Eastern European and Baltic countries that addressed the past became democratic sooner than former Soviet republics that chose to forgive and forget communist human rights abuses. Nevertheless, lustration breeds distrust in new democracies on the part of those affected by it and truth commissions seem inimical to democracy because of their inability to bring perpetrators to justice, while the relationship of other transitional justice methods with trust remains theoretically and empirically contentious.[4] The EU has played a minor role in redressing the communist past by allocating small funds to education and memorialization projects, but the aid has remained modest, coming through only fifteen years after the region took its first steps toward revisiting the past.[5]

The second set of questions relates to the sequencing, nature, and goals of transitional justice programs. Does the order in which transitional justice methods are enacted matter in any way? Does the adoption of some methods (e.g., access to secret files) facilitate or preclude the use of others (such as truth commissions)? Do

[2] Ruti Teitel, *Transitional Justice* (Oxford: Oxford University Press, 2001), 148–149.

[3] Tricia Olsen, Leigh Payne and Andrew Reiter, *Transitional Justice in Balance. Comparing Processes, Weighting Efficacy* (Washington, DC: United States Institute of Peace Press, 2010), 146.

[4] Idem. Also Cynthia Horne and Margaret Levi, *Does Lustration Promote Trustworthy Governance? An Exploration of the Experience of Central and Eastern Europe* (January 2003), available at: http://www.colbud.hu/honesty-trust/horne/LeviHorne.doc (accessed on 18 August 2011).

[5] John Gledhill, "Integrating the Past: Regional Integration and Historical Reckoning in Central and Eastern Europe," *Nationalities Papers*, 39(2011): 481–506.

specific judicial and nonjudicial methods complement or undermine each other? Is there a temporal "window of opportunity" beyond which efforts to work through the past are rendered severely crippled or meaningless for victims and societies at large? In which ways have competing pasts shaped transitional justice programs after 1989? Why have these programs emphasized truth and justice far more than reconciliation? Why does radical lustration remain unpopular in countries that need it the most? Why has a key transitional justice method such as the truth commission been generally overlooked in Eastern Europe, and why have commissions in that part of the world been mostly academic in nature, emphasizing truth but almost never reconciliation? Comparative multi-country analyses suggest that trials, truth commissions, amnesties, lustration, and reparations are implemented, on average, within the first six years after the regime change.[6] The finding supports Helga Welsh's "window of opportunity" thesis, which argues that transitional justice can be pursued successfully only immediately after the regime change,[7] but many post-communist countries have implemented transitional justice well beyond this limited time frame. Indeed, the Romanian truth commission was created in 2006, in Central Europe and the Baltic states trials of Soviet perpetrators have extended well into the 2000s, and Poland, Romania, and Serbia enacted late lustration after 2003. There is some evidence that "transitional democracies sequence their mechanisms by adopting amnesties first, trials later, and restorative justice mechanisms many years after the transition,"[8] but the literature remains silent on whether the adoption of some methods precludes the enactment of others and whether facing competing pasts influences the speed, scope, and outcome of specific programs.

This volume seeks to answer some of these interrelated questions by looking closely at Romania, a purportedly marginal country that remains understudied, although it exemplifies the region's middle road of adopting a moderate transitional justice program – more sustained and substantive than in most former Soviet republics, but less so than in Central Europe. To some, the choice of a country study, rather than a multi-country comparison, unnecessarily privileges description over theory building, but I argue that this shortcoming is only superficial. Given the differences in the nature of the past regimes that need to be addressed, the type of regime change, the varying post-communist political and economic conditions, the adopted transitional justice methods, and the order in which they were implemented, few post-communist countries are truly comparable. A study accounting for all these differences in a handful of countries would go beyond a single volume,

6 Olsen et al., *Transitional Justice in Balance*, 107.

7 Helga Welsh, "Dealing with the Communist Past: Central and East European Experiences after 1990," *Europe-Asia Studies*, 48(1996): 413–428.

8 Olsen et al., *Transitional Justice in Balance*, 107.

whereas one including all or most countries of the region would gloss over important details, operate simplifications, or risk making mistakes in data collection and interpretation. A country study allows comparisons among social segments and local communities that reveal differences between victims, victimizers, and bystanders; contrasts in time that address the problem of sequencing; and rich contextualization that explains which state, non-state, domestic, and international actors have shaped the politics of memory and which specific memory projects have facilitated the rule of law, observance of human rights, and liberal democracy more generally. As a comparative politics specialist, I remain convinced that case studies represent key building blocks of theory development.

The volume is organized thematically, investigating each method separately as a facet of a larger, more ambitious program, instead of chronologically, as a narrative account of different actors, initiatives, policies, and outcomes. To help readers navigate the material, the volume includes a time line of transitional justice efforts (see Chapter 10, Table 10.1), but the analysis reconstructs, evaluates, and compares the different methods as distinct efforts designed to reckon with specific legacies of the recent past. The interactions, overlap, and synergy between various methods are duly recognized, and the methods are compared both among themselves and with similar programs enacted in other post-communist countries. Such a thematic approach necessarily relies on a selective reading of the numerous Romanian actors, factors, and events relevant for this volume's topic. As such, for reasons of space, some names and events of secondary importance are not mentioned here – a limitation this analysis duly acknowledges. Note that names, places, and events are invoked to construct and illustrate larger theoretical arguments, not to rank specific victims and victimizers or to recognize some as being more deserving or guiltier than others.

More importantly, this is a volume about post-communist efforts to reckon with the communist past, not one that delves in great detail into the pre-1989 human rights abuses that various transitional justice methods have tried to rectify. As such, the book is concerned with the political negotiations and state–civil society interactions centered on addressing and redressing the past, more than with establishing which communist actors were responsible for which crimes and human rights infringements against which specific victims at which particular moments in time. The book therefore should be read as a political science case study of post-communist policies and initiatives, not as a history of the communist institutions and the overwhelming array of military, bureaucratic, police, and secret police resources that successive communist leaders have pulled together to organize murder, engage in mass surveillance, or inflict injustice. True, the following paragraphs sketch in very broad strokes the human rights violations in need of redress, showing that the history of the Romanian communist regime amounted to another "tale of unrequited injustice,"[9] but readers are invited to supplement these presentations with information drawn from the growing literature on Romanian communism, which includes scholarly studies, memoirs of former victims, and books of interviews with former communist officials and Securitate agents.[10]

Finally, my theoretical perspective draws on transitional justice more than memory studies, and in doing so privileges the relationship between state and civil society actors and the responsibility of the post-communist state in overcoming the repressive past over the way in which individual, collective, or social memories have been reconstructed and reshaped since the collapse of communism. True, 1989 opened the "floodgates of memory" and resulted in a "cavalcade of stories of victimization" during communist times, as historian Maria Bucur reminded us, and it is important to record these truth-telling initiatives.[11] Equally true is that some memory scholars

9 I borrow this term from Janna Thompson, *Taking Responsibility for the Past. Reparation and Historical Justice* (Cambridge: Polity Press, 2002), vii.

10 For an official historical narrative, see Comisia Prezidenţială pentru Analiza Dictaturii Comuniste din România, *Raport Final*, (Bucharest, 2006), available at: http://www.presidency.ro/static/ordine/RAPORT_FINAL_CPADCR.pdf (accessed on 24 August 2011). Lavinia Betea has conducted personal interviews with former Communist Party leaders. See Lavinia Betea, *Maurer şi lumea de ieri. Mărturii despre stalinizarea României* (Arad: Editura Fundaţiei Ioan Slavici, 1995); Lavinia Betea, *Alexandru Bârlădeanu despre Dej, Ceauşescu şi Iliescu* (Bucharest: Evenimentul Românesc, 1997); Lavinia Betea, *Convorbiri neterminate. Corneliu Mănescu în dialog cu Lavinia Betea* (Iaşi: Polirom, 2001); and Lavinia Betea, *Poveşti din Cartierul Primăverii* (Bucharest: Curtea Veche, 2010). Major publishing houses like Humanitas, Polirom, and Curtea Veche have published victims' memoirs and scholarly analyses of communist repression, as explained in Doina Jela, "Gulagul şi Holocaustul în conştiinţa românească – perspectiva unui editor de carte," *Caietele Echinox*, 13(2007): 205–211. Victims wrote powerful testimonials of their prison experience: Corneliu Coposu, *Confessions* (Boulder: East European Monographs, 1998); Nicolae Corbeanu, *Vara transfugului* (Bucharest: Humanitas, 2002); Ioan Corpaş, *Secvenţe din fostele închisori politice* (Bucharest: Humanitas, 2003); Ion Diaconescu, *Temniţa, destinul generaţiei noastre* (Bucharest: Nemira, 2003); Ion Diaconescu, *După temniţă* (Bucharest: Nemira, 2003); Constantin C. Giurescu, *Five Years and Two Months in the Sighet Penitentiary (May 7, 1950-July 5, 1955)* (Boulder: East European Monographs, 1994); Ioan Ioanid, *Închisoarea noastră cea de toate zilele* (Bucharest: Humanitas, 1999), 3 volumes; Nicolae Mărgineanu, *Un psiholog în temniţele comuniste. Documente preluate din arhiva* CNSAS (Iasi: Polirom, 2006); E. Pătraşcu Buse, *Lumea pierdută* (Bucharest: Humanitas, 2003); Annie Samuelli, *Woman behind Bars in Romania* (London: Frank Cass, 1997); and Nicole Valery-Grossu, *Binecuvântată fii, închisoare* (Bucharest: Univers, 2002). Also Gheorghe Boldur-Lăţescu, *The Communist Genocide in Romania* (New York: Nova Science Publishers, 2005); Virgil Ierunca, *Fenomenul Piteşti* (Bucharest: Humanitas, 1990); Stelian Tănase, *Anatomia mistificării* (Bucharest: Humanitas, 2003); Ruxandra Cesereanu, ed., *Comunism şi represiune în România. Istoria tematică a unui fratricid naţional* (Iaşi: Polirom, 2006); Ruxandra Cesereanu, *Gulagul în conştiinţa românească. Memorialistica şi literatura închisorilor şi lagărelor comuniste* (Iaşi: Polirom, 2005); Marius Oprea, *Bastionul cruzimii. O istorie a Securităţii (1948–1964)* (Iaşi: Polirom, 2008); and Sharon Rushton, *No Easy Shore* (no place: Rushton Press, 2011). In addition, a number of authors have compiled volumes of historical documents collected from different archives.

11 Maria Bucur, *Heroes and Victims. Remembering War in Twentieth-Century Romania* (Bloomington: Indiana University Press, 2009), 223–224.

have noted that "memory matters politically" for attempts to legitimate current regimes[12] and that "the power of memory" is related to "the memory of power" in "contentions over interpretations of historical experiences between official history and social memory," "the appropriation of these interpretations for political action, critique and consent," and "the formation of political subjects through remembering and forgetting."[13] Nevertheless, memory studies limit the discussion in two important ways. First, *memory* relates directly to only a subset of the methods and practices that legal scholars and political scientists recognize as part of transitional justice – that is, to the so-called backward-looking, not the forward-looking, processes, to use Claus Offe's terminology.[14] Indeed, memory is tied to commemoration rituals that periodically re-actualize past events and underscore their importance for what Helga Welsh termed "the politics of the present," but not so much to lustration, which, through its capacity to cleanse the political elite of tainted elements, is related to the future as much as to the past.[15] Second, only some memories that the population at large employs, individually and collectively, to commemorate victims of state-perpetrated violence are echoed in political debates about guilt and moral responsibility. A catalog of memories, even complete and updated, might tell us little about state efforts to redress past human rights transgressions and the instrumentalization of that past by political actors, whereas transitional justice studies place these questions at the core of the analysis. Jeffrey Olick recognized the limitation of memory studies, which examine memory as individual and collective, social and political, mythic and oppositional, official and vernacular often without making clear distinctions among these terms, when he proposed an "integrated paradigm" to evaluate the impact of the social on what he pertinently called "collected," instead of "collective," memory.[16]

THE REPRESSIVE COMMUNIST PAST

The history of Romanian communism (1945–1989), as it emerges from the works published to date, echoes Eva Hoffman's prescient observation that Romania's most serious problem is "the shortage of a usable past," because the past has represented

[12] Jan-Werner Muller, "Introduction: The Power of Memory, the Memory of Power and the Power over Memory," in *Memory and Power in Post-War Europe*, ed. Jan-Werner Muller (Cambridge: Cambridge University Press, 2002), 1–35.

[13] Ching Kwan Lee and Guobin Yang, *Re-envisioning the Chinese Revolution: The Politics and Poetics of Collective Memories in Reform China* (Washington, DC: Woodrow Wilson Center Press, 2007).

[14] Claus Offe, *Varieties of Transition. The East European and East German Experience* (Cambridge: Polity Press, 1996).

[15] Welsh, "Dealing with the Communist Past," 415.

[16] Jeffrey Olick, "Collective Memory: The Two Cultures," *Sociological Theory*, 17(1999): 333–348.

"a negative capital, an almost pure deficit"[17] – a handicap, more than an asset – in the quest for democratization. Romania's history, Hoffman further noted, is marked "by discontinuity more than continuities, by oppression more than by independence, by various forms of authoritarianism more than by liberalism."[18] The communist period was no exception, as the regime employed a combination of many sticks and few carrots to maintain its unchallenged control over the country. Stalinism was an ideology "for all seasons," as Vladimir Tismaneanu suggested,[19] but there were perceptible differences in the way it informed the political game over the years. During the early decades of communism (1945–1964), leader Gheorghe Gheorghiu-Dej, the Communist Party, and their insidious secret political police, the Securitate, engaged in systematic campaigns of human rights infringements that often involved murder, terror, and deportation. After Nicolae Ceauşescu took over the leadership of the party-state in 1965 and instituted his dynastic "socialism in one family," as the only sultanist-cum-totalitarian regime in Europe was jokingly called,[20] outward terror gave way to more subtle repression exerted through a mass surveillance program that targeted dissenters, opponents, and apolitical citizens alike. As fewer people were thrown into prisons for refusing to obey the regime, the number of individuals placed under constant surveillance increased, more people were co-opted into the party-state structures, which themselves grew in number over time, and larger social segments became dependent on the regime for their livelihood and social advancement. During the 1980s, as the economic situation became extremely dire and living standards plummeted to European lows, human rights abuses somewhat faded in the background and Romanians became concerned primarily with their economic survival. The country's increased autarchy and isolation on the international scene, the ubiquitous and insidious secret informers, and the ever depleted reserves of interpersonal trust and social capital meant that Romania had a very weak civil society unable to oppose the communist regime and provide a voice to its critics. Citizens survived by keeping silent, accepting manifold compromises, negating their basic moral principles, turning a blind eye to injustice inflicted on relatives, neighbors, and friends, downgrading their life expectations, living parallel solitudes that often

17 Eva Hoffman, *Exit into History. A Journey through the New Eastern Europe* (New York: Penguin Books, 1993), 292.

18 Idem, 293.

19 Vladimir Tismaneanu, *Stalinism for All Seasons: A Political History of Romanian Communism* (Berkeley: University of California Press, 2003).

20 "The Lost World of Communism: Socialism in One Family," documentary (2009), available at: http://www.cosmolearning.com/documentaries/the-lost-world-of-communism-socialism-in-one-family-2009/ (accessed on 24 August 2011), and Juan Linz and Alfred Stepan, *Problems of Democratic Transition and Consolidation: Southern Europe, South America, and Post-Communist Europe* (Baltimore: Johns Hopkins University Press, 1996).

drew little support from within and outside their immediate family, and even silently rejoicing when their enemies and rivals got in trouble with the authorities.

To its many victims, the psychological repression of Ceauşescu's late communism and its Orwellian paraphernalia felt as stifling and oppressive as the outward terror of Gheorghiu-Dej's early communism, although fewer of the human rights abuses perpetrated by the Ceauşescu regime qualified as crimes indictable in courts of law. Regardless of whether the victim's worst fear was to be thrown in prison or to be confined into the psychiatric ward, the struggle between the individual and the state was a very unequal battle, as there was "very little justice to be had when the state decides on a policy of violence against its own citizens," as Noel Calhoun contended.[21] The all-powerful state, whose daily presence was aggrandized by rumors, insinuations, half-truths, threats, and even jokes spread by secret agents drawn from all walks of life, was able to "close off nearly all channels of assistance, leaving citizens with nowhere to turn: the police and courts are in the grip of the hostile state; the press will not risk printing their stories; even friends and neighbors may be reluctant to get involved." In short, "by mobilizing the full armory of violence and terror," the state was able to render victims "utterly powerless" and to ensure "not only its impunity, but the secrecy of its crimes as well."[22]

The number of people who became victims of communist repression from 1945 to 1989 remains subject of controversy, and the mere body count is compounded by the difficulty of measuring its magnitude and impact. An enumeration of fatalities may create a misleading picture, as communist terror was greater than the sum of its casualties or the tally of its perpetrators. To a certain extent, suffering was a personal journey to hell, a lonely experience whose full dimensions cannot be described to or comprehended by non-victims. Citizens of democracies can never grasp the multiple shades of utter fear that paralyzed those arrested during the 1950s, sometimes with a knock on the door in the middle of the night, with helpless children witnessing their horror and humiliation. Even Eastern European bystanders, who neither cooperated with the authorities nor fell victims to their repression campaigns, had a hard time accepting the innocence of those unjustly thrown into communist prisons, although they themselves had to navigate the multitude of limitations that the regime imposed on a daily basis. As Timothy Snyder reminds us, total rounded figures computed for those who were arrested, imprisoned, murdered, persecuted, harassed, disappeared, exiled, humiliated, or simply prohibited to live a normal life desensitize the reader and hide the fact that each one of those lives was shattered and remained an unfulfilled promise.[23] Neither do tallies of perpetrators – those who

[21] Noel Calhoun, *Dilemmas of Justice in Eastern Europe's Democratic Transitions* (New York: Palgrave MacMillan, 2004), 1.

[22] Idem.

[23] Timothy Snyder, *Bloodlands. Europe between Hitler and Stalin* (New York: Basic Books, 2010).

committed human rights abuses with their fist, club, pen, or word – offer a more complete picture of how repression ubiquitously seeped into personal lives, divided families, eroded local communities, and fractured society.

At the center of communist repression was the political police, the specialized arm of the hegemonic Communist Party, to which it reported and which it obeyed. In 1989, the Securitate employed 15,087 secret officers (popularly known as *securişti*), 507,003 informers (*informatori*) not belonging to the Communist Party, and an unknown number of collaborators (*colaboratori*) drawn from party ranks, in a total population of 21.5 million.[24] That same year, the Stasi employed 102,000 full-time officers and 174,000 part-time informers (known as *inoffizielle Mitarbeiter*, unofficial collaborators) in East Germany, a country of 16.7 million inhabitants.[25] Although the Securitate and the Stasi were the largest state agencies in their respective countries, at least 3.4 percent of adult Romanians and only 2.5 percent of adult East Germans collaborated with the communist secret political police that was responsible for the vast majority of politically motivated human rights abuses perpetrated by the communist state. These small percentages fail to convey the full force of the dreaded political police and its secret agents, their enlarged presence in the citizens' daily lives, and the morbid fear they inspired. Neither can they reflect the peculiar nature of party dictatorship, which maintained a specialized division of labor that allowed secret agents who worked as one in a mass to feel few scruples and little responsibility for their decisions. Their willingness to play along with the Securitate with hardly any reservations explains why after 1989 most secret agents claimed that their actions were benign.

Among the victims of Romanian communism were the 600,000 political prisoners of 1948–1964 and the 81,000 political prisoners of 1945–1948 and 1965–1989, including the 80,000 peasants arrested in 1945–1952 for opposing collectivization. Some 30,000 of these peasants were sentenced to jail time in trials open to the public.[26] Around 200,000 other "enemies of the state" were deported to Bărăgan and Dobrogea from 1949 to 1962.[27] During the Black Night of 18 June 1951, 44,000 residents of the Banat and Mehedinţi regions were relocated to Bărăgan, where 2,000

[24] Gabriel Catalan and Mircea Stănescu, "Scurtă istorie a Securităţii," *Sfera politicii*, 12 (2004): 42, and Cristina Anisescu, *Dinamica de structură şi rol a reţelei informative în perioada 1948–1989*, available at: http://www.comunism.ro/images/anisescuagentura.pdf (accessed on 29 August 2011).

[25] H. Müller-Enbergs, *IM-Statistik* 1985–1989 (Berlin: BStU, 1993), 55; John Koehler, "Revenge versus the Rule of Law," *New York Times* (1999), available at: http://www.nytimes.com/books/first/k/koehler-stasi.html (accessed on 29 August 2011); and Steffen Kröhnert and Samuel Skipper, *Demographic Development in Eastern Germany* (Berlin: Berlin-Institut fur Bevolkerung und Entwicklung, 2010).

[26] Dorin Dobrincu and Constantin Iordachi, eds., *Ţărănimea şi puterea. Procesul de colectivizare a agriculturii în România (1949–1962)* (Bucharest: Polirom, 2005), 21.

[27] Comisia Prezidenţială pentru Analiza Dictaturii Comuniste din România, *Raport Final*, 161. Historians like Andrei Pippidi consider these figures inflated.

of them lost their lives as a result of harsh living conditions.[28] Add 1.1 million people secretly monitored and 507,003 individuals recruited as secret informers throughout the communist period.[29] Some secret informers were children as young as nine, who were compelled to provide information on their playmates, parents, relatives, and neighbors at an age when they could hardly understand the world surrounding them and the difference between good and evil.[30] Armed resistance centered on the Nucşoara group, which the Securitate apprehended in 1958.[31]

Stalinist repression went down in history for the Piteşti reeducation experiment, which used brutality and torture to turn prisoners into new people apt to form the bedrock of the new communist state. Between 1949 and 1952, young political prisoners jailed in the Piteşti prison were terrorized and cruelly beaten, compelled to confess real and imaginary crimes against the state, brainwashed, and reeducated to betray their friends and publicly abjure their families. The tortured were turned into torturers, ready to apply to others the coarse methods of extreme physical degradation, constant psychological pressure, and personal alienation from the deepest emotional ties they themselves endured. This last step, meant to prove the prisoner's full transfiguration into the new person, ensured that distrust among reeducation victims would render unlikely cooperation between them in the event of an uprising. According to former participants, at that stage the tortured contemplated suicide, a "luxury" they were denied.[32]

Religious denominations were hard-hit by communist persecution campaigns. Initially, the majority Orthodox Church was targeted for repression by an atheist regime bent on curbing religiosity and weakening the Church's considerable social base. Many Orthodox clergymen and faithful were arrested and imprisoned – often for the support they had provided to the interwar Iron Guard – nuns and monks were forced to leave the monasteries, seminaries and theological schools were closed, and

[28] Liviu Stan, "Rusaliile Negre. Deportarea în Bărăgan," *Obiectiv Vocea Brăilei* (8 September 2011).

[29] Lavinia Stan, "Moral Cleansing Romanian Style," *Problems of Post-Communism*, 49(2002): 56.

[30] Not all the crimes of the communist period were directly attributable to the Romanian authorities. At the end of World War II the invading Soviet troops captured 100,000 "prisoners" in Iaşi, and forcefully deported 150,000 ethnic Germans from Romania. Comisia Prezidenţială pentru Analiza Dictaturii Comuniste din România, *Raport Final*, 161.

[31] Aurora Liiceanu, *Rănile memoriei. Nucşoara şi rezistenţa din munţi* (Bucharest: Polirom, 2003), and Alina Mungiu-Pippidi and G. Althabe, *Secera şi buldozerul. Scorniceşti şi Nucşoara. Mecanisme de aservire a ţăranului român* (Bucharest: Polirom, 2002).

[32] Ierunca, *Fenomenul Piteşti*; Dumitru Bacu, *Piteşti. Centru de reeducare studenţească* (Hamilton: Cuvântul Românesc, 1989); Eugen Magierescu, *Moara Dracilor. Amintiri despre Piteşti* (Alba Iulia: Fronde, 1994); Gila Safran Naveh, "Violence as Culture: 'Educating' Political Prisoners in Romania," in *Cultural Shaping of Violence: Victimization, Escalation, Response*, ed. Myrdene Anderson (West Laffayete: Purdue University Press, 2004), 258–267; and Mircea Stănescu, *Reeducarea în România comunistă (1945–1952). Aiud, Suceava, Piteşti, Braşov* (Iaşi: Polirom, 2010).

the regime appointed subservient patriarchs.[33] Over time, the Orthodox Church leadership accepted collaboration with the regime, and some of its prominent hierarchs rushed in singing sycophantic praises to the communist leaders, condemning outspoken priests who criticized the authorities, defrocking disobeying priests, and providing secret information obtained through confession to the Securitate. Some 600 Greek Catholic priests, including all six of their bishops, who refused to convert to Orthodoxy were imprisoned in 1948. None of the arrested bishops were ever brought to trial, and only three bishops survived the prison.[34] That same year, the Romanian communist authorities unilaterally denounced the concordat with the Holy See and refused to obey by its terms. In 1948–1964, 130 Roman Catholic priests were arrested or confined to forced domicile, including the Bishop of Alba Iulia, and at least 96 Protestant priests and students were sentenced to prison between 1957 and 1964.[35] In 1982, the communist authorities banned the Yoga-based Transcendental Meditation relaxation technique, dismantled the Institute for Research in Pedagogy and Psychology in Bucharest where the technique was used for research, ousted from the party the apparatchiks who introduced it, and transferred to unskilled posts more than 250 university professors, researchers, scholars, philosophers, and writers who used that form of meditation.[36]

The most important revolts against the Ceauşescu regime – the strikes of the Valea Jiului miners in 1977 and of the Braşov industrial workers in 1987 – were brutally quashed by the party-state, with the help of the army and the Securitate troops. In 1977, miners denounced legislation ending their disability pensions and raising the retirement age from fifty to sixty-five and asked to talk to top party leaders. First cabinet ministers and then Ceauşescu himself negotiated with the miners, promising better working conditions and no retaliatory measures. After the introduction of draconian measures designed to reduce food and energy consumption and to sell stocks against hard currency, in 1987 workers at the Red Flag factory in Braşov took to the street to reach the headquarters of the county party leadership in search of answers for being denied salary payment. In both cases, retaliation was harsh. Based on photographs taken during the strikes, the Securitate identified the most vocal protesters and singled them

33 Cristian Vasile, *Biserica Ortodoxă Română în primul deceniu comunist (1945–1959)* (Bucharest: Curtea Veche, 2005), and Lucian Leustean, *Orthodoxy and the Cold War. Religion and Political Power in Romania, 1947–1965* (London: Palgrave, 2009).

34 Cristian Vasile, *Între Vatican şi Kremlin. Biserica Greco-Catolică în timpul regimului communist* (Bucharest: Curtea Veche, 2004), and Lavinia Stan and Lucian Turcescu, *Religion and Politics in Post-Communist Romania* (New York: Oxford University Press, 2007).

35 Idem, 535–536.

36 Doina Jela, Cătălin Strat and Mihai Albu, *Afacerea Meditaţia Transcedentală* (Bucharest: Humanitas, 2004).

out for punishment. Protesters who were also Communist Party members were expelled or sanctioned. In 1977, some 4,000 miners were relocated to other localities, others were brought before the courts and sentenced to up to five years of "correctional work" for disturbing the social order, and still others were beaten in the local Securitate headquarters.[37]

The list of victims further includes an unknown number of people confined to psychiatric wards for speaking their mind against the authorities.[38] Best known among them was Vasile Paraschiv (1928–2011), a postman who in 1963 was abusively evicted from his apartment by a militia man who needed a place to stay. In 1968, Paraschiv was arrested after renouncing his Communist Party membership. Afterward he was repeatedly confined to psychiatric wards and subjected to harsh treatment. When trying to set up a free labor union, he was kidnapped by the Securitate, which portrayed him as mentally disturbed and did everything in its power to reduce him to that state of mind.[39] His predicament was shared by other victims in whose name the Securitate opened secret files and collected information about their "subversive activities."

Under communism, ethnic minorities had their rights and freedoms negated or diminished. During the early stages, most Hungarian political elite members were arrested by Romanian and Soviet authorities or forced to take exile in Hungary. Hungarian intellectuals and community leaders were interned, while the Magyar Popular Union – the main political vehicle of the Transylvanian minority – was subordinated to the Romanian Communist Party, and its leadership endured several arrest campaigns from 1949 to 1958. Cultural and economic associations of ethnic minorities were dismantled and their assets confiscated by the communist state. Whereas some Transylvanian Hungarians supported the communist ideology, others became a target of the Securitate for siding with the 1956 Hungarian revolution, because their sympathy was thought to reflect nationalist more than pro-democratic sentiment. The Securitate extended its information network among Hungarian clergy and teachers suspected of fueling secessionist sentiments among youth.[40] Germans and Jews were allowed to emigrate if the Romanian state

[37] Ruxandra Cesereanu, "Greva minerilor din Valea Jiului, 1977," 22 (3 August 2004); Ruxandra Cesereanu, "Revolta muncitorilor din Braşov, 1987," 22 (2 December 2003); and Stejărel Olaru and Marius Oprea, *The Day We Won't Forget. 15 November 1987* (Bucharest: Polirom, 2003).

[38] Nanci Adler, Gerard O. W. Mueller and Mohammed Ayat, "Psychiatry under Tyranny: A Report on the Political Abuse of Romanian Psychiatry during the Ceausescu Years," *Current Psychology: Research & Reviews*, 12(1993): 3–17.

[39] Andrei Crăciun and Adrian Grama, "Vasile Paraschiv – nebunul care a învins Securitatea," *Evenimentul Zilei* (6 February 2008), and "Twenty Years after Fall, Ghost of Ceausescu's Government still Haunts Romanians," France 24 (25 December 2009).

[40] Comisia Prezidenţială pentru Analiza Dictaturii Comuniste din România, *Raport Final*, 526–527.

received payments from their friends and relatives abroad, but all ethnic minorities suffered greatly during the 1970s and the 1980s, when Ceauşescu instituted his national-communism and cult of personality.[41]

Abusive confiscations took place throughout the communist period. After 1945, Romania moved quickly to nationalize property belonging to individuals, organizations, and religious and ethnic communities to ensure the preeminence of state-controlled property in the new command economy. In 1945 large land properties were expropriated, and in 1950 residential units of "bourgeois exploiters" were nationalized without compensation, although the 1948 communist constitution guaranteed private property, limited expropriations to instances of public utility for which owners were duly compensated, and excluded residences from the categories of assets to be nationalized.[42] The state then took possession of abandoned residences and dwellings of owners who were unable to repay debts to the state, refused to return to Romania after traveling abroad, or crossed the border illegally. After 1973, families were allowed to own only one dwelling, and the state was permitted to requisition without just compensation additional dwellings not sold within a year. In 1994, parliament announced that the communists confiscated 241,068 residential units, but other sources referred to as many as 640,000 confiscated dwellings, affecting close to 800,000–900,000 individuals.[43]

Surely, for many Romanians, as for many other Eastern Europeans, the history of 1945 to 1989 also included rays of hope, an appreciation of the simple joys of life, and pride in personal and professional accomplishments – that is, positive connotations that analysts of communist politics tend to negate, trivialize, or ignore. Ultimately, for victims, perpetrators, and bystanders alike, communism was a family photo album, the collection of past deeds and feelings, aspirations and disappointments, successes and failures, love and hate, friendship and rivalry. The normalcy of communist times that many communist diehards bitterly regret, ordinary citizens casually invoke, and younger generations sometimes assume suggests that, at least for some categories of population, the totalitarian, repressive communist past remains nothing but "a foreign country," to paraphrase David Lowenthal.[44] Indeed, opinion polls conducted in 2010 suggested that a majority of Romanians (59 percent) considered that communism was a good idea, and only 7 percent of them suffered directly

[41] I thank Levente Salat for providing guidance on the topic of ethnic minorities under communist rule. Email communications with Levente Salat, 27 March 2012 and 1 April 2012.

[42] *Constituţia Republicii Populare Române 1948*, available at: http://legislatie.resurse-pentru-democratie.org/const_1948.php (accessed on 22 July 2011).

[43] Lavinia Stan, "The Roof over Our Head: Property Restitution in Romania," *Journal of Communist Studies and Transition Politics*, 22(2006): 184.

[44] David Lowenthal, *The Past Is a Foreign Country* (Cambridge: Cambridge University Press, 1985).

as a result of communist policies.[45] The results are surprising, given the fact that Romania experienced the most restrictive Stalinist regime that deprived citizens of their basic rights and necessities on an unprecedented scale. The responses make sense, however, when we remember that Romania had the largest percentage of Communist Party members among all European communist countries, communism continues to be praised for its nationalist overtones and the ephemerid equality for all that it preached to the masses, and respondents were reluctant to declare themselves victims and thus single out a personal experience that was shared at the time by most of the population.[46]

After the 1989 revolution, which toppled one of the most sinister European dictatorships, Romania had more reasons than its neighbors to work through the recent past vigorously and resolutely. First, the communist regime was not brought about by free and fair elections, but was imposed by Soviet troops on an ethnically diverse and politically fragmented country at the end of World War II. Generations of Romanians contested the regime's legitimacy out of dissatisfaction with their country's perceived subordination to Moscow, which was denounced even after the country acquired a measure of independence from the Soviet Union and when it became evident that Romanian communists subjugated the Romanian population. Second, up to the very last moment the rule of unrepentant dictator Ceauşescu remained one of the strictest in the region, permitting neither opposition ("voice") nor emigration ("exit") to individuals discontent with his increasingly megalomaniac and erratic policies.[47] Ceauşescu, whose unchallenged rule echoed Asian personality cult more than European authoritarian-bureaucratic communism, openly rejected Gorbachev's reforms. Third, regime change was achieved through the region's only bloody revolution, which resulted in over 1,100 dead and 3,350 wounded.[48]

Notwithstanding these reasons, lack of a vigorous civil society meant that, after the 1989 revolution, political power reverted from the Ceauşescu family, their sycophantic supporters, and self-interested clients to second-echelon Communist Party officials organized as the National Salvation Front. Rather disingenuously, the Front

45 Lavinia Stan, *Communist Nostalgia in Romania* (12 December 2010), available at: http://laviniastan.wordpress.com/2010/12/12/communist-nostalgia-in-romania/ (accessed on 25 August 2011). The posting reports the results of a poll conducted, under the aegis of the Institute for the Investigation of Communist Crimes and the Memory of Romanian Exile, between 22 October and 1 November 2010 on a sample representative of the population.

46 Dennis Deletant, "Romania, 1945–89: Resistance, Protest and Dissent," in *Revolution and Resistance. Challenges to Communist Rule*, eds. Kevin McDermott and Matthew Stibbe (Oxford: Berg, 2006), 81–100.

47 John Moran, "The Communist Torturers of Eastern Europe: Prosecute and Punish or Forgive and Forget?," *Communist and Post-Communist Studies*, 27(1994): 95–109.

48 Peter Siani-Davies, *The Romanian Revolution of December 1989* (Ithaca: Cornell University Press, 2006).

claimed that it represented popular desires to build liberal democracy and a free market economy. In reality, the Front envisioned "salvation" for its self-appointed leaders more than for the people as a whole. It sought to lengthen the political careers of its most prominent figures despite public criticism of their involvement with the communist regime and insisted that the mad dictator (Ceauşescu), more than the entrenched system (communism), was responsible for the country's economic bankruptcy and political malaise. Because the leader was gone, they claimed, a modified version of communism could represent the country's best chance for future prosperity. Instead of engineering the transition away from communist repression and control, the Front made every effort to slow down political and economic change and, whenever possible, to turn it to its own advantage.

PARAMETERS OF POST-COMMUNIST TRANSITIONAL JUSTICE

In many ways, transitional justice is a misnomer, as not all endeavors that aim to come to terms with the recent past are undertaken by countries transiting between political regimes, and not all such efforts strictly pertain to or aim at delivering justice. Indeed, recently consolidated democracies like Canada and Australia have rectified past injustices inflicted on their aboriginal populations. The transition these countries experienced before reckoning with the past affected mentality more than political institutions. In addition, transitional justice scholars and practitioners acknowledge truth and reconciliation, besides justice, as goals of the working-through-the-past project and agree that both judicial and nonjudicial methods can be successfully employed to this end. This is partly the reason why post-communist Europe has avoided the literal translation of transitional justice, preferring formulae such as "coming to terms with history" (*Geschichtsbewältigung*) and "working through the past" (*Vergangenheitsaufarbeitung*) in Germany, "providing justice" (*igazságtétel*) in Hungary, "delivering justice during transition" (*sprawiedliwosc czasow przemiany*) in Poland, "assuming the past" (*asumarea trecutului*) in Romania, "dealing with the past" (*vyrovnani se s minulosti*) in the Czech Republic, or "disclosing the files" (отваряне на досиетата) in Bulgaria.[49]

Notwithstanding these linguistic nuances, the concept of transitional justice reflects the Eastern European politics of memory in more ways than one. First, only after the communist regimes collapsed in 1989 and the region opted for democratization as political transformation were these countries in a position to turn their

[49] The terms were compiled by Helga Welsh, "Beyond Lustration: Transitional Justice in Central and Eastern Europe," paper delivered at the Meeting of the Council for European Studies, Montreal, Canada, 15–17 April 2010. I thank the author for making available a copy of the presentation to me.

attention toward the crimes of communism, many of which had been left unaddressed for decades. In this respect, these countries, Romania included, differed from the former Soviet Union, where communist leader Mikhail Gorbachev allowed for the selective acknowledgment and condemnation of Stalinist crimes as early as 1987 and where the collapse of communism and the dismantling of the Union in 1991 represented a within-regime change more than a transition from one political system to another.[50] Second, for most of the region's citizens transitional justice was meant, first and foremost, to deliver justice to former victims or their descendants, to encourage authorities to recognize the injustices inflicted on ordinary citizens, to identify former perpetrators publicly, and to force them to assume responsibility for their human rights abuses before the courts. While the truth about communist repression and, to a lesser degree, reconciliation between victims and victimizers were by-products of post-communist transitional justice, many politicians and citizens have considered redress incomplete, inadequate, and even illegitimate unless perpetrators were tried in court. Therefore, the reckoning with the communist past has revolved primarily around the quest for justice.

Remember that Romania, together with post-communist Europe, underwent one of the most radical regime changes among all regions that ever engaged in transitional justice, as the distance that separated the totalitarian communism they left behind from the Western-style liberal democracy they wished to build was greater than in Latin America, Africa, and Asia. During the late communist regime of the 1980s, Eastern Europe experienced "wide repression" that targeted a larger number of citizens, but subjected them to less gruesome crimes than the "deep repression" of military juntas of Latin America.[51] At the same time, no Latin American junta ever aimed to totally change politics, economy, society, and culture to the degree envisioned by European communist states. This is why post-communist transitional justice has been undertaken in a far more complex domestic environment than in other post-dictatorial settings. The structure of the communist party-states – which penetrated every social layer, school, enterprise, state agency, and voluntary association – the party's control over the most mundane aspects of public and private life, the subordination to the party of all branches and levels of the government machinery, and the pervasive use of state surveillance against powerless citizens have raised a host of difficulties other regions did not face. At the same time, the far-reaching transformations undertaken in post-communist Europe after 1989 meant that transitional justice was, for

[50] Jon Elster, *Closing the Books: Transitional Justice in Historical Perspective* (New York: Cambridge University Press, 2004), 67, and Calhoun, *Dilemmas of Justice*, 27.

[51] Tina Rosenberg, *The Haunted Land: Facing Europe's Ghosts after Communism* (New York: Vintage, 1996).

both state and civil society actors, one among many other political priorities, some more urgent and legitimate than others.

Romania's case has been complicated by an additional layer. All post-communist European countries have had to deal with two dictatorial pasts – the communist regimes and their Nazi predecessors – but Romania has had three historical periods to make right again: the dictatorship of 1940–1944, the communist regime of 1945–1989, and the December 1989 revolution. The need to address these periods of human rights abuses simultaneously convinced some politicians and civil society groups that these pasts were in fact competing for the rather meager resources that the post-communist reform program made available to the working-through-the-past project. Indeed, successive Romanian governments have not tackled all three pasts with the same degree of intensity and urgency. Official transitional justice efforts addressed the revolution well before they addressed the 1945–1989 period, perhaps because the crimes of the revolution were more recent, the victims were more impatient and vocal, the revolution was perceived as more gruesome than the long-forgotten Stalinist crimes and more significant for democratization, the country's new leaders were unwilling to condemn a regime with which they once collaborated, and some politicians benefited personally from the advantages granted to the revolutionaries. At times the competition between these pasts relented, advocates of transitional justice related to one past taking inspiration from the methods applied to redress another. For example, supporters of lustration often compared it to de-Nazification, while the presidential commission that analyzed communist crimes emulated the body that studied the Holocaust.

Following scholars and practitioners working in the area, this analysis understands transitional justice as the set of judicial and nonjudicial measures implemented by civil society actors, local and national governments, and international organizations in view of redressing the legacy of massive human rights abuses.[52] In the case of post-communist Romania, the methods employed to "assume the past" have ranged from court trials, truth commission, and access to secret files to a tribunal of opinion, memorialization, and public commemorations. Some were initiated by the president (the truth commission and official condemnation of communist crimes), the government (the amendments that expanded the lustration program in 2006), parliament (legislation returning assets to initial owners or granting citizens access to the secret files compiled on them), or the courts (the indictment of Stalinist perpetrators Alexandru Drăghici or the sentences handed down to those responsible for

[52] International Center for Transitional Justice, *What Is Transitional Justice?* (New York, 2011), available at: http://ictj.org/about/transitional-justice?gclid=CKDu_eem5qoCFQrf4AodZlU49g (accessed on 23 August 2011); Ruti Teitel, *Transitional Justice* (New York: Oxford University Press, 2002); and David Baker, "Civil Society and Transitional Justice: Possibilities, Patterns and Prospects," *Journal of Human Rights*, 2(2003): 297–313.

the death of dissident Gheorghe Ursu). Others originated with political parties (the informal lustration of some party leaders running for public office in the 1996 and subsequent elections), victims' organizations (lustration and the truth commission), religious denominations (the restitution of abusively confiscated church property, including places of worship, and religious artifacts) other civil society groups (the citizens' opinion tribunal and the restitution of dwellings). Some methods (property restitution, lustration, public identification of former secret agents, as well as education and memorialization programs) have been suggested and supported by international actors such as the EU, the European Court of Human Rights, the Council of Europe, and NATO.

Most methods have had at least a veneer of legitimacy and were capable to deliver a measure of justice, truth, and/or reconciliation, but the trial of the communist dictator Nicolae Ceauşescu and his much despised wife Elena – Romania's first attempt to address its communist past – amounted to a mock, show trial reminiscent of the court proceedings organized during the first decade of communist rule more than the legal scrutiny that other communist leaders – Erich Honecker and Egon Krenz in Germany, General Wojciech Jaruzelski in Poland, and Todor Zhivkov in Bulgaria – faced before the courts of law. In more ways than one, this sham trial represented the "original sin" of the Romanian transitional justice attempts; a handicap that the country was able to overcome only after years of internal squabbles and accusations (see Chapter 2). While legitimate, other methods of redressing the past have not been all equally successful, because they had limited scope, were not fully enacted, did not enjoy support from the political elite or victims' groups, or were implemented too late and too hesitantly.[53] In line with my previous research, this volume considers transitional justice policies beyond their adoption and discusses their implementation and outcomes, together with the way in which they were perceived by the general public (through opinion polls) and were promoted or undermined by various political and social actors, including the executive and legislative branches of government, the court system and the Constitutional and Supreme Courts, victims' organizations, political parties and interest groups, as well as international actors.

This volume offers a scorecard of the most important procedures through which Romania has dealt with its communist past during the first two decades of post-communist transition (1989–2009). The time frame begins with the 1989 revolution, which marked Romania's exit from communism, and ends five years after the country gained acceptance into the EU, arguably the most important event

[53] Lavinia Stan, "Neither Forgiving, Nor Punishing?: Transitional Justice in Romania," in *After Dictatorship: Transitional Justice and Democratic Consolidation: Lessons from Eastern Europe and Latin America*, ed. Vesselin Popovski (Tokyo: United Nations University Press, 2012), 200–210.

in its modern history. Some of the methods analyzed here – especially lustration, court trials, access to secret files, the truth commission, and property restitution – were selected because the literature considers them important markers of the post-communist *Vergangenheitsbewältigung*. Memorialization, the citizens' opinion tribunal, and forensic investigations were added because of their capacity to show the involvement of civil society groups in a process that has been generally regarded as the exclusive turf and obligation of the state. A number of processes required presentation because they led to the implementation of other important methods (i.e., lustration rests primarily on access to secret files, while the truth commission led to the official condemnation of communist crimes). The theoretical questions that drive this analysis, the relations between methods and their sequencing, and the time when different initiatives were publicly debated determined the order in which these methods are presented.

Transitional justice is often considered a necessary, if not sufficient, requirement during the early stages of democratization, although not all new democracies have chosen to "prosecute and punish" perpetrators of human rights violations, to unveil the truth and to educate the public about the repressive past, to sideline officeholders tainted by collaboration, or to bring victims and victimizers together in reconciliation programs. For example, post-Franco Spain democratized in the absence of transitional justice, and post-Nazi Germany postponed the adoption of meaningful restorative programs for close to twenty years. In these countries impunity was perpetuated, victims were unable to forget, and perpetrators were unwilling to acknowledge wrongdoing. At the same time, most citizens supported the building of the new democracy in the absence of truth, justice, and reconciliation delivered through transitional justice. These cases suggest that at least some post-dictatorial societies and political leaders might wish to forgive and forget to preempt violence, avoid undertaking costly compensation programs, remove "a highly emotional and controversial issue from the political agenda … that may be crowded with other serious priorities,"[54] and permit politicians tainted by association with the ancient regime to continue their careers.

While ignoring the past was a possibility in Romania, it became apparent during the 1989 revolution that significant segments of the population rejected the forgive-and-forget policy on which the new rulers insisted. Former victims, young students, and reconstituted "historical" parties warned that those who forget the past are doomed to repeat it and argued strongly in favor of redressing communist abuses, instead of ignoring them. The elite reproduction that Romania experienced after the 1989 events kept the honest assessment of the crimes and abuses of communist times in the public eye, because the new leaders' refusal to condemn the

[54] Calhoun, *Dilemmas of Justice*, 4–5.

communist regime placed the irreversibility of the regime change into question. As the new rulers were mostly second-echelon Communist Party leaders who believed that communism had been a worthy political project perverted by Ceauşescu's megalomania and were unwilling to move the country closer to Western-style liberal democracy, the very gains of the 1989 revolution (multiparty free elections, a new constitution, and a revamped governmental structure) were seemingly threatened. In addition, the country's bloody exit from communism and the revolutionary leaders' decision to summarily try, condemn, and kill Ceauşescu took the forgive-and-forget option off the table. The crimes of the revolution were too recent and too gruesome to simply ignore them, and the new leaders themselves opened the possibility and underscored the importance of working through the past when they hastily put Ceauşescu on trial. As we shall see, it was just a matter of time for civil society groups and opposition political parties to ask the new authorities to redress the other crimes of the communist regime.

ROMANIAN TRANSITIONAL JUSTICE ACTORS

As in other transitional justice settings, in Romania the main actors that shaped transitional justice efforts were state, non-state, domestic, and international. Overall, the Romanian efforts to reckon with the communist past have been reluctantly moved forward by the civil society and systematically blocked by political elites. The advocates of a radical break with the communist regime have been drawn primarily from among the communist-era victims and their surviving relatives. Among them were members of pre-communist political parties and governmental structures, collaborators of the royal family, individuals involved in the anticommunist resistance during the 1940s and the 1950s, Orthodox, Greek, and Roman Catholic, Protestant and neo-Protestant faithful persecuted for their religious beliefs, outspoken critical intellectuals, persons who unsuccessfully tried to illegally cross the border to escape to Western Europe, and workers and miners who revolted in 1977 and 1987. As explained earlier, some of them were imprisoned and tortured, others lost their jobs, others were relocated to different regions or were forced to emigrate, still others were spied upon and placed under constant surveillance, while another group lost its property to communist authorities.

Several independent agencies funded by the state have been entrusted with explicit transitional justice responsibilities. None of these institutions have retained their independence from the political elite, which often made financial support conditional on verdicts or investigations benefiting the government at the expense of the opposition. The National Council for the Study of Securitate Archives, created in 2000 as custodian of the Securitate archive, makes secret files available to citizens of Romania (and more recently citizens of other NATO countries) and determines, based on the secret files and personal interviews, whether a person collaborated with the Securitate as a political police engaged in human rights infringements. The Council houses in its stacks the third largest Eastern European political police archive formed of close to 2 million files that describe the activity of both victims and secret informers. Embroiled in public scandals that almost completely blocked its activity in the mid-2000s, the Council is led by an eleven-member leadership nominated by political parties. Its most important investigations pertain to unveiling former Securitate agents from among post-communist political luminaries. A deficient legislative framework, opposition from the intelligence services, and its own politicized leadership have negatively affected the Council's ability to fulfill its transitional justice mandate (see Chapter 3).

The Institute for the Investigation of Communist Crimes in Romania was set up in 2006 by Liberal Prime Minister Călin Popescu-Tăriceanu under the leadership of historian Marius Oprea, who at the time served as an advisor to the prime minister. After the Liberal Party joined the opposition in 2009, the Institute was renamed the Institute for the Investigation of Communist Crimes and the Memory of Romanian Exile, its mandate was enlarged to include the investigation of post-communist human rights infringements (related most notably to the miners' descent on Bucharest in 1990, the so-called *mineriada*), and its leadership was entrusted to Vladimir Tismăneanu, the former chair of the Presidential Commission for the Analysis of the Communist Dictatorship in Romania, and a scientific council formed of both Romanian and foreign scholars (see Chapter 5). With its small team of historians, the Institute has published original research, offered a range of educational projects, and gathered evidence necessary for the indictment of communist-era perpetrators, which it submitted to the courts.

Since his departure from the Institute, Oprea has carried out transitional justice projects, most notably forensic investigations, within the small Center for the Investigation of Communist Crimes, which has received no funding from the government but has secured assistance from the German Konrad Adenauer Foundation. With extremely limited resources and the support of volunteers, the Center remains the only Romanian institution engaged in locating the remains of former communist-era victims who lost their lives in extrajudicial executions carried out by the Securitate troops. Its exhumations program has covered several Transylvanian counties where anticommunist resistance extended during the 1950s (see Chapter 9).

Under the leadership of Tismăneanu, the Presidential Commission for the Analysis of the Communist Dictatorship in Romania worked during 2006 as an academic, history commission responsible to compile an expert report that detailed the criminal character of the communist regime and to submit it to the president before the country gained acceptance into the EU on 1 January 2007. Because it lacked subpoena powers, had not more than six months at its disposal, conducted no public hearings with victims, did not travel to various regions of the country, and included mostly humanistic intellectuals but no legal experts, and its work was vigorously contested by the opposition Social Democrats and Greater Romania Party, the Commission used primarily archival materials and previously published works as documentation for its final report. Because of its predominantly academic character, purportedly inspired by the Commission of Inquiry for the Assessment of History and Consequences of the SED Dictatorship in Germany (Enquete Kommission zur Aufarbeitung von Geschichte und Folgen der SED-Diktator in Deutschland) that operated in 1992 in Germany,[55] the Romanian Commission had a relatively minor impact on the way the political elites, the intellectuals, and the general public in that country have viewed the communist past (see Chapter 5).

Created in 2005, the Property Fund compensates initial owners whose property rights were recognized by the courts, but whose assets cannot be returned in kind either because they were destroyed or because they were sold to third parties. The Fund offers shares only to owners of abusively confiscated property who had received no just compensation for their loss. Since its creation, the Fund has been affected by frequent public scandal and mismanagement and contested by the owners, who must wait for over three years to have their ownership right recognized by four different governmental agencies before the Fund can disburse compensation. Beside the Fund, a National Agency for Property Restitution works as the central governmental body that recognizes demands for the restitution of nationalized dwellings (see Chapter 6).

A number of civil society groups have supported transitional justice. The Association of Former Political Prisoners in Romania, constituted in 1990 in Bucharest, has branches throughout the country and a membership that diminished from 98,700 in 1990 to 45,000 in 2009.[56] It has been the country's most important organization of communist-era political prisoners, deportees, and their relatives. In the mid-1990s, the smaller Association of Former Political Prisoners and Anticommunist Fighters was created by communist-era political prisoners with ties to the interwar fascist Iron Guard, which subscribed to nationalism, Orthodoxism, and anti-Semitism. It commemorates mostly Iron Guard members imprisoned, tortured, or killed by the Securitate, keeping silent on the crimes the Guard perpetrated during pre-communist times. The Association of Owners of Property Abusively Confiscated by the State was set up in 1999 in Bucharest by property owners, their

[55] Vladimir Tismaneanu, "Democracy and Memory: Romania Confronts Its Communist Past," *Annals of the American Academy of Political and Social Science*, 617(2008): 169.

[56] Asociaţia Foştilor Deţinuţi Politici din România, *Memoriul Asociaţiei Foştilor Deţinuti Politici din România* (2009), available at: http://www.bumbacari.net/news.php?extend.3 (accessed on 23 June 2011).

descendants, and legal representatives to fight for property restitution and equitable compensation. With an initial membership of 11,000, the Association is Romania's most vocal organization of initial homeowners.[57] Constituted in 1991 in Bucharest, the ICAR Foundation provides medical rehabilitation for victims of communism in Bucharest, Iaşi, and Craiova, through programs funded by international organizations and private donors.[58]

Other associations have local, not national, membership or represent much smaller victims' groups. Created in 2009, the Association of Owners Abusively Deprived of Their Property, Former Deportees and Refugees represents property owners, deportees, and refugees seeking compensation and redress. In mid-2009, it had 210 members, exclusively drawn from the southern town of Craiova.[59] Former owners are also represented by the Association for Private Property and the Community of Legitimate Owners and Descendants in Romania, both headquartered in Bucharest, and by the more obscure Association of Victims of the Bolshevik Communist System and Its Legacy of Râmnicu-Vâlcea. Since 1997, the Bucharest-based Association of Victims of Magistrates represents those who believe they suffered as a result of court decisions rendered by corrupt communist and post-communist judges. Homeowners residing in France and Germany are represented by the French Association for Defending Property Rights in Romania of Paris and the Restitution in Romania of Munich.

To these voluntary associations, add the Gheorghe Ursu Foundation, set up by relatives of the engineer who, in 1986, was murdered while jailed in the Bucharest Militia dungeon (see Chapter 2). Ursu was arrested after being denounced by two workmates for keeping a journal critical of the communist leadership and policies. The Foundation, which includes Ursu's close relatives, maintains a website and has drawn support from European politicians and Romanian intellectuals. The Ion Gavrilă Ogoranu Foundation was set up in 2008, two years after Ogoranu's death, to commemorate the leader of the Făgăraş anticommunist fighters group, active between 1948, when the country turned communist, and 1955, when the Securitate arrested most of the group's members. After being sentenced to death in absentia

57 Damiana Oţoiu, "La (re)construction de la propriete privee en Roumanie post-communiste. 'Anciens' vs. 'nouveaux' proprietaires?," paper delivered at the At the Frontier of Land Issues: Social Embeddedness of Rights and Public Policy workshop, Montpellier, France, 17–19 May 2006, available at: http://www.mpl.ird.fr/colloque_foncier/Communications/PDF/Otoiu.pdf (accessed on 26 July 2011).

58 ICAR Foundation, *Who Is ICAR Foundation* (2010), available at: http://www.icarfoundation.ro/ (accessed on 1 September 2011), and Damiana Oţoiu, "Negocier la (re)constitution de la propriete privee en Roumanie postsocialiste. (Nouveaux) acteurs, (anciennes) strategies," *Options Mediterraneennes*, A92 (2009): 65–75.

59 Asociaţia Persoanelor Deposedate Abuziv Foştilor Deportaţi Refugiaţi din România, *Ştiri*, *Legea 290/2003*, *Legea 10/2001*, *Legea 247/2005* (7 August 2009), available at: http://caritas-craiova.piczo.com/stiri,legea2902003,legea102001,legea2472005,?cr=5&linkvar=000044 (accessed on 23 June 2011).

in 1955, Ogoranu managed to hide from the communist authorities for twenty-one years until the late 1970s, when his sentence was commuted. Whereas some have praised him for his anticommunist activity, others have considered his early affiliation with a youth fascist organization reprehensible.[60]

The need to address the legacy of the communist regime has also been stressed by organizations uniting the victims of the revolution, which remain preoccupied primarily with finding the truth about the December 1989 events, publicly unmasking the involvement of post-communist leaders in those events, and securing financial compensation and other benefits for their members, who are referred to as revolutionaries. Best known among these groups has been the Association 21 December 1989, set up in 1990 in Bucharest by some of those who, during the revolution, took to the streets and defied the police and army forces deployed by the Ceauşescu regime. The Association has actively advocated for resolute transitional justice, including radical lustration, but other organizations of revolutionaries that include National Salvation Front leaders have seen such radical proposals as ill-disguised attempts to block the careers of politicians like Ion Iliescu and Petre Roman, the first post-communist president and prime minister, respectively.

In addition, the humanistic intellectuals and former anticommunist dissidents have lent support to some transitional justice methods (the truth commission, lustration, and access to secret files), while mostly rejecting efforts to unveil collaborators from among their groups, the intelligentsia, and the political parties they support. The Group for Social Dialogue of Bucharest and the Timişoara Society, located in the town where the revolution first started, were both created after the 1989 revolution to "promote real democracy" by providing viewpoints alternative to those proposed by the former communists turned into the country's first post-communist rulers.[61] Although few in number and elitist in view, these very vocal intellectuals have proposed some of the most coherent political programs advanced by the civil society. The Civic Alliance was created in 1990 by 216 respected writers, philosophers, and anticommunist dissidents "to channel social energies supporting faith, humanism and democracy."[62] The Alliance was most active in the early 1990s, when its members gained seats in parliament and it launched a number of programmatic documents, including the Declaration for National Reconciliation of March 1991 (see Chapter 4).[63] Its transitional justice programs, mostly related to the

60 Monica Ciobanu, "Rewriting and Remembering Romanian Communism: Some Controversial Issues," *Nationalities Papers*, 39(2011): 216.

61 Domniţa Stefănescu, *Cinci ani din istoria României. O cronologie a evenimentelor decembrie 1989-decembrie 1994* (Bucharest: Maşina de Scris, 1995), 47.

62 Ibidem, 104.

63 Alianţa Civică, *Declaraţia de Reconciliere Naţională* (13 March 1991) available at: http://www.aliantacivica.ro/documente/Declaratia%20de%20reconciliere%20nationala%20-%2013%20martie%201991.htm (accessed on 14 December 2011).

Sighet Memorial Museum, have been run through the nonprofit Civic Academy Foundation, led by poet Ana Blandiana and writer Romulus Rusan.

The repeated calls for truth, justice, and reparations of these civil society groups have been blocked by political elites drawn primarily from among the former Communist Party. Throughout 1989–2009, the center-left remained strong and united around the conservative faction of the National Salvation Front, the Party of Social Democracy, whereas the center-right was weak and divided among a multitude of political formations. The Social Democrats inherited the organizational skills, financial resources, and territorial organization of the Communist Party, which penetrated every town, workplace, and apartment block. Together, these advantages turned them into a formidable political actor that won the largest number of parliamentary seats in each post-communist election organized until 2008 (in 1990, 1992, 1996, 2000, and 2004).[64] The Social Democrats remained an important voice even when they were unable to form the government in 1996–2000 and 2004–2008 and when they acted as the official opposition. Providing safe haven to former communist officials and secret political police agents, the party constantly opposed transitional justice in principle and deed. Lacking leadership, financial resources, a clear vision for the future, and managerial experience to lead the country, the center-right failed to deliver accountable and transparent governments in 1996–2000 and 2004–2009. Despite electoral promises to work through the recent past, under the rule of the Democratic Convention, the Justice and Truth Alliance, and the Democrat-Liberals, transitional justice was the result of the personal initiative of individual politicians (including senator Constantin Ticu Dumitrescu, President Traian Băsescu, and Prime Minister Călin Popescu-Tăriceanu) more than the expression of a coherent governmental strategy.

In a country where the Communist Party membership extended to one-third of the adult population, one in two citizens depended on the party-state for their livelihood, and hundreds of thousands of individuals (including children) spied on their relatives, neighbors, and friends for the benefit of the Securitate, the position of the Social Democrats toward the past has not significantly departed from the wishes of the population. That party, however, was not the most formidable obstacle to transitional justice. The chauvinistic Greater Romania Party made it its mission to rehabilitate communist officials and secret collaborators and to recast the communist period as the epitome of Romanian civilization, a time when the country gained unprecedented international status, albeit not for its commitment to freedom and democracy, but for its apparent independence from Moscow in matters

64 As a result of the 2008 parliamentary elections, the Democrat Liberals gained one seat more than the Social Democrats, which ran in alliance with the Conservatives. For the election results, see Lavinia Stan and Răzvan Zaharia, "Romania," *European Journal of Political Research*, 48(2009): 1087–1099.

of foreign policy. By blending virulent nationalism, irredentism, and anti-Semitism with a discourse emphasizing Romanian cultural superiority, the party and its leader, Ceauşescu's sycophantic court poet Corneliu Vadim Tudor, systematically attacked transitional justice proponents, mocking them, laughing at them, smearing them, and whenever possible, destroying their lives, careers, and reputations. In this war of words, bottom-up calls for reckoning with communist-era crimes have been promptly dismissed as a witch hunt and a desire to take revenge on hardworking individuals who collaborated with an oppressive regime not for personal gain, but out of a genuine altruistic impulse of helping their country.

At the same time, among the actors inimical to the process of reckoning with the communist past were also the tenants who occupied confiscated dwellings with the authorities' permission before and after 1989. Although some were poor workers who moved from village to town to work in industrial factories, many others were privileged party nomenklatura members who had access to special food stores, medical clinics, and holiday resorts. Until 1989, all these tenants rented dwellings from the state, paying low rents that did not reflect the real market value of the property. They continued to abusively occupy these large historical houses, located in leafy residential areas, even after 1989.[65] The Association of Tenants Living in Nationalized Dwellings has branches in the most important towns. The Association of Tenants Who Acquired Ownership through Law 112/1995 represents tenants who, after 1995, bought the confiscated dwelling in which they lived.[66]

Tenants and secret agents were not the only ones to benefit from communist-era infringements of other people's rights. Since 2003, the Motherland and Honor Solidarity Foundation has provided financial help to and has protected the interests of former Securitate officers and post-communist intelligence agents.[67] Former Communist Party leaders and activists, political and militia officers, prosecutors and judges have not created civil society associations because they could face public condemnation as a result, and after 1989 they retained enough political clout to advance their personal interests directly through official channels. In addition, former communist perpetrators have gained a public voice as members of formations successor to the Communist Party and the Communist Youth League: the Social Democratic Party (which formed the government during 1990–1996 and 2000–2004), the Democratic Party (renamed the Democrat-Liberal Party, a government partner since 2004), and the Greater Romania Party (represented in parliament

[65] Stan, "The Roof over Our Head," 180–205.

[66] Daniela Benea, "Musceleni, la şedinţa pentru modificarea Legii Chiriaşilor," *Evenimentul Muscelean* (28 October 2008).

[67] "SRI a fătat o vacă de muls pentru securişti," *Ziarul de Iaşi* (25 July 2003), and Gabriel Andreescu, "Cazul Grigore Opriţă: a început vânătoarea zăpăciţilor şi a aiuriţilor," *Observator Cultural*, 180 (August 2003).

until 2008).[68] Tenants and former perpetrators have consistently blocked transitional justice attempts.

By and large, the Romanian transitional justice has been conducted with little meaningful support from international actors. During the 1990s, foreign governments and international organizations were generally disinterested in the Romanian redress, being content to remind the authorities of the democratic obligation to uphold the right to property of the owners (individuals, religious denominations, or ethnic communities) who had lost their assets abusively under the communist and interwar fascist regimes. As Romania refused to adopt the controversial lustration policy, the country was not mentioned when the Council of Europe and the European Court of Human Rights pointed to the undemocratic and unjust elements of banning former communist decision makers and secret agents from post-communist governmental posts. Starting in 1999, the European Court began to hear property restitution cases lodged by Romanian plaintiffs and, as a result of its decisions, compelled the Romanian authorities to redesign the national property restitution program. Several years before accepting Romania as a member, the EU began to offer modest financial assistance to educational and memorialization programs, while refusing to launch a more sustained program to facilitate an honest reckoning with the recent past in its member states.

THE OUTLINE OF THE VOLUME

The following chapters present a comprehensive assessment of the most important ways in which Romania has come to terms with its communist past. Having presented the main research questions that drive this study, the nature of the human rights trespasses perpetrated by the Gheorghiu-Dej and Ceauşescu regimes, and the most important factors that have shaped the effort to reassess the communist past, this chapter serves as an introduction to the volume. Chapters 2 through 9, which offer a wealth of empirical evidence, are dedicated to the most important transitional justice methods employed in the country.

Our journey into Romania's transitional justice program begins by considering court trials launched against Communist Party officials and militia and Securitate officers involved in human rights abuses. As Chapter 2 explains, for many former victims, reckoning through the courts has remained the best – nay, the only acceptable – approach to deal with communist crimes, and this is why the scarcity of the court trials and their inability to force perpetrators to assume responsibility for their past actions has been regarded as disappointing by civil society actors. Chapter 3 discusses access of the ordinary citizens to the secret Securitate files, and the numerous

[68] Stan and Zaharia, "Romania," 1087–1099.

public scandals that have surrounded the secret files since their opening in 2001. Romania's winding road to lustration, a method that for many Western scholars uniquely characterizes Eastern European efforts to reassess the communist past, is detailed in Chapter 4. The focus is then shifted in Chapter 5 to the presidential truth commission and the official condemnation of the communist regime delivered only days before the country joined the EU. Chapter 6 weaves together the return of abusively confiscated dwellings and places of worship transferred in 1948 from the minority Greek Catholic Church to the majority Orthodox Church as facets of the property restitution process. Two of the most important demands put forward by former political prisoners – compensation and rehabilitation – are examined in Chapter 7, whereas Chapter 8 surveys the changes operated in the way in which the communist regime, its victims, and perpetrators, and its role in the history of modern Romania are presented in pre-university history textbooks. Chapter 9 investigates a range of transitional justice methods initiated and implemented by civil society actors: unofficial truth projects, the citizens' opinion tribunal, forensic investigations, and memorialization.

The volume's concluding chapter tentatively responds to the two sets of questions that drive this research. First, it inquires about the role of sequencing transitional justice methods, demonstrating that the use of some approaches (public identification of former perpetrators, property restitution) precludes or limits the use of others (lustration, compensation); timing is of essence, as justice delayed is justice denied; sequencing matters, but political actors can only partially determine it; the relationship between official, state-sponsored and vernacular, civil society-sponsored *lieux de memoire* is indirect; and the nature of the communist past led to a preference for truth and justice – at the expense of reconciliation – and in turn determined the choice of methods (file access more than truth-telling initiatives, and an academic, not truth, commission). Second, the chapter suggests that when victims do not accept it, a forgive-and-forget policy deeply divides the post-dictatorial society and undermines trust in the new democratic institutions. In such cases, post-authoritarian countries must engage in transitional justice immediately after the regime change, as early reckoning with the past can allow the government and the civil society to choose from among a larger number of methods. The process of working through the past is significantly helped when important foreign actors (such as the EU) support it or at least do not send mixed messages (condemning and praising it at different times, criticizing methods on procedural grounds, while praising them on moral grounds, without specifying clear guidelines on how to improve the procedure). While Romania serves as a starting point, this discussion is relevant for other post-communist countries.

2

Court Trials

Criminal prosecutions have an important role to play in times of transition to democracy, not only because "in the public imagination, transitional justice is commonly linked with punishment and the trials of *ancien regimes*," but also because legal responses "serve to condemn and delimit abuses of past state power," "challenge past state criminality, and therefore go to the core illegitimacy of past rule."[1] In countries marred by legacies of past human rights violations, Ruti Teitel explains, court trials "play a significant foundational role in laying the basis of a new liberal order" by contributing to the social good, fostering the rule of law, repairing the harm caused by the crime, breaking with the myths of the old regime, enabling and unveiling the truth about the past, offering "normative legalism that helps to bridge periods of diminished rule of law," affirming the primacy of individual rights and responsibilities, exposing and delegitimizing the predecessor regime, and legitimizing the new legal and political order.[2] Few of these correlations are empirically demonstrated, but experts suggest that, on a more pragmatic level, justice may aim at controlling behavior (by deterring the offender from reengaging in violence and the victim from resorting to vengeance or social disruption) and reasserting social values and beliefs (by shaming the offender and changing his beliefs regarding the victims and the larger society and by restoring the victim's confidence in the state and the legal system).[3] Transitional justice scholars know that court trials have reached these goals when they are capable to facilitate "the construction of a permanent, unmistakable wall between the new beginnings and the old tyranny."[4] The gesture of "breaking the cycle of impunity

1 Ruti Teitel, *Transitional Justice* (New York: Oxford University Press, 2000), 26–27.

2 Idem, 28, 30.

3 Hugo van der Merwe, "Delivering Justice during Transition: Research Challenges," in *Assessing the Impact of Transitional Justice: Challenges for Empirical Research*, eds. Hugo van der Merwe, Victoria Baxter, and Audrey R. Chapman (Washington, DC: United States Institute for Peace, 2009), 122.

4 Otto Kirchheimer, *Political Justice: The Use of Legal Procedure for Political Ends* (Westport: Greenwood Press, 1961), 308, cited in Teitel, *Transitional Justice*, 29.

and the social illusion that no justice is available for the destitute," Rolando Ames and Felix Reategui contended, "can have a paradigm-shift quality to it: if justice can be done and if the powerful can be called to task (even if not properly punished) for their past wrongdoings, then the notion of politics as a realm where 'things do happen' can prevail."[5] Or, as Samuel Huntington wrote, "prosecution is necessary to assert the supremacy of democratic values and norms and to encourage the public to believe in them."[6] In addition, prosecutions are known to open the gates to retributive justice, commonly understood as punishment by the state of perpetrators following a process of judging guilt and imposing penalties proportional to the nature of the crime.

Of all Eastern European countries, Romania has conducted the second largest number of court trials related to the recent past, a veritable "justice cascade" unique in the region.[7] According to official estimates, by 2004 the Romanian military and civilian prosecutors had opened as many as 4,495 investigations, which involved 3,500 medical probes, 10,000 field trips, more than 1,000 on-site visits, and close to 1,100 gun tests. Around 41,000 people, including perpetrators, witnesses, and victims, were interrogated and interviewed as part of these proceedings. The military courts indicted 245 individuals in 112 trials. In one case, the charges rested on documentation contained in 250 files that included 4,000 statements identifying close to 1,000 victims.[8] With a handful of notable exceptions, however, all of these cases dealt with the crimes perpetrated during the December 1989 revolution – the bloody confrontation between state agents and peaceful, unarmed demonstrators in which 1,104 persons died and 3,352 others were wounded[9] – and the Valea Jiului miners' descent on the capital in June 1990, when angry miners damaged public buildings such as the University of Bucharest, ransacked the headquarters of prominent opposition parties, and attacked ordinary citizens in the name of protecting the country's budding democracy and its "revolutionary"

5 Rolando Ames Cobián and Félix Reátegui, "Toward Systemic Social Transformation: Truth Commissions and Development," in *Transitional Justice and Development: Making Connections*, eds. Pablo De Greiff and Roger Duthie (New York: Social Science Research Council, 2009), 156.

6 Samuel Huntington, *The Third Wave: Democratization in the Late Twentieth Century* (Norman: University of Oklahoma Press, 1991), 213.

7 Ellen Lutz and Kathryn Sikkink, "The Justice Cascade: The Evolution and Impact of Foreign Human Rights Trials in Latin America," *Chicago Journal of International Law*, 2(2001): 1–33.

8 The case involved the miners' decent on Bucharest. Dorin Petrişor, "Iliescu scapă de procesele mineriadei şi revoluţiei," *9AM News* (21 June 2007).

9 Peter Siani-Davies, *The Romanian Revolution of December 1989* (Ithaca: Cornell University Press, 2005), 97. Also John Sislin, "Revolution Betrayed? Romania and the National Salvation Front," *Studies in Comparative Communism*, 29(1991): 395–412; Steve Roper, "The Romanian Revolution from a Theoretical Viewpoint," *Communist and Post-Communist Studies*, 27(1994): 401–410; and Richard A. Hall, "The Uses of Absurdity: The Staged War Theory and the Romanian Revolution of December 1989," *East European Politics and Societies*, 13(1999): 501–542.

leaders.[10] By contrast, the Romanian judiciary has largely overlooked the many crimes perpetrated by the communist repression apparatus from 1945 to 1989 (see Chapter 1).

Romania is not the only post-communist country that showed reluctance to prosecute perpetrators of communist crimes and apparently worked on the premise that "there had been a guilty elite minority who should be punished, and an innocent majority of the former nomenklatura who should remain untouched."[11] A survey of post-communist court proceedings organized until 2007 revealed the scarcity of such cases even in countries with far more commitment to working through their communist past promptly and thoroughly. With the exception of Germany, no post-communist country brought more than three dozen communist-era perpetrators before the courts to assume responsibility for their crimes. The cases in which communist decision makers and army, police, and secret police officers were found guilty for their crimes and served prison time were even fewer.[12] Polish martial law ruler General Wojciech Jaruzelski, German leader Erik Honecker, and Bulgarian communist strongman Todor Zhivkov were all dragged in front of the courts to explain their role in repression, but none of them served prison time commensurate to their past crimes. In Albania, the judiciary's continued dependence on the executive has greatly hampered efforts to use court cases for redressing communist crimes. In a country where economic shortages had overshadowed human rights trespasses, communist leaders were indicted not for their numerous and heinous political crimes, but for their endemic corruption, access to food and medical services, and lavish spending – a decision interpreted by the public to reflect the legal impossibility and the lack of political will to hold communist leaders responsible for their political crimes.[13]

10 Tom Gallagher, *Modern Romania. The End of Communism, the Failure of Democratic Reform, and the Theft of a Nation* (New York: New York University Press, 2005); Ariadna Combes, Mihnea Berindei and Anne Planche, *Mineriada. 13–15 iunie 1990. Realitatea unei puteri neocomuniste* (Bucharest: Humanitas, 2010); and Sorin Ilieşiu and Alin Rus, *Raport-rechizitoriu despre fratricidul din 13–15 iunie 1990* (2010), available at: http://www.projects.expertvision.ro/luju/static/attachments/article/303/Raport%20-%20Rechizitoriu%20despre%20Dec%201989.pdf (accessed on 28 July 2011).

11 James Mark, *The Unfinished Revolution. Making Sense of the Communist Past in Central-European Europe* (New Haven: Yale University Press, 2010), 36.

12 Lavinia Stan, ed., *Transitional Justice in Eastern Europe and the Former Soviet Union: Reckoning with the Communist Past* (London: Routledge, 2009). Germany is an exception. During the 1990s, 79,108 investigations yielded 993 prosecutions and fewer than 100 convictions. In 1990–1996, 52,050 probes were launched in communist crimes, but only 139 convictions were handed down. David Wroe, "East German Victims Lament Lack of Justice," *The Local* (5 November 2009) and John Koehler, "Revenge versus the Rule of Law," *New York Times* (1999), available at: http://www.nytimes.com/books/first/k/koehler-stasi.html (both accessed on 29 August 2011); and A. James McAdams, *Judging the Past in Unified Germany* (Cambridge: Cambridge University Press, 2001).

13 Robert Austin and Jonathan Ellis, "Albania," in *Transitional Justice in Eastern Europe and the Former Soviet Union: Reckoning with the Communist Past*, ed. Lavinia Stan (London: Routledge, 2009), 181–183.

Only a handful of secret officers and none of the former Communist Party leaders have been convicted for involvement in communist crimes in the Baltic republics, where it is widely accepted that after 1940 both the Nazi (German) and the Soviet (Russian) regimes engaged in genocide against Baltic residents.[14]

Raluca Grosescu and Raluca Ursachi identify five reasons that explain the low number of cases brought before the courts in post-communist Romania. First, the continued political clout of former communist decision makers explains why, after 1989, the courts refused to hear cases dealing with communist crimes on grounds that those crimes were prescribed because they did not amount to war crimes, crimes against humanity, or genocide. Tainted members of the executive have cooperated behind closed doors with tainted judges, prosecutors, and police members to procrastinate investigations, keep evidence hidden from the public eye, warn indicted perpetrators of their impeding arrest, and sometimes even facilitate their escape. The lenient verdicts reached in cases related to communist crimes, the unwarranted lengthening of court proceedings, and the courts' reluctance to hear such cases demonstrates that Romanian judges "lack the impartiality and independence (from political parties and the surviving Securitate) to do their job."[15] As in other post-communist countries, in Romania new judges "are not as personally committed to absolving those who violated human rights under communism, but they are still professionally mediocre and timid in their approach to former and present hierarchical superiors," and their decisions "depend much more on their reading of the hierarchy of power in their environment than on the content of any laws."[16] In addition, opposition parties promoted court trials only to the extent that they hurt Ion Iliescu, proclaimed as the archenemy of democratization as a result of his undemocratic political choices as the first post-communist president. This rhetoric, which echoed the arguments justifying the Ceauşescu trial, focused the blame on one single person, overlooked the repressive nature of the larger political system, and ignored the role in human rights violations of tainted political actors other than the top leader.[17]

Second, the country's most vocal civil society groups – representing the communist-era victims and humanist intellectuals – have preferred to advocate for

[14] I thank Eva-Clarita Pettai for drawing my attention to this point. Also Lavinia Stan, "The Former Soviet Union," in *Transitional Justice in Eastern Europe and the Former Soviet Union: Reckoning with the Communist Past*, ed. Lavinia Stan (London: Routledge, 2009), pp. 234–240.

[15] Valerian Stan, "Răul communist: amnezie şi amnistie," *New York Magazine* (17 June 2009).

[16] Avizier Tucker, "Paranoids Must Be Prosecuted. Post-Totalitarian Transitional Justice," in *Retribution and Reparation in the Transition to Democracy*, ed. Jon Elster (New York: Cambridge University Press, 2006), 183–185.

[17] Alexandru Gussi, *La Roumanie face a son passé communiste. Memoires et cultures politiques* (Paris: L'Harmattan, 2011), 16.

a generic Trial of Communism that would indict and condemn all human rights violations committed from 1945 to 1989 and underscore the responsibility of all Communist Party officials and Securitate secret agents instead of lending support to specific court cases, because the latter required a familiarity with the law that group members did not possess.[18] The Group for Social Dialogue and the Civic Academy waged a rhetorical "intellectual trial" of the communist regime, but the accusations were couched in general terms that gave few details on what the Trial of Communism would entail precisely and were fraught with imprecise legal terms and justifications untenable in a court of law. Few serious legal scholars have been active politically in Romania as part of civil society organizations; many of them preferring instead to run for political office on behalf of various parties or to open their own legal practices to represent the interests of politicians involved in corruption more often than those of victims of human rights abuses. The ideological and policy divisions separating various groups and organizations further weakened the civil society and prevented it from promoting common transitional justice projects, court trials included.

Additionally, Grosescu and Ursachi suggested that three legal obstacles have hampered the use of trials as a method of post-communist justice, severely restricting the number of cases brought in front of the courts. The first was the presidential pardon Decree 11 that Nicolae Ceauşescu signed on 26 January 1988 to coincide with the anniversary of his seventieth birthday.[19] The Decree annulled all prison convictions of up to ten years, halved convictions over ten years, and commuted the death punishment into prison terms of twenty years. Because the overwhelming majority of the crimes committed by state authorities against political opponents and dissidents under his rule (including torture, serious bodily injury, maltreatment, illegal detention, abusive opening of correspondence, and violation of private domicile) were punishable with convictions of up to ten years, the Decree effectively amnestied the crimes of the Ceauşescu regime – other than manslaughter and imprescriptible crimes – and allowed the courts to hear only cases related to crimes committed by state authorities during the very last two years of dictatorship, from January 1988 to December 1989.[20] Civil society activists did not ask for and political

[18] Raluca Grosescu and Raluca Ursachi, *Justiţia penală de tranziţie. De la Nurnberg la postcomunismul românesc* (Bucharest: Institutul de Investigare a Crimelor Comunismului din România, 2009), 182.

[19] "Decret nr. 11 din 26 ianuarie 1988 privind amnistierea unor infracţiuni şi reducerea unor pedepse" (26 January 1988), available at: http://www.legex.ro/Decret-Nr.11-din-26.01.1988–860.aspx (accessed on 24 November 2011).

[20] Grosescu and Ursachi, *Justiţia penală de tranziţie*, 112–113, and Raluca Ursachi and Raluca Grosescu, "Transitional Criminal Justice in Post-Communist Romania," paper presented at the Crimes of the Communist Regimes conference, Prague, the Czech Republic, 24–26 February 2010, available at: https://www.ustrcr.cz/data/pdf/konference/zlociny-komunismu/Raluca_Grosescu.pdf (accessed on 10 December 2011).

decision makers did not take the initiative to annul the pardon decree. It was only in 2006 that the annulment featured among the recommendations handed down by the Presidential Commission for the Analysis of the Communist Dictatorship in Romania (see Chapter 5). Nevertheless, although he courageously agreed to serve as the first state representative to officially condemn communist crimes, President Traian Băsescu did not include the annulment among the recommendations to which he personally subscribed. Prosecutor General Codruţa Kovesi did very little to implement the recommendation, although she had been appointed by Băsescu's Democrat-Liberal Party in 2006. As such, Ceauşescu's pardon remains in effect at the time of this writing. If the pardon decree were annulled, the window of opportunity for judging maltreatment and the violation of correspondence and domicile would have extended only to 1993, and for torture acts, until 1998.[21] Ceauşescu's pardon was complemented by the Decree-Law 3 of 4 January 1990, which Iliescu signed as leader of the National Salvation Front Council, the self-appointed revolutionary force that wrested power from the dictator.[22] This more restricted amnesty program annulled all crimes punishable with prison time of up to three years. It benefited the militia, army, and Securitate officers and soldiers who beat up peaceful protesters in December 1989; individuals who helped the communist authorities to quash those revolts, intimidate the protesters, and cover up the crimes perpetrated by state agents; and the "revolutionaries" who broke communist laws that were still in effect at the time of the protests.

The expiry of the statutes of limitations for communist crimes represented a second legal obstacle that seriously impeded criminal prosecutions. According to the communist Penal Code adopted in 1968, which remained in force until 2006 when a new code was passed, the statute of limitations expired in fifteen years for murder, eight years for torture, and three years for maltreatment and illegal detention.[23] As such, "even in the absence of the 1988 amnesty, after the fall of communism [in 1989] the Prosecutor's Office could incriminate only killings committed after 1975, acts of torture committed after 1982, or abusive inquiries committed after 1987,"[24] thus leaving most communist human rights violations outside the scope of criminal prosecutions. Because of the expiry of the statute of limitations, most communist crimes committed under the rule of the Stalinist dictator Gheorghe Gheorghiu-Dej during the late 1940s and the 1950s could not be prosecuted once the country started to democratize in 1989. Successive post-communist prosecutor generals have insisted that courts that agreed to hear

21 Idem, 7.

22 "Decret-Lege nr. 3 din 4 ianuarie 1990," *Monitorul Oficial al României, partea I* (5 January 1990).

23 The communist Penal Code was republished in 1997. See "Codul Penal al României. Lege nr. 15 din 21 iunie 1968," *Monitorul Oficial al României* (16 April 1997).

24 Ursachi and Grosescu, "Transitional Criminal Justice in Post-Communist Romania," 7.

cases related to those crimes disregarded ex post facto issues and the principle of nonretroactivity, despite the fact that before 1989 the courts were unable to hear cases related to communist crimes.

Whereas Ceauşescu's amnesty decree remained in force, in 1993 the Romanian courts accepted the argument put forth by prosecutors investigating crimes committed during the 1950s that the statute of limitations should be suspended for communist crimes, as the Penal Code called for, if the criminal investigation had been obstructed in any way. According to the prosecutors, until 1989 "the members of the state and Communist Party apparatus had a privileged status before the law, their political position offering them actual immunity."[25] That observation has been echoed by numerous scholars, including Avizier Tucker, who noted that during communist times "a broad nomenklatura class was above the law, above the judges in the hierarchy," and its members "were able to do as they wished with impunity, limited only by the balance of power within the elite itself."[26] This suspension created a precedent by recognizing that, for crimes committed by communist leaders, the statute of limitations should start on 22 December 1989, the day when the leaders' political positions no longer protected them from prosecution because their protector, Ceauşescu, abdicated his political office by leaving Bucharest on board a helicopter. However, even in the case of communist leaders, the statute of limitations expired in 2005. A further attempt by the Institute for the Investigation of Communist Crimes to convince the courts to ignore the 2005 deadline was rejected by the prosecutor general's office, which argued that nothing prevented the indictment of communist crimes from 1989 to 2005 in a country where access to court was free.[27] Although formally Article 21 of the Constitution of 1991 recognized free access to justice, during Iliescu's first two presidential terms (1990–1996) there was little room, if any, for prosecutors to investigate communist crimes and for courts to hear those cases, as access to courts was systematically infringed by the new government, as evidenced by the case of the Greek Catholic Church, which was unable to convince the courts to hear its arguments favoring the return of its property (Chapter 6).

The third insurmountable legal obstacle was the communist authorities' refusal to recognize the crimes of the communist regime as imprescriptible crimes against humanity for which the statute of limitations does not apply. Genocide and war crimes were recognized as imprescriptible by the Penal Code of 1968, while crimes against humanity were not, although Romania ratified the Convention on the Non-Applicability of Statutory Limitations to War Crimes and Crimes against

25 Idem.

26 Tucker, "Paranoids Must Be Prosecuted," 183.

27 Grosescu and Ursachi, *Justiţia penală de tranziţie*, 115.

Humanity.[28] The reason why the communist authorities evaded their international obligation to introduce these crimes in the Penal Code related to the fact that those stipulations applied to persecutions on political grounds committed in time of peace, a provision that could have applied retroactively to crimes perpetrated under the Gheorghiu-Dej regime. That communist decision and the failure of the post-communist decision makers to adopt a new penal code immediately after 1989 have meant that "framing the communist crimes in the category of imprescriptible crimes as defined by the socialist Criminal Code [in force until 2006] is problematic"[29] because they cannot be legally considered war crimes, as they were committed during times of peace. Neither could they be considered acts of genocide, because their aim was not to exterminate an ethnic, racial, or religious group, as the 1968 Convention stipulated. True, the initial definition proposed by Raphael Lemkin in the aftermath of World War II also involved attacks against political and social groups, and only at the last moment did the final text of the Convention leave out repression against political groups, at the pressure of the Soviet Union and its satellite countries.[30] However, the definition of "genocide" introduced in the Romanian legislation and accepted internationally excluded aggression against political groups, which characterized most of the crimes committed by the communist regime in that country.

That Soviet leaders tried to protect themselves by imposing a restricted understanding of genocide not covering the liquidation of their political opponents and the Romanian communists avoided international condemnation by excluding crimes against humanity from the Penal Code is understandable, given their obsession with covering up their human rights violations and keeping up the appearance of legality. Less justified has been the willingness of successive Romanian post-communist governments – especially those boasting anticommunist credentials like the Democratic Convention (1996–2000) and the Liberal and Democrat-Liberal Parties (after 2004) – to perpetuate impunity by not including crimes against humanity in the Penal Code after 1989. This situation likely resulted from the reproduction of communist elites after the regime change, a reproduction that was more pronounced in Romania than in Poland and Croatia and comparable to the levels registered in the Russian Federation. Indeed, a large comparative elite study conducted in Eastern

28 *Convention on the Non-Applicability of Statutory Limitations to War Crimes and Crimes against Humanity* (26 November 1968), available at: http://www2.ohchr.org/english/law/warcrimes.htm (accessed on 10 December 2011).

29 Grosescu and Ursachi, *Justiţia penală de tranziţie*, 115.

30 Ronaldas Racinskas, "Historical Justice for Europe: Why, When and How?," in *European Public Hearings on Crimes Committed by Totalitarian Regimes. Crimes Committed by Totalitarian Regimes: Reports and Proceedings of the 8 April European Public Hearing on Crimes Committed by Totalitarian Regimes*, ed. Peter Jambrek (Ljubljana: Slovenian Presidency of the Council of the European Union, 2008), 16.

Europe uncovered that the percentage of Romanian government members who had belonged to the communist nomenklatura dropped from 74.2 percent for the first post-revolutionary government of Petre Roman (1989–1990) to 44.2 percent for the Social Democrat government of Nicolae Văcăroiu (1992–1996). The nomenklatura included the top communist party and state officials, and as such, the percentage of former lower-echelon communists in post-communist governments was even higher. Even the self-avowed, anticommunist Democratic Convention governments of 1996–2000 included 7 to 9 percent former nomenklatura members within their ranks. That percentage jumped to 18.5 once the Social Democrats returned to government in 2000.[31] Because neither the executive nor the legislative took the initiative to amend the Penal Code in view of condemning crimes against humanity, prosecutors and judges refused to apply the international legal principles that Romania accepted as early as 1968. Instead, they gave precedence to domestic law in cases related to communist-era human rights violations, although by doing so they infringed Article 20 of the 1991 Constitution, which provided not only that "constitutional provisions concerning the citizens' rights and liberties shall be interpreted and enforced in conformity with the Universal Declaration of Human Rights, with the covenants and other treaties Romania is a party to," but also that "where any inconsistencies exist between the covenants and treaties on the fundamental human rights Romania is a party to, and the national laws, the international regulations shall take precedence, unless the Constitution or national laws comprise more favourable provisions."[32]

Equally puzzling was Romania's acceptance as a member state of the EU when its domestic legal instruments only partly and highly selectively reflected the country's international commitments and the insistence of Western and Romanian scholars and practitioners on excluding political crimes from the definition of genocide, thus upholding an understanding of the term that perpetuates the Soviet view by condemning Nazi racial and ethnic crimes, but absolving communist political violations. An attempt by the Institute for the Investigation of Communist Crimes in 2008 to convince the Ministry of Justice to fully integrate the 1968 Convention into the national Penal Code such that crimes against humanity would be imprescriptible "irrespective of the date when they were committed" was rebuked by the Ministry on grounds that it infringed the principle of the non-retroactivity of the law, which a country committed to the rule of law like Romania could not tolerate.[33] The Ministry

31 Raluca Grosescu, "Conversia elitelor comuniste din România în perioada de tranziţie: 1989–2000," in *De ce trebuie condamnat comunismul* (Bucharest: Institutul de Investigare a Crimelor Comunismului din România, 2006), 249.

32 *Constituţia României din 1991*, available at: http://www.cdep.ro/pls/dic/act_show?ida=1&idl=1 (accessed on 26 July 2011).

33 Ursachi and Grosescu, "Transitional Criminal Justice in Post-Communist Romania," 9.

introduced instead a reference to the Rome Statute of the International Criminal Court of 1998, which echoes the Convention, but is applicable to crimes committed after April 2002, when it entered into force. As such, communist-era human rights violations are not recognized as crimes against humanity in Romania. The courts "have not applied international treaty provisions directly, even though lawyers have invoked them in some instances, but have used international treaties in interpreting national laws referring to human rights"[34] in ways that have perpetuated impunity.

Note that, in reviewing the possibility to hold communist decision makers responsible in a court of law, the Romanian judiciary, as its other Eastern European counterparts, has had to choose between the authority of the written law and the requirements of substantive justice. Communist law had protected state agents, but after the regime change of 1989 their human rights trespasses became morally condemnable. Even though the requirements of substantive justice called for putting perpetrators on trial, the legal basis of such court proceedings was weak at best. As such, in almost all cases, the reasons for the decisions hinged on political judgments about the legitimacy of the communist regime, which many judges were unwilling to seriously question.

Finally, the long time span separating the moment when most crimes were committed (during the first decades of communist rule) from the moment when they could be brought to court (after 1989) further explains the limited number of court trials. The Stalinist rule of the 1940s to 1960s was brutal, whereas the communist regime of the 1970s to 1980s was much milder (see Chapter 1). As they infringed basic rights that were guaranteed even by communist constitutions and resulted in gross human rights violations, Stalinist crimes were likelier to result in conviction, if brought before the courts. By contrast, the widespread surveillance of late communism destroyed many lives and thwarted many careers but was comparatively less punitive and therefore less likely to lead to conviction. The calculated choice of post-communist leaders to forego criminal investigation of more recent crimes and to indict perpetrators of older crimes backfired, because perpetrators of Stalinist crimes were older and frailer, if not already deceased. The difficulty of piecing together evidence that communist authorities tried hard to erase, the lack of proof connecting high-ranking communists to indictable crimes, and the public support for communist leaders widely believed to have upheld national interests in the face of Soviet pressure further made it unpalatable to mount convincing court cases against party officials and secret police agents involved in repression.

The fact that a country like Romania conducted so many trials in relation to the *cris de liberté* of December 1989 (which marked a rather short period of extreme repression) and so few in relation to the communist regime (which extended for

[34] Redress, *Romania Country Report* (May 2003), 3, available at: http://www.redress.org/downloads/country-reports/Romania.pdf (accessed on 3 October 2011).

forty-five years) is counterintuitive because the victims of the revolution (barely reaching 4,500) were fewer than the number of Romanians affected by communist repression (e.g., in 1990, there were 98,700 surviving former communist-era political prisoners, and they formed just one category of victims among others).[35] The discrepancy can be explained by analyzing the way in which Romania's first post-communist political leaders and the general public weighted these two competing pasts. Notwithstanding its longer duration and larger number of victims, the Stalinist regime was not on the minds of Romanians after the regime change of 1989. The past with which they had to reckon at the onset of transition was Ceauşescu's more recent sultanism-cum-totalitarianism,[36] not Gheorghiu-Dej's more distant rule. Compared to Ceauşescu's egregious economic infringements, the crimes of the revolution seemed more urgent and more gruesome, having resulted in the death of unarmed students and peaceful protesters. In addition, for the general public, the effort to prosecute communist crimes lost most of its expiatory significance once revolutionary leaders like Iliescu and Silviu Brucan blamed the Ceauşescu family, not the communist system, for the country's bankruptcy, argued that Ceauşescu's economic policy of depriving the people of food, heat, medicine, and electricity had turned almost all Romanians into victims, and presented themselves as the main victims of Ceauşescu's repression, despite their long-standing affiliation to the nomenklatura.[37] Prosecuting the crimes of the revolution but not those between 1945 and1989 benefited the new leaders by signaling their resolve to break with communist practice, while covering up their own tainted past.

This chapter examines the reluctance of the Romanian judiciary – which remained largely dependent on the executive from 1989 to 2009 – to prosecute communist-era perpetrators, the reasons why notorious communist-era torturers did not have to assume responsibility for their crimes, and the impact of amnesty presidential decrees on transitional justice. The successful court trials dealing with communist crimes, in which the hearings were brought to completion and concluded in conviction (the Gheorghe Ursu cases), are contrasted to the "limited criminal sanction" cases of the notorious communist torturers Alexandru Drăghici, Alexandru Nicolschi, and Gheorghe Crăciun, which were never heard or were discontinued before the courts reached a verdict, to tease out the factors that facilitated or impeded the sentencing of former communist decision makers.[38]

35 The figure represents the membership of the Association of Former Political Prisoners in Romania (Chapter 1).

36 Juan Linz and Alfred Stepan, *Problems of Democratic Transition and Consolidation: Southern Europe, South American, and Post-Communist Europe* (Baltimore: Johns Hopkins University Press, 1996), 344–365.

37 See Gussi, *La Roumanie face a son passé communiste*.

38 I borrow the "limited criminal sanction" term from Teitel, *Transitional Justice*, 46–51.

Throughout Eastern Europe, demands for transitional justice through court procedures have clustered around major incidents of police brutality against protesting citizens. As such, it is important to break down the Romanian communist period according to levels of dissent and repression, bearing in mind that any such classification would necessarily simplify reality. Apart from the 1989 revolution, the country registered the highest levels of repression during the first two decades of communist rule (1945–1964), in 1977, and again in 1987 (see Chapter 1). Between these temporal markers we can mention the isolated cases of Ursu; Radio Free Europe/Radio Liberty correspondents Monica Lovinescu and Emil Georgescu; anticommunist social and political activists Doina Cornea and Vasile Paraschiv; dissident writers Paul Goma, Mircea Dinescu, and Andrei Pleşu; and a number of individuals apprehended by the Securitate while trying to illegally cross the Western border to freedom. Repression methods ranged from harassment and smear campaigns to imprisonment and staged accidents all the way to murder. As we shall see, the courts have heard only one of these cases.[39]

Identifying 1977 and 1985 as years of high-level repression in no way means that the Ceauşescu regime was benevolent at other times, only that the number of gross human rights violations committed by state agents was significantly lower at other times. With the help of a massive Securitate secret network, the authorities opened mail, eavesdropped on phone conversations, monitored victims' every move by sending agents in plain clothes to pursue them in the streets, and collected information on their political convictions, marital infidelity, and personal preferences. Although some of these activities infringed constitutionally protected basic human rights like the secret of the correspondence, they did not constitute crimes serious enough to be heard by post-communist courts. As the Securitate placed hundreds of thousands of people under surveillance, the sheer number of cases would have overwhelmed the Romanian courts.

As with other transitional justice methods, court trials have been vigorously and vociferously promoted by representatives of civil society organizations and adamantly blocked by state authorities and major political formations, which harbor former communist perpetrators. Only a handful of cases were brought before the courts until 2009, although the first criminal charge against communist officials was filed with the prosecutor general on 2 September 1991 by the Association of Former Political Prisoners in Romania, representing the country's most organized victims' groups (see Chapter 1). The complaint listed as many as 264 persons allegedly responsible for various crimes during communist times. An investigation was initiated, but subsequently discontinued and never resumed, ostensibly as a result of political pressure, as some of those implicated still wielded considerable influence.

[39] Stan, ed., *Transitional Justice*, 128–151, and Ursachi and Grosescu, *Justiţia penală de tranziţie*.

Because they were committed well before 1989, most of these crimes can no longer be prosecuted because of the statute of limitations.[40]

THE TRIAL OF NICOLAE AND ELENA CEAUŞESCU

In a step unprecedented in the region, Romania's very "exit into history" coincided, and was brought about, by the speedy trial and execution of its much-feared communist dictator and his wife. Samuel Huntington, Elin Skaar, and other respected scholars considered Ceauşescu's trial as a sign of resolute transitional justice, in sharp contrast with what ordinary Romanians know: that the trial was a show trial reminiscent of those once conducted by the communist authorities, and that, in many ways, it tainted further attempts to honestly come to terms with the recent past.[41] Indeed, as Michael Kraus rightly contended, transitional justice in Romania "initially focused on several high profile trials of former [communist] leaders, while ignoring the machinery that facilitated the system of terror."[42] The new revolutionary leaders, President Iliescu and Prime Minister Peter Roman, defended the haste with which the trial hearings and executions took place by claiming that due process could not take precedence over the bloody confrontations waged in the streets, the ever-mounting number of civilian casualties, and the real possibility that the country might descend into chaos and civil war. While not downplaying the gravity of the 1989 events but recognizing their seriousness, their critics have underscored the fact that the speedy trial allowed the new rulers to blame the leader, not the communist system, for the country's malaise, without giving Ceauşescu the chance to elaborate on the role that second-echelon apparatchiks like Iliescu and Roman's parents had played in repression. The trial allowed the revolutionary forces to terminate Ceauşescu and thus completely shatter the hopes of his loyal army and secret service members that the tide could be reversed. However, its many flaws prevented the trial from accomplishing the very task for which it was organized: bestowing a measure of much-needed legitimacy on the new self-appointed "revolutionary" government. Instead of bringing Romanians together, the trial deeply divided them, sped up the formation of numerous political opposition groups, exposed the new rulers to an unprecedented wave of criticism that culminated in the University Square demonstrations of June 1990, and even absolved Ceauşescu of part of his guilt in the eyes of some ordinary citizens longing for the job security of communist times. In short, the

40 Ursachi and Grosescu, *Justiţia penală de tranziţie*, 9.

41 Huntington, *The Third Wave*, and Elin Skaar, "Truth Commissions, Trials or Nothing?: Policy Options in Democratic Transitions," *Third World Quarterly*, 20(1999): 1117.

42 Michael Kraus, "Settling Accounts: Post-Communist Czechoslovakia," in *Transitional Justice: How Emerging Democracies Reckon with Former Regimes*, vol. 2, ed. Neil Kritz (Washington, D.C.: United States Institute of Peace, 1995), 542–544.

trial resulted in "high-jacked justice," albeit of a different kind than that identified in the former Yugoslavia by Jelena Subotic.[43]

The trial's real loser was the dictator's wife, Elena Ceauşescu, described as a "gargoyle of grandiosity" by Eva Hoffman and perceived by ordinary Romanians as a veritable harpy who exerted control over the country by controlling her powerful husband.[44] Despised for her pretense of scientific notoriety and vain intellectual ambitions, the uneducated Elena occupied high-ranking positions in the party-state apparatus but was involved in the 1989 massacres less directly and intimately than other communist officials who managed to avoid the death squad.[45] Popular wrath was also directed against Ceauşescu's children, who became the protagonists of a well-staged cloak-and-dagger drama. In December 1989, Ceauşescu's heirs – Valentin, Zoe, and Nicu – were hastily arrested, jailed in the Bucharest Militia, and charged with undermining the national economy by using their privileged position to usurp party assets. Afterward, valuable possessions were confiscated from Valentin's home and moved to the National Art Museum collection. In late 1990, Ceauşescu's three children were released from prison, and in January 1996, charges against them were dropped. Half a year later, Nicu died of cirrhosis, thus ending a life wasted in alcoholism, substance abuse, and continuous excesses. The reclusive Zoe, who barely came out of her Bucharest apartment in a well-guarded effort to preserve her anonymity, died of cancer in 2006. In 2003, the courts awarded Valentin most of the valuables confiscated in 1989, thus turning him into one of the main beneficiaries of the property restitution program at a time when other initial owners were denied the assets that had been rightfully theirs (see Chapter 5).[46] There was no attempt on the part of the new revolutionary leaders to prosecute the members of the extended family of Nicolae Ceauşescu and Elena (née Petrescu), who had greatly benefited from the despotic regime but sought no public office after 1989. Until 1989, twenty-seven of Ceauşescu's relatives occupied high-ranking state and party positions, whereas Elena's only brother, Gogu, remained a trade union leader all his life. At the time of this writing, Ceauşescu's relatives have either died or are very old, and none hold public office.[47]

[43] Jelena Subotic, *Highjacked Justice: Dealing with the Past in the Balkans* (Ithaca: Cornell University Press, 2009).

[44] Eva Hoffman, *Exit into History. A Journey through the New Eastern Europe* (New York: Viking Press, 1993), 321.

[45] D. Golebiewska, G. Brycki, and W. Sochacki, "A Mixed Bag of Communist Trials," *World Press Review*, 43(1996), available at: http://scilib.univ.kiev.ua/doc.php?5779544 (accessed on 28 December 2007); Dan Ionescu, "Old Practices Persist in Romanian Justice," *Report on Eastern Europe* 1(9 March 1990): 44–48; Michael Shafir, "The Isolation of Romania and the Fall of Nicolae Ceausescu," *Report on Eastern Europe* 1(5 January 1990): 28–32.

[46] Personal interview with Damiana Oţoiu, Bucharest, 29 June 2011.

[47] For a memoir written by a family member, see Mihaela M. Ceauşescu, *Nu regret, nu mă jelesc, nu strig* (Bucharest: Editura Meditaţii, 2004).

The trial, which addressed the crimes committed by Ceauşescu during both his 1965–1989 despotic rule and the 1989 revolution, was hastily conducted on the morning of 25 December 1989 in Târgovişte, a small town some 100 kilometers away from Bucharest, by an ad hoc military "people's tribunal" that handed down the death sentence after less than two hours of deliberation. The court hearings were organized on Christmas Day to symbolically mark the death of the Antichrist, incarnated as a communist dictator who remorselessly persecuted the church and his people. The defiant Ceauşescu stood accused of genocide and undermining the state order during the 1989 revolution, the destruction and neglect of industrial property, and the bankruptcy of the state economy from 1965 to 1989. He was faulted for refusing "to engage in dialogue with the people" as a leader, appearing in public "dressed luxuriously, at a time when ordinary people had their salami rationed to 200 grams per day," orchestrating starvation and "genocide against the Romanian people," denying the people central heating and electricity during the 1980s, and most importantly, "enslaving the Romanian spirit"[48] and driving Romanians to despair. The written indictment, which extended on merely two pages and was prepared by an upstart prosecutor, thus levied accusations couched in very general terms and provided no sound rationale for linking the very harsh charges to the non-existing evidence.

The content and format of the indictment reflected the desire of the new leaders to avoid incriminating the communist regime and to condemn solely the dictator as much as they reflected the speed at which the trial was organized and the amateurism of the prosecutors, defense counselor, and judges who agreed to bestow a veneer of legality on what amounted to regicide. Instead of citing lack of "dialogue," "clothing," "salami," "central heating and electricity," and "enslavement," the charges could have well referred to the many human rights infringements condoned, sponsored, or ordered by the dictator: the selling of German and Jewish citizens against hard cash; the illegal placing in jail, under house arrest or in psychiatric wards of those who criticized the leader and his policies; the death of so many women who underwent illegal abortion after Ceauşescu implemented his pro-natal policy in 1967; the arrest, torture, illegal deportation, and disappearance of miners and workers who participated in the 1977 and 1987 strikes; or Ceauşescu's involvement in communist repression as a Central Committee member from 1952 to 1964. Almost all of these instances of oppression and terror would have also incriminated high-ranking leaders of the 1989 revolution, who had occupied key leadership positions under the Gheorghiu-Dej and Ceauşescu regimes (first and foremost, Iliescu and Brucan), and even members of the panel of judges (most notably, Army General Victor Atanasie Stănculescu).

[48] *Transcriptul 'procesului' Nicolae şi Elena Ceauşescu* (2008), available at: http://www.ceausescu.org/ceausescu_texts/revolution/trial-ro.htm (accessed on 30 July 2011).

As no hard evidence was brought forth to substantiate the charges of political crimes, especially the contention that Ceauşescu was directly responsible for the death of 60,000 people during the December 1989 clashes between state troops and peaceful demonstrators, the indictment mostly echoed the economic crimes levied in post-communist Albania against the family of communist dictator Enver Hoxha. The report prepared by Genc Ruli and presented to the Albanian parliament in mid-1991 audited the luxurious spending of the communist elite and showed that "the country's new leaders felt that in a nation so stricken by poverty and shortages, the public would be more inclined to support actions that focused on financial abuses."[49] The Ruli report, which read like a detailed grocery list more than a serious indictment, accused the Hoxha family of trifle trespasses: from 1989 to 1990, they consumed "2 tons of meat, 7 tons of salami, 523 liters of oil, 3.1 tons of butter, 321 liters of *raki*, alcoholic beverages and wine, 250 liters of beer, 5.3 tons of fruit and citrus products, 114 kilograms of olives ... and 1.8 kilograms of coffee."[50] In the same vein, Ceauşescu was reminded of the gulf separating his luxurious clothes – which were dull in comparison to those regularly exhibited by Libya's colorful dictator, General Muammar Gaddafi – from the insufficient daily salami intake of ordinary Romanians. The contrast was meant to demonstrate the shallowness of a regime that claimed to represent paradise on earth when, in fact, it starved its people and failed to provide them with basic necessities. Nevertheless, Ceauşescu's decadent lifestyle, ubiquitous personality cult, or "scientific" food rationing plan hardly demonstrated the regime's criminal character.

The trial was a show trial because of its significant procedural and substantial flaws that prevented it from setting what Paul Ricoeur called "the just distance" (*la juste distance*) between crime and punishment, victim and perpetrator, or perpetrator and the rest of the society.[51] As key members of the judging panel later admitted, the judges knew in the morning that Ceauşescu had to be executed by afternoon[52]; no hard evidence was produced to substantiate the claim that Ceauşescu was the only, or even the primary, state dignitary responsible for the loss of human lives before or during the revolution; the charges exclusively targeted the person (Ceauşescu) but remained silent on the mechanism of communist terror and the institutional bases of the dictatorship; the number of casualties (60,000) cited as proof of Ceauşescu's repressive policies was grossly inflated and unsubstantiated; Elena's guilt of

49 Austin and Ellis, "Albania," 181.

50 Idem.

51 Paul Ricoeur, *La mémoire, l'histoire, l'oubli* (Paris: Seuil, 2000), 413.

52 Dinu Săraru and Victor Atanasie Stănculescu, *Generalul Revoluţiei cu piciorul în gips* (Bucharest: Rao, 2005). Silviu Brucan, the *eminence grise* of the National Salvation Front, also admitted in his memoires that the outcome of the trial was predetermined. Silviu Brucan, *De la capitalism la socialism şi retur. O biografie între două revoluţii* (Bucharest: Nemira, 1998).

intellectual fraud did not warrant the death penalty, making the punishment highly disproportionate to her crimes and thus infringing basic legal principles; and the two defendants were granted neither a strong defense (as even their counselor accused them of crimes) nor the right to appeal (as the death sentence was carried out by the firing squad only minutes after the improvised military court handed it down). In addition, the principle of non-retroactivity was grossly overlooked when, at the start of the proceedings, Ceauşescu was told he would be judged not according to the communist law in effect at the time when the crimes took place, but according to the new law passed by the National Salvation Front Council, the new formation that had just deposed him. In reply, Ceauşescu urged the judge to read the constitution, but the court mocked his request.[53]

Carried out during highly volatile times without observing minimal rules of procedure, the trial represented victors' justice, because Ceauşescu was convicted on the basis of unsubstantiated charges just because the new revolutionary forces could do so. While at the time few Romanians gave him the benefit of the doubt and many believed that he had to go as quickly as possible, Ceauşescu denounced the legality of the trial and rejected the legitimacy of the people's tribunal. Of course, the ad hoc military tribunal reflected the will of the people far less than the interests of the unelected new leaders, who sought to consolidate their power and block a possible counterrevolution by discrediting Ceauşescu. The revolutionary leaders saw the trial as the fundament of the new political order they created, and handsomely rewarded the prosecutors, judges, and army officers who participated in the proceedings with speedy promotions, while making sure that the trial outcome was the one desired by Iliescu and his Salvation Front collaborators, many of who had formerly been supporters of the much-despised dictator. The trial's hasty organization was entrusted to army General Stanculescu, a former collaborator of Ceauşescu, who became first Minister of National Defense and then Minister of Economy in the first two revolutionary governments of Prime Minister Petre Roman (1989–1991). Defense Counselor Constantin Lucescu became head of the Bucharest Military Court, while his trial assistant, the unknown army Officer Mugurel Florescu, was appointed deputy prosecutor general. Gelu Voican Voiculescu and Virgil Măgureanu, two trial observers who were appointed by the National Salvation Front Council – the leadership body of the revolutionary forces that ousted Ceauşescu – played key roles in the post-communist intelligence services: the former as deputy prime minister of the first Roman government and supervisor of the recreation of the Securitate along the lines of its former departments (28 December 1989–28 June 1990), and the latter as the first director of the Romanian Information Service (March 1990–April 1997), heir to the Securitate's domestic repression branch. Voican Voiculescu

[53] *Transcriptul 'procesului' Nicolae şi Elena Ceauşescu.*

and Măgureanu were rumored to have worked for the Securitate, but allegations were never proven. The only trial participant who kept his distance from Iliescu and the Social Democrats was Prosecutor Dan Voinea, who shot to fame after the Democratic Convention won the elections of 1996, occupying the position of military prosecutor with the Supreme Court of Justice from 1997 to 2000. He led the investigations related to the revolution of December 1989 and the miners' descent on Bucharest in 1990, without ever succeeding to finalize them and bring them before the courts. For this reason, in March 2009 he was dismissed from his post and forced to retire.[54]

In addition, this trial conducted by the military people's tribunal was not only a misleading "ritual of rupture" – to use Claus Offe's metaphor – but also an evident perversion of justice (what the Germans call *Rechtsbeugung*), because military and people's tribunals represent a contradiction in terms, as one term refers to a vertical hierarchy that selects its members according to well-known rules, while the other suggests a body freely elected by civilians.[55] This contradiction was never satisfactorily addressed by the military organizers of the trial, the National Salvation Front collective leadership, or Iliescu, who hoped to derive legitimacy from the proceedings and thus protect themselves against a reversal of fortune. Because of its many flaws, however, the trial eroded the Romanians' trust in the willingness of the new soi-disant revolutionary leaders and of the weak, corrupt, and self-interested judiciary to shed light on communist atrocities. This is partly why Ceauşescu's grave in the Ghencea cemetery in Bucharest remains a site of pilgrimage and recollection for some communist nostalgics. The trial also showed that transitional justice cannot be carried out with unjust procedures and disregard for due process and that communist injustice cannot be rectified or healed by another injustice.

OTHER COURT TRIALS AND PROCEEDINGS

A handful of other court cases have related to communist-era perpetrators. The trial of the killers of Ursu, an engineer who wrote critically about the communist regime in his journal during the 1980s, and the so-called Bus Trial, which referred to the suspected killing by the Securitate of young people arrested for taking hostage a local bus, were brought to completion. Notorious torturers Alexandru Nicolschi, Alexandru Drăghici, and Gheorghe Crăciun died before the courts could find

54 Romulus Cristea, "Un dosar incomod pentru cei care au fost la putere," *RomâniaLiberă* (16 June 2006).

55 Claus Offe, "Disqualification, Retribution, Restitution: Dilemmas of Justice in Post-Communist Transitions," *Journal of Political Philosophy*, 1 (1993): 17–44.

them responsible for their many crimes perpetrated during the 1950s.[56] Observers have detected a qualitative difference between trials initiated in the early stages of post-communism and those launched later. Whereas earlier trials were marked by serious procedural flaws that turned them into show trials (as was Ceauşescu's trial), later trials were less of a spectacle for the benefit of a population hungry for revenge, and instead, they took the form of drier legal exercises that endeavored to observe the letter and the spirit of the law.[57] Nonetheless, these court proceedings were also affected by a host of problems: the statute of limitations lapsed for some crimes before the sentence was handed down, some of the accused were old and frail, others avoided prosecution by leaving the country, and the young defendants in the Bus Trial were as much victims of the Securitate as perpetrators of terrorist acts. Importantly, none of these cases addressed the most gruesome and recent communist crimes or convicted the most notorious individuals who masterminded or executed those crimes (the Securitate officers and prison guards and the Communist Party leaders).

One high-profile set of trials related to a documented case of murder of a political prisoner in communist prisons under Ceauşescu's rule. On 21 September 1985, the 59-years-old Ursu entered the infamous jail of the Bucharest Militia, located on Rahova Street. For close to a year, Ursu had been closely watched by the Securitate for establishing and maintaining contact with Romanian emigrant writers and Radio Free Europe/Radio Liberty journalists who voiced critical views of Ceauşescu's megalomania. Then, two female workmates denounced Ursu for keeping a diary that recorded negative comments toward the party-state and Ceauşescu personally. Instead of being prosecuted for his political views, Ursu was charged with an invented illegal possession of hard currency, which was deemed a crime by communist law. Within two months of entering the prison, Ursu reportedly died of "natural causes," but after 1989, prison doctors admitted that the death was a homicide resulted from cruel beating.

A criminal investigation initiated by the military prosecutor in 1990 ended five years later when a former inmate, Marian Clita, confessed to having killed Ursu. Ursu's relatives raised serious doubts about the confession in the light of strong evidence of police involvement. In 2000, Clita and four high-ranking police officers were convicted, but the court was forced to apply the Ceauşescu's presidential pardon decree of 1988. As a result, Clita's sentence was halved, and no punishment was imposed on the police officers. After public protests against this judgment, three other officers were charged in the Ursu case. In 2001, a court upheld a challenge of the defendants against the legality of the proceedings and dismissed the case,

56 Grosescu and Ursache, *Justiţia penală de tranziţie*.

57 Idem.

a decision that the prosecution subsequently appealed.[58] Then, in mid-July 2003 the Bucharest Court of Appeals Judge Viorel Podar ruled that former head of the Criminal Investigations Department of the Bucharest Militia Tudor Stănică and his deputy Mihail Creangă were guilty of ordering Ursu's killing. The prosecution argued that the officers ordered prisoner Clita to "exercise acts of violence" against Ursu, and forbade the guards on duty from offering Ursu any medical help that might have saved his life. They were sentenced to twenty-two years' prison terms, eight years' suspension of civil rights, military downgrading, and payment of Lei 1 billion (around 35,000 USD) to the three surviving members of the Ursu family. The new prison sentence was again halved by Decree 11/1998.

As a result of this court decision, an arrest warrant was issued for Stănică's and Creangă's immediate apprehension, which could not be carried out because the arresting policemen had once been subordinates of the two retired officers, and each time they raided the homes of Creangă and Stănică the two mysteriously disappeared. The two officers appealed the verdict to the Supreme Court, as did the prosecutor general on grounds that it was too harsh. On 10 October 2003, the Supreme Court upheld the original verdict, cutting down the sentence to twenty years in prison. Within a month, Stănică and Creangă were arrested. The upholding of the verdict was in large measure the result of pressure applied by the Finnish member of the European Parliament Astrid Thor, who on 21 August 2003 urged the EU ambassadors to Bucharest to keep a close eye on the Ursu trial because it amounted to "a case of injustice" resulting from "years of delays and abuse of justice."[59]

While in prison Stănică obtained a copy of Ursu's (legally unavailable) Securitate file, which he studied to prepare another appeal alleging that Ursu had been an informer for the Securitate, which had him killed for disobedience. Stănică's efforts to exonerate himself were highly disingenuous. Before 1989, Stănică was one of the most feared communist criminal investigators, nicknamed the Beast of Rahova. Former prisoners reported that, while at Rahova under Stănică's rule, they were savagely beaten on the head, face, and groin, were left hanging from large wall hooks for hours until their hands and feet went numb and were denied basic medical treatment, and women prisoners were obliged to perform oral sex with the guards. After 1989, Stănică became a successful businessman and the head of the doomed Credit Bank.[60]

58 Idem, 9–10.

59 *Un parlamentar UE cere monitorizarea 'dosarului Ursu'*, Fundaţia Gheorghe Ursu (no date), available at: http://gh-ursu.ong.ro/ziua_spt.htm (accessed on 31 July 2011), and Gianina Buzea, "Cazul Gheorghe Ursu, o ruşine pentru justiţia română," 22 (10 June 2002).

60 Adrian Artene, "Dreptate pentru Ursu," *Ziua* (15 July 2003), and Cristian Levant, "Surse din Parchetul General dezvăluie: Informaţii clasificate, pe mâna torţionarilor lui Ursu," *Evenimentul Zilei* (10 November 2003).

The Ursu family moved one step closer to attaining justice in 2004, when General Eugen Grigorescu received a three-year prison term for facilitating the disappearance of the diary that prompted the Securitate to place Ursu under arrest. When Ursu was arrested in 1985, Grigorescu ordered the search of his apartment and the confiscation of his journal. After the collapse of the communist regime in 1989, Grigorescu was one of the former Securitate officers retained by the Information Service, which the new revolutionary rulers wrongly presented to the country as a completely new institution, untainted by ties to the communist political police. In fact, the Service was the heir to the domestic repression branch of the Securitate, inheriting its personnel, cases, archives, and even methods. As though to confirm the fears of civil society representatives who championed the forced retirement of communist-era secret agents, Grigorescu used his new position with the Information Service to destroy the evidence that demonstrated his communist-era involvement in the Ursu case. Ursu's relatives complained of Grigorescu's suspended sentence, because without the threat of actually going to jail, Grigorescu was unlikely to return the diary.[61] At the time of this writing, the Ursu family has not yet located the journal.[62]

The Ursu family also collected enough evidence against the much-feared Colonel Gheorghe Vasile, the head of the Securitate Direction for Criminal Investigations at the time of Ursu's arrest, and Marin Pârvulescu, Ursu's interrogator, to bring them in front of the courts on charges of murder and torture. Although lodged only months after the collapse of the communist regime, the cases dragged for several years after they were assigned to another prosecutor in 1993 and the Information Service refused to assist the investigation by releasing the Securitate documents needed to prove the charges. The political change that followed the elections of 1996, which brought the Democratic Convention to government and University of Bucharest Professor Emil Constantinescu to the presidency, failed to speed up the investigation. The cases were reassigned to another prosecutor, and then assigned back to the one who had helped launch the investigation in the early 1990s. Investigations ceased with Vasile's death in the 2000s.[63] In 2008, the Institute for the Investigation of Communist Crimes sent to the Military Chamber of the Supreme Court of Justice a report detailing the crimes committed by Pârvulescu, but the petition resulted in no indictment.[64] The prosecutors' reluctance to investigate former Securitate

[61] Nicoleta Savin, "25 de ani de la asasinarea lui Gheorghe Ursu," *Realpolitic* (1 December 2010). Grigorescu served one year in jail.

[62] In 1990, the journal was read by several members of the Group for Social Dialogue before being taken over by the Information Service.

[63] Ovidiu Simonca, "Sub presiunea societății civile. Interviu cu Adrian Ursu," 22 (28 July 2003).

[64] Institutul de Investigare a Crimelor Comunismului din România, *Sesizare penală în cazul inginerului Gheorghe Ursu* (20 June 2008), available at: http://www.valerianstan.ro/files/Sesizare%20penala%20in%20cazul%20inginerului%20Gheorghe%20Ursu%20(iunie%202008).pdf (accessed on 31 July 2011).

officers and to recognize their crimes as crimes against humanity has blocked all these cases.[65]

In March 2002, in the so-called Bus Trial, former Minister of Interior Tudor Postelnicu (1987–1989) and eight militia and Securitate officers were sentenced to prison terms of six to seven years for the death of three young people who, on 24 August 1981 in the Timiş county, took hostages from among the passengers of a local bus using guns and ammunition stolen from the local militia headquarters the night before. They asked for hard currency and passports to leave Romania in exchange for the hostages. When the Securitate troops assailed the bus, the captors killed the bus driver and five other passengers, including women and children, before being apprehended. One of them hanged himself in the hospital, and the other two were killed by the Securitate agents while trying to escape. By the time this sentence was handed down, Postelnicu had already served five years jail time after being convicted in two other cases related to the 1989 revolution. As such, the courts decided against his rearrest.[66] The Bus Trial's long duration reflected the ambivalence of the Romanian political elite and the judiciary toward the case. Because the captors behaved as violent terrorists, killing innocent people when the Securitate turned down their demands, many legal minds believed that the three had no right to vindication and that the real victims of this unfortunate case were the innocent passengers murdered on the bus. There were, however, suspicions that two captors were shot not because they tried to flee, but because their summary execution had been ordered by top communist party-state officials.[67]

Three other cases were brought before courts, but they were never fully heard. Romania has tried to prosecute the communist officials involved in the waves of arbitrary arrests, torture, and murder that took place from the late 1940s to 1964, the year when most political prisoners were released. Only two torturers were placed under investigation, and both of them were individuals marginalized by Ceauşescu. The choice to channel all efforts into prosecuting two old individuals involved in crimes that were hideous, to be sure, but had taken place decades earlier was seemingly prompted both by their lack of support from the second-echelon communist leaders who took over the reign of the country from Ceauşescu and by the perception that earlier communist rule had infringed on human rights more than late communism. As some former Securitate officers have insisted, Romanian communism was malign under Gheorghiu-Dej, when torture was widely used against large

[65] The reluctance has been noted by Ursu's son. *Fiul dizidentului Ursu acuză justiţia română că pactizează cu foştii securişti* (no date), available at: http://www.luju.ro/opinii/interviu/exclusiv-fiul-disidentului-ursu-acuza-justitia-romana-ca-pactizeaza-cu-fostii-securisti?pdf (accessed on 31 July 2011).

[66] "Tudor Postelnicu şi-a executat pedeapsa, a decis instanţa militară," *Mediafax* (29 April 2002).

[67] "Tudor Postelnicu şi alţi opt foşti ofiţeri de Securitate şi Miliţie îşi aşteaptă sentinţa," *Gazeta de Sud* (21 February 2002).

categories of victims, and benign under Ceauşescu, when authorities preferred to employ soft methods like secret surveillance. Political support and public apathy explain, for example, why the head of the foreign branch of the Securitate, General Nicolae Pleşiţă, was never convicted for torturing dissident writer Paul Goma or for ordering the killing of members of the Romanian section of the Radio Free Europe (Noel Bernard and Vlad Georgescu) despite concrete evidence demonstrating his involvement.[68]

From 1952 to 1965, first as Minister of State Security and then as Minister of Interior, Alexandru Drăghici consolidated the Securitate into a repression tool accountable only to the top party-state leadership. As he stated in one of his most suggestive declarations, "the Securitate is the instrument of the party; it is obliged to respect the law, but we can turn the law into what we want."[69] He encouraged the use of terror to crush anticommunist resistance and extended repression to Communist Party leaders like Lucreţiu Pătrăşcanu, who fell in disgrace for his outspoken criticism of the forced collectivization campaign. Once he assumed the party leadership, Ceauşescu launched an investigation into Drăghici's activity and involvement in Pătrăşcanu's condemnation to death. To be sure, Ceauşescu did not seek to uncover the true extent of earlier communist repression – as he himself had played an important part in it – but sought political capital and legitimacy by blaming his predecessor for those atrocities. The investigation was abandoned in 1968, not before Drăghici was stripped of all his positions in the party-state apparatus. In 1991, former political prisoners asked for his investigation, but Drăghici managed to flee the country by relocating to Budapest. Two years later he was condemned in absentia not for his role in masterminding some of Romania's worst repression incidents, but for ordering the killing of a certain Ibrahim Sefit, who had dared to confront him in 1954. When approached by the Romanian prosecutors, the Hungarian authorities refused to extradite him, and as a result, Drăghici peacefully died in Budapest on 12 December 1993.[70] At the time of this writing, Drăghici's portrait is still displayed in the hallways of the Romanian parliament, alongside the portraits of other former ministers.

Alexandru Nicolschi (whose real name was Boris Grunberg) was a Soviet agent and a recognizable leader of early communist repression in Romania. In 1946 to 1947, he ordered massive waves of arbitrary arrests, before becoming deputy director of the then newly created Securitate in 1948. Nicolschi, who for Romanians represented the epitome of calculated sadistic cruelty, was responsible for the arrest

68 Cornel Oprea, "Pleşiţă, diplomaţii şi terorismul de stat," *România Liberă* (8 November 2007).

69 Cristian Troncotă, "Securitatea – Începuturile," *Magazin Istoric*, 10(October 1998), available at http://www.itcnet.ro/history/archive/mi1998/current10/mi24.htm (accessed on 29 May 2008).

70 Vladimir Tismaneanu, "Alexandru Drăghici şi teroarea comunistă în România," *Cotidianul* (27 Aprilie 2006).

of writer Lena Constante, the torture of Liberal politician Adriana Georgescu, the execution of Lucreţiu Pătrăşcanu in April 1954 following a mock trial of a predetermined outcome, and the introduction of the Piteşti experiment in prisons that housed student political prisoners, and ignored evidence of gruesome torture in his many visits to detention centers.[71] After the Romanian Communist Party leaders distanced themselves from Moscow in the 1960s, Nicolschi was forced into retirement without being denied the luxuries reserved for the nomenklatura. He died in 1991 of a heart attack, on the very day when he was presented with a subpoena from the prosecutor general to appear in court and face former political prisoners.[72]

In December 1998, the Association of Former Political Prisoners and Anticommunist Fighters asked the state prosecutors to investigate Gheorghe Crăciun, the former head of the notorious Aiud political prison (1958–1964), for his involvement in the crime of genocide. In response, the prosecutors charged Crăciun with premeditated murder on grounds that his actions were gruesome, but did not amount to genocide because they neither targeted individuals for their ethnic, religious, or racial identity nor sought to exterminate such groups as a whole. The indictment, filed in September 2000, rested on the depositions of eleven witnesses who described how Crăciun had blatantly disregarded the rights of the inmates and had subjected them to a calculated extermination regimen designed to kill them through reeducation. By the time the prosecutors interrogated him, the former prison guard was gravely ill, deaf, and partly paralyzed. He died in 2001, before his case even reached the courts.[73]

An important role in preparing some of the documentation that exposed the crimes of former communist perpetrators was played by the Institute for the Investigation of Communist Crimes, an independent state agency created by Liberal Prime Minister Călin Popescu-Tăriceanu at the initiative of Marius Oprea, a historian known for his studies on the Securitate.[74] The Institute was the result of the bitter competition that ensued soon after the general elections of 2004 between the Liberal prime minister and the Democrat President Traian Băsescu, which divided the Liberals and the Democrats soon after they won the right to form the government under the umbrella of the Justice and Truth Alliance electoral bloc. Hopeful that early elections would give his Democrats the votes needed to appoint a

71 Lena Constante, *The Silent Escape: Three Thousand Days in Romanian Prisons* (Berkeley: University of California Press, 1995); Adriana Georgescu, *In the Beginning Was the End* (Bucharest: Memoria Cultural Foundation, 2003); and Lavinia Betea, *Lucreţiu Pătrăşcanu – Moartea unui lider comunist* (Bucharest: Curtea Veche, 2006).

72 Dennis Deletant, *Communist Terror in Romania: Gheorghiu-Dej and the Police State, 1948–1965* (New York: St. Martin's Press, 1999).

73 Andrei Muraru, "Ne mor torţionarii, doamnă Kovesi!," *Observatorul cultural* (28 July 2011).

74 Oprea first presented the proposal for a new transitional justice institution to President Băsescu, but was refused.

majority cabinet without the backing of other political formations, Băsescu started a relentless campaign of undermining the Liberals and cornering Popescu-Tăriceanu to either submit to his policy priorities or to step down. After the Liberals responded in kind, both the prime minister and the president used the "politics of memory" as a powerful political tool, each vying for the anticommunist center-right electoral vote, which until then had supported the "historical" Liberal and Christian Democrat Parties. To prove their impeccable anticommunist credentials, the prime minister and the president supported the creation of different transitional justice institutions – the Institute in the case of Popescu-Tăriceanu and the Presidential Commission for the Analysis of the Communist Dictatorship in Romania in the case of President Băsescu (see Chapter 5). This is how the Institute was established as an independent body directly subordinated to the Prime Minister's Office, which also provides its funding. Because at the time of its creation Romania already had a governmental agency with attributions related to the reevaluation of the communist past – the National Council for the Study of Securitate Archives – the Institute had to look for a distinct niche. It found it in the "investigation of communist crimes," which it interpreted as the responsibility to help the courts to mount trials against communist torturers.

As such, from 2006 to 2008, the Institute sent to state prosecutors seven letters detailing the crimes of communist perpetrators. These letters, together with twenty others filed by former political prisoners, were included in the Case File 35 (see discussion later in the chapter). Whereas some of these letters offered precise information about the victimizers and their crimes, others were vague, listing political luminaries as perpetrators in the absence of evidence linking them to specific crimes. The efficacy of these letters was also affected by the fact that the Institute staff included no legal scholar who could sort evidence admissible in court from the information presented in the letters. In none of these cases were indictments or arrest warrants issued by Prosecutor General Kovesi, a political figure appointed by the Democrat-Liberal Party, although that party's leaders had supported other methods of working through the past, such as the history commission.[75] Instead of recognizing communist-era crimes like torture and kidnapping as crimes against humanity, prosecutors continued to treat them as mere abuse of office, for which the statute of limitations applied.[76] This is the reason why historian Cosmin Budeanca characterized the interaction between the Institute and the justice system as a "cat and mouse game" in which the Institute historians tried to prove the guilt of communist perpetrators by compiling the legal

75 Muraru, "Ne mor torţionarii, doamnă Kovesi!"

76 George Rădulescu, "Marius Oprea: 'Suntem conduşi de circa 10.000 de ticăloşi'," *Adevărul* (21 January 2010).

documentation needed for their indictment only to see prosecutors downplaying the charges and refusing to bring the torturers to court.[77]

Taken together, these other court proceedings provide important lessons for the way in which the Romanian judiciary has dealt with communist crimes after 1989. The Drăghici case indicted high-ranking Securitate officials, but the charges did not relate to the political repression that the accused had coordinated for close to twenty years as Minister of Interior. As such, even if ending in the conviction of the accused, it would have contributed little to shedding light on the nature of communist repression. However, the case created the precedent of suspending the statute of limitations for cases launched against top communist dignitaries, thus allowing the crimes of the former regime to be examined in the courts.[78] A former high-ranking communist official was sentenced to jail time in the Bus Trial, but the sentence was reduced for political reasons. The Ursu trials found former communist decision makers responsible, but not the institutions they served (the militia and the Securitate). Although it led to no conviction, the Crăciun case was the only one to show the crimes that occurred in the Aiud prison not as the abuses of a single person (the prison director), but as a systematic state policy masterminded and conducted by the ruling Communist Party and its repressive arm – the Securitate.[79]

THE TRIAL OF COMMUNISM

The Trial of Communism became a recurring theme for anticommunist civil society organizations whenever they sought to underscore the incompleteness of democratic reforms. On 29 November 1990, the Civic Alliance demanded, in the name of the Romanian people, the condemnation in courts of the communist ideology that "inspired, perpetrated and covered up crimes" of the party leaders and Securitate agents who "terrorized the people for four decades by controlling the state and installing the most ferocious dictatorship" and of all "unjust communist laws, state structures and institutions."[80] This call, which targeted what the victims of communist repression saw as the "horrendous communist Holocaust,"[81] was embraced by the Group for Social Dialogue, but afterwards neither the Group nor the Alliance took the time or had the expertise to compile the evidence that would help prosecutors to indict communist perpetrators.

77 Personal interview with Cosmin Budeanca, Bucharest, 28 June 2011.

78 Grosescu and Ursachi, *Justiţia penală de tranziţie*, 183–184.

79 Idem, 194.

80 Domniţa Stefănescu, *Cinci ani din istoria României. O cronologie a evenimentelor Decembrie 1989-Decembrie* 1994 (Bucharest: Editura Maşina de Scris, 1995), 23.

81 "AFDPR cere Guvernului să condamne Holocaustul roşu," *România Liberă* (30 June 2003).

Evidence was brought forward by organizations representing former political prisoners and the Institute for the Investigation of Communist Crimes. In 2003, the ICAR Foundation approached the courts with the request for the presidency and the government to condemn the crimes of communism. Unprepared to take such a step, the ruling Social Democrats responded that during communism all Romanians, including the Communist Party members and secret agents, had suffered to an extent and that the legacies of communism had already found a "social and moral solution."[82] In the end, the judges agreed with the presidency and rejected the request.

In 2006, all petitions registered against communist officials and Securitate officers were gathered together in Case 1304/P/2008, known as the Trial of Communism. Military prosecutors denounced the extermination regimen imposed at Sighet. Ioan Roşca laid twenty-three charges against the communist authorities, ranging from the destruction of the monarchy and Romania's complete and forced Sovietization to the "programmed extermination" of Romanian citizens and political prisoners. Cicerone Ioniţoiu levied sixteen charges against party officials. Prosecutors opened files connected to the death of Roman Catholic priests between 1949 and 1969, Gheorghe Jijie and Grigore Caraza denounced their abusive arrest during the early decades of communist rule, Neculai Mercaş and Ion Bugan complained about being tortured and kidnapped under Ceauşescu's rule, while some faithfuls asked prosecutors to investigate the conditions under which the communist authorities dismantled the Greek Catholic Church. The documentation included the indictments prepared by the Institute for the Investigation of Communist Crimes against Gheorghe Enoiu and the Securitate officers who recruited children as informers, and the seven complaints filed by the Romanian Federation of Former Political Prisoners Anticommunist Fighters against cruel prison guards who tortured prisoners and denied them medical treatment.

Two years after it registered the documentation, in July 2008, the Military Section declined to evaluate the cases, on grounds that civilians, besides military personnel, took part in the crimes that made the object of those complaints. The Civil Section in turn forwarded the cases to the Section Investigating Organized Crime and Terrorism, as some of the crimes were related to those fields. In January 2009, that section decided not to launch investigations into the involvement of high-ranking members of the party-state leadership because the statute of limitations for those crimes had lapsed. It further decided not to investigate the crimes against humanity that occurred before 30 July 1969 – the date when Romania ratified the 1969 Convention mentioned earlier – because the Convention could not be applied retroactively and Penal Code stipulations called for the application of the most

[82] B. Petriceicu, "NUP în 'procesul comunismului'," *România Liberă* (1 August 2003).

favorable law when the Romanian legislation diverged from international law. In those cases, the section argued the most favorable rule meant to recognize the prescriptibility of the crimes. On 19 October 2010, Supreme Court of Justice Prosecutor Iuliu Molcuţ formulated his conclusion in the Trial of Communism.[83] According to him, none of the post-1969 crimes indicated in the documents represented crimes against humanity, and the fifteen-year period during which those crimes could be prosecuted after the collapse of the communist regime had already passed by the time charges were registered. Thus, the prosecutor decided against launching investigations related to the crimes described in the petitions. His decision, which came as no surprise to former victims, was ignored by the general public, which by then was preoccupied with the impact of the EU accession and the global financial crisis on the frail Romanian economy.

CONCLUSION

Post-communist Romania presents a paradox. Whereas its courts have heard a large number of cases, most of these cases have dealt with the exit from communism (the 1989 revolution), and only a handful of them with the communist crimes perpetrated from 1945 to 1989. The scarcity of these latter cases did not make court trials more efficient or capable to establish a persuasive hierarchy of guilt. Ceauşescu's trial blamed the person, not the system, for communist crimes and allowed his former collaborators to extol the merits of communist institutional arrangements and national unity around the country's leaders. Even though it brought Romanians instant revenge on the despised couple that for twenty-five years had invaded their bedrooms, dictated their diet, deprived them of basic necessities of life, forced them into submission, robbed them of critical thinking, and indoctrinated them with nationalist propaganda, the trial and the ensuing execution did not help Romanians to understand what happened to them and why. Because the communist leaders most closely associated with Stalinist repression, Drăghici and Nicolschi, died before going to trial, little was revealed about the mechanism of repression or the institutional ties between the Securitate and the Communist Party during the first decades of communist rule. The public ignored the Bus Trial, whereas the extended coverage received by the Ursu trials, in which some minor figures of communist repression stood accused, painfully underscored Romania's failure to prosecute notorious torturers drawn from the ranks of the nomenklatura and the secret police.

The contribution of civil society to advancing the process of reckoning through trials has been markedly uneven. Through a combination of perseverance, skillful

[83] *Cauza intitulată generic procesul comunismului – Ordonanţă* (19 October 2010), available at: http://www.universulromanesc.com/ginta/showthread.php?t=919 (accessed 12 January 2012).

appeals to foreign politicians, and sheer determination, the relatives of Ursu obtained justice, although the accused were not punished proportional to their crimes, the procedures were repeatedly procrastinated and, in the course of the court hearings, the accused added insult to injury by portraying Ursu as a Securitate secret informer. The Association of Former Political Prisoners has shown the same determination in pursuing justice through the courts, demanding the indictment of notorious communist human rights abusers months after the 1989 regime change. However, the Romanian courts heard none of the cases called for by former prisoners, either because the accused died before the trials began or because the prosecutors refused to even indict those perpetrators. Instead of supporting these cases, other victims' groups (like the ICAR Foundation) and groups of intellectuals (e.g., the Civic Academy and the Group for Social Dialogue) have advocated a generic Trial of Communism with little chances of assigning blame.

As in other post-communist countries, in Romania court trials have represented weak instruments of attaining justice and setting the historical record straight. The old age and frail health of key victimizers, the high burden of proof, the pardon decrees and the statute of limitations, the reproduction of communist-era magistrates, and the tendency of police and army forces to cover up the mistakes of their members have concurred in rendering court trials few in number, limited in scope, and weak in effectiveness. Given the Stalinist nature of the Ceauşescu regime and the lack of a negotiated transition from communism to democracy, communist perpetrators were not protected by an amnesty law designed to usher in the regime change of 1989. Informally, the pact of silence that linked together former communist perpetrators who successfully secured public posts in post-communist times reinforced the pardons granted by Ceauşescu and Iliescu, perpetuated impunity for communist crimes, and undermined the rule of law. In policies that echoed Latin America more than Central Europe, successive Romanian post-communist governments have shrouded the most brutal human rights violations in the cloak of honorable intentions and the defense of national interests, although thousands of people were raped, tortured, and murdered. Two decades after the country opted for democracy, Romanians can hardly celebrate "the end of euphemism" resulted from the failure to prosecute the top communist decision makers for their crimes and compel them to "do time."[84]

[84] The end of euphemism (*El fin del eufemismo*) was celebrated in 2001 by the Argentineans, when Judge Gabriel Cavallo invalidated the Due Obedience and Full Stop amnesty laws. Horacio Verbitsky, "El fin del eufemismo," *Página/12* (6 March 2001), available at: http://members.tripod.com/doska_/democKracia/ElFallo.htm (accessed on 31 July 2011).

3

Public Access to Secret Files

Court trials have generally focused on the most gruesome human rights violations of the early decades of communist rule, whereas file access was meant to redress the widespread surveillance program of late communism. In December 1999, the Romanian parliament took the first steps toward allowing ordinary citizens to read the secret files compiled on them by the notorious political police, the Securitate, when it passed Law 187 on Access to Securitate Files and Unveiling the Securitate as a Political Police. Two years later, in 2001, in a move widely commented by the local press, the newly established National Council for the Study of Securitate Archives released the first such files to the former victims of secret surveillance. Nevertheless, for the next five years citizens could access only a tiny portion of the extant archives. Limitations were political more than technical in nature. Surprisingly, it was former President Emil Constantinescu, celebrated as the leader of the pro-democratic and anticommunist forces, who restricted public access by declaring, without any legal basis, the files of the most prominent post-communist politicians as "state secrets" protected from the public eye.[1] That controversial decision, handed down months after the adoption of Law 187/1999 but before Constantinescu's presidential mandate expired in November 2000, became known to the public only in the mid-2000s, when it was criticized for negating the very spirit of file access and for protecting elected officials tainted by association with the communist regime. It was only in 2006 that President Traian Băsescu ordered the transfer to the Council of 1,300,000 secret files in view of being opened to the Romanian citizens. Since then, the Council has granted access to an increased number of applicants and reached more definitive conclusions when asked to confirm or disconfirm the involvement with the Securitate of post-communist luminaries.

Romanian citizens thus had to wait for over a decade to read their secret files. Although that might seem an unpardonably long time span, in reality the country

[1] "Dosarul lui 'Felix', secretizat de SRI-ul şi CNSAS-ul lui Constantinescu," 22 (3 March 2011).

was not the last to unlock its secret vaults. East Germany was the first in the region to grant file access in mid-1990, when its parliament passed a law that spearheaded the post-unification opening of the vast majority of the Stasi secret dossiers. In Hungary, Act XXIII of 1994 offered limited access to very few secret files, but later amendments enlarged the number of dossiers opened to the public. Act 140 of 1996 allowed Czechs to examine their own files, whereas Slovaks were recognized that right only in mid-2002, when parliament created the Institute for National Memory, an independent governmental agency serving as custodian of the secret archives. Poland legislated partial access in 1997, when those who were "wronged" by the communist regime, but not those who served as secret informers, were permitted to read their own dossiers. In Slovenia, draconic privacy laws have continued to severely limit file access, which remains restricted as a result. In 2006, Albania reluctantly opened some secret files to discredit selected post-communist politicians more than to allow the truth about the communist past to come out. With the exception of the Baltic states, none of the former Soviet republics have recognized this right, because some of them have remained non-democracies after 1991, and most of the secret KGB files were transferred to Moscow and were thus outside their reach. In short, access to the archives of the communist secret police has varied across countries and in terms of when the laws were passed, who may view the files, and how many documents were made public.[2]

Access to secret files by ordinary citizens remains a strictly Eastern European method of reckoning with the past. In other regions of the world no such extensive archives were ever compiled, and truth commissions and court trials have fulfilled truth-seeking needs, permitting the public disclosure of the identity of victims and victimizers, the nature of the crimes, the state mechanisms of repression, and the chain of command linking army and police agents to the top leaders of the dictatorship. Commissions offer information in a top-down manner, and their conclusions can be influenced by the national and international political actors who created them. When commissions study distant events, their efforts to piece together the past enlighten generations that have little, if any, direct experience with the repression. When the object of study is the immediate past, the "truth" they propose in their final reports often complements, and sometimes even competes with, the truth known by the previously terrorized population that directly lived and experienced it. The truth delivered through court trials is equally partial – as trials remain few – evidence is shaped by strict rules of procedure, and important details about the past remain hidden because of the victimizers' reservations to incriminate themselves.

[2] Lavinia Stan, ed., *Transitional Justice in Eastern Europe and the Former Soviet Union: Reckoning with the Communist Past* (London: Routledge, 2009).

By contrast, access to secret files democratizes truth seeking by allowing victims to control the process and ordinary citizens to contrast the truth contained in the files with their own recollection of past events. Instead of supporting the version of events detailed in the final report or before the court of law, the state blesses the truth-seeking process as such when it agrees to open the secret files to citizens. While it can decide which documents the citizens can access, the state cannot directly control how those documents are interpreted by those who read them. Instead of reconstructing truth at the national level, file access underscores the significance of personal histories that might never enter a commission's report or a court of law, because they are too insignificant or devoid of evidentiary value. It also allows ordinary citizens to reclaim their right to privacy that the secret police took away from them, as human rights activist Gabriel Andreescu noted.[3] Once a state opens the files, the reconstruction of the past belongs not only to historians, but also to those who lived during times of repression. That is important because, as historian Maria Bucur wrote, "if the picture of Romanian communism viewed from the inner sanctum of the Politburo in Bucharest is one of unchanging authoritarianism with grotesque elements of a cult of personality, this angle provides very little insight into how people lived it."[4]

This chapter presents the extant Securitate archives, the legal framework that permitted their opening, and the limitations of file access as a method to redress the past and to uncover the truth about communist repression. Because file access as a transitional justice method has been shaped by the secret archive, the chapter overviews the Securitate as a state repressive agency, its information network, and its secret collections. On the basis of visits to the stacks of the Securitate archive and the reading room of the archive custodian, I outline the extant Securitate archival collections and briefly explain the political negotiations that led to file openings.[5] Attention is given to two government agencies that have decided the fate of the files: the National Council, responsible for giving access to as many files as possible, and the Information Services, keen on keeping under lock as many files as possible to

[3] Personal interview with Gabriel Andreescu, Bucharest, 29 June 2011.

[4] Maria Bucur, *Heroes and Victims: Remembering War in Twentieth-Century Romania* (Bloomington: Indiana University Press, 2009), xiii.

[5] Details on the political negotiations that preceded the opening of the secret files are provided in Stan, *Transitional Justice in Eastern Europe*, 128–151; Lavinia Stan, "Access to Secret Files: The Trials and Tribulations of a Romanian Law," *East European Politics and Society*, 16(2002): 55–90; Lavinia Stan, "Moral Cleansing Romanian Style," *Problems of Post-Communism*, 49(2002): 52–62; and Lavinia Stan, "Spies, Files and Lies: Explaining the Failure of Access to Securitate Files," *Communist and Post-Communist Studies*, 37(2004): 341–359. Also Dragoş Petrescu, "Dilemmas of Transitional Justice in Post-1989 Romania," *Lustration and Consolidation of Democracy and the Rule of Law in Central and Eastern Europe*, eds. Vladimíra Dvořáková and Anđelko Milardović (Zagreb: Political Science Research Center, 2007), 127–151.

protect the identity of former Securitate agents. In addition, the chapter comments on the way in which information in the files has been interpreted, ponders on the criteria for labeling a person a former secret agent, and investigates file access as a truth-seeking method of revisiting the past.

THE COMMUNIST SECURITATE AND ITS SECRET ARCHIVES

The Securitate was set up in 1948 with help from the Soviet People's Commissariat for Internal Affairs (known as the NKVD) as a secret political police responsible for eliminating political opponents to consolidate communist power, ensure compliance with the regime, gain acceptance for its public policies, and shape public sentiment. It also acted as a praetorian guard to the communist leaders, protecting their every step. Its two main departments conducted operations both inside the country and abroad – this latter set of activities, directed against democratic and communist countries alike, constituting the Securitate's claim to patriotism. The Securitate's methods, goals, and personnel changed over the years. During the first two decades of communist rule, uneducated officers engaged in summary executions, illegal house arrests, imprisonment, and deportations, but after 1964 the Securitate preferred subtler control that no longer aimed to physically annihilate dissenters, but tried to persuade them to renounce their fight, to discredit them, or to encourage them to leave the country (see Chapter 1).

The political police employed full-time agents and part-time informers drawn from all walks of life. On 22 December 1989, the day when Nicolae Ceauşescu relinquished control over the country by fleeing Bucharest on board a helicopter, the Securitate employed 13,275 officers and 984 civilian personnel, divided roughly equally between the Bucharest office and the territorial branches.[6] The number of full-time agents varied over the years, according to the needs of the Securitate, fluctuating from as few as 3,549 in 1948 to as many as 72,697 in 1956 and 23,381 in 1983.[7] Of the Securitate agents, 90 percent were Communist Party members – a percentage demonstrating the intimate link between the ruling party and its repression agency. From 1945 to 1989 there were 507,003 informers in total, a number that included 29,613 former sympathizers of the fascist Iron Guard, 10,367 members of

6 Stan, "Moral Cleansing Romanian Style," 55. On 10 April 2004, the *Ziua* daily cited a total of 15,312 employees, including 10,114 officers and 1,228 civilians. Virgil Măgureanu, the first director of the Romanian Information Service, claimed that on 22 December 1989, the Securitate personnel totaled 14,259 military cadres, including 8,159 officers, 5,105 warrant and noncommissioned officers, and 984 civilian personnel. Dennis Deletant, *Ceausescu and the Securitate: Coercion and Dissent in Romania, 1965–1989* (Armonk: M. E. Sharpe, 1995), 392.

7 Florica Dobre, Florian Banu, Camelia Duică, Silviu B. Moldovan, and Liviu Ţăranu, *Trupele de Securitate (1949–1989)* (Bucharest: Nemira, 2004).

the interwar ruling Peasant and Liberal Parties, as well as 2,753 political prisoners. Most informers were elderly (above fifty years of age) and well educated (having completed high school or university studies). The number of active informers steadily increased from 73,000 in 1968 to 144,289 in 1989.[8]

The agents could have their identity covered, partially covered, or fully covered, with the former being the highest position in the political police ranks. Most secret officers were engaging in domestic surveillance, recruiting and monitoring the activity of the informers, identifying targets (victims), gathering and analyzing data received from informers, designing strategies to collect information, intimidating victims, preempting information leaks and keeping informers loyal, and reporting the results of investigations to their superiors. As any other communist institution, the Securitate received plan targets from the party leadership that it endeavored to meet and exceed with patriotic zeal, occasionally by resorting to unorthodox methods. Under pressure to maintain a wide information network, some Securitate officers manufactured informer files for people who never agreed to spy and never submitted information about others. While occasionally engaged in counterterrorist actions, the investigation of economic crime, and the protection of national state security, the Securitate remained a political police whose primary role was to quash opposition to the communist leaders, ideology, and policies.

The most important cleavage dividing the informer network related to party membership, party members who acted as secret agents being known as "collaborators," and nonparty members being labeled "informers," a difference not always translated in the kind of information each group provided. As communism matured, the party took greater care to hide the identity of its members who had turned into Securitate informers. After analyzing the activity of the Ministry of Interior, in 1968 the party's Central Committee decided to prohibit the Securitate from using party and state leaders as secret collaborators and from compiling files on them. After 1968, archived secret documents on informers-turned-party members were destroyed, an operation laconically noted in special memos kept by the political police. According to some estimates, as many as 230,000 files and attached folders describing the secret activities of party members were destroyed by 1974.[9] These decisions did not apply to documents on informers who were not Communist Party members, whose ties to the Securitate were not guarded as well.

According to the services provided to the political police, the informer network divided among informers (*informatori*), supporting individuals (*persoane de sprijin*),

[8] Stan, "Moral Cleansing Romanian Style," 55.

[9] Declaration delivered in 1998 by the Romanian Information Service deputy director Mircea Gheordunescu. See "Recursul la discurs," 22 45(1998): 5–8.

residents (*rezidenţi*), and hosts of meeting places (*gazde ale caselor de întîlniri*).[10] Under the guidance of the Securitate officer, informers and supporting individuals collected data on specific targets. Residents were trusted individuals who maintained regular contact with up to thirty supporting individuals to transmit information from them to the officer. Residents were usually selected from among retired secret agents and informers whose loyalty to the political police was unquestionable and personal behavior was beyond reproach, by Securitate standards. The hosts were individuals who made a room of their residence or workplace available for the Securitate officers to secretly meet informers. With the information available to date, we cannot estimate the percentage of each one of these categories in the total Securitate network.

The recruitment process included ranking and verifying potential candidates, selecting the candidate for recruitment, designing the recruitment plan, and securing the candidate's secret, truthful, and loyal collaboration. Selected for their support for the regime, the quality of the information they could provide, and their openness to collaborate secretly, candidates were recruited for different intelligence projects. Agents detailed the recruitment strategy in reports approved by their superiors. Informers were contacted by the agent or resident on a monthly basis and were instructed to pass urgent information to the Securitate between the meetings by way of conspiratorial addresses, hidden places, postal boxes, or codes for sending data in writing or by phone. Agents and residents met with informers secretly in predesignated meeting places. Securitate agents met at least twice a year with supporting individuals. After recruitment, the agent continuously verified the members of his information network to ensure their loyalty.

The reasons why citizens became victims of the Securitate or decided to collaborate with it varied among individuals, social groups, and time periods. During the 1950s, when the communist regime wanted to assert its political monopoly and root out opposition from interwar parties and anticommunist resistance groups, the main criteria included social class and status, political and social involvement, personal wealth, and even descent. State dignitaries, leaders of parties and movements, revolting peasants, their families, and those who assisted them in any way were targeted. During the 1960s, thousands of political prisoners returned home, but in 1971 Ceauşescu launched his cultural revolution and thwarted active resistance. Telling a joke that mocked Ceauşescu became a good enough reason to target an individual. The Securitate monitored "individuals under surveillance, information network members, former political prisoners, individuals condemned for security

[10] The 1987 top secret "Instructions on Setting Up and Using the Securitate Informer Network" explained the difference between these four categories. For more details, see Marius Oprea, *Banalitatea răului. O istorie a Securităţii în documente 1949–1989* (Bucharest: Polirom, 2002), 478–492.

crimes, subject to prevention actions, refusing to return from abroad, trying to cross the border illegally, or seeking permission to emigrate or marry foreign citizens, foreign citizens visiting Romanian embassies in a non-official capacity, Romanians maintaining unofficial ties to foreigners, and foreigners living in Romania."[11]

The reasons why individuals accepted collaboration ranged from misplaced patriotism and the desire to help their country to financial rewards, permission to travel abroad, university entrance for their offsprings, the promise of moving from rural to urban areas, or the prospect of promoting their career and obtaining leadership positions in their work field. Others did it out of revenge, to get back at old enemies. Fear motivated those who believed that the Securitate would not accept refusal, an intuition reflecting reality, as the secret police closely monitored individuals who refused collaboration. Agents saw refusal as a personal defeat to be swiftly avenged. In his memoirs, for example, World War II veteran George Mârzanca revealed that in 1952 Nicolae Popa tried to recruit him as an informer. His refusal prompted Popa to enter Mârzanca's name on the Securitate blacklist. Within a month Mârzanca was arrested and condemned to prison for imagined crimes. When he realized the mistake of Mârzanca's arrest, another Securitate officer told him, "you had the misfortune of being included on the black list as a dangerous element by our intelligence agent, and even if this was a mistake we cannot do anything in your case."[12] A special category, which involved individuals who accepted collaboration out of blackmail, included former political prisoners who wished to redeem their past mistakes and endear themselves with the regime while in prison or after their liberation. Former political prisoner Cezar Zugravu described four successive attempts to recruit him, and the agents' sweeping promises, which were too good to ever become reality.[13] However, once repression abated after 1965, turning down a collaboration proposal seldom entailed more than "occasional psychological pressure and chicaneries,"[14] because refusal was rationalized as a failure on the part of the agent to anticipate the candidate's response.

The nature of the collaboration ran the gamut, although secret agents were instructed to recruit only individuals who "accepted to collaborate candidly, secretly and in an organized manner."[15] Reluctant informers gave few short reports that

[11] The Minister of Interior Order 001050 of 25 May 1977, cited in Lavinia Stan, *Inside the Securitate Archives*, Woordrow Wilson Center for International Scholars, Cold War International History Project, 4 March 2005, para. 12, available at: http://www.wilsoncenter.org/article/inside-the-securitate-archives (accessed on 17 September 2011).

[12] G. Mârzanca, *Patru ani am fost … 'bandit.' Confesiuni* (Bucharest: Vasile Carlova Press, 1997), 10, 18.

[13] C. Zugravu, "Securitatea m-a programat 'turnător'," *Memoria* 10(1995): 60.

[14] Bogdan Iancu, "Post-Accession Constitutionalism with a Human Face: Judicial Reform and Lustration in Romania," *European Constitutional Law Review*, 6(2010): 48.

[15] Oprea, *Banalitatea răului*, 478–492.

included only trivial information they believed was not detrimental to victims. Taking no pleasure in reporting, realizing the unethical nature of their collaboration, and helping themselves more than the Securitate, these informers kept the meetings with the liaison officer or the resident short and refrained from passing judgment on the victim's activity. These cases were isolated, as the Securitate agents either terminated the relationship or encouraged the informer to provide quality data. Other informers relished in their new role, writing detailed reports about what they saw and heard in the victim's company, even designing strategies to penetrate further into the victim's inner space. Informers included in the Atlas program (professionals attending conferences abroad, physicians and scientists studying abroad, citizens visiting their emigrated relatives) gave reports each time they returned to Romania as a condition to being allowed to travel abroad in the future. These reports presented the individuals with whom the informers met, the events they attended, the places they visited, and other people's remarks on Romania's domestic and foreign policy.

Equally varied were the reasons why informers ceased their activity. Securitate agents had to terminate collaboration with individuals with a criminal record, who did not collaborate loyally, or who disclosed their ties to the political police to their friends and relatives. When and how collaboration ceased depended on the agent more than the informer. Collaboration ended abruptly when the informer died, left the country, or cut links to the agent. In these latter cases, the informer rapidly joined the ranks of the victims he once spied upon, being placed under surveillance. In other cases, collaboration continued for years without having real substance, when the informer provided trivial reports at increasingly longer intervals of time. In these cases, the agent ended the collaboration, convinced that the informer could no longer supply relevant data. The personal chemistry between agents and informers constituted another factor in pursuing or terminating such relationships.[16]

The multifaceted activity of the political police was reflected in the trail of documents it produced until 1989, which together constitute the secret archive. Reflective of the "graphomania" that Milan Kundera spoke about as early as 1981,[17] the secret files were spun by "directors of the terror machine," who recorded and documented almost everything they did because they "were unashamed and unafraid of a negative historical verdict" and believed that the Communist Party would be eternal and of world-historical significance.[18] The Evidence Service, set up in 1951, created a

[16] A detailed analysis of the recruitment and activity of secret informers is offered by Mihai Albu, *Informatorul. Studiu asupra colaborarii cu Securitatea* (Iaşi: Polirom, 2008). The book also reveals that the Securitate recruited informers from among children, who had no secret file in case they accepted collaboration.

[17] Milan Kundera, *The Book of Laughter and Forgetting* (New York: Penguin, 1981), 2.

[18] J. Arch Getty and Oleg V. Naumov, *The Road to Terror: Stalin and the Self-Destruction of the Bolsheviks, 1932–1939* (New Haven: Yale University Press, 1999), xi.

system that identified the Securitate informers and victims, and received, registered, and classified the files opened for such individuals. Twenty years later, the Service was replaced by the Center for Information and Documentation, which until 1989 included the archive and the card system. The Center studied materials revealing the enemy's methods and means against state security and the Securitate's actions against the enemy; organized the card system that allowed names of individuals to be matched with corresponding files; received and registered archival documents; provided data, copies, and photocopies of original documents to the Securitate departments, militia, Procuratura, the courts, and other state organs; and registered, organized, and conserved the Securitate archives.[19] After the Center acquired IBM computers and asked Stasi engineers to install them, the Securitate became the first institution in Romania to use high-performance, large-capacity computerized systems.[20]

The Securitate files contained several types of documents, all written in the official "wooden language" (*limbă de lemn*) that subordinated individuality to the collective. An assortment of documents revealed the type of file. Victim files contained information notes provided by secret informers under code names and by Communist Party members under their real names, term reports submitted by the case officer to his superiors, which often bore the superior's decision ("Approved," "Take further action," "Ask for information from Department S," among others), periodical evaluations of the information accumulated to date, action plans (*planuri de măsuri*) that case officers compiled for the near future, requests for information from other Securitate departments, handwritten excerpts from letters sent and received by the victims, photographs of the victims, and copies of medical records, together with an assortment of other forms and memos. Informer files included the collaboration pledge, the profile of the informer, the dossier of recruitment, and the information notes the informer provided on his victims.[21]

The secret archives included several types of files. Information surveillance files (*dosare de urmărire informativă* or DUI), bearing the victim's name, included one or several bound volumes of 300–400 pages each assigned a unique number. These files, which might include notes, reports, syntheses, and photographs of individuals monitored by the Securitate, were opened for special cases that had to be solved within a year. Information network files (*dosare ale reţelei informative*), bearing the informer's name, usually accompanied attached folders (*mape-anexă*) containing all

19 Florin Pintilie, "Constituirea arhivei Securităţii," *Profil* 2(March 2004): 6–8.

20 Reportedly, the Securitate first installed the computers and then told Ceauşescu of the purchase.

21 The structure of the secret file is explained in detail in Carmen Chivu and Mihai Albu, *Dosarele Securităţii. Studii de Caz* (Iaşi: Polirom: 2007). The volume includes a chapter on jokes and humor lifted from the secret files.

the written reports the informer supplied to the Securitate. Criminal investigation files (*dosare de anchetă penală*) were opened for crimes against national security, as defined by the communist legislation. There were strict regulations – not always observed – on when, who, and how to open and close these files, and which documents to attach and in what order.[22]

Case files (*dosare de problemă*), which gathered information on social groups considered problematic from a security viewpoint, could be opened only with the approval of the Securitate top leader and were closed when the issue at hand was solved. Individuals monitored as part of larger cases had informative verification folders (*mape de verificare informativă*), which were archived when the Securitate considered the persons to no longer pose a threat to the regime.[23] The case files related to "Arts and Culture" (on writers and artists), "Bourgeois Political Parties" (on the interwar political parties), "Anticommunist Resistance Movement" (on the resistance groups active during the early decades of communism), "Eterul" and "Meliţa" (on the Radio Free Europe/Radio Liberty), "Central Press" (on the press), "Religious Cults and Sects" (on registered and nonregistered religious denominations and groups), "Transcendental Meditation" (on the 1980s movement), and "Agricultural Collectivization" (on the vast campaign of collectivization carried out from 1949 to 1962).[24] The Securitate also prepared regular reports on the popular mood (*starea de spirit*) that were submitted to the party leadership and revealed "not only what the informers reported on people's attitudes but also the sources of anxiety for Party leaders (as evident in the categories for which they requested information)."[25]

All documents included in nominal victim or informer files were bound together in carton covers, with the front cover bearing the victim's or informer's alias. Sometimes the front page bore the conspiratorial alias assumed by the informer but, if the same person acted during two time periods under different aliases, the resulting informer volumes were classified as one single file. Once archived, each file was preserved in carton boxes bearing the number code recorded in the card system. Part of the archive was lost because documents were deposited in

22 Pintilie, "Constituirea arhivei Securităţii," 6–8.

23 Such folders were also opened for former political prisoners after their release and were archived when the person died or was believed that he "gave up all hostile activity." A journalist traveling to Romania was placed under surveillance during his stay, and information was collected in a personal file attached to the "Foreign Journalists" case file. If the journalist manifested a "hostile attitude" toward the regime by making critical remarks or writing negative reports, a personal information file was then opened for him.

24 Stan, *Inside the Securitate Archives*, para. 22.

25 Gail Kligman and Katherine Verdery, *Peasants under Siege: The Collectivization of Romanian Agriculture, 1949–1962* (Princeton: Princeton University Press, 2011), 25.

precarious conditions in dirty, humid, and overcrowded rooms, or even prison cells before the 1970s.[26]

The Securitate also confiscated and archived over 110,000 manuscript pages to stop their publication or distribution. The confiscations generally occurred as a result of surprise searches carried out in the homes of philosophers, writers, former political prisoners, or ordinary citizens who confided their dissatisfaction with everyday life to personal diaries. Among those who lost manuscripts were philosopher Lucian Blaga, poet Ion Caraion, and pre-communist party leader Constantin Titel Petrescu. According to human rights activist Gabriel Andreescu, in 1991 the Romanian Information Service transferred to the National Archives eighty manuscripts that, it argued, had been confiscated by the Securitate in an effort to protect their authors, without elaborating on what "protection" meant in the communist context.[27] In 2000, a list of authors whose manuscripts were found in the secret archives was published for the authors to reclaim the writings. By 2004, only thirty-seven individuals had asked for manuscripts totaling some 50,000 pages. The remaining 60,000 pages were transferred to the National Council and are available to researchers on request. They belonged to 105 individuals, including Orthodox priest Gheorghe Calciu-Dumitreasa, monk Nicolae Steinhard, theologian Dumitru Stăniloae, literary critics Ion Negoiţescu and Ovidiu Papadima, poet Vasile Voiculescu, folklorist Ovid Densuşianu, former political prisoners Paul Goma and Marcel Petrişor, writer Petre Tuţea, and pre-communist politician Ion Puiu. The diary of Gheorghe Ursu was never recovered (see Chapter 2).

The General Documentary Card System consisted of alphabetically organized cards listing the names of all individuals with personal secret files, including all those monitored by the Securitate; persons sentenced for crimes against state security; members of the fascist Iron Guard and pre-communist parties; pre-communist state dignitaries; agents of the Siguranţa, the pre-communist information service; army officers with anticommunist activity; individuals who legally or illegally left Romania; persons known for their critical stance against Ceauşescu, the party, and the ideology; and foreign travelers visiting Romania. Case files did not feature in the card system, which was strictly nominal. Each informer card specified the person's name, parents' names, birth date and place, nationality, citizenship, political membership, education level, occupation, known foreign languages, position, and workplace. The cards classifying informer files further mentioned recruitment date

26 The Bucharest warehouse I visited stored around 800 meters of archive the Romanian Information Service used to train archivists, included six vertical rows of carton boxes marked "Operative Archive," and could be accessed only with two keys entrusted to two different persons. The warehouse was located in a permanently guarded military unit that could be entered only with special permit.

27 Personal interview with Gabriel Andreescu, Bucharest, 29 June 2011.

and name of recruiting officer, contact officer, and conspiratorial name.[28] Specially trained agents accessed the card system, each being responsible for two to three letters of the alphabet. Over the years, the system was enlarged by adding cards with variants of the names with a file. For example, when the file "Stan" was received, additional cards for "Stana," "Stancu," and "Stanca" were created.

The archive was divided into fonds (*fonduri*). The victims' operative surveillance files and the pre-communist information service archives constituted the operative or information fond (*fondul operativ sau informativ*). The oldest extant documents in the Securitate archive, dated 1917, had been drafted by the royal intelligence service, Siguranţa. The inoperative fond (*fondul neoperativ*) received the personnel files of Securitate, army and militia officers and civilian personnel, payroll records, administrative and secretarial memos, and other materials without operative value. The criminal investigation fond (*fondul de anchetă penală*) included the files related to criminal investigations and the prison files of persons sentenced or investigated for "actions against state security." The network fond (*fondul de reţea*) consisted of the files of active and retired informers, as well as candidates to recruitment who refused to collaborate with the Securitate. The documentary fond (*fondul documentar*) included reports, analyses, notes, and work plans that detailed the activity of the Securitate and of pre-communist state agencies and political parties, together with other materials of interest. Finally, the correspondence fond (*fondul corespondenţă*) included mail between Securitate and Ministry of Interior units and between them and other state institutions and party structures.[29]

In December 1989, there were 1,901,530 extant Securitate files, of which 1,162,418 referred to victims (individuals or groups); 507,003 were informer files; 154,911 were attached folders with information notes and reports; 29,281 represented "documentation"; 47,917 were correspondence files; and 317,258 were unfinished files.[30] Official reports claimed that the Securitate archive totaled 35 kilometers of documents, of which 25 were victim files, 4 were informer files, and 6 were attached folders, but local historians and former political prisoners disputed the numbers, pointing out that the Stasi archive totaled 188 kilometers for a population of 14.5 million (compared to Romania's 22.5 million inhabitants). Every meter of the Securitate archive contains 5,000 documents, and every file is on average 200 pages in length.[31] The extant archive, which includes documents in hard copy and electronic format, excludes the secret files of 239,000 Communist Party members destroyed after 1968;

28 "Evidenţa reţelei informative a aparatului de securitate," *Sfera politicii* 52(1997): 39.

29 Florin Pintilie, "Păstrare şi acces la documentele Securităţii aflate în arhivele SRI," 22 (17 November 1998).

30 Stan, "Moral Cleansing," 56.

31 Stan, "Spies, Files and Lies," 422.

1,800 documents on deceased informers and older archived documents shredded in 1977; 130,000 files lost in December 1989; and documents illegally destroyed in the early 1990s.[32]

After the collapse of the communist regime, the Securitate was dismantled, and its archives and personnel transferred to nine different intelligence services formed along the lines of the former Securitate departments. The most important Securitate successors have been the Romanian Information Service, heir to the domestic repression branch, and the External Information Service, heir to the foreign branch. Until 2006, the Romanian Information Service stored 60 percent of the Securitate archive in its military units, and its refusal to hand over the archive to the National Council drastically restricted the file access program.

ACCESS TO SECRET FILES

The Securitate's place in the Romanian imaginary was comparable with the Stasi's in East Germany, but Romanians were not as quick to ask for access to secret files. "Stasi buildings formed a focal point of unrest in 1989,"[33] historian Gary Bruce noted, and "demonstrators simply had to point to the Stasi building," as "a simple finger point summarized years of repression and a morally bankrupt regime."[34] By contrast, the pro-democratic forces active in post-communist Romania had to provide an elaborate justification for convincing the country's new leaders of the need to condemn the communist regime, open the secret vaults, and more generally reckon with the past, although the Romanian communist regime affected at least as many social categories as its East German counterpart, driving them to even greater despair during the 1980s, when mere survival consumed individuals, families, and communities. At least as many Romanians as East Germans understood the unequivocal signs of economic deprivation, political persecution, and cultural annihilation to which the communist regime subjected them.

Different was the justification offered for those crimes, which in Romania were deemed acceptable by former Communist Party leaders and Securitate agents who skillfully invoked the national interest. Although as a result of his show trial Ceauşescu was found guilty of crimes that warranted the harshest sentence in the books (the death penalty), the post-communist leaders who masterminded the trial claimed that his rule was one of personal "excesses," not systematic crimes perpetrated by his henchmen. The faults of the pre-1989 regime were therefore

[32] Stan, *Inside the Securitate Archives*, para. 29.

[33] Gary Bruce, "East Germany," in *Transitional Justice in Eastern Europe and the Former Soviet Union: Reckoning with the Communist Past*, ed. Lavinia Stan (London: Routledge, 2009), 16.

[34] Idem, 17.

attributable to the dictator, not to the communist regime. By selectively reading history, the new rulers insisted that Ceauşescu, the delusional Conducător responsible for the bleak 1980s, was also the one who preserved national integrity in the face of Hungarian demands for autonomy, placed Romania on the international map by playing the West against the Soviets, made Romanians masters of their own land by exporting the country's Germans and Jews and keeping Transylvanian Hungarians under his thumb, and encouraged the rewriting of world history to acknowledge Romania's overlooked contribution to human progress.[35] By extension, the Securitate included a highly professional corps animated by the noblest desire of defending the country against its numerous and ever-insidious internal and external enemies. Moreover, the post-communist leaders claimed that they themselves had been sidelined and persecuted by the mad dictator, Ion Iliescu when transferred from Bucharest to the Timiş county in 1971, Silviu Brucan when placed under house arrest in a decrepit Bucharest suburb in 1987, and Alexandru Bârlădeanu after he signed, together with other Communist Party leaders, a letter critical of Ceauşescu at the beginning of 1989.

The miraculous transformation of the new leaders from Ceauşescu's close collaborators and nomenklatura members to the most important victims of communist persecution and the country's only hope for political stability, state sovereignty, and national dignity explains the absence of calls for promptly opening the secret archives. For many Romanians fed on nationalist communist propaganda, to pry open the files meant to sign the death certificate of the Securitate, to retire its patriotic agents, and to unveil publicly its secret operations, all to the great loss of the country and the enormous benefit of its many enemies. Moreover, the lack of a strong civil society, which meant that few Romanians were organized in state-free groups with coherent political goals, and the extended Communist Party membership, which made people dependent on the party for their livelihood, prevented citizens from storming the Securitate buildings.

As a result, after 1989 the secret files remained hidden from the public eye, but not from the new rulers, who used them copiously to discredit opposition leaders, or from the former Securitate agents, in whose hands the information included in the files turned into an efficient secret weapon allowing them to become the new entrepreneurial elite. Until the 1996 elections, a stream of secret documents appeared on the black market, being traded against influence, money, or public posts. If the information leaks were random, the Social Democrat government and President Iliescu might have opted for opening the archives, because file access would have rendered such leaks worthless. The leaks were in fact controlled by political leaders and secret

[35] Alexandru Gussi, *La Roumanie face a son passé communiste. Memoires et cultures politiques* (Paris: L'Harmattan, 2011).

agents interested in preventing the opposition Democratic Convention, ever more popular, to access valuable secret information after the elections of 1996. If Iliescu had feared that President Emil Constantinescu and his Democratic Convention would throw open the doors of the secret archives, as many Romanian voters hoped, he was utterly mistaken. The Convention had no desire to unveil the files and, by doing so, compromise its supporters and collaborators who had served as secret agents. The inexperienced Convention-appointed heads of the two information services were unwilling to effect meaningful change. Soon after the 1996 elections, it became clear that the archives were to remain locked.

They were out of sight, but not out of mind for the Christian Democrat Senator Constantin Ticu Dumitrescu, a former political prisoner who made it his personal crusade to legislate lustration and access to secret files. With great difficulty, after being ostracized by his party, scorned by the Social Democrats, and vilified by the Greater Romania Party, in 1999 Dumitrescu had the satisfaction to see parliament adopt his legislative proposal. Law 187/1999 permitted citizens – both former victims and former victimizers – to read the files compiled on them by the Securitate. According to the law, Romanian citizens (and later citizens of other NATO countries) could read their own files, obtain copies of documents and statements detailing their collaboration or lack thereof with the Securitate, and find out the names of those who contributed information to the files. The archive custodian, the National Council for the Study of Securitate Archives, was created as an autonomous governmental agency meant to deposit and analyze the Securitate archives transferred from other institutions (including the two main information services, as well as the Ministries of Justice and Defense) and to identify Securitate officers and informers from among public officials and ordinary citizens.

Even though it opened the secret archives, the law had several glaring shortcomings. First, file access and file interpretation was entrusted to the National Council for the Study of Securitate Archives, whose leaders were appointed by the Senate according to party interests, not selected from among independent civil society representatives. Over the years, several Council leaders proved unable to resist pressure from the parties that appointed them to protect the identity of party members with a tainted past. Second, the files remained housed in locations inaccessible to the file custodian, which had to ask the file holders, the information services, or the ministries whether the files existed and could be consulted. Neither the services nor the ministries provided unrestricted access to their vast collections, thus allowing the Council to declare some individuals as non-collaborators although the Securitate archive provided evidence of their involvement with the political police. Third, only files not touching on national security could be made public, but the law offered no clear definition of the term. While legally the information services and the Council jointly decided which files were to be opened and which were to remain close, in practice the services controlled the process, because only they knew how large the archive was and what kind of files it contained.[36] Fourth, the law targeted only a narrow category of former secret agents who engaged in political police activities that damaged the lives and careers of their victims, but not the Communist Party leaders under whose orders the Securitate operated and the secret agents working abroad or for Romanian export-import monopolies. Because the party controlled the Securitate, the secret archives included no files on the party leaders morally responsible for repression (most notably, Ion Iliescu) or secret agents enjoying privileged ties to the party leadership (such as Dan Voiculescu, who worked for an export-import monopoly before 1989), although these categories should have shared the blame for the vast surveillance program that encroached the people's basic human rights.[37]

By 2005, the Council received only 10,000 secret files of minor political significance, but Romania's accession to the EU in 2007 refueled transitional justice efforts. As a result of President Băsescu's personal intervention, from 2005 to 2006 the Romanian Information Service transferred to the Council 1,306,000 files (that is, twelve linear kilometers) and the card system that cataloged them. These include the archives of the communist-era local army units, which are still to be processed.[38] Still, some 102,000 files related to national security remained under lock, unavailable to the general public.[39] The delay with which the archive changed hands raised serious doubts about the documents' authenticity, with some observers believing that the Romanian Information Service altered, replaced, and modified so many files that the archive entrusted to the Council in 2006 significantly differed from the archive as it was in December 1989.[40]

Overall, Romanians have demonstrated a level of disinterest in secret files unmatched by the eagerness with which the mass media has followed public scandals related to the dossiers. According to the Council, by 20 December 2011 a total of 34,249 Romanians asked to read their secret files. Of those, 32,489 were given an answer, either by being invited to read their files or by being told that they were "unknown" to the Securitate. There were cases in which the files of the individuals

[36] Mircea Marian, George Rădulescu, and Bogdan Costache, "SRI şi CNSAS au secretizat la discreţie dosarele Securităţii," *Adevărul* (31 August 2006).

[37] Personal interview with Gabriel Andreescu, Bucharest, 29 June 2011.

[38] Personal interview with historian Cosmin Budeanca, Bucharest, 28 June 2011.

[39] The Romanian Information Service retained close to 75,000 of those files, and the External Information Service 27,000. Adrian Mogoş, "Trei oficiali CNSAS au anunţat Ambasada SUA că au fost distruse 1.000 de dosare," *Jurnalul Naţional* (30 March 2011).

[40] In a discussion with representatives of the United States Embassy in Bucharest, National Council leaders claimed that many files lacked key documents, some files of former political prisoners were reported as missing, and as many as 1,000 files had been destroyed by the Romanian Information Service after 1989. Mogoş, "Trei oficiali CNSAS au anunţat Ambasada SUA."

"unknown" to the Securitate were found as a result of re-verifications.[41] The number of requests has remained low because of the logistical difficulties faced by petitioners outside Bucharest, where the Council is located. An early proposal, put forth by civil society representatives and supported by some Council leaders, to open local offices of the National Council that would act as custodians of the collections of the Securitate located outside Bucharest was abandoned for lack of funds and personnel shortage.[42] The centralized model retained to date, which brought all Securitate archives to the headquarters in the capital, impedes access, because petitioners have to visit Bucharest to read their secret file. Although Romania has a smaller territory than the United States or Canada, poor infrastructure still makes travel a risky, costly, and time-consuming endeavor avoided by petitioners. During the late 2000s, the new Council leadership sought to clear the backlog of access applications by solving more applications than it received in some years. Effective file access has been deterred by an imperfect law that favored the services over the Council and by the slow transfer of secret archival documents to the Council. According to the procedure followed until 2006, the Council had to petition the services, which released the file or not, according to its political priorities. Because nobody knew which files were extant, it was difficult to contradict the Romanian Information Service when it refused to hand over the files of well-known victims or victimizers. The Council received the bulk of files housed with the Information Service in 2006, the criminal files in 2007, the files and catalog cards of individuals who suffered administrative sentences in 2010, and only parts of the archives housed with the Ministry of Interior.[43] It takes time and personnel to record, arrange, and store the newly received secret files in its own deposits.

Soon after its creation, the National Council registered a deficit of credibility that took considerable time to overcome. It partly stemmed from factors the Council was in no position to control: a deficient legislative framework that included a restrictive definition of secret collaboration; the late transfer of the secret files; and the appointment of its leaders from among personalities supported by political parties but who never worked in an archive. However, other factors were within the Council's control: its leaders' refusal to consult the shelves directly, frequent information leaks, questionable public statements, allegiance to political parties, and multiple commitments as writers, university professors, and media gurus; the Council's acceptance

[41] Letter to the author from Dragoş Petrescu, President of the National Council for the Study of Securitate Archives, 20 December 2011.

[42] Personal interview with Cosmin Budeanca, Bucharest, 28 June 2011, and email communication with Claudiu Secaşiu, member of the leadership of the National Council for the Study of Securitate Archives, 7 December 2011.

[43] Letter to the author from Dragoş Petrescu, President of the National Council for the Study of Securitate Archives, 20 December 2011.

to keep files of post-communist politicians under lock; and the many partial or inaccurate verdicts it handed down.[44] Frustration has been voiced by historians, who denounced the different standards applied to researchers unaffiliated with the National Council, whom Council members see as competition, the arbitrary criteria that govern the accreditation process, and the slow pace of photocopying original secret documents.[45]

FILE ACCESS AND THE POLITICS OF MEMORY

Reading secret files is a unique experience for those who engage in it, mostly former victims in whose name the files were drafted and who were spied on, often without even knowing that they presented a security interest for the communist regime. The exercise of opening the file confirms that the victim, whose life was so ordinary and unimportant, survived a regime that, until 1989, seemed unassailable and well entrenched. The opening symbolically attests to the victory of the victims over the all-powerful system that ordered the surveillance operation and deployed all its might, resources, and agents to harass ordinary citizens and to contain their anti-regime actions. It implicitly transfers ownership of the file and its contents from the political police that compiled it and the dictatorial system that applied repression to the victim whose life is narrated in the secret documents.[46] It further guarantees that surveillance was discontinued, the secret officers and informers named in the file were retired, and the citizen is no longer seen as a security threat and a target by the state apparatus. Most importantly, the opening of the files breaks the secrecy that surrounded those documents and the informers' identity and represented the cornerstone of political police action under dictatorial rule.

At the same time, the reader cannot miss the discrepancy between the past he remembers and the reality the secret agents narrated laconically, impersonally, and often inaccurately. What emerges from the files is a series of snapshots taken by the political police from various angles and with various ends that suited them. Agents read events and evaluated victims exclusively from the viewpoint of their support or opposition to the regime, in the process retaining intimate details often used for blackmail (by threatening to publicly disclose the victims' homosexuality or adulterous relations). Not every detail of life was recorded secretly, as many former victims have discovered after accessing their files. In 2001, for example, writer

44 For some of those verdicts, see Stan, "Moral Cleansing Romanian Style," and Gabriel Andreescu, "Cazul Vasile Vetişanu şi aplicarea Legii 187/1999," *Revista Română de Drepturile Omului*, 25(2003): 63–81.

45 Personal interview with Cosmin Budeanca, Bucharest, 28 June 2011.

46 The state's ownership over the secret archives was the main argument why file access has not been granted in Russia. See Stan, ed., *Transitional Justice in Eastern Europe*, 222–246.

Stelian Tănase read his 500-page-long file from 1983 to 1989 and found that he was placed under surveillance shortly after the publication of his first novel in 1982. The monitoring intensified when he refused to rework two other novels to make them acceptable to censorship, deciding instead to send them abroad for possible publication. After reading the file, Tănase noted that it lacked important pieces of evidence, but remained informative because, through it, "one could get a glimpse of a house through a door left ajar."[47] To highlight the discrepancy between his real life and the life the Securitate recorded for him, Tănase published his personal diary and the file together in a single volume suggestively titled *At Home We Whisper*.[48]

Not all information included in the files is accurate, as informers lied by omission, distortion, exaggeration, or ignorance of the Securitate's goal of nailing a person down as a state security threat.[49] Let me provide two examples to illustrate this point. First, after reading the secret files that described the armed resistance of his group, Ion Gavrilă Ogoranu declared that

> the Securitate's clashes with us are described truthfully enough, but details were introduced to excuse their failures, by claiming that they fought against larger numbers [of anticommunist fighters], they were fewer, their guns did not function properly, or the fights occurred during the night when darkness gave us an advantage. They always found scapegoats to explain why we were not destroyed and why they suffered losses.... When it comes to the truth and the lie in the files, some documents are true, others include details that favor them, still others are partly made up so that we take all the blame, and a few are totally invented for them [the Securitate agents] to explain their inefficiency to their superiors.[50]

Second, on 17 October 1988, Corneliu Popa, the economic deputy director of the Constantin Tănase Theatre, delivered a note describing the cocktail reception organized by the cultural attaché of the French Embassy to Bucharest to honor a visiting French jazz group. After listing the names of the Romanian and foreign participants, describing the program, and commenting on the menu, Popa mentioned that Tănase was also present. His note went on to include short evaluations of the party's success and the guests' civilized behavior and mentioned the exact time when the Romanians left. In the note, Popa used his own name.[51] As only a line of the note referred to Tănase, Popa was likely asked to describe the party, not to denounce

47 Stelian Tănase, *Acasă se vorbeşte în şoaptă. Dosar & jurnal din anii târzii ai dictaturii* (Bucharest: Compania, 2002), 10.

48 Idem.

49 Mihaela Miroiu, "Delaţiunea ca obligaţie, cruciadă şi voluptate," 22 (29 September 2006).

50 Cited in Florian Banu, *Adevăr şi ficţiune în documentele Securităţii* (no date), 3, available at: http://www.cnsas.ro/documente/istoria_comunism/studii_articole/arhiva_securitatii/Adevar%20si%20fictiune.pdf (accessed on 22 September 2011).

51 Tanase, *Acasă se vorbeşte în şoaptă*, 71.

Tănase. By commenting on the food, Popa probably believed that he solved the difficult predicament of serving the political police, while limiting the damage done to the people he mentioned. Little did he know that his deposition was used as evidence for Tănase's efforts to contact foreign citizens who could help take his manuscript abroad.

Of the wealth of information contained in the files, the most sought after has remained the identity of the secret informers. True, the mass surveillance system was masterminded by the Communist Party and the operations were carried out by full-time Securitate officers, but it was the informers who approached the victims, pried open their personal space, infringed on their privacy, selected the information of value and interest, and transmitted it to the officers. It was very unlikely for a victim to meet a Securitate officer and not recognize him for what he was, as most officers wore their uniforms most of the time. It was equally unlikely that a victim could identify the informer from among the people with whom he came in daily contact, because both the Securitate officers and the informers took great care to protect the secrecy of the collaboration from the victim and everybody else. Condemnation has been directed primarily against the informers, those who delivered information under a code name, not against the casual sources, those who wrote notes under their real names and thus can be easily identified in the secret files. For all these reasons, Romanians, as other Eastern Europeans, have been interested in the shadowy informers more than the party leaders and Securitate officers involved in surveillance. For this exact reason, most readings of secret files have primarily sought to separate informers from among the victim's relatives, friends, neighbors, schoolmates, or workmates.

Many analysts have lamented the fact that the transitional justice priority of identifying informers by accessing the secret archives overlooks the informers' relatively low position within a repression apparatus dominated by party leaders and Securitate officers, the informers' efforts to provide trivial data of little operative value, and the fact that candidates could hardly refuse recruitment. But low position did not necessarily mean low importance, because informers were key cogs in the repression mechanism that often shaped investigations by interpreting basic facts, statements, and gestures. Arguably, without its informers the Securitate could never have maintained such a tight grip on the population, as without soldiers the Latin American military juntas could never disappear so many opponents. Moreover, the identity of party leaders and Securitate officers can be found in sources outside the secret archives, whereas few documents stored with other state agencies detail the secret activities of the informers. This is why access to secret files has been so intimately linked to the identification of informers, not Securitate officers or party activists. Refusing collaboration was dangerous, but not impossible, although the candidate for recruitment had to give up the prospect of qualifying for many material benefits associated with being a Securitate spy and daring the political police exposed him and his family to the threat of surveillance. Nonetheless, the fact that refusal was not impossible is proved by the fact that ultimately only a tiny fraction of the Romanian population (less than 3 percent) agreed to spy on others (see Chapter 1). Extremely few volunteered to join the ranks of the Securitate. As to the argument that informers often provided irrelevant information, note that even the most trivial and apolitical information could have greatly damaged a victim's well-being, as the cases of Popa and Tănase mentioned earlier show.

In Romania, three groups have contributed to the identification of former Securitate informers: those who read their own files, journalists who read other people's files, and the Council. For many victims, the fact that a name appeared in an information note was sufficient proof of that person's collaboration. One instance was often enough to convince the victim of the other person's guilt, without hearing the other side. Journalists have tried to give informers a chance to explain their actions, but different standards have been applied to different cases, and evaluations were occasionally made without giving victims any voice. These unofficial "verdicts" formulated by the public have paralleled those reached by the Council, constrained by the provisions of Law 187/1999 that neither victims nor journalists must observe. According to the law, persons are branded informers only if they collaborated with the Securitate "as a political police," that is, a repressive agency that infringed human rights. To determine collaboration with the political police, the Council should have interviewed victims and found out whether the notes submitted to the Securitate negatively affected the lives of these victims. The procedure seemed lengthy and the determination difficult. As such, the Council grounded the verdict in the existence of a collaboration pledge (demonstrating the informer's willingness to spy and his understanding of the information process) and information notes on victims (that demonstrated the fulfillment of the pledge) and supplemented this information by conducting interviews with the informers.[52] Ironically, the victim has been excluded from the process, the information has been drawn from incomplete archival fonds, and the verdicts have often been tainted by the political allegiances of Council leaders, who reach decisions through a majority vote. Unsurprisingly, the Council's official verdicts have often contradicted the unofficial assessments of the victims and the press.

From a transitional justice viewpoint, the public identification of Securitate informers cannot be dissociated from the public reaction to the disclosure and the consequences of those identifications on the post-communist political parties and civil society groups to which the former informers belonged at the time of the disclosure.

[52] This disproves the view that all secret documents are alike. See Monika Nalepa, *Skeletons in the Closet: Transitional Justice in Post-Communist Europe* (New York: Cambridge University Press, 2010).

Since the Council started to provide access to the secret archives, thousands of victims and informers have read their files and hundreds of informers have been unmasked by the mass media for their ties to the Securitate, but significantly fewer have been declared as such by the Council (see Chapter 4). Among those who once secretly reported on others were writers (Adrian Marino, Ioan Groşan, Stefan Augustin Doinaş, Petru Dimitriu, and Paul Comarnescu), philosophers (Constantin Noica), university professors (Central European University historian Sorin Antohi), musicians (Ducu Bertzi), sportsmen (soccer players Gică Popescu, Ladislau Boloni, and Rodion Cămătaru), religious leaders (Orthodox Metropolitan of Banat Nicolae Corneanu, Bishop of Argeş Calinic Argatu, and Baptist Minister Petru Dugulescu), journalists (Dan Ciachir), former political prisoners (Dan Amedeo Lăzărescu, Alexandru Paleologu, Constantin Bălăceanu Stolnici, and Mircea Ionescu Quintus), and post-communist politicians (Liberal Mona Muscă, Social Democrat Rodica Stănoiu, Democrats Cristian Rădulescu and Adrian Vilău, Greater Romania Party leader Corneliu Vadim Tudor, Christian Democrat Vasile Lupu, and Francisc Baranyi of the Democratic Union of Magyars). Hundreds of other individuals have been unmasked officially or unofficially as former Securitate agents.

The outrage that followed public disclosures of informers' names was generally disproportional to the damage they inflicted on their victims, reflecting instead the degree of perceived honesty exhibited by each former agent. Honesty related both to the willingness to publicly disclose one's tainted past after 1989 and the choice to refrain from delivering moralizing speeches about secret collaboration and from presenting oneself as a champion of file access and lustration. As a rule, the public commended and even forgave those who disclosed their own secret activities, praising their courage and integrity, even when the Securitate documents showed little signs of past moral rectitude. By contrast, former informers unveiled by the Council, the press, or their former victims felt the pains of public ostracism, lost their social standing and moral ground, and were even compelled to keep a low public profile. Judging from the secret notes he wrote from 1950 to 1988, the rush with which he defrocked priests who criticized the communist regime, and the decision to keep his church closed in December 1989 and to refuse entrance to the peaceful protesters who sought refuge from the army troops shooting at them, Metropolitan Corneanu was one of the worst communist offenders. He was also the first luminary to publicly confess collaboration, a gesture that almost overnight transformed him into a beacon of moral rectitude. When Corneanu later called on others to admit to their collaboration, his words rang true, given his willingness to stand public scrutiny.[53] By contrast, Bălăceanu-Stolnici kept silent and repeatedly denied any wrongdoing when

53 Lavinia Stan and Lucian Turcescu, *Religion and Politics in Post-Communist Romania* (New York: Oxford University Press, 2007).

the press accused him of collaboration in 2007. The Council eventually published details on how he volunteered to become an informer and then sold his friends and relatives against money, a doctoral degree, speedy promotion at his workplace, and acceptance into the Academy of Sciences.[54] After the disclosure, Bălăceanu-Stolnici lost his television show and kept a very low public profile.

Probably the most disappointing case was that of former Liberal Minister of Culture Mona Muscă, a politician who advocated the lustration of public officials with a hidden past. In what was later interpreted as a most cynical move, in 2005 Muscă helped initiate a lustration bill modeled after the Timişoara Declaration (see Chapter 4), which called for the marginalization from public life of all "those who were part of the power structures and the repressive apparatus of the communist regime."[55] In mid-2006, the press published documents indicating that Muscă collaborated with the Securitate during the 1970s, when she taught Romanian language to foreign students at the University of Timişoara. As both her collaboration pledge and her information notes were found in the secret archive, the Council branded her an informer, a verdict reaffirmed on appeal. After the Liberal Party expelled her from its ranks, Muscă gave up her deputy seat, and then withdrew from politics, having lost all her credibility.

While Muscă remains the only Romanian politician to voluntarily renounce public office, she was one of tens of politicians unmasked as Securitate informers. Former informers have been identified in virtually all political parties, and they uniformly kept silent about their past, in the hope that their collaboration would remain hidden, first because Romanians were denied file access in the 1990s, and then because access did not extend to the files of politicians, which were kept under lock for touching on national security. When unveiled as former spies, all these politicians claimed that either their secret notes were trivial or their secret activity served the greater good and protected national interests. That the Social Democrats tried to block access and downplay the repressive character of communist surveillance was to be expected, as the formation was rooted in the Communist Party. But the unveiling of former Securitate agents from among parties that promised de-communization showed their propensity to see file access and public identification as tools to settle scores with political rivals more than to redress the communist past. As Raluca Grosescu rightly pointed out, these parties' "militant actions sprang from dishonest grounds," because they wished to derive legitimacy from transitional justice programs they themselves refused to fully implement within their own ranks.[56]

54 Ionuţ Baias, "Mircea Dinescu: Bălăceanu-Stolnici s-a autopropus pentru colaborare cu Securitatea," *Hotnews* (3 December 2007).

55 "Legea lustraţiei," 22 (13 July 2005).

56 Raluca Grosescu, "The Role of the Civil Society and Anticommunist Political Actors in the Romanian Transitional Justice Partial Failure," in *Lustration and Consolidation of Democracy and the Rule of*

Following these revelations, the post-communist political parties and civil societies groups to which former informers belonged at the time of the disclosure have registered serious loss of credibility and legitimacy, because it was assumed that these parties and groups knew of the informers within their ranks, refused to expose them publicly, and instead facilitated their political careers. The damage has been greater for parties that included de-communization in their political platform or among their electoral promises (such as the Liberals and the Christian Democrats) because their public anticommunist discourse contrasted with the communist-era careers of some of their tainted leaders. Equally damaging has been the unmasking of religious figures because their past spying activities opened the possibility that they had offered information obtained through confession and informing on others was seen as incompatible with the moral standing of the church. Whereas the public has not looked favorably to the priests unveiled as former secret agents, the Romanian Orthodox Church has adopted a policy of non-expulsion, if not one of forgiveness toward tainted clergy.[57] The National Council has been the most serious casualty of this war of words, having been delegitimized by its refusal to brand well-known informers as former Securitate agents (Tudor because of political pressure, and Antohi because of his personal friendship with some Council leaders). By contrast, the revelations related to the past of apolitical luminaries – writers, philosophers, musicians, and sportsmen – have left their public standing relatively untouched, gaining little echo among fans and supporters, who continued to give their idols the benefit of the doubt and to argue that secret collaboration did not diminish these personalities' contribution to their respective fields of work.

CONCLUSION

Romania's experience with public access to secret files provides important transitional justice lessons. First, communist repression was greater than the sum of the individual cases on which the Securitate worked, and as such, the truth about those times can be pieced together only by going beyond the secret archive to collect information from other archives (especially the Communist Party collections), personal interviews with victims and perpetrators, communist-era governmental reports, memoires written by those who lived during those times, as well as graduation diplomas, medical records, photographs, and other objects that the Securitate had taken out of their usual context and inserted into the file.

Law in Central and Eastern Europe, eds. Vladimíra Dvořáková and Anđelko Milardović (Zagreb: Political Science Research Center, 2007), 190.

57 Stan, "Spies, Files and Lies," and Adriana Mica, "Forgiveness and Disclosure Scandals in Romania," in *Forgiveness: Probing the Boundaries*, eds. Stephen Bloch-Schulman and David White (Oxford: Inter-Disciplinary Press, 2009), 257–274.

Second, until a full picture of the damage inflicted through monitoring is constructed, suggestions that Ceauşescu's mass surveillance was relatively benign in comparison to Gheorghiu-Dej's terror defend a political police that never admitted to being a repressive apparatus bent on destroying opposition to the regime. For some observers, the existence of a trail of documents attests to the fact that the political police was a law-abiding structure that sought to be productive, efficient, and correct, but the files reveal that few of the Securitate's victims raised threats to national security and that in more than one occasion the secret police served its own interests more than the country's.

Third, given the National Council's credibility deficit, the unofficial assessments arrived at by victims and journalists have received more attention than the Council's official verdicts, which often were overturned by the courts or by the Council itself. As such, the mass media has been the most important actor to judge the communist past, thus substituting itself to the state agency in charge of the process. Indefatigable journalists have read the secret files, corroborated different pieces of information, interviewed witnesses, and publicized cases of communist-era injustice, but their relatively low standards of investigation and dependency on politicians raise serious questions about both the quality of these revelations and the reasons behind them.

Fourth, the public has condemned the denunciations of communist times, reprehensible and self-serving as they were, less than the post-communist lie and the informers' insistence on no wrongdoing. Out of fear of facing the consequences of their actions, many informers missed the opportunity to set the record straight, reveal important aspects of their questionable past, and show remorse immediately after the collapse of the communist regime. The refusal to assume responsibility received public condemnation, while voluntary acceptance of responsibility often led the public to forgive the most gruesome and long-standing collaboration.

Fifth, the task of reading the Securitate files cannot be accomplished without contextualizing their production as corpora delicti and without remembering the wooden language with which the communist regime used to bestow a veneer of legitimacy to its crimes. Not only that the secret file converts all other discourses into a legal discourse and all the documents it contains into pieces of evidence, but the narrative that couches past events is replete with communist terms in need of deconstruction and reconstruction: enemy of the people, traitor of the country, subversive activities, dissatisfaction with party policies, reactionary propaganda, among others. For the Securitate agents who busied themselves with file compilation, the ultimate goal was not so much to act as a trustworthy biographer but rather "to erase all incongruities in a synthetic characterization, a characterization ideally reduced down to one incriminating sentence,"[58] as Cristina Vătulescu noted. The fact that the political police branded a person an informer or a traitor of the country should not be taken at face value, as many observers have already noted. Patchy and altered as they are, however, the extant secret files remain powerful tools in rewriting the record of communist repression. Therefore, to completely discard them, as philosopher Gaspar Miklos Tamas argued when suggesting that all secret files should be sent to the bottom of the Danube River, seems totally unwarranted.[59]

Sixth, it is true that access to secret files has included no reconciliatory dimension, but at the same time fears that their dark secrets might lead to civil war have proved completely unfounded. No victim has sought revenge on the secret agents who once made his life a living hell, and very few of them have publicly denounced the secret informers mentioned in the files. The society was not divided by the opening of secret files but rather by the decision of communist leaders to pit one social group (the Securitate agents) against another (the victims).

Last, ordinary citizens have proved that they know how to read the files and distinguish angels from devils, as they know best how their lives intertwined with and were affected by the Securitate agents. The ability to set the historical record straight still lies with the researchers, who are called to offer the grand narratives that would link these personal stories together and detail the communist repression mechanism, but file access to ordinary citizens has turned out to be a powerful truth-searching and truth-telling initiative, as though to prove skeptics wrong.

[58] Cristina Vatulescu, *Police Esthetics. Literature, Film, and the Secret Police in Soviet Times* (Stanford, CA: Stanford University Press, 2010), 192.

[59] Cited in Stan, ed., *Transitional Justice in Eastern Europe*, 122.

4

Lustration

Any discussion of lustration in Romania must necessarily start with the definition of the term. During the early 1990s lustration was legislated in Germany and Czechoslovakia as an accusation-based procedure permitting the government to dismiss or demote selected communist decision makers from selected post-communist public offices. Lustration, which involved job loss or demotion to a non-lustratable position, targeted the individuals who had worked in the Communist Party leadership or for a range of communist repressive agencies (connected mostly with the army, the police, and the secret police). In spite of the German and Czech precedent, Hungary in 1994 and Poland in 1997 labeled "lustration" a substantially different, confession-based process that only in exceptional cases led to job loss. In those two countries, public officials who chose to hide their past involvement with the communist secret police had their names disclosed to the public. Politicians who planned to run in elections, not those nominated to public office, could potentially be affected by the unveiling, if voters chose to consider these candidates' tainted past, alongside their managerial skills and ideological or policy preferences.[1] Thus, by the end of the 1990s, two strikingly divergent vetting procedures were known by the same name. Nevertheless, in Romania this conflation of terms was seen as morally indefensible, because it baselessly brought together substantially different processes. Former political prisoners, civil society representatives, and anticommunist politicians supportive of transitional justice have never embraced this more recent understanding of lustration, which they believed to imply only partial vindication for the damage once inflicted by former communist decision makers, given the fact that most of them could retain their public office following the vetting. Whenever they have been asked, these voices emphatically pointed out that Romania adopted

[1] Lavinia Stan, ed., *Transitional Justice in Eastern Europe and the Former Soviet Union: Reckoning with the Communist Past* (London: Routledge, 2009), and Monika Nalepa, *Skeletons in the Closet: Transitional Justice in Post-Communist Europe* (New York: Cambridge University Press, 2010).

the lustration law only in 2006, but that law was never fully implemented, and as such, no politicians ever lost public office because of their past collaboration with the communist regime. In that country, a lustration process that leads to no job loss largely remains a contradiction in terms.

Notwithstanding the lateness and inefficiency of lustration leading to job loss, post-communist Romania has endeavored to effect elite renewal through a combination of 1) official public identifications of former communist secret agents operated first by the National Council for the Study of the Securitate Archives and then by the regular courts, 2) confession-based secret statements offered to the party leadership by political party members, electoral candidates, and nominees to public office, as well as 3) wild purges carried out discretionarily by the executive after each alternation in government (following the parliamentary elections of 1996, 2000, 2004, and 2008, as well as the Social Democrats' withdrawal from the government in late 2009). Some of these measures were confession based, others were accusation based.[2] Some led to job loss, others did not. Some were official and carried out in virtue of laws discussed and adopted by parliament or decisions passed by the executive, whereas others had an unofficial character, being implemented discretionary by the leadership of various political parties.

To an extent, all these lustration-related processes have aimed to change the composition of the Romanian post-communist elites in areas as diverse as politics, economy, the justice system, mass media, and education by sidelining former communist decision makers and secret agents. The intimate ties between the Communist Party and the Securitate, together with their joint control over almost all aspects of life and the political, economic, and cultural elites, made communist Romania a state where management positions were predominantly occupied by party members and/or Securitate agents. Writer Horia Roman Patapievici captured the ubiquitous penetration of state structures by the Securitate and the party when he remarked that "90 percent of the personnel in ministries dealing with propaganda or foreign partners were Securitate collaborators," in 1989 "the top leadership of the main ministries down to bureau heads was represented by Securitate officers whose identity was covered, residents or collaborators," and "in every institution the party secretary, administrators and managers were all part of the Securitate information network."[3]

[2] I borrow these two terms from Monika Nalepa, "Lustration," in *Encyclopedia of Transitional Justice*, eds. Lavinia Stan and Nadya Nedelsky (New York: Cambridge University Press, in press), pp. 46–51. Roman David proposes a different classification of lustration systems by distinguishing among exclusive, inclusive, and reconciliatory systems based on dismissal, exposure, and confession, respectively. Roman David, *Lustration and Transitional Justice. Personnel Systems in the Czech Republic, Hungary and Poland* (Philadelphia: University of Pennsylvania Press, 2011). I thank Roman for making a copy of his volume available to me.

[3] Horia Roman Patapievici, cited in "Din nou despre moştenirea fostei Securităţi," 22, 36(1998).

Given all these, Patapievici concluded that the Romanian communist state was "totally integrated into the Securitate surveillance structures."[4]

An analysis of the arguments for and against lustration brought to the attention of the Romanian Parliament during discussions of various lustration bills between 1990 and 2007 and a public debate to which both legislators and civil society representatives were invited to take part in May 2006 revealed generally feeble support for lustration. Advocates of lustration saw individuals tainted by past collaboration with the communist regime as potential enemies to democracy and free market economy, supporters of ideological principles that privileged the community over the individual, and the command, planned economy over free market. They considered communist decision makers as open to blackmail by former secret agents who knew their past and ready to rely on the ties that brought together communist leaders, state-owned enterprise directors, and Securitate secret officers and informers to defraud public resources and to engage in corruption schemes detrimental to the public good. For its proponents, the marginalization of individuals with a tainted past amounted to a much-needed national catharsis, a moral cleansing program, a "return to normalcy," a resolute break with the repressive past, its culture of secrecy, unaccountability, patronage, and discretion, and a *vote de blâme* for the "mentality instituted in Romania through Sovietization and communization in May 1945."[5] The vetting process represented an "absolute necessity" and a "moral filter" that would unmask "the 'servants of evil' who stole decades of our history" because "hygiene in politics is as useful as hygiene in our personal life," as one Liberal deputy put it.[6] Lustration further constituted a measure of retributive justice for the former victims of communist crimes – a way to "give minimal moral satisfaction to the millions of victims who suffered because of communism and its servants"[7] and were killed during the December 1989 revolution and a guarantee that "a new genocide would never be possible again."[8] No less important was the fact that lustration prevented post-communist violence by negating former communists access to the resources that would allow them to wreak havoc on the country and prepared Romania for accession into the European Union as a "clean and unbroken" member state.[9] In short, "democracy is but an empty word without lustration," as Deputy Gabriel Sandu claimed.[10]

4 Idem.

5 Historian Andrei Cioroianu, a Liberal Party member, cited in Lavinia Stan, "Witch-hunt or Moral Rebirth? Romanian Parliamentary Debates on Lustration," *East European Politics and Societies* (6 April 2011), 10, available at: http://eep.sagepub.com/content/early/2011/04/05/0888325411403922.full.pdf+html (accessed on 21 August 2011).

6 Ion Dumitrescu, cited in Stan, "Witch-hunt or Moral Rebirth?," 10.

7 Gheorghe Gabor, cited in idem.

8 Liberal Viorel Arion, cited in idem, 11.

9 Idem.

10 Idem.

By contrast, critics of lustration considered it "legally, politically and morally unacceptable," "unconstitutional and even anti-constitutional," a "discriminatory imbecility," a "confused, ambiguous, legally imperfect" proposal amounting to witch hunt and modern inquisitorial techniques, an "uninspired anachronism, a wasps' nest empoisoning the country," an aberrant policy, an "exercise in hypocrisy and intolerance," even an "unnecessary stupidity."[11] That was because one cannot condemn part of the Romanian history (that is, the 1945–1989 communist period) or punish "valuable" and "patriotic" individuals (as the communist officials and secret agents supposedly were); the country should focus on more important and urgent socioeconomic priorities, and the lustration proposal ran counter to European values of political inclusion by "artificially creating categories of population that were denied their basic human right" of being elected to public office.[12] Additional arguments referred to the fact that guilt was not directly commensurate with the political office (because "a county First Secretary might have been responsible for more numerous and more gruesome human rights infringements than a Central Committee member," although the latter was higher up on the communist ladder) and that the responsibility of the top commanders "who had the right and power to decide" had to be distinguished from that of Securitate officers "who had engaged in atrocious acts" or of the almost 4 million regular party members who simply obeyed orders and supposedly "did not know what they were doing."[13] For a number of Romanian political luminaries, lustration's Achilles heel was represented by its inability to distinguish well-intentioned, patriotic informers who helped their country in dangerous times from the evil, mercantile spies who offered information out of sheer greed, moral turpitude, or revenge.[14]

The May 2006 public debate on lustration organized by the Liberal leaders of the Chamber of Deputies represented the only time when the Romanian Parliament sought the opinion of civil society representatives on the renewal of the post-communist political and economic elites through vetting. While several non-state organizations found a zest to contribute prescient written opinions, conspicuously absent from the debate were the intellectuals inside and outside the Group for Social Dialogue. The Group's inability to speak with a single voice in favor of a core transitional justice method enacted in post-communist Europe was borne out of the diversity of positions toward lustration among its members, who included a handful of former communist officials alongside many anticommunist dissidents and even many more writers and philosophers who, during communist

[11] Idem, 14.

[12] Senator Gheorghe Dumitraşcu, quoted in "Şedinţa Senatului din 25 martie 1992", *Monitorul Oficial al României, partea II-a* (26 March 1992): 2–10.

[13] Senator Radu Câmpeanu, idem.

[14] Senator Corneliu Vadim Tudor, idem.

times, retreated into "resistance through culture," a philosophy that advocated political inaction toward the dictatorial regime and a return to classical philosophical themes remote from the reality faced by ordinary Romanians. Some Group members have repeatedly lent support to lustration over the years, but others have dismissed it as an unwanted and inappropriate policy premised on collective guilt. As early as 1996, Vladimir Tismaneanu, who headed the Presidential Commission for the Analysis of the Communist Dictatorship in Romania a decade later (see Chapter 5), qualified lustration as an "extremely dangerous" measure that left open the possibility for a "collective massacre" of former communist decision makers, individuals he despised but to whom he could not deny their civic rights.[15] In 1999, Emil Hurezeanu, a former reporter with Radio Free Europe/Radio Liberty, quipped that lustration was "aberrant," "inopportune, useless, and ridiculous," because "it is possible that many successes of Romania's partial democracy were made possible through the administrative skills of the honest members of the old communist regime."[16] Weeks before lustration was debated in parliament in 2006, Dan Pavel, former editorialist with the Group's weekly 22, indicted lustration as a "tardy, unjust, and illogical" proposal, "the most disagreeable act of injustice of post-communist times," and a gesture of "blind revenge" that could tremendously hurt the Romanian democracy.[17] Another constant and vocal critic was Andrei Cornea, who both in 1990 and in 2012 maintained that lustration was misguided because "a person should answer only for her own actions and a blanket policy that sees her solely as part of a group is not only undemocratic but also far from the best European humanist tradition."[18]

During the 1990s, demands for elite renewal stemmed from concerns with the reproduction of communist officials and Securitate agents in political and economic leadership positions after the December 1989 revolution. Started in Timişoara as anticommunist, the revolution ended in Bucharest as merely anti-Ceauşescu, with the civil society realizing that the National Salvation Front "participated in a counterrevolution. Through diversion, disinformation, violence, calumny against new political parties, Romania was steered toward neo-communism."[19] The backbone of the Salvation Front, which claimed to embody Romania's hopes for democratic

[15] Vladimir Tismaneanu, cited in Vladimir Tismaneanu and Mircea Mihăeş, *O tranziţie mai lungă decât veacul. România după Ceauşescu* (Bucharest: Curtea Veche, 2011), 28.

[16] Cited in "Faţă în faţă," Radio Free Europe (30 May 1999). According to the Romanian press, both historian Marius Oprea and President Traian Băsescu have publicly alleged that Hurezeanu was a former Securitate collaborator.

[17] Dan Pavel, "Lustraţia – tardivă, nedreaptă, ilogică," *Ziua* (17 April 2006).

[18] Andrei Cornea, "Legea lustraţiei – o eroare," 22 (6 March 2012).

[19] Christian Democrat Deputy George Şerban, author of the Timişoara Declaration, quoted in "Şedinţa solemnă comună a Camerei Deputaţilor şi Senatului din 22 decembrie 1997," *Monitorul Oficial al României, partea a II-a* (12 January 1998): 1–8.

change, remained the former Communist Party and its satellite youth, workers, and women's organizations – all of which had supported the repressive regime to the very end. As communist Romania lacked a strong civil society that could present alternatives to the party-state, the revolution resulted in elite reproduction, not elite replacement. The second echelon of the communist leadership (party apparatchiks, county first secretaries, and Communist Youth League leaders) replaced the first echelon (the family of dictator Nicolae Ceauşescu and their close collaborators) and became the new political and economic elite. Former communist officials and Securitate agents constituted a majority in the cabinets formed after the 1990, 1992, and 2000 elections, the largest parliamentary caucus in 1990–1996 and 2000–2004, and important percentages of deputies and senators in 1996–2000. All three post-communist presidents (Ion Iliescu, Emil Constantinescu, and Traian Băsescu), seven of the nine prime ministers (Petre Roman, Nicolae Văcăroiu, Victor Ciorbea, Mugur Isărescu, Adrian Năstase, Emil Boc, and Mihai-Răzvan Ungureanu, but not Radu Vasile or Călin Popescu-Tăriceanu), as well as scores of ministers and deputy ministers, deputies, and senators were drawn from the ranks of the communist state, party, economic, or student leadership.[20] According to analysts, half of all members of the first post-communist legislature (1990–1992) had occupied political positions before 1989, while "survey data from the fourth legislative term in the post-Ceauşescu era show that five out of six [members of parliament] were registered as [Communist] party members before 1989," demonstrating that Romania experienced more modest rates of elite replacement than other Eastern European countries.[21] A comparative elite study uncovered that the percentage of Romanian government members who had belonged to the communist nomenklatura dropped from 74.2 percent for the first post-revolutionary government of Petre Roman (1989–1990) to 44.2 percent for the Social Democrat government of Nicolae Văcăroiu (1992–1996). The nomenklatura included the top Communist Party and state officials, and as such, the percentage of former lower-echelon communists in post-communist governments was likely higher. Even the self-avowed anticommunist Democratic Convention governments of 1996–2000 included 7–9 percent nomenklatura members among their ranks. That

[20] Roman's family was part of the nomenklatura, Văcăroiu worked for the Committee of Central Planning, which handed down plan targets to state enterprises, Ciorbea was a judge and prosecutor from 1979 to 1987, Isărescu worked for the Institute of International Economics from 1971 until after the 1989 revolution, and Năstase was a judge before marrying the daughter of Minister of Agriculture Angelo Miculescu (1969–1981). Boc was leader of the Union of Communist Student Associations in the University Babeş-Bolyai of Cluj-Napoca and in 1985 was reportedly recruited into the Securitate troops. See George Bara, "Este Emil Boc lustrabil? Istoria politică a premierului României," *Napoca News* (20 May 2009).

[21] Gabriella Ilonszki and Michael Edinger, "MPs in Post-Communist and Post-Soviet Nations: A Parliamentary Elite in the Making," *Journal of Legislative Studies*, 13(2007): 142–163.

percentage jumped to 18.5 percent once the Social Democrats returned to government in 2000.[22]

As time passed, another set of concerns fueled demands for lustration: Romania's high corruption levels, the involvement of former communist officials and Securitate agents in some of the most notorious scandals revolving around embezzlement, cronyism, clientelism, and nepotism, and their uncanny ability to transform themselves and their close relatives and friends into successful entrepreneurs and prosperous businessmen. Independent research has demonstrated that the most significant factor predicting membership in the new business elite was past membership in the communist elite, a finding echoing press reports that unveiled the collaboration of Romania's richest entrepreneurs with the Securitate and Ceauşescu's family.[23] The Securitate agents' involvement in corruption scandals, along with the inability and/or unwillingness of governments representing both the successors to the Communist Party and their pro-democratic political rivals, was denounced by the anonymous author of Armageddon 7 (see Chapter 9) and scores of books and newspaper articles, some more documented than others.[24] Despite their declared commitment to effect democratization and raise living standards, the Romanian political elites have had difficulty to accept the need for governmental accountability and efficiency, to set aside their group interests to promote the common good, to abstain from promoting their relatives into positions of power and responsibility and from relying on client-patron networks, and to dissociate public resources from their personal purse. Although formations remain divided by policy and ideological preferences into center-left and center-right parties, they remain remarkably similar in their use of high political corruption as a tool to promote their group interests. The widespread belief is that this generalized political corruption, which leads to chronic waste of public resources, governmental inefficiency, and democratic deficit, has been fueled by former secret agents and communist factory managers (what journalist Andrei Cornea called the "directocracy" [*directocraţia*]) who have used the old boys' networks and connections to their advantage.[25] These occult networks cross party lines, but have apparently been more resilient and prevalent within the

22 Raluca Grosescu, "Conversia elitelor comuniste din România în perioada de tranziţie: 1989–2000," in *De ce trebuie condamnat comunismul* (Bucharest: Institutul de Investigare a Crimelor Comunismului din România, 2006), 249.

23 Roman David, "Lustration Laws in Action: The Motives and Evaluation of Lustration Policy in the Czech Republic and Poland (1989–2001)," *Law and Social Inquiry*, 28(Spring 2003): 414 fn 63.

24 Among articles blaming corruption on former communist officials and Securitate agents, see Pavel Lucescu, "De ce ne interesează CNSAS?," *Monitorul de Iaşi* (12 March 2003); Cristian Oprea, Christian Levant, Lidia Moise, and Alina Mihai, "Am făcut operaţiuni din ordinul serviciilor secrete," *Evenimentul Zilei* (15 March 2003); Cornel Nistorescu, "Cazul Temeşan, spre final," *Evenimentul Zilei* (15 March 2003); and Bogdan Ficeac, "Căutaţi securistul," *România Liberă* (30 October 2003).

25 Andrei Cornea, *Directocraţia şi sfârşitul tranziţiei în România* (Bucharest: CSPAC, 1995).

ranks of the successors to the Communist Party than among anticommunist forces. Since joining the EU, its Corruption Perception Index has improved from 2.6 in 2006 to 3.6 in 2011, but Romania has constantly ranked among the countries with the highest levels of corruption and bribe in the region.[26]

OFFICIAL LUSTRATION POLICIES

In Romania, the first lustration demand took the form of Article 8 of the Timişoara Declaration of 11 March 1990, which asked for amendments to the electoral law that would ban Communist Party leaders, state dignitaries, and secret political police agents from being included on party lists for the first three consecutive post-communist elections (that is, a total of twelve years) and communist officials from running in presidential elections.[27] Similar demands were put forth by the Civic Alliance in its Declaration of National Reconciliation of 13 March 1991, which read that "until 2000, the following persons cannot be promoted to positions of power and responsibility in the state: former members of the Central Committee of the Romanian Communist Party, former Securitate agents, and former activists who renounced their professions and were remunerated by the Communist Party for their political and ideological work."[28] These lustration calls received a cold shoulder from the new rulers, as they would have cut short the political careers of many Salvation Front leaders, especially that of President Iliescu, who served as the first secretary of the Iaşi County Council (1974–1979) and deputy first secretary of the Timiş County Council (1971–1974).[29] The failure of the Timişoara Declaration to gather support left an indelible mark on subsequent lustration proposals as it was felt that, to launch the lustration process, the country had to condemn communism, a step few Romanians were willing to take given the success with which the new leaders had discredited Ceauşescu and rescued his former aids as "patriotic elements." The weakness of the civil society, the Communist Party's extended membership of

[26] The scores ran from 10, the least corrupt country, to 1, the most corrupt country. Transparency International, *Corruption Perception Index* 2010 *Results* (2010), available at: http://www.transparency.org/policy_research/surveys_indices/cpi/2010/results (accessed on 21 August 2011).

[27] "The Timişoara Declaration," *Report on Eastern Europe* (6 April 1990): 41–45.

[28] Alianţa Civică, *Declaraţie de Reconciliere Naţională* (13 March 1991), available at: http://www.aliantacivica.ro/documente/Declaratia%20de%20reconciliere%20nationala%20-%2013%20martie%20 1991.htm (accessed on 15 December 2011).

[29] Lavinia Stan, "Moral Cleansing Romanian Style," *Problems of Post-Communism*, 49(2002): 52–62, and Lavinia Stan, "Romania: In the Shadow of the Past," in *Central and Southeastern European Politics since* 1989, ed. Sabrina P. Ramet (Cambridge, UK: Cambridge University Press, 2010), 379–400. In July 1992, the Romanian parliament debated the possibility to create a commission to study the Securitate files of legislators elected in the May 1990 elections, but the talks led to no concrete action. Domniţa Ştefănescu, *Cinci ani din istoria României. O cronologie a evenimentelor Decembrie 1989-Decembrie 1994* (Bucharest: Editura Maşina de Scris, 1995).

nearly 4 million members, and the people's recollection that they had failed to act against the regime and had been accomplices to the dictatorial experience further accounted for the poor receptivity of lustration among ordinary citizens, opinion leaders, and politicians.

Subsequent lustration calls were launched in parliament as legislative proposals, confidence motions, amendments to electoral laws, or as part of the yearly commemorations of the 1989 revolution to which all political formations eagerly paid their respects. Resistance to vetting came from all formations, especially from the Social Democrat Party, which included many former communist officials, and the nationalistic Greater Romania Party, which openly represented the interests of the former Securitate agents (see Chapter 1). Although all legislative proposals in favor of lustration were lodged by the so-called historical parties, not all positions against lustration originated with the Social Democrats and the nationalist camp. From 1990 to 1996 the government and the opposition were split over the issue, with individuals on both sides joining hands in blocking these proposals.

In late 1996, the Democratic Convention formed the government, and academic Emil Constantinescu assumed the presidency with promises to renew the political elite and unmask communist officials and secret agents from among its midst. Nevertheless, hopes for the country's moral cleansing completely vanished on 20 March 1997, when in a surprise move, President Constantinescu laid waste to his unparalleled capital of legitimacy by vehemently insisting that the very results of the 1996 elections – the alternation in government from the Social Democrats to the Democratic Convention – had rendered Article 8 of the Timişoara Declaration obsolete and lustration redundant. According to him, implementing lustration would demonstrate the rulers' "weakness, incompetence and incapacity to use the power given to [them] by the people."[30] This position stirred condemnation from civil society groups that felt betrayed by the haste with which the president reneged his electoral promises. It also showed that even the political actors most supportive of lustration preferred elite renewal through "wild" executive purges to orderly processes controlled by the legislative.

Constantinescu's statement, which effectively stopped the lustration law in its tracks, explains why, in the years that followed, his Democratic Convention joined hands with the opposition to render toothless the only serious lustration proposal ever discussed in parliament. After over 100 amendments were introduced by the government and the opposition, Law 187/1999 on Access to the Securitate Files and the Unveiling of the Securitate as a Political Police (popularly known as the Ticu Law after Senator Constantin Ticu Dumitrescu, who initiated it in 1997) allowed

[30] Constantinescu received Timişoara Society's Speranţa (Hope) prize. Emil Constantinescu, *Timpul dărâmării, timpul zidirii* (Bucharest: Universalia, 2002).

the vetting of neither communist officials nor secret agents, but rather hoped that politicians with a tainted past would voluntarily refrain from running in elections or from seeking party support to qualify for public office.[31] The National Council for the Study of the Securitate Archives was set up as an independent governmental agency mandated to investigate the past of public officials and electoral candidates based on the secret files, but investigations were rendered meaningless because the Council had no direct access to the archives, still housed with the Romanian Information Service and the External Information Service in closed military units inaccessible to the Council, and most files of post-communist politicians were kept under lock for touching an ill-defined "national security" (see discussion later in the chapter).

After 2000, when Iliescu regained the presidency and his Social Democrats formed the government, the word "lustration" was never again uttered in parliament. Civil society groups and opposition legislators unsuccessfully tried their best to keep the issue in the public eye, echoing the widespread belief that former Securitate agents fueled the country's endemic corruption and the popular support for unveiling former Securitate agents from among post-communist politicians.[32] By 2004 the elite's failure to renew itself had become a matter of concern for a growing number of Romanians, ever more dissatisfied with their corrupt politicians. The Timişoara Society lamented the fact that "communism did not disappear, it privatized itself."[33] For one outspoken journalist, the former Communist Party secretaries and youth leaders had transmogrified into "prosperous businessmen and successful politicians, genuine capitalists" who would bring "pull, tricks, rapt and lies, corruption, wooden language"[34] into European politics once the country was allowed to join the Union. Another newspaper warned that the communist decision makers have retained "the reflexes of a system that did not fully disappear in 1989," "were raised in the communist double discourse, and were told not to say what they really think." Given

[31] Lavinia Stan, "Lustration: The Story of a Failure," *Studia Politica. Romanian Political Science Review*, 6(2006):146.

[32] An opinion poll conducted by the Institute for Social Studies (Institutul de Studii Sociale) in April 2003 showed that 70 percent of respondents saw a direct link between the former Securitate and the high levels of post-communist corruption, and 80 percent supported the public identification of former secret agents. See "Sondaj ISS pentru urechile lui Onisoru," *Ziua* (24 April 2003). But according to a poll conducted in March 2002, 60 percent of respondents agreed that the information services had been reformed along democratic lines, 50 percent argued that the services no longer targeted citizens because of their political opinions, 52 percent contended that the services served the national interest, and 74 percent suggested that good Securitate experts should continue to work for the post-communist information services. Radu Tudor, "Televiziunea Română s-a întrecut pe sine," *Ziua* (25 March 2002).

[33] Idem, 150.

[34] A 2004 declaration of journalist Teodor Flueraş, quoted in Stan, "Lustration: The Story of a Failure," 150.

their tainted background, they should "let others, unaltered by socialist-scientific training," to occupy public office and "make decisions on our behalf."[35]

Lustration was resurrected as a political topic before the 2004 general elections, when Traian Băsescu and his Justice and Truth Alliance challenged Adrian Năstase and his Social Democrats. For Democrat leader Emil Boc, Romania had to effect "a second revolution, end the Iliescu era," and "forever marginalize the communist structures that engaged in political police actions before 1989," because the first fifteen years of post-communism had shown that "the victim and its torturer cannot sit together at the same table."[36] Hours before the vote, Băsescu openly endorsed elite renewal in a televised confrontation, when he wondered, "What curse [was put in effect] for the people to have to choose between two former communists, Adrian Năstase and Traian Băsescu? In fifteen years no other [politician], untainted by communist habits, emerged.... Maybe it's time for another candidate to come before the people."[37] His candor carried rhetorical appeal, helping Băsescu to gain the trust of the voters and to win the presidency.

In 2005, months after being sworn into office, President Băsescu denounced "the lack of will, power and capacity to break with the old [communist] system,"[38] without naming those responsible for stalling or effecting that break, and then publicly declared his personal support for lustration in view of appeasing civil society groups that doubted his commitment to the program after the press listed him among longtime Securitate collaborators. While parliament registered an unprecedented number of legislative proposals on lustration and the civil society renewed its demands for vetting, public debates were generally marked by skepticism and the belief that the ruling Alliance was unable to support the implementation of such a radical project. An opinion poll conducted in early 2006 revealed the ordinary Romanians' ambivalence toward that policy. Some 37 percent of respondents believed that those who had collaborated with the Securitate should be banned from running in future elections, 32 percent believed that they should give up their public office, and 12 percent believed that they should be held accountable for hiding the truth about their past. Around 43 percent were of the opinion that many former Securitate agents occupied high-ranking posts in the administration and the economy. As many as 56 percent agreed that Băsescu was unable to destroy the lingering influence of the Securitate network, while 48 percent believed that Romania did not fully break with its communist past. Some 48 percent thought that the Romanian Information Service resembled the Securitate,

[35] "Aţi auzit de Punctul 8?," *Evenimentul Zilei* (29 July 2004).

[36] Stan, "Lustration: The Story of a Failure," 151–152.

[37] Idem, 152.

[38] Idem, 154.

but for a majority of respondents the Service played after 1990 a role that was mostly positive.[39] When all hope seemed lost, with an impeccable sense of political timing, the cabinet of Liberal Prime Minister Popescu-Tăriceanu introduced lustration stipulations in a governmental decision meant to clarify Law 187/1999, which governed the activity of the National Council.[40]

That clarifying decision was Emergency Governmental Ordinance 16/2006, which expanded confession-based lustration in Romania and entrusted the National Council with the task of verifying personal statements signed by public office holders and detailing their past collaboration or non-collaboration with the Securitate.[41] The final verdicts regarding public office holders and electoral candidates were to be published in the state gazette, *Monitorul Oficial*. At that point, if the published verdict differed from the personal statement (presumably because the statement denied, whereas *Monitorul Oficial* certified, past collaboration), the Council had to notify the courts, as the act of offering a false declaration was a legal offense punishable with loss of public office. In an effort to dislodge unreformed and un-repenting older members of the judiciary suspected of a tainted past, collaboration with the Securitate of judges and prosecutors holding or seeking administrative leadership positions in the court system or the prosecutor's offices or elected to the Superior Council of the Magistracy led to disqualification even when there was no evidence that collaboration endangered fundamental human rights and liberties. The ordinance affected only politicians who occupied public offices at the time when the ordinance came into effect and those who sought future appointments, not those who had discontinued their political careers by 2006.

As lustration depended on a highly corrupt, politically tainted, and notoriously inefficient judiciary that has consistently opposed vetting, those identified as former Securitate agents represented a small fraction of all secret agents active in post-communist politics. Politicians could have lost their public office if they provided a false statement, but the incentive to misrepresent the past was canceled out by the fact that statements were not made public. Because of these reasons, from 2006 to 2007 no public office holders lost their positions because they lied about their past, although by late 2007 the names of 2,958 former secret agents appeared in *Monitorul Oficial*, a handful of whom occupied public office. Lustration was bitterly contested by a number of prominent politicians, mostly drawn from the Communist

[39] Ovidiu Banches, "Nomenclaturiştii, mai vinovaţi decât securiştii," *Ziua* (9 May 2006).

[40] "Legea 187/1999 privind accesul la propriul dosar şi deconspirarea Securităţii ca poliţie politică," *Monitorul Oficial al României, partea I* (9 December 1999).

[41] "Ordonanţa de Urgenţă nr.16 din 22 februarie 2006 pentru modificarea şi completarea Legii nr. 187/1999 privind accesul la propriul dosar şi deconspirarea Securităţii ca poliţie politică," *Monitorul Oficial al României, partea I* (27 February 2006).

Party successor formations.[42] The fiercest opponent was Dan Voiculescu, the wealthy leader of the Conservative Party, unveiled by the National Council as former secret agent "Felix" on the basis of Securitate documents. Rather than acknowledging his tainted past, repenting for his former activity, and asking forgiveness from his victims, which included his own relatives, Felix vehemently contested the verdict and asked the Constitutional Court to review the constitutionality of the entire lustration legislation.[43] In January 2008, in a politically motivated ruling that contradicted seven of its earlier decisions, the Court found Emergency Ordinance 16/2006 unconstitutional, invalidated all verdicts that the Council had handed down up to that moment, and threatened to shut down the Council completely.[44] To avert this possibility, which did not seat well with its supporters, the Popescu-Tăriceanu cabinet extended the life of the National Council by limiting its mandate to storing the secret documents and granting citizens access to their files, while transferring the right to decide who was (or not) a former Securitate agent from the Council to the courts.[45] The controversial Court decision elicited no response from the Presidential Office, which took no notice of it, although President Băsescu had won the 2004 elections on a de-communization campaign. By 2008, however, lustration's purchasing power had been seriously affected by lack of political will on the part of the main parties and the haphazard verdicts handed down by the Council.

The passing of a new bill on 28 February 2012 sought to resurrect lustration. The bill adoption was the ruling Democrat-Liberal Party's attempt to salvage its popularity, chronically affected by street protests in which thousands of people voiced dissatisfaction with governmental measures requiring ordinary citizens to shoulder the effects of the global financial crisis while protecting the interests of the political and economic elites. As a party harboring former communist decision makers, the Democrat-Liberals never wholeheartedly embraced lustration, but paid lip service to a policy that could weaken their Social Democrat rivals and was keenly supported by their Liberal archenemies, with whom they did not want to compare unfavorably. In 2012, the ruling majority accepted to support the bill only after Teodor Mărieş, the Association 21 December 1989 president, ended 100 days of hunger strike. The bill was a reworked version of a proposal introduced in 2006 by four Liberal legislators, including Deputy Mona Muscă,

[42] The figure was computed on the basis of the Annual Reports of the National Council. See Lavinia Stan, "Reckoning with the Communist Past in Romania: A Scorecard," *Europe-Asia Studies*, vol. 64, no. 8 (2012), pp. 1–20.

[43] Octavian Hoandră, "Colaborarea ca memorie," *Ziua* (19 Iunie 2006).

[44] Curtea Constituţională, "Decizie nr.51 din 31 ianuarie 2008 referitoare la excepţia de neconstituţionalitate a dispoziţiilor Legii nr. 187/1999 privind accesul la propriul dosar şi deconspirarea poliţiei politice comuniste," *Monitorul Oficial al României, partea I* (6 February 2008).

[45] "Ordonanţa de Urgenţă nr.24 din 5 martie 2008 privind accesul la propriul dosar şi deconspirarea Securităţii," *Monitorul Official al României, partea I* (10 March 2008).

later unmasked as a Securitate informer. After much procrastination and political wrangling, in May 2010 the Chamber of Deputies adopted the proposal, while the Senate petitioned the Constitutional Court against its constitutionality. The Court agreed that lustration infringed the constitution by blocking some citizens' access to elected positions, running counter the nonretroactivity principle, and failing to individualize guilt.[46] In response, the law was reworded to target only nominated public offices, thus placing the Democrat-Liberal leader, Băsescu, outside of its scope, as the presidential position is elected. To avoid the vetting of Prime Minister Mihai Răzvan Ungureanu, head of the External Information Service from 2007 to January 2012, the Democrat-Liberals further excluded Communist Youth League leaders from among the categories banned from occupying public office.[47] A close collaborator of Băsescu, Ungureanu served as an alternate League leader from 1985 to 1989.

At the time of this writing, the bill is being reexamined by the Constitutional Court, with little chances of gaining the approval of either the Court or the Senate as a result of its serious flaws. Besides arbitrarily excluding the Communist Youth League in a move serving the interests of the ruling majority more than the country's need for truth, the bill affects neither former Securitate agents who continued their spying activities as agents of post-communist intelligence services (because their identity and files remain secret) nor those whose secret files were never publicly open (mostly high-ranking Communist Party leaders like Iliescu or post-communist politicians like Băsescu). These two groups were allegedly closer to the communist repressive state, and better able to hide their past by destroying the files, than the categories slated for lustration. The bill further provides for the removal of all communist-era prosecutors, thus failing to individualize guilt, while its implementation rests on a judiciary resistant to cleanse its own ranks of tainted magistrates. Although by the time the bill passes most communist decision makers would have retired from public life, analysts fear that the Democrat-Liberal government includes an increasing number of covered Securitate officers with a vested interest in thwarting the honest implementation of even the mildest lustration program.[48] Although it affected no elected officials, the bill offered moral reparation to former

[46] Curtea Constituţională, "Decizia nr. 820 din 7 iunie 2010 referitoare la obiecţia de neconstituţionalitate a dispoziţiilor Legii lustraţiei, privind limitarea temporară a accesului la unele funcţii şi demnităţi publice pentru persoanele care au făcut parte din structurile de putere şi din aparatul represiv al regimului communist în perioada 6 martie 1945 – 22 decembrie 1989," *Monitorul Oficial al României, partea I* (23 June 2010), available at: http://www.cdep.ro/proiecte/2006/200/80/2/decizie282.pdf (accessed on 8 March 2012).

[47] "Sedinţa Camerei Deputaţilor din 28 februarie 2012," *Monitorul Oficial al României, partea II-a* (9 March 2012).

[48] Alina Mungiu-Pippidi, "Când demilitarizăm România?," *România Liberă* (1 March 2012).

communist-era victims, the Timişoara Society declared.[49] The more pessimistic Liberal Party leader Crin Antonescu reminded that Romania failed to enact lustration as a result of the inexistence of political elites alternative to the communist one, the manifold complicities among political parties, and the willingness of international actors to work with former communists rather than to support lustration. For Antonescu, whose party did not attend the meeting in which the bill was passed, the Democrat-Liberals' efforts were demagogic because lustration was never that party's cause.[50]

THE NATIONAL COUNCIL FOR THE STUDY OF SECURITATE ARCHIVES VERIFICATIONS

Until 2008, the National Council was the only public institution legally mandated to decide whether a person was a Securitate agent. It made that determination on the basis of secret documents and interviews with individuals suspected of collaboration. Since 2008, the courts have made such assessments, based on documentation received from the Council, which retains a key role in disclosures by deciding what information reaches the courts and which individuals are placed under investigation and in which specific order. Two different procedures have been observed for verifying the politicians' past. The Council has automatically investigated electoral candidates who run in elections and persons who occupy a slate of top public offices, ranging from those of president of the republic and cabinet member to judges and university presidents. In addition, any Romanian citizen and institution can ask the Council to verify elected or appointed state officials at all levels, as well as leaders of officially registered religious groups, mass media, and private and public universities. The results of final verifications are published in *Monitorul Oficial* after the courts recognize the person as a former Securitate agent.

To determine the number of Securitate informers and officers unveiled by the Council is an arduous task. A tally of the totals offered in the Council's annual reports suggests the Council unveiled 1,355 Securitate officers and 2,000 informers between 2000 and 2010. A more detailed breakdown shows that from 2000 to late 2011, the Council identified 773 officers and 189 informers from among those who occupy public positions (see Table 4.1), and an unknown number of secret agents were unveiled at the request of those who read their files (Table 4.2 presents the number of registered and solved identification requests, without revealing which

[49] "Preşedintele Societăţii Timişoara: Legea Lustraţiei e o victorie parţială," *Evenimentul Zilei* (2 March 2012).

[50] Marius Vulpe, "Antonescu: Lustraţia, demers ratat. PDL, campionul unei cauze care nu i-a aparţinut niciodată," *Evenimentul Zilei* (5 March 2012).

TABLE 4.1. *Securitate officers and informers identified in Monitorul Oficial (2000–2010)*

	2000	2001	2002	2003	2004	2005	2006	2007	2008	2009	2010	2011
Number of officers	–	–	–	38	27	38	40	283	54*	48	145	100
Number of informers	15	12	0	0	7	13	3	8	3*	18	80	30

Source: National Council for the Study of Securitate Archives, January 2012.
Note that from 2000 to 2008 the Council decided the identification, whereas after 2008 the courts fulfilled that role.
* One of those was branded a Securitate agent by the courts.

solutions included identifications).[51] The courts overturned the Council's verdict of collaboration in the case of four individuals identified as informers and two identified as officers.[52] Compare these numbers with the estimated 13,275 officers and 400,000 to 1,000,000 informers the Securitate employed before 1989 (see Chapter 1). If the pace of public disclosures remains unchanged, the Council will need ninety years to unveil all Securitate officers and at least 200 years to name all secret informers, an excruciatingly slow progress that renders verifications meaningless. At the time of this writing, none of the deputies and senators who provided false statements regarding their collaboration with the Securitate renounced their public office.[53] As such, Romanians confidently maintain that lustration has affected no one in their country, although the program has included the investigation of thousands of individuals within and outside the political elite.

The many commissions and omissions of the legislative framework, the bitter divisions among National Council leaders and their ever-shifting political allegiances,

[51] The two tables were constructed based on letters received from Dragoş Petrescu, president of the National Council for the Study of Securitate Archives, and dated 20 December 2011 and 10 January 2012. I thank Dragoş Petrescu and Mariana Draghici for supplying this information to me promptly.

[52] According to the letter addressed to the author by Dragoş Petrescu and dated 10 January 2012. For additional details, see National Council for the Study of Securitate Archives, *Lista persoanelor pentru care Consiliul a solicitat instanţei constatarea calităţii de colaborator al Securităţii, în temeiul Art. 3 din Legea 293/2008* (no date), available at: http://www.cnsas.ro/colaboratori.html (accessed on 22 August 2011).

[53] The senator is Dan Voiculescu, who is deputy speaker representing the National Liberal Party. Seven deputies were unveiled as former informers (including former Liberal leader Mona Muscă) and two others as former Securitate officers (including Mircea Tudor, brother of Greater Romania Party Corneliu Vadim Tudor). See Alina Mungiu-Pippidi, "Anticomunismul ca politică publică," *România Liberă* (4 August 2011).

TABLE 4.2. *Unveiling Securitate informers and officers at the request of those who accessed their files (2000–2010)*

Year	2000–2001	2002	2003	2004	2005	2006	2007	2008	2009	2010
Solved requests for unveiling informers	1	9	54	87	49	270	330	610	739	847
Case files prepared in view of unveiling officers	0	216	278	43	70	158	402			
Case files discussed and voted on by Council leaders	–	0	47	18	56	0	0			
Case files submitted to courts								210	298	337

Source: National Council for the Securitate Archives, December 2011.
From 2000 to 2008 the Council decided when a person had served as a Securitate agent, while after 2008 the courts fulfilled that role.

Romania's weak and self-serving judiciary, which remained subservient to the executive and legislative branches of government, and lack of political will on the part of government and opposition forces rendered the Council's verdicts highly interpretable during its first years of activity. Instead of becoming the solution to Romania's dilemma of dealing with the communist past, by 2008 the Council turned into one of its major stumbling blocks, a shortcoming that the government tried to bypass by giving the courts the right to hand down verdicts on collaboration with the Securitate.

After its creation, the Council rapidly lost credibility. First, its leaders claimed that the Council verified over 20,000 candidates who ran in the local and parliamentary elections in 2000.[54] However, it was impossible for the Council to form an opinion on so many individual cases only months after it was set up, because it hired an insufficient number of investigators compared to the large number of files it had to go through; its access to the secret archive was not direct, but mediated by institutions with a vested interest in disclosing no secret information; and it had very little time to conduct reliable identifications thoroughly and impartially, by consulting secret documents, interviewing candidates, and formulating its first verdicts. After the press questioned its leaders, it emerged that the Council provided inaccurate information and took shortcuts that rendered verifications highly superficial

[54] Lavinia Stan, "Access to Securitate Files: The Trials and Tribulations of a Romanian Law," *East European Politics and Society*, 16(2002): 172.

and unreliable. To mitigate lack of time and personnel and to meet high public expectations to quickly solve thousands of cases, the Council interpreted, and in the process misinterpreted, the law.

Instead of interviewing candidates before publicly identifying them as secret collaborators, the National Council published their names without confronting them, thus overlooking their testimonies and leaving verdicts open to appeal on technical grounds. Instead of verifying all electoral candidates, the Council looked only at those proposed by a handful of parties likely to gain parliamentary representation, without informing the public about the reduced scope of investigations. Instead of analyzing a plurality of archives, the Council used only the Romanian Information Service documents, although the Service held only 60 percent of the Securitate archive and relevant archives were housed with the External Information Service and the Ministries of Defense and Justice. Instead of examining the files directly by going to the shelves, as the law called for, the Council asked the Services to search the archive's card system, thus ignoring the risks of the Services misreporting their findings, the card system not reflecting the archive adequately, and the Securitate identification of informers being erroneous. Instead of admitting that verdicts were provisory and could be altered (even reversed) once new information became available, the Council claimed they were final. Instead of arriving at verdicts on the basis of dispassionate analysis of the evidence at hand, Council leaders allowed their political and personal preferences to dictate their positions. In 2004, rather than releasing the verdicts before local elections were organized, the Council made them public afterward, making the exercise of unmasking spies redundant, as mandates of elected officials could not be legally revoked. The Council's loss of credibility was so dramatic that by 2008 few Romanians had any interest in the Securitate agents identified from among electoral candidates.

The Council's credibility further suffered because of its inability to unmask notorious Securitate agents and informers, its decision to declare some agents as non-collaborators despite the overwhelming evidence implicating those persons, and its reluctance to unveil agents from among the friends of Council leaders. During its first years of activity, the Council mostly unmasked deceased secret agents and low-ranking Securitate officers. In 2004, the Council leaders appointed by the Social Democrats and the Greater Romania Party voted against branding Greater Romania Party leader, poet Corneliu Vadim Tudor, as a Securitate informer, although secret documents showed that he identified Octavian Paler, George Ivaşcu, and Dan Hăulică as writers engaged in "ideological subversion" to the Securitate leader Iulian Vlad.[55] After the press showed in 2006 that the Central European University

55 "Corneliu Vadim Tudor, următorul pe lista CNSAS," *Evenimentul Zilei* (19 July 2006), and "Problema CNSAS, un simptom al unei crize mai grave," 22 (2 March 2004).

History Professor Sorin Antohi acted as a Securitate informer from 1976 to 1982 and suggested that the Council knew of Antohi's collaboration as early as 2002, it became evident that for four years the Council leaders had protected their friend from being publicly exposed.[56] In addition, different standards were apparently applied to different electoral candidates, depending on their political clout. Democrat leader Băsescu admitted that, as a communist commercial ship commander, he filed thousands of reports with the Securitate, but insisted that none of them offered damaging information on his peers. The Council readily embraced that viewpoint, announcing that Băsescu was "clean as a whistle" and had infringed no human rights.[57] Democratic Union of Magyars Deputy Ludovic Rakoczi was also clean, but the Council first unmasked him as a Securitate informer, thus exposing Rakoczi to public condemnation before finally declaring him innocent.[58]

All in all, until 2008 the Council felt no need to revisit the criteria for collaboration it applied across cases and to adopt a set of unified conditions that would point unequivocally to political police activities. Journalist Carol Sebastian was declared a secret agent only on the basis of his collaboration pledge, although he never provided the Securitate with important information and he took the time to warn the person whom he was asked to spy on. Similarly, the Council declared Liberal politician Mona Muscă as an informer based on information notes in which she provided only positive evaluations of the people she had to report on. In the case of Greater Romania Party leader Corneliu Vadim Tudor, the absence of the written pledge absolved him of any wrongdoing, although his secret file included scores of denunciations. The file of Christian Democrat Deputy Vasile Vetişanu did not include a written pledge, but he was branded a secret collaborator.[59] More importantly, the Council failed to apply the legal stipulation that included among secret collaborators the former Communist Party leaders with decisional, juridical, or political responsibilities over the Securitate (Article 5.5 of Law 187/1999). Such a provision would have applied to Ion Iliescu, who had overseen the Securitate while a county party leader in Timiş and Iaşi, and Gheorghi Prisăcaru, a post-communist senator

[56] "Sorin Antohi a recunoscut colaborarea cu Securitatea," *Ziarul de Iaşi* (5 September 2006).

[57] Andrei Pleşu also admitted that, while a member of the National Council leadership, he read an information note submitted by Băsescu to the Securitate. Mirela Corlăţan, "Nota lui Băsescu către Securitate, văzută de Andrei Pleşu," *Evenimentul Zilei* (29 September 2010). In February 2011, long after Pleşu ceased his relationship with the National Council, the Council admitted that his wife became a Securitate informer in the late 1960s, and a Securitate victim in 1985–1986. See National Council for the Study of Securitate Archives, "Adeverinta nr. 748/22.02.2011" (23 March 2011), available at: http://www.cnsas.ro/documente/adeverinte/2011/748%20Plesu%20%28Petrulian%29%20Lacramioara%20Maria%20Catrinel.pdf (accessed on 9 March 2012).

[58] Stan, "Moral Cleansing Romanian Style," 59–60.

[59] Gabriel Andreescu, "Cazul Vasile Vetişanu şi aplicarea Legii 187/1999," *Revista Română de Drepturile Omului*, 25(2003): 63–83.

who served as adviser to the last communist Prime Minister Constantin Dăscălescu (1982–1989).

Loss of credibility also resulted from the questionable actions of the Council leaders, who were criticized for media overexposure, hiring former Securitate officers as investigators, firing young pro-lustration historians like Gabriel Catalan and Mircea Stănescu, failing to present annual reports to parliament as the law required, refusing to share basic information with the press, and taking sides in the political debate that preceded elections. By giving in without opposition to the Romanian Information Service demands to keep most files under lock for reasons of national security, refusing to provide information to the press, slowing down verifications of political luminaries, and resisting calls to investigate notorious communist perpetrators, the first Council leader, historian Gheorghe Onişoru, gave the impression that he wanted to stall, more than to unblock, the reevaluation of the communist past.[60] Controversy followed Onişoru's removal when elections for a new president failed to confirm Ticu Dumitrescu, the father of Law 187/1999, as the Council president, although the Justice and Truth Alliance parties had encouraged the Council leaders nominated by them, who formed a majority in the Council leadership, to vote for Dumitrescu. Disappointed with the result of the vote, Dumitrescu joined the chorus of journalists and intellectuals who denounced the duplicity of the Council leaders who chose their president and suggested that his defeat had been decided in secret negotiations masterminded by President Băsescu and his Democrats.[61]

No analysis of the Council's activity can disregard the tremendous opposition it faced from the Romanian Information Service and segments of the political class tainted by past collaboration. While claiming to be a new information service distinct from the political police, the Service refused to turn the Securitate archive over to its legal custodian, mounting opposition even after President Băsescu ordered the transfer of dossiers to the Council in 2005. Important political parties gave no support to the public identification of the Securitate informers, and the judiciary refused to prosecute electoral candidates who signed false declarations regarding their noninvolvement with the political police. Instead of encouraging its members to disclose their former ties before the 2000 elections, the Social Democrat Party reminded them that Law 187/1999 did not forbid former agents to run for public office. The party pledged to support its members even if irrefutable evidence exposed them as longtime Securitate collaborators. The Greater Romania Party went a step further by denouncing the Council as a "political police" that allegedly sold top secret Securitate files to foreign

[60] Marius Oprea, "Onişoru, vinovat pentru criza CNSAS," 22 (4 October 2005), and Miron Damian, "Şantajul Român cu Informaţii," *Cotidianul* (7 August 2006).

[61] Ovidiu Bancheş, "Ticu Dumitrescu: FSN conduce CNSAS," *Ziua* (12 May 2006).

agencies and announcing that territorial organizations that aided the Council in his investigations would be immediately dissolved.[62]

Given the manifold shortcomings that have plagued the activity of the Council, some observers might take solace in the government's decision to transfer the prerogative of declaring a person a Securitate secret collaborator from the Council to the courts. However, three cases heard in 2008 by judges with the Bucharest Court should give us pause. In all three cases, which discussed the alleged collaboration of Dan Troncotă, Vasile Bărbat, and Vasile Nechita, the judges overturned the collaboration verdict proposed by the National Council, refusing to apply the law. In part under the influence of the Council, the judges argued that collaboration was evidenced by the presence of a written and signed collaboration pledge and of notes providing information that infringed the fundamental human rights of those named in the notes. These cases prompted analyst Gabriel Andreescu to call for cases on collaboration to be forwarded to magistrates with the expertise to judge these files, for compelling judges hearing such cases to disclose their own ties to the communist regime before taking up the cases, and for the law to be amended so as to include more precise definitions of "collaboration" and "collaborators."[63] At the time of this writing, the Romanian judiciary has implemented none of these recommendations.

UNOFFICIAL CONFESSION-BASED IDENTIFICATIONS OF PARTY MEMBERS

In 1996, at a time when the Romanian political elite showed little inclination to embrace lustration and to open the secret archives, some political formations asked their members who wished to be considered for elected or appointed public office to make their past ties to the Securitate known confidentially to their party leadership in advance of the local and general elections organized that year.[64] As part of this unofficial campaign, inspired from the confession-based lustration proceedings introduced in Hungary in 1994, candidates provided signed statements briefly describing their past activities to the leaders of their county or town organizations. The statements were not disclosed to other party members, the press, or the public at large, and as such, they did not expose tainted candidates to public censure. The information they provided could not be verified against the secret archives, which were closed at the time, but leaders of some local party organizations conducted

[62] Stan, "Access to Securitate Files," 169.

[63] Gabriel Andreescu, "Necesitatea judecătorilor specializaţi în cazurile de colaborarea cu Securitatea ca poliţie politică," *Noua Revistă de Drepturile Omului*, 5(2009): 13–26.

[64] Idem, 155.

personal interviews with the candidates who disclosed their ties to the Securitate.[65] These disclosures were not required of the party leaders who received the statements and of the party members who sought no public office. There were significant differences between local party structures – some requiring most candidates to informally disclose a lot of details about their past, others asking for vague and general statements only on an exceptional basis. However, these unofficial statements allowed the party leaders, who controlled nominations for public office and inclusion on electoral lists, to disqualify some former Securitate agents from public office.[66] No systematic study of such declarations has been conducted to date, and as such, it is impossible to say how many statements were submitted, how many were taken into consideration, how many candidates were denied office as a result, and how truthful each statement was.

The opposition Democratic Convention embraced these unofficial vetting efforts to show commitment to the elite renewal project implied by the 1989 revolution, to gain an electoral advantage over and additional legitimacy relative to the Social Democrats and the Greater Romania Party, which were known for harboring notorious communist decision makers, and to preempt and counteract the increasingly numerous press reports that exposed some of its most prominent leaders as former Securitate agents. Regardless of whether or not the statements were able to marginalize politicians, their very introduction proved that at least some Romanian political formations were ready to start the elite renewal process by screening their own ranks.

The same requirement to provide written declarations was further adopted by the Civic Alliance, a civil society organization that has constantly advocated the need for a clean break with the communist past and practices (see Chapter 1). On 26 April 2000, well after the Civic Alliance renounced its status as a political party, the candidates for the Alliance's national leadership positions were asked to provide, in front of the public notary, written statements that they did not collaborate with the Securitate. Only candidates untainted by collaboration were considered for the leadership posts at the Alliance's congress organized weeks later.[67]

After the National Council for the Study of Securitate Archives began to publicly disclose the names of Securitate agents in 2000, the slow pace of identifications prompted the civil society to encourage political parties to continue the informal

65 A series of interviews I conducted in 1999 for a project on local governments revealed that some local chapters of the National Peasant Party Christian Democrat and the National Liberal Party launched such disclosure campaigns ahead of the 1996 elections and were planning to restart them in view of the 2000 elections. Those interviews were conducted in the counties of Arad, Argeş, Constanţa, Galaţi, and Mureş.

66 This was suggested to me in 1999 by party leaders from Argeş.

67 "Cronologie," 22 (7 December 2010).

screening of candidates for public office. The Coalition for a Clean Parliament monitored the integrity of candidates who ran in the 2004, 2007, and 2008 elections for the Romanian and European parliaments, the Coalition for a Clean Government screened cabinet members appointed in 2005, and the Coalition for Clean Universities vetted the leadership of public universities in 2009 through 2010. These screenings, carried out by civil society groups and independent think tanks such as the Romanian Academic Society, used noninvolvement with the Securitate as a criterion for integrity, published black lists of corrupt officials, and denounced parties that appointed tainted individuals to positions of power and responsibility.[68] They were seen as successful attempts on the part of the civil society to assume an active political role in augmenting the quality of Romanian democracy.[69] Anticommunist formations like the Christian Democrats and the Liberals took those criteria into consideration, the Social Democrats and the Greater Romania Party ignored them, while the Democrats (rebaptized as the Democrat-Liberals) adopted them selectively.

"WILD" EXECUTIVE PURGES

Whereas successive post-communist legislatures have procrastinated the adoption of lustration as a method of banning former communist decision makers from public office, all post-communist executives formed in the wake of alternations in power (that followed the 1996, 2000, 2004, and 2008 general elections) engaged in widespread purges of the local and national public administration, the judiciary, the management of firms jointly owned by the state, as well as the leadership of national radio and television, public utilities, hospitals, and school boards. The purges were "wild" because the elected parliament monitored neither their scope (the number of state agencies included in the purge) nor their depth (the number of positions within each state agency), and until 2001 those demoted or removed from their posts had few legal means at their disposal to contest the government's decision as Romania lacked a law on public administration. More importantly from a transitional justice viewpoint, only in 1996 were the reasons for dismissal directly related to involvement with the communist regime, and even then the criteria were applied very discretionary and not uniformly across positions, state agencies, and counties. These purges were not conducted on the basis of a law discussed in parliament

68 Coaliţia pentru o Românie Curată, *Listele negre realizate de echipa Alianţa pentru o Românie Curată* (2008), available at: http://www.romaniacurata.ro/listelenegre.php (accessed on 22 August 2011).

69 Peter Gross and Vladimir Tismaneanu, "The End of Postcommunism in Romania," *Journal of Democracy*, 16(2005): 146–162, and Alina Mungiu, "The Coalition for a Clean Parliament," *Journal of Democracy*, 16(2005): 154–155.

by parties representing both the government and the opposition. Rather they were grounded in decisions of cabinets that represented only the ruling formations and were directed expressly against the political opposition. As such, they were bitterly criticized as clear instances of antidemocratic behavior and unwelcomed dictatorial impulses that threatened the rule of law.[70]

Seven years into the post-communist transition, the Democratic Convention launched the first such wild purge after the 1996 elections by announcing that 15,000 experts supportive of its reform program were ready to take over key positions from Social Democrats public officials who had stalled the transition to democracy and free market. The announcement was part of the Contract with Romania, the Convention's governing program, styled after the American Republicans' campaign document launched before the Congressional elections of 1994. During the electoral campaign, the Democratic Convention pledged to implement its Contract, which promised better living standards, within 200 days of forming the government.[71] It led to a massive dismissal campaign that made room for new appointments in the public administration, public utilities, the national radio and television boards, joint public-private firms, hospitals, and even schools.[72] The government insisted that the dismissed Social Democrat public officials had obtained their positions in virtue of connections more so than superior training and managerial skills, that they had badly misused their posts, and that many of them were former communist-era managers who after 1989 retained their public office under the protection of the revolutionary rulers. Nevertheless, the press rapidly discovered that the newly appointed public officials had similarly weak credentials, political considerations had driven most appointments, and the Convention had multiplied the number of offices to reward its many supporters.[73] Because of the Convention's "suicidal government style," as historian Mircea Stănescu qualified it, the 1996–2000 period went down in history for levels of governmental inefficiency, waste, and corruption that exceeded

[70] Seven opposition legislators criticized the purges after the 1997 elections, four after the 2000 elections, twenty-seven after the 2004 elections, and two after the purges operated in October 2009. The opposition and the government included different political parties each of these times. In response, the government acknowledged each of the purge campaigns, but defended them on various grounds.

[71] Tom Gallagher, *Modern Romania. The End of Communism, the Failure of Democratic Reform, and the Theft of a Nation* (New York: New York University Press, 2005), and Dan Pavel and Iulia Huia, *Nu putem decât împreună. O istorie analitică a Convenţiei Democratice, 1989–2000* (Iaşi: Polirom, 2003).

[72] Alina Mungiu-Pippidi, "Romania: From Procedural to European Integration," in *Democratization in Central and Eastern Europe*, eds. Mary Kaldor and Ivan Vejvoda (London: Continuum, 2002), 136–138.

[73] Lavinia Stan, "Comparing Post-Communist Governance: A Case Study," *Journal of Communist Studies and Transition Politics*, 18(2002): 77–109.

those registered in 1989–1996 and strongly resembled the Phanariote rule of the nineteenth century, when public posts were sold to the highest bidder.[74]

Although the opposition Social Democrats lamented these purges, after winning the elections of 2000 they set out to reverse the effects of the purges by dismissing the Democratic Convention sympathizers and rehiring their own supporters. A campaign similar in scope and depth to the 1996 one was thus launched, with equally debatable effects on the efficiency, accountability, transparency, and legitimacy of the public administration. This time also, the purges went far beyond the bureaucracy, affecting appointments in joint firms and the mass media. The ruling Social Democrats presented the dismissal of leaders of the national television as an effort to modernize the station, but the opposition saw it as "a way to create positions for the Social Democrat clients," subordinate the television to the government, and institute censorship by cutting down the airtime offered to opposition parties and presenting the cabinet exclusively in a positive light.[75] The bureaucracy was affected by these uncontrolled and highly discretionary dismissals seriously enough for the opposition Democrats and Liberals to introduce a motion of no confidence against the government in 2002 to denounce the systemic corruption and mismanagement that encroached on the public administration.[76] The motion was unsuccessful.

By the time new elections took place in 2004, Romania endeavored to fulfill the EU accession requirements, which called for renouncing political appointments in public administration to turn it into a professional, competent bureaucracy. Law 215/2001 on Public Administration prohibited further *epurations* of public officials, but the ruling Democrats and Liberals were unable to refrain from dismissing Social Democrats and hiring their own clients instead.[77] The wild purges were relaunched, although the experience of the 1996 and 2000 campaigns left no doubt as to their negative consequences on the performance of the governmental agencies whose leaders were sidelined. Dismissals of hospital managers were considered an "immoral solution,"[78] those of school principals provoked chaos and abuse,[79] while those of public

74 The comparison was suggested by Social Democrat Deputy Adrian Gheorghiu. "Şedinţa Camerei Deputaţilor din 16 noiembrie 1999," *Monitorul Oficial al României, partea II-a* (26 November 1999), 16. Also personal interview with historian Mircea Stănescu, Bucharest, 29 June 2011.

75 Greater Romania Party Deputy Smaranda Ionescu, cited in "Şedinţa Camerei Deputaţilor din 30 martie 2004," *Monitorul Oficial al României, partea II-a* (8 April 2004).

76 "Şedinţa Camerei Deputaţilor din 19 martie 2002," *Monitorul Oficial al României, partea II-a* (29 March 2002).

77 "Legea nr. 215/2001 a administraţiei publice locale," *Monitorul Oficial al României, partea I* (23 April 2001).

78 Social Democrat Deputy Claudiu Aprian Pop, cited in "Stenograma Camerei Deputaţilor din 7 February 2006," *Monitorul Oficial al României, partea II-a* (17 February 2006).

79 Social Democrat Deputy Ioan Chelaru, cited in "Stenograma Camerei Deputaţilor din 17 octombrie 2005," *Monitorul Oficial al României, partea II-a* (24 October 2005).

administrators inspired an unsuccessful motion of confidence introduced by the Social Democrat opposition against the government in 2005.[80]

The purges enacted after the 2008 elections were conducted by the Emil Boc cabinet, supported by the Democrat-Liberals (the former Democrats) and their erstwhile rivals, the Social Democrats. Their collaboration protocol, which was thin on policy strategies, detailed the allocation of over 3,000 bureaucratic posts, a fact suggesting that the cabinet pursued a position-seeking more than a policy-seeking strategy. At the national level, there were twenty minister portfolios, eighty deputy minister posts, and hundreds of counselors, directors, and deputy directors, each with their own advisors, secretaries, and supporting staff. At the local level, there were forty to fifty posts of leaders of prefectures, local branches of ministries and state agencies in each county. The total number reached 10,000 posts at all state levels.[81] This time, the dismissed public officials petitioned the courts, which sided with them against the government by invoking Law 215/2001 that prohibited wild purges. Court decisions were handed down after public servants were replaced with Democrat-Liberals, but the Boc government refused to reverse its personnel decisions, even after judges ordered the reappointment of those dismissed. By 2010 two, sometimes three, persons occupied the same public post, with none of them doing the job but all being handsomely remunerated from the national budget.[82]

CONCLUSION

Of the lustration-like processes that post-communist Romania enacted in view of renewing its elites, the ones that led to the widest personnel turnovers were the executive wild purges, which were also the least related to the communist past, because involvement with the *ancien regime* influenced dismissals only in 1996 and never constituted the most important reason for job loss. Together with Albania, Romania is perhaps the Eastern European country that made the most use of executive purges, with significant negative impact on the efficiency and professionalization of its public administration.[83] The unofficial vetting program introduced by the Democratic Convention before the 1996 elections and continued by civil society

80 "Şedinţa Camerei Deputaţilor din 29 martie 2005," *Monitorul Oficial al României, partea II-a* (5 April 2005).

81 Lavinia Stan and Diane Vancea, "Old Wine in New Bottles: The Romanian Elections of 2008," *Problems of Post-Communism*, 56(2009): 1096–1109, and Lavinia Stan and Răzvan Zaharia, "Romania," *European Journal of Political Research*, 48 (2009): 1098.

82 Lavinia Stan and Răzvan Zaharia, "Romania," *European Journal of Political Research*, 49(2010): 1153, and A. Simina, "Cum pregăteşte Boc a treia politizare neconstituţională," *Evenimentul Zilei* (3 February 2010).

83 Robert Austin and Jonathan Ellis, "Albania," in *Transitional Justice in Eastern Europe and the Former Soviet Union: Reckoning with the Communist Past* (London: Routledge, 2009), 176–199.

groups during the 2000s blocked the careers of an unknown number of former communist decision makers, but was unable to convince political formations and voters to withdraw support from well-known former communist officials. The least effective from the viewpoint of dismissals, which Romanians still consider key to any effective lustration program, have been the official investigations conducted by the National Council, whose activity has been impacted by a multitude of factors, only some of which have been under its control.

In Romania, the absence of lustration allowed the executive to engage in wild purges and prompted political parties and civil society groups to adopt unofficial vetting programs as alternative methods of "informal reckoning" based on untransparent criteria more than the mediation, restorative justice and reparations that Andrew Woolford and R. S. Ratner associated with the term.[84] Romania exemplifies the case of a new democracy where public officials whose fortunes were tied to the *ancien regime* prolonged their careers after the regime change and stalled elite renewal through whatever means possible. Elite replacement through lustration might infringe basic human rights, rely too heavily on the secret files, and place former decision makers at a considerable disadvantage, but its absence signals a disturbing political continuity with which few Romanians were comfortable, especially after a revolution as bloody as the one of 1989. Early lustration with job loss might not have completely preempted the purges, but would have been more transparent and predictable, would have allowed both the government and the opposition forces to decide which categories were banned from which positions and for how long, and would have taught the persons slated for lustration the value of observing human rights and repenting for the support they provided to the dictatorial regime. Instead, the lessons learned by those dismissed from public office through executive purges and unofficial vetting campaigns have downplayed the value of the rule of law that these purges repeatedly violated and suggested that only personal connections and party support make or break one's career.

[84] Andrew Woolford and R. S. Ratner, *Informal Reckonings. Conflict Resolution in Mediation, Restorative Justice and Reparations* (New York: Routledge-Cavendish, 2008).

5

The Commission and Official Condemnation

Despite their increased popularity in Latin America, Africa, and Asia, truth commissions have remained an overlooked solution to come to terms with the human rights abuses perpetrated in communist Europe.[1] Since the start of the democratization process in the early 1990s, only Germany, the Baltic republics, Uzbekistan, Romania, and Moldova have employed inquiry commissions as truth-seeking methods.[2] When the communist regimes collapsed in 1989, truth commissions were not yet recognized internationally as an effective truth-seeking and truth-telling method, and as such, they did not represent a model worth considering in the post-communist world. Even after the German Parliament created the Commission of Inquiry for the Assessment of History and Consequences of the SED Dictatorship in Germany (Enquete Kommission zur Aufarbeitung von Geschichte und Folgen der SED-Diktator in Deutschland) in 1992, neighboring countries did not follow suit, as access to the secret files, court trials, official condemnations, and apologies were the preferred methods to reckon with the communist past. When the fiftieth anniversary of the end of World War II was celebrated in 1995, international organizations, victims groups, and foreign governments asked European countries to reevaluate their collaboration with the Third Reich. In reply, twenty-four commissions were created to investigate the recent past, three of them in the Baltic republics in late 1998: the International Commission for the Evaluation of the Crimes of the Nazi and Soviet Occupation Regimes in Lithuania (Tarptautine komisija

[1] I made this argument in Lavinia Stan, "Truth Commissions in Post-Communism: The Overlooked Solution?," *Open Political Science Journal*, 2(2009): 1–13, available at: http://www.bentham.org/open/topolisj/openaccess2.html (accessed on 28 January 2012).

[2] The Truth and Reconciliation Commission of Yugoslavia examined the crimes perpetrated during the Yugoslav wars of the 1990s, not those of the communist regime. In 1999, Uzbekistan created an inquiry commission analyzed in Brian Grodsky, "Justice without Transition: Truth Commissions in the Context of Repressive Rule," *Human Rights Review*, 9(September 2008): 281–297, and Brian Grodsky, *The Costs of Justice: How New Leaders Respond to Previous Rights Abuses* (Notre Dame: University of Notre Dame Press, 2011).

Naciu ir Sovietinio okupaciniu rezimu nusikaltimams Lietuvoje ivertinti), the Estonian International Commission for Investigation of Crimes against Humanity (Inimsusevastaste Kuritegude Uurimise Eesti Rahvusvahelise Komisjon), and the Commission of Latvian Historians (Vesturnieku Komisija). These international presidential commissions were initially meant to limit their analysis to those republics' collaboration with Nazi Germany and involvement in the Holocaust, but following intense public discussions, their mandates were extended to cover both the Nazi and the Soviet occupation regimes of 1940–1991.[3] The Baltic commissions inspired no similar investigative bodies in other post-communist countries.

The Presidential Commission for the Analysis of the Communist Dictatorship in Romania was created in 2006 – two years after the International Commission on the Holocaust in Romania ended its activity – to provide President Traian Băsescu with the scientific, expert report needed to officially condemn the crimes of the communist regime before the country's acceptance into the EU on 1 January 2007. The Romanian presidential councilors and civil society representatives who envisioned the independent inquiry body drew little inspiration from commissions constituted outside of Eastern Europe when they decided the terms, mandate, and composition of the Presidential Commission, relying instead almost exclusively on the earlier Romanian and German models.[4] Therefore, the Romanian Commission resembled a history commission more than a truth commission and was more academic in nature than bodies created in South Africa, Chile, Sri Lanka, or other Latin American, African, and Asian countries. At the same time, this was the first commission examining communism that clearly served as a template for another investigative body. The presidential Commission for the Study and Evaluation of the Totalitarian Communist Regime in the Republic of Moldova (Comisia pentru Studierea şi Aprecierea Regimului Comunist Totalitar din Republica Moldova), set up in 2010 in the independent republic that was once a constituent territory of Greater Romania, understood its mission in terms that closely echoed those of its Romanian counterpart.

As in other post-dictatorial settings, in Romania official truth seeking and truth telling have been the most common demands from below. Although information on past abuses may surface from a variety of different sources and the civil society can play a definite role in both processes, many victims prefer a government-sponsored

3 Eva-Clarita Onken, "The Politics of Finding Historical Truth: Reviewing Baltic History Commissions and Their Work," *Journal of Baltic Studies*, 38(2007): 109–116.

4 Vladimir Tismaneanu suggested that the German commission served as a model for the Romanian commission, but the commission secretary claimed that the German commission was never mentioned during the initial stages that led to the creation of the Romanian commission. It was only after the Romanian commission completed its mandate that references to the German commission were made. Personal interview with Cristian Vasile, Bucharest, 30 June 2011.

investigation because it serves several objectives at once. As Kathleen Smith reminded us, "by informing relatives of the fates of the missing, a formal study can offer a form of reparation; by releasing official documents of repression, it can offer historians invaluable sources for investigation and directly shape public consciousness; finally, if it discloses the identity of perpetrators, it may act as a surrogate for a court."[5] An official report further demonstrates that at least the state actors who commissioned it, if not the political elite as a whole, are ready to assume responsibility for past human rights abuses and to distance themselves from the criminal past by breaking the silence that veils the repression, the nature of the crimes, the chain of command that linked state leaders to soldiers and secret agents, the fate of the victims, and the identity of the victimizers. Whereas analyses signed by historians could be considered to reflect personal viewpoints on historical events and processes, even when executed with utmost care and attention to detail, official reports have an additional political dimension because they involve recognition of a certain historical narrative on the part of the government, serve political purposes complementary to truth telling, and enjoy higher levels of publicity and media attention than any history books written by knowledgeable researchers. By creating the Presidential Commission, President Băsescu hoped that "officially constructed narratives about the evils of dictatorship would bind democratizing societies and elites to the new political regime by providing them with a convincing moral case for the rejection of the values of the previous regime,"[6] James Mark remarked.

This chapter presents the political background that led to the creation of the Romanian Presidential Commission for the Analysis of the Communist Dictatorship in Romania, discusses its mission, structure, and activity, critically examines its final report and recommendations, and further ponders on the public echo of the official condemnation of the communist regime by the president that the commission was able to facilitate. Several authors have written on this commission, and those studies provide much more detail about the reasons why and the conditions under which this body emerged.[7] By contrast, this chapter goes a step further to evaluate

5 Kathleen Smith, *Remembering Stalin's Victims. Popular Memory and the End of the USSR* (Ithaca: Cornell University Press, 1996), 4.

6 James Mark, *The Unfinished Revolution. Making Sense of the Communist Past in Central-Eastern Europe* (New Haven: Yale University Press, 2010), 27.

7 Rodica Palade, "Raportul nu e un rechizitoriu," 22 (19–25 December 2006); A. Gabor, "Note de lectură asupra Raportului Tismăneanu," *Anuarul Facultății de Teologie Ortodoxă*, 6(2006): 185–208; Charles King, "Remembering Romanian Communism," *Slavic Review*, 66(2007): 718–723; Vladimir Tismaneanu, "Confronting Romania's Past: A Response to Charles King," *Slavic Review*, 66(2007): 724–727; Michael Shafir, "Raportul Tismăneanu: Note din public şi din culise," *Tribuna* (1–15 March 2007); Lavinia Stan, "Comisia Tismăneanu între adevăr şi reconciliere," 22 (2–8 March 2007); Valerian Stan, "Tismaneanu Report: Another Delay in the Trial of Communism," *New York Magazine* (6 February 2007); Cosmina Tănăsoiu, "The Tismaneanu Report: Romania Revisits Its Past," *Problems of Post-Communism*, 54(2007): 60–69; Monica Ciobanu, "Criminalizing the Past

the commission's success and impact according to a set of criteria proposed by the literature recently published on such commissions.

Before delving into an analysis of the Romanian case, this chapter should identify as precisely as possible the kind of commission it examines. The confusion of terms evident in the scholarly literature dealing with commissions complements the confusion in the declarations made by members of the Romanian Presidential Commission, who sometimes referred to the commission as an academic body and other times as a truth commission. In 2006, Mark Freeman distinguished truth commissions from five other types of bodies created in various countries at different times, but even after his work was published some researchers have continued to conflate all such bodies into a single umbrella category labeled "truth commissions."[8] Freeman's typology, however, underscores significant differences between commissions that, if overlooked, can affect our expectations vis-à-vis the effectiveness of these bodies. For him, truth commissions (defined as temporary, nonjudicial, and autonomous bodies that usually complete their work with a final report that includes recommendations for future governmental action), should be distinguished from ad-hoc inquiry commissions (national, usually parliamentary bodies mandated to look at human rights issues), event specific bodies (concerned with investigating past events that were well defined in time), thematic commissions (analyze a specific topic), institutional bodies (investigate the involvement in human right violations of the members of a given institution), and sociohistorical commissions (deal with historical injustice and are known as historical commissions to other authors).[9]

While all these investigative bodies examine some kind of human rights violations, the nature and timing of those crimes differ among commissions, as does the way in which they arrive at and deliver the truth. Of particular interest are the differences between historical and truth commissions identified by Eva-Clarita Pettai,[10] because the other commissions listed by Freeman are far more restricted in scope than the Romanian example. Whereas truth commissions investigate relatively recent past human rights abuses, historical commissions deal with crimes that took place several decades before those commissions were set up. Because of this temporal difference, historical commissions tend to rely heavily on written and archival

and Reconstructing Collective Memory: The Romanian Truth Commission," *Europe-Asia Studies*, 61(2009): 313–336; Ruxandra Cesereanu, "The Final Report on the Holocaust and the Final Report on the Communist Dictatorship in Romania," *East European Politics and Societies*, 22(2008): 270–281; and V. Tismaneanu, "Democracy and Memory: Romania Confronts Its Communist Past," *The Annals of the American Academy of Political and Social Science*, 617(2008): 166–180.

8 Mark Freeman, *Truth Commissions and Procedural Fairness* (New York: Cambridge University Press, 2006). I thank Eva-Clarita Pettai for bringing Freeman's typology and work to my attention.

9 Carol Gluck, *Thinking with the Past: Japan and Modern History* (Berkeley: University of California Press, 2008).

10 I thank Eva-Clarita for sharing with me her work on this important theme.

documents to arrive at their conclusions, whereas truth commissions can also make use of extensive public hearings with both surviving victims and victimizers during which numerous testimonials are duly recorded. As a consequence, many historical commissions work in relative isolation from the general public and deliver truth ex cathedra, whereas truth commissions center on the victims' plight and attempt to allow victims to "own" that truth by engaging in extensive outreach programs. Differences also extend to membership. Whereas historical commissions are composed mainly of academics (historians and legal experts) and individuals who did not directly and personally suffer the human rights violations under investigation, truth commissions include representatives of former victims (and sometimes even victimizers, as was the case with the South African Truth and Reconciliation Commission). Moreover, the final reports compiled by historical commissions closely resemble extensive and detailed history books that purportedly follow "scientific" methods of data collection and data analysis, whereas truth commissions are concerned both with describing the past and with making recommendations aimed to redress those injustices and to make sure they will not be repeated in the future. Not surprisingly, these characteristics have informed the reception of these commissions (and their work); truth commissions generally having a much wider impact on the general public and the political elites than historical commissions, whose audience is often primarily academic. As this chapter will show, the Romanian presidential commission can more easily be assimilated to historical commissions, given its mandate, membership, activity, results, and reception.

THE POLITICAL BACKGROUND

Given the fact that Germany set up an inquiry commission as early as 1992 and the South African Truth and Reconciliation Commission gained international respect for its work by the mid-1990s, it is surprising that no political and civil society actors have seriously demanded the creation of an analogue investigative body in Romania during the first fifteen years of post-communist transition. Several possible explanations come to mind, although a complete list is difficult to provide. First, in Romania as in other post-communist countries, the absence of an investigative commission resulted from "the historically defensible but also comfortable conviction that the dictatorship was ultimately imposed from outside" by the Soviet tanks and "the uneasy knowledge that almost everyone had done something to sustain the dictatorial system," as Timothy Garton Ash pertinently suggested.[11] Second, in transitional

[11] Timothy Garton Ash, "Trials, Purges and History Lessons: Treating a Difficult Past in Post-Communist Europe," in *Memory and Power in Post-War Europe: Studies in the Presence of the Past*, ed. Jan-Werner Muller (Cambridge: Cambridge University Press, 2002), 265–282.

justice terms Romania has generally followed the example of other countries only very selectively. An analysis of Romanian newspaper reports published during the first two decades of post-communism reveals that the South African commission had almost no echo among Bucharest intellectuals, politicians, and human rights activists, who saw few parallels between the racially based apartheid and the ideologically based communist regime and few advantages to the effort of bringing victims and victimizers together in televised sessions broadcast to the general public, as the nature of communist rule had blurred the lines between those two groups and greatly inflated the category of victims. Romania and South Africa belong to two different regions, have different socioeconomic and religious makeup, and experienced different dictatorships and regime changes. In addition, the German Commission reminded Romanians of the inquiry parliamentary commissions they had hoped would illuminate the casualties perpetrated by various state agents (representing the army, the police, and the secret police) during the 1989 revolution. The continuous clout of former communist officials in all governmental institutions rendered those commissions highly ineffective, as they uncovered little new information about those events and identified no former perpetrators other than those already tried.[12] The Baltic example was not emulated because in those republics the communist regime was studied alongside the Holocaust – two repressive pasts that neither the political formations successor to the communists (the Social Democrats and the Greater Romania Party) nor their opposition (the Democratic Convention) wanted to investigate together.

In Romania, the study of the Holocaust was dissociated from that of the communist regime; two different commissions were created to analyze these two regimes. By 2003, President Ion Iliescu was approaching the end of his second full presidential mandate, contemplating ways to crown his political career and establish his political legacy. Throughout the post-communist period, both as president of the republic (1990–1996 and 2000–2004) and as senator representing the opposition (1996–2000), Iliescu constantly opposed government efforts to work through the communist past, because such an exercise delegitimized him by exposing his own prolonged involvement with the repressive communist regime. His checkered biography included an extended and often uncritical association with the communists.

[12] For example, the Senatorial December 1989 Commission was initiated by film director Sergiu Nicolaescu, who also acted as its chair. It worked from 1990 to 1992, producing a report that was only partially publicized, interviewing no victims, conducting extensive talks with the army and Communist Party officials responsible for quashing the revolts, and reiterating inaccurate information provided by these respondents without checking it against other sources of information. Nicolaescu eventually published a book summarizing the activity and conclusions of the commission. The volume was strongly criticized by victims groups. See Sergiu Nicolaescu, *Revoluţia, începutul adevărului* (Bucharest: Editura Topaz, 1995).

He joined the Communist Party as an activist in 1953 at the age of 23 – at a time when thousands of Romanians were jailed for their political views – and soon afterward entered the top party leadership, the nomenklatura, serving as a member of the Central Committee, the Minister of Youth, and close collaborator to dictator Nicolae Ceauşescu from 1967 to 1971. After 1989 Iliescu claimed victim status because in 1971 Ceauşescu demoted him from national to county party leadership and some years later sidelined him even further by appointing him to the relatively unimportant position of head of the state-owned printing press Politics (Politica) headquartered in Bucharest.

In June 2003, a letter to the United States Holocaust Memorial Museum of the Romanian Social Democrat government became an example of selective negationism by denying that the Holocaust ever took place within the country's boundaries, a view supported by many Romanian politicians and citizens alike, despite extensive historical evidence to the contrary. Shortly afterward Iliescu deepened the controversy when he publicly stated that the Holocaust was not unique to the Jews, but affected other ethnic groups as well.[13] These two incidents, which Israeli government officials and international Jewish organizations vehemently contested, precipitated the creation of the International Commission on Holocaust in Romania on 22 October 2003, under the chairmanship of Nobel laureate Elie Wiesel, born in Sighetul Marmaţiei, a northern Romanian town close to the border with Ukraine (and also the site of the well-known Sighet Memorial discussed in Chapter 9). The commission, popularly known as the Wiesel Commission, was mandated "to research the facts and determine the truth about the Holocaust in Romania during World War II and the events preceding this tragedy"[14] and was composed of both Romanian and foreign scholars and activists. After several working meetings, the Wiesel Commission submitted its final report to President Iliescu on 11 November 2004 and published it soon afterwards. The Wiesel Commission inspired the commission that analyzed communism.

The Presidential Commission for the Analysis of the Communist Dictatorship in Romania was born out of President Traian Băsescu's refusal in mid-2005 to support the enactment of lustration legislation in the absence of an official report that "scientifically" documented communist crimes. During the 2004 presidential elections, Băsescu gained the support of victims, intellectuals, and human rights groups who advocated for resolute transitional justice. That was no small accomplishment, given the fact that before 1989 the authorities considered Băsescu, a long-term

[13] "Romania's Iliescu says Holocaust comments taken out of context," *Haaretz* (29 July 2003), and Irina Culic, "Re-Writing the History of Romania after the Fall of Communism," *History Compass*, 3(2005): 12.

[14] International Commission on the Holocaust in Romania, *Final Report*, Bucharest (11 November 2004), 4, available at: http://www.inshr-ew.ro/pdf/Final_Report.pdf (accessed on 26 July 2011).

Communist Party member, trustworthy enough to serve as Romania's representative in Anvers, the Netherlands, a position he could not occupy without the consent of the Securitate. After the collapse of the Ceauşescu regime Băsescu embarked on a successful political career as a leader of the Democratic Party, the reformist wing of the National Salvation Front, heir to the Communist Party that ruled the country unchallenged from 1945 to 1989.[15] As journalist Sabina Fati pointed out, "Băsescu participated in the Roman and Stolojan cabinets (1990–1992) and had no difficulty accepting the country's incomplete transition to democracy or President Iliescu's *mineriade* strategy" that brought the miners of the Valea Jiului to Bucharest to "defend" the revolutionary government against peaceful protesters denouncing the former communist leaders who gained a new lease on their political lives as members of the new cabinet.[16] In 2004, Băsescu's final debate with Social Democrat presidential contender Adrian Năstase, known for his personal ties to the communist nomenklatura, was widely interpreted as a pro-lustration declaration because it suggested that it was time for new political leaders, untainted by collaboration with the Ceauşescu regime, to lead Romania into the future. The statement won Băsescu much-needed electoral support, but also burdened him with an obligation that he might not have been prepared to fully assume.

For the first few months of his presidency, Băsescu showed reluctance to support genuine institutional reforms and transitional justice more broadly. For example, he appointed several known former Securitate agents to high-ranking government posts and presidential advisor positions and turned a blind eye to civil society demands for launching the generic Trial of Communism that would publicly unveil the names of the Communist Party leaders and Securitate officers responsible for human rights abuses (see Chapter 2). In addition, Băsescu seriously hesitated when asked to replace the heads of the Romanian Information Service and the External Information Service, Costin Georgescu and Cătălin Harnagea, respectively. Although appointed by the Democratic Convention in 1997, during their mandates the two had consistently ignored the legislative framework that made the National Council for the Study of Securitate Archives the sole custodian of the extant Securitate archives and ordered the transfer of those archives from the services to the council. To add insult to injury, the two heads hid the fact that former Securitate officers continued to work for the intelligence services in high-ranking leadership positions and that several agents were involved in corruption scandals. For some local observers, Băsescu's reluctance to sideline the two service heads immediately after he assumed

[15] *Biografie Traian Băsescu* (no date), available at: http://www.presidency.ro/?lang=ro (accessed on 26 July 2011).

[16] Sabina Fati, "(Anti)comunismul lui Băsescu şi jocurile politice ale PNL," *Observator Cultural* (April 2006).

the presidency demonstrated that, for him, the task of gaining the support of the intelligence services took precedence over unrestricted access to secret files and indirectly confirmed reports about a past of secret collaboration that Băsescu was never capable to convincingly disconfirm.

In February 2005, the civil society's increasingly insistent calls for de-blocking transitional justice prompted several Securitate officers to publicly defend the communist regime and, by doing so, their own actions, which often hinged on gross human rights abuses. For former victims, the televised intervention of former Securitate General Nicolae Pleşită was particularly upsetting. Rather than repenting for his past mistakes and asking for forgiveness, Pleşită nonchalantly declared that he was not sorry for having tortured Paul Goma while the dissident writer was in prison for collecting signatures on a petition that asked the communist authorities to respect human rights, and he admitted that the Securitate killed dissidents, not only harassed them, as the Social Democrats and the Greater Romania Party leaders had insisted.[17] Pleşită's misplaced candor was denounced as simply "revolting," while Băsescu's ruling Democrats were again called to launch the Trial of Communism, because "there is no statute of limitations for communist crimes, the same as there is none for Nazi crimes."[18] The incident occurred at a time when frequent leaks of information from the secret files were damaging the Justice and Truth Alliance government more than the Social Democrat opposition, because the latter included a larger number of former Communist Party officials, from among whom the Securitate had not been permitted to recruit secret informers without party approval (see Chapter 3). Băsescu himself came under fire when former President Emil Constantinescu (1996–2000) alleged that the president had collaborated with the Securitate while stationed in Anvers, a collaboration allegedly corroborated by twelve documents.[19] As a result of this heated war of words, President Băsescu was cornered to pledge his support for the "complete" public identification of former Securitate agents, irrespective of the "collateral damage" that the Justice and Truth Alliance government had to sustain as a result of such a bold political move.[20] Two weeks later, an open letter signed by writer Radu Portocală was the first to ask the president to create an international expert commission mandated to study the communist crimes of 1945 to 1989 and to access all relevant archives "in order to obtain a complete picture of the terror and crimes" committed during those times and, thus,

17 Horia Tabacu and Vlad Teodorescu, "Generalul Locotenent (r) Nicolae Stan: Elena mai trăia cu trei înalţi activişti. Doi sunt în viaţă," *Evenimentul Zilei* (29 September 2011).

18 Writer Maria Spiridon, cited in "Fără un process al comunismului sfidări de genul Pleşiţă sunt oricând posibile," *România Liberă* (9 February 2005).

19 Christian Mititelu, "Securitatea 'nedreptăţită'," *Evenimentul Zilei* (30 November 2005).

20 "Deconspirarea foştilor securişti, indiferent de 'pierderile colaterale'," *România Liberă* (18 February 2005).

"allow for future indictments and court verdicts."[21] Portocală's open letter explicitly drew on the precedent established by the Wiesel Commission, which could serve as a template for investigating communist crimes.

The proposal was received with much skepticism by political formations successors to the Communist Party, which instead contended that historians alone could provide such an analysis, because only they had the required scientific tools and knew how to interpret archival documents correctly. By contrast, politicians like Băsescu were required "to remove the social legacies of the communist regime, the mentalities of those times,"[22] not set up "useless" investigatory bodies. A different view was voiced by political analyst Dan Pavel, for whom the proposal stemmed from the desire "to see whether the new president is different from his predecessors" – that is, sympathetic to transitional justice. For Democrat Senator Paula Ivănescu, the work of the commission was necessary because "it would be nice to know our communist past, start with a clean slate, and not repeat past mistakes."[23] In addition, Portocală's well-argued proposal scored a victory when it was embraced by the *România Liberă* newspaper, a daily of countrywide circulation known for its unflinching anticommunist stance, whose journalists reminded President Băsescu that his predecessor had already formed the Commission on the Holocaust, declared 9 October as the Day of the Holocaust, and formally recognized the government's participation in the crimes directed against the Jewish people. For Romanians, the daily further made the case: it was equally important that authorities assume the crimes of the communist regime, because their victims had remained largely ignored.[24]

From April 2005 to March 2006, cinematographer Sorin Ilieşiu, a member of the Group for Social Dialogue and of the Civic Alliance, single-handedly initiated four petitions calling for the official condemnation of communist crimes by the president and the courts.[25] The first two appeals, titled the Appeal for the International Condemnation of the Criminality and Illegitimacy of Communism and the Appeal for Romania, expressed surprise that President Băsescu demanded "concrete evidence" of communist crimes, asking him instead to support lustration, the legal

[21] Radu Portocală, "Deconspirarea crimelor comuniste," *Ziua* (3 March 2005).

[22] Augustin Bolcaş, vice president of the Greater Romania Party, quoted in "Reacţii privind un eventual process al comunismului," *Ziua* (3 March 2005).

[23] Idem.

[24] "Statul român trebuie să-şi asume întregul trecut," *România Liberă* (26 March 2005).

[25] The Declaration for Romania of 28 April reiterated the lustration call of the Timişoara Declaration of 1990. The Appeal for Romania, initiated on 14 June, received support from major non-governmental organizations and victims groups. On 19 October, Ilieşiu asked Băsescu to condemn the communist regime as illegitimate and criminal on the basis of an unofficial report Ilieşiu published by the BBC Romanian Service two weeks earlier. On 10 March 2006, Ilieşiu reiterated this demand and presented a report documenting communist crimes. "Societatea civilă cere condamnarea oficială a regimului communist," BBC Romanian Service (10 March 2006), available at: http://www.bbc.co.uk/romanian/news/story/2006/03/060310_condamnare_comunism.shtml (accessed on 26 July 2011).

rehabilitation of former political prisoners, the official condemnation of the communist regime, the unrestricted opening of all Securitate archives, the rewriting of textbooks to document communist-era human rights violations, and the view that the statute of limitations was inapplicable to communist crimes, which were therefore indictable. The last petition, which gained support from forty nongovernmental organizations and victims groups and over 700 Romanian university professors, political luminaries, intellectuals, and human rights activists; received endorsement from the respected Group for Social Dialogue, which pointed out that the Civic Alliance and its Sighet Memorial Museum had amassed a considerable database of victims' testimonials, together with 93,000 official incarceration reports that attested to the crimes of the communist regime. Transitional justice supporters could rely either on this extensive research output or on the eleven-page unofficial report prepared by Ilieşiu, the Group believed.[26] If a commission was to be formed, Ilieşiu argued, its members should be appointed from among the personalities who made up the Scientific Council of the International Center for Studies on Communism sponsored by the Civic Academy Foundation (Chapter 1).[27] Civil society representatives appointed according to nonpolitical criteria were to supplement the membership of the commission, whose chair should be Stephane Courtois of the Centre National de Recherches Scientifiques in Paris, the author of the monumental *The Black Book of Communism*.[28] The investigative body should make its conclusions available ahead of Romania's accession to the EU.[29] This recommendation was noted, but few scholars proposed by Ilieşiu became commission members.

Despite public pressure, President Băsescu was slow to warm up to the proposal. In July 2005, he openly declared that the lustration law, the official apology to former victims, and the condemnation of totalitarian communism were not among his priorities and all these measures would have been "politically ineffective" in the absence of "scientific documentation" put together by a commission of experts. "We all know that we had television program for only two hours a day and the people were poorly fed," the president boldly declared, "but we should go beyond our personal experiences and explain all these [deprivations]

[26] "Recunoaşterea, asumarea şi condamnarea genocidului communist," 22 (22 March 2006). Ilieşiu's accusations against the communist regime were later included in the final report of the Presidential Commission.

[27] Those were Thomas Blanton of the National Security Archives in Washington, DC, Helmut Muller-Enbergs of the Gauck Authority in Berlin, Dennis Deletant of the University College of London, and Russian dissident Vladimir Bukovski, together with Romanian historians Şerban Papacostea and Alexandru Zub.

[28] Stephane Courtois, *The Black Book of Communism: Crimes, Terror, Repression* (Cambridge: Harvard University Press, 1997).

[29] O. Bancheş, "Sorin Ilieşiu cere Preşedintelui înfierarea regimului criminal la 11 martie," *Ziua* (26 January 2006).

in a scientific document drafted by renowned people, because only then would these issues be able to sustain a political gesture such as an apology delivered to the victims of communism."[30] In response, some local observers wondered "why does President Băsescu not understand that we are talking not about those who eat poorly and endured cold [during the 1980s], but about the tragedy of those killed, deported, tortured, and imprisoned by a criminal regime?"[31] Former President Emil Constantinescu scolded Băsescu for "profoundly offending" former victims with his insensitive remarks, which were interpreted to question the sufferings of communist times.[32] Other political analysts reminded the president that political will more than extensive documentation was needed to condemn a regime as profoundly unjust as the communist one.[33]

To prove that his policy options matched his public declarations, in February 2006 Băsescu requested parliament to augment the powers of the information services and subordinate the services directly to the president, instead of the legislature, thus prompting journalists to deplore "the revival of the old Securitate,"[34] because the proposal went against much-needed reforms of the secret services that significantly cut down their responsibilities and powers. Reigning in the information services was deemed necessary because, according to independent reports, the number of secret agents was exceeding the number of Securitate officers in 1989, although Romania's total population had diminished in post-communist times and the country declared itself to be a democratic state where intelligence services no longer engaged in widespread surveillance programs targeting political crimes.[35] Băsescu's widely broadcast effusions of sympathy for the old Securitate officers who had to work for protection firms because they had been forced to take early retirement led to suggestions that he wanted to secure their loyalty. These statements further enraged the public, the more so because the president never once spoke about the plight of the former victims, whose pensions were several times smaller than those of the retired secret officers who once made their lives difficult. He also ignored the fact that their generally poor health conditions prevented the former political prisoners from taking any kind of job to round up their meager incomes. Misplaced as they might have seemed, these opinions reflected Băsescu's long-held position that, as most other Romanian

[30] R. Ristache, "Traian Băsescu nu e preocupat de condamnarea regimului totalitar," *România Liberă* (7 July 2005).

[31] Cornelia Doru, cited in Ristache, "Traian Băsescu nu e preocupat de condamnarea regimului totalitar."

[32] Cited in "Recunoaşterea, asumarea şi condamnarea genocidului communist," 22 (22 March 2006).

[33] Vladimir Tismaneanu, cited in Andrei Bădin, "Nu cred în legenda celor două Securităţi, una bună şi alta rea," *Adevărul* (10 April 2006).

[34] Dan Bucura, "La mila securiştilor," *Adevărul* (17 February 2006).

[35] Andrei Bădin, "Mai mulţi ofiţeri de informaţii pe cap de locuitor decât în perioada comunistă," *Adevărul* (4 April 2006).

citizens, he lived comfortably during communist times, when he had money, social standing, and job security. There were thus few points of convergence able to help President Băsescu understand the plight of the former victims.[36]

Taken together, these public declarations and policy options made President Băsescu increasingly unpopular with some important constituencies who had helped him win the presidential vote only months earlier – victims, intellectuals, and civil society representatives. In April 2005, for the first time since his election as president, Băsescu was unceremoniously booed while visiting the headquarters of the National Council for the Study of Securitate Archives in Bucharest – an open gesture of censure that reportedly took him completely by surprise.[37] That very public show of disapproval, which gained a lot of attention from the local mass media, apparently convinced the president to approve the commission's formation days later.

Two important events that added urgency to the creation of the investigative body explain the broader context in which President Băsescu decided to give in to civil society demands. First, in January 2006 the Council of Europe voted on a resolution proposed by Goran Lindblad, chair of the Swedish delegation to the Parliamentary Assembly, that "strongly condemned" the "massive human rights violations committed by totalitarian communist regimes," which included "individual and collective assassinations and executions, death in concentration camps, starvation, deportations, torture, slave labor, and other forms of mass physical terror," and expressed "sympathy, understanding and recognition for the victims of these crimes."[38] Although the proposal did not receive the two-thirds of the votes in the Parliamentary Assembly required for adoption, it showed readiness on the part of the European Christian Democrats, Democrats, Liberals, and even some Social Democrats in the Council of Europe to condemn the crimes of Eastern European communist regimes.

36 Băsescu repeatedly declared that communism was a benevolent regime, from his point of view. For such a statement, see "Băsescu a furat idea anticomunismului şi i-a prostit pe intelectuali," Ziare.com (20 December 2010), available at: http://www.ziare.com/basescu/presedinte/marius-oprea-basescu-a-furat-ideea-anticomunismului-si-i-a-prostit-pe-intelectuali-1063547 (accessed on 7 July 2012). Three years after condemning the communist crimes, in 2009, he shocked journalists by stating that "Ceauşescu would have been a great president in the history of the Romanians, if he served [in that post] for only ten years." "Băsescu: Ceauşescu rămânea un mare preşedinte în istorie, dacă stătea doar zece ani," *România Liberă* (5 November 2010), available at: http://www.romanialibera.ro/actualitate/politica/basescu-ceausescu-ramanea-un-mare-presedinte-in-istorie-daca-statea-doar-zece-ani-204863.html (accessed on 11 February 2012).

37 L. Ruse and F. Negroj, "Băsescu a încasat primele huiduieli de când e preşedinte," *Gândul* (5 April 2006).

38 Parliamentary Assembly of the Council of Europe, *Report on the Need for International Condemnation of Crimes of Totalitarian Communist Regimes, Doc.* 10765 (16 December 2005), available at: http://assembly.coe.int/Documents/WorkingDocs/Doc05/EDOC10765.htm (accessed on 30 July 2011).

Second, after being counseled by his advisors, President Băsescu declared that Romania had to assume its communist past before its admission into the EU in January 2007, although transitional justice was never among the formal accession requirements imposed on Romania (or any other post-communist country) as a candidate state. This position might have been meant to avoid reiterating the political embarrassment Romania faced during the months that preceded its admission into the North Atlantic Treaty Organization (NATO) in March 2004, when its government was bluntly requested to ensure that former Securitate agents who were once involved in anti-NATO operations would not gain access to the most sensitive NATO documents.[39] During those discussions, NATO officials pointed out that former Securitate agents who once engaged in anti-NATO operations were unworthy of trust and could even hurt the interests of the organization if allowed access to its secrets. At the same time, Băsescu seized the EU accession as a unique chance to break with the previous Social Democrat government (2000–2004) and to underscore the need to cleanse the political elite from its most tainted elements.[40] Given the context in which it was created, the Presidential Commission seemingly sought to provide "impartial assessments or 'balance sheets' of the recent past," as President Băsescu and the Commission chair Vladimir Tismaneanu repeatedly claimed, as much as "to make the liberal democratic case for an utter rejection of a criminal dictatorial past."[41]

THE COMMISSION'S MISSION, STRUCTURE, ACTIVITY, AND FINAL REPORT

The Tismaneanu Commission had to draft a scientific document that analyzed the entire communist regime (1945–1989), focusing on "the main institutions that made possible the perpetuation of the communist regime, the gross human rights violations, and the role of some political leaders."[42] As Monica Ciobanu pointed out, "given its mandate – to reveal the institutional mechanisms of communist repression, to recommend legal reforms for compensating the victims of repression, and to outline the criminal and illegal nature of the former regime – the Commission ... can properly be described as a historical truth commission."[43] This, and the German inquiry body it chose as a model, set it apart from truth commissions. First,

[39] Sabina Fati, "Orniss-securişti – siguranţa naţională," 22 (23 June 2003).

[40] John Gledhill, "Integrating the Past: Regional Integration and Historical Reckoning in Central and Eastern Europe," *Nationalities Papers*, 39(2011): 481–550.

[41] Mark, *The Unfinished Revolution*, 32.

[42] "Comisie pentru studierea crimelor comunismului," BBC Romanian Service (April 2006), available at: http://www.bbc.co.uk/romanian/news/story/2006/04/060405_comunism_basescu.shtml (accessed on 26 July 2011).

[43] Ciobanu, "Criminalizing the Past," 322.

as a presidential body, the Romanian Commission enjoyed much less support from among formations represented in parliament than similar parliamentary bodies with mandates encompassing truth and reconciliation. Opposition from the Social Democrats and Greater Romania Party was to be expected, given their constant efforts to block meaningful reckoning with the communist past. Nonetheless, the Commission drew little support even from within the ruling Justice and Truth Alliance – from the Liberals, who saw it as Băsescu's attempt to outdo his erstwhile political rival, Prime Minister Călin Popescu-Tăriceanu, who created the Institute for the Investigation of Communist Crimes in Romania as an independent transitional justice agency, and even from some Democrats, who considered transitional justice a non-priority and even a dangerous political move because of their strong ties to the former Securitate.

Second, the Commission had no subpoena powers, being thus unable to compel former victimizers to testify and to provide much needed information on the nature of their crimes. This, and the fact that they had only six months to complete the Commission's work, prompted commission members to use exclusively archival documents, memoires, and previously published reports as sources of information, effectively transforming the Commission into an academic body. No former victims were interviewed to corroborate the facts, no public meetings were organized to report partial research results, and no outreach program was launched to educate the public about the investigations or to solicit additional information. The Commission included a handful of former victims, and the report presented a wealth of data but, as mentioned earlier, it delivered the truth primarily ex cathedra, as expert-driven and scientific in nature, without allowing victims individually or collectively to own the new historical narrative and occasionally even reporting inaccurate basic facts on those who had endured the wrath of the communist authorities. For example, the Commission's final report pronounced Constantin Dobre, one of the leaders of the Valea Jiului miners' strike of 1977, dead – a mistake that was soon corrected.

As such, its contribution to reconciliation at either the individual or the national level was rather limited, a fact acknowledged publicly by the former communist-era victims. Tellingly, two years after the Commission wrapped up its work, the Association of Former Political Prisoners declared that national reconciliation in a post-conflict society like Romania "requires not only an apology for political and human rights abuses and not only individual justice for each victim as a reason to forgive and forget," but also represents "a long-term process that has to be experienced by the society as a whole in order to be effective."[44] Interestingly, the Commission's

[44] *Contribution to the UPR 2008 by ICAR Foundation and the Association of Former Political Prisoners – Romania* (2008), available at: http://lib.ohchr.org/HRBodies/UPR/Documents/Session2/RO/ICAR_ROM_UPR_S2_2008_FoundationandtheAssociationofFormerPoliticalPrisoners_uprsubmission.pdf (accessed on 3 October 2011).

final report mentioned the word "reconciliation" once, in relation to the post-1954 Soviet-Yugoslav relations, not the need to bring victims, victimizers, and bystanders together in post-communist times.[45]

The University of Maryland political science professor Vladimir Tismaneanu, author of the first English-language history of Romanian communism, *Stalinism for All Seasons: A Political History of Romanian Communism*, was named commission chair and given a free hand to decide on the Commission's composition, research tools, methodology for data gathering and data analysis, and structure of the final report.[46] Ilieşiu praised Tismaneanu's appointment, seeing it as a guarantee that the Commission would facilitate Romania's moral renewal by unveiling the truth,[47] but others took issue with Tismaneanu's background, family, and political connections, often raising anti-Semitic accusations and unfair charges against him in the hope of destroying his credibility. Given the short time it had on its hands, the relatively long time period under investigation, and the level of detail it wanted to report, the Commission became one of the largest commissions ever created, with nineteen members and twenty-one experts. The nomination process ran into problems when dissident Goma refused to sit on the Commission, and two other members withdrew after public protests pointed to their former ties to the Securitate.[48] Despite Tismaneanu's sustained efforts to ensure representativeness and diversity, the Commission membership was drawn primarily from among anticommunist intellectuals, although some members were publicly known for their

45 Comisia Prezidenţială pentru Analiza Dictaturii Comuniste din România, *Raport Final* (Bucharest: Presidential Commission for the Analysis of Communist Dictatorship in Romania, 2006), 67, available at: http://www.presidency.ro/static/ordine/RAPORT_FINAL_CPADCR.pdf (accessed on 1 October 2011). The report was subsequently published in book format as Vladimir Tismăneanu, Dorin Dobrincu, and Cristian Vasile, eds., *Comisia Prezidenţială pentru Analiza Dictaturii Comuniste din România. Raport Final* (Bucharest: Humanitas, 2007). The word was pronounced during the 1989 revolution in Timişoara by a protesting public speaker, but subsequently neither the civil society nor the political elite identified reconciliation among transitional justice goals.

46 Vladimir Tismăneanu, *Stalinism for All Seasons. A Political History of Romanian Communism* (Berkeley: University of California Press, 2003).

47 "Comisie pentru studierea crimelor comunismului."

48 Metropolitan of Banat Nicolae Corneanu stepped down after being criticized for accepting the appointment in spite of his documented past as a long-term Securitate informer. The nomination of Central European University History Professor Sorin Antohi was revoked after the press revealed that he not only served as a secret agent during communist times but also engaged in academic fraud by declaring that he completed his doctorate when in fact he did not and published a series of books that no libraries and bookstores ever carried. The revelations led to Antohi's dismissal from the Central European University, where he was also part of the administration at the time. Whereas Corneanu recognized his mistake and made his collaboration public during the early 1990s, Antohi refused to admit he was in the wrong. In a letter that sounded more as a threat than an exercise in atonement, Antohi promised he will make a comeback. For his letter, see "Sorin Antohi: Am turnat la Securitate," *Cotidianul* (5 September 2006), and Arina Petrovici, "Sorin Antohi – între sferturi de adevăr şi jumătăţi de minciună," *Observator Cultural*, 344 (2006).

professional qualifications as historians, involvement with civil society groups, or prominence in the diaspora. For some analysts, the overrepresentation of individuals critical of the communist regime gave "those perceiving the communist past through a more favorable lens" the chance to contest the legitimacy of the report, thus undermining the Commission's contribution to national reconciliation and the public reception of its final report.[49] For other observers, the large number of members with no background in historical research and the fact that some members made only a limited contribution to the investigation devalued the scientific contribution of the final report, making it less of an objective historical document based on dispassionate scientific research and more a political statement prone to fuel the endless fight among political parties representing the government and the opposition. Two additional factors fueled criticism and cast a shadow over the results of the Commission's investigations. On the one hand, the absence of legal scholars "contributed to the often imprecise and confusing usage of concepts such as genocide, repression or dictatorship."[50] On the other hand, the fact that several commissioners belonged to or were close to the Group for Social Dialogue meant that the Commission's claim to conducting its work in a scientific – implying ideologically neutral – manner became tainted by the Group's poignant politically active agenda and well-publicized ideological options.

The Commission's 700-page final report, submitted to President Băsescu in November 2006, was published first electronically and then in book format. The text, which was the most comprehensive and multidimensional presentation of the communist period undertaken in Romania until that time, condemned the communist regime as criminal, illegal, and illegitimate, identified the secret political police and the state propaganda as the regime's two main pillars, underscored the continuity between the Gheorghe Gheorghiu-Dej's Stalinist regime of 1945 to 1964 and Nicolae Ceauşescu's nationalist-communist cult of personality of 1965 to 1989, named scores of communist officials involved in state repression (including first post-communist President Ion Iliescu, the father of the first post-communist Prime Minister Petre Roman, Valter Roman, and even Tismaneanu's own father), and presented the fate of national minorities as part of "the overall history of state-sponsored crimes, repression, and mass persecutions."[51] An extensive section was devoted to detailing the empirical evidence concerning the criminal and illegitimate nature of the communist regime. The report concluded with a long list of recommendations pointing to additional transitional justice measures meant to provide remedy to a country scarred by the criminal dictatorship.

49 Ciobanu, "Criminalizing the Past," 325.

50 Idem.

51 Tismaneanu, "Confronting Romania's Past," 726.

Analysts and victims groups faulted the report for providing only a superficial overview of the Ceauşescu regime; embracing an extremely broad definition of the term "victim of communism" that extended beyond those who had been deported, tortured, or executed; ranking groups and individuals who protested against the communist regime at different times; including members of the interwar fascist Iron Guard among the victims of communism (although many fascist supporters were identified as such); giving too much credit to individual dissident intellectuals and comparatively too little to organized protest groups gathering the workers; avoiding to report on the widespread cooperation of the Romanian population with the communist regime; delivering an uneven report whose different sections overlapped; extending the narrative beyond the 1989 to present the aftermath of the revolution, the *mineriade* (the descent of the Valea Jiului miners on Bucharest in 1990 and 1991), and the elite continuity between the communist and post-communist periods; and presenting the dominant Orthodox Church as co-opted by and supportive of communist policies and leaders, although some clergy and faithful had openly opposed the regime and its antireligious policies.[52] Among criticisms was the charge that the characterization of Romanian communist repression as involving genocide was highly problematic, both because the amassed data insufficiently proved that repression met the definitional criteria of genocide and because the concept was applied to social, economic, and even cultural cases.[53] Pages 158–167 of the report offer the definition of the term consecrated by the United Nations Convention on the Prevention and Punishment of the Crime of Genocide of 1948 and then immediately argue that an instance of genocide is represented by "the torture and imprisonment in conditions of extermination of political prisoners," without explaining how that was possible if political and social groups were not included in the definition of genocide.

True to his word, on 18 December 2006 President Băsescu condemned the communist regime as criminal in a parliamentary meeting attended by former Presidents Constantinescu (Romania), Lech Walesa (Poland), and Jelio Jelev (Bulgaria), as well as Commission members. The Greater Romania Party and Social Democrat Party legislators stridently contested Băsescu's speech, unsuccessfully seeking to halt the session and silence the president, and threatened to throw some Commission members over the balcony of the parliament's meeting room, from where they were watching the session. Băsescu was not the first Romanian high-ranking politician to

[52] Vasile Ernu, Costi Rogozanu, Ciprian Şiulea, and Ovidiu Ţichindeleanu, *Iluzia anticomunismului. Lecturi critice ale Raportului Tismăneanu* (Chisinau: Cartier, 2008).

[53] Gabriel Andreescu, "Raportul privitor la dictatura comunistă: Lumini şi umbre (I)," *Ziua* (21 December 2006); G. Andreescu, "Raportul privitor la dictatura comunistă: Lumini şi umbre (II)," *Ziua* (28 December 2006); and Dan Tapalagă, "Raportul Tismăneanu notat cu şapte. Un interviu cu Michael Shafir," *Ziua de Cluj* (12 January 2007).

condemn the crimes of the communist regime, but he was the first to do so officially. In 1997, President Constantinescu condemned communist crimes in a private message sent to the Sighet Memorial, which also asked forgiveness from the Romanian people, but his gesture failed to de-block the Trial of Communism because the Justice and Interior Ministries claimed to have no documents related to sentences handed down in civil cases, which accounted for half of all convictions pronounced against political dissidents until 1989.[54] Compared to Constantinescu, President Băsescu went a step forward and made his political gesture official by pronouncing the condemnation before the house at a time when his Democrats enjoyed much weaker parliamentary representation than Constantinescu's Democratic Convention once had.

EVALUATING THE SUCCESS AND IMPACT OF THE COMMISSION

The Tismaneanu Commission was the product of unique national circumstances, and its success must be judged against that background. At the same time, the literature suggests several criteria for evaluating success. As Eric Wiebelhaus-Brahm contended, truth commissions are successful when they 1) bring their work to completion, 2) finish the report, submit it to the president, and have the government publicly release it for dissemination, 3) produce recommendations that are widely publicized, 4) uncover a great number of victims, and 5) fulfill moral obligations to victims and create conditions for individual and societal reconciliation. These five dimensions look at whether the commission's activity delivers concrete investigation results that are disseminated outside the commission to both the political elite and the general public. When these conditions are met, commissions can be further assessed in terms of their long-term contribution to 1) democratic development and 2) human rights practices.[55] While the Tismaneanu Commission was not a truth commission per se, I will apply these criteria to evaluate its impact both because no similar blueprint for success was developed in relation to historical commissions and because these criteria are applicable to these latter inquiry bodies.

When judged by the first set of criteria, the Tismaneanu Commission appears to have been a very successful transitional justice institution. First, the Commission was able to complete its work by the deadline, producing a final report that was

54 Romulus Rusan, cited in "Recunoaşterea, asumarea şi condamnarea genocidului communist," 22 (22 March 2006).

55 Eric Wiebelhaus-Brahm, *Truth Commissions and Transitional Societies. The Impact on Human Rights and Democracy* (London: Routledge, 2010), 8–10. The charge to fulfill a state's obligation under international human rights law to investigate and prosecute those responsible for human rights violations or its investigations contribute to subsequent prosecutorial efforts to try perpetrators does not apply to the Romanian case.

endorsed by all its members, without exception. Second, the Commission submitted the report to the politician who created it, President Băsescu, both by the November 2006 deadline that Tismaneanu initially indicated and in time for Băsescu to deliver the official condemnation before the country gained EU membership. The complete version of the report was made available to the wider public soon after its submission. Third, the report included recommendations that were well publicized and meaningful because they called for substantial legislative changes (the adoption of a lustration law, the legal rehabilitation and compensation of victims, the criminalization of any type of apology for the communist regime and its leaders), continued institutional reforms (a call for unlimited access to archives relevant for the study of communism), and key memory projects (the opening of a Museum of Victims of Communism, as well as education and research programs). Fourth, the Tismaneanu Commission chose not only to uncover a great number of victims who suffered under both the Gheorghiu-Dej and the Ceauşescu regimes, but it also named numerous perpetrators, both Communist Party leaders and Securitate agents, pointing to their individual relationship to the repressive apparatus and their personal responsibility for specific human rights violations. At the same time, however, the Commission was unable to facilitate national reconciliation, for reasons outlined earlier.

More than five years after the Commission wrapped up its activity, it is evident that its contribution to democratic development and human rights practices has remained negligible, as it facilitated only one of the processes outlined by Wiebelhaus-Brahm. The Tismaneanu Commission informed the society about communist crimes, but at the same time the number of Romanians knowledgeable about the past did not significantly increase, as opinion polls released after the report's publication have indicated.[56] Despite inspiring animated discussions within the country's intellectual and political circles, the report remained generally unknown to the larger population, especially the younger generations. A poll conducted in March 2010 at the Academy of Economic Studies in Bucharest revealed that barely one-fifth of all students recognized the official names of the Tismaneanu and Wiesel Commissions, and that the Tismaneanu Commission was the second least-known commission created by Băsescu during his first presidential mandate (2004–2008).[57]

[56] Lavinia Stan, *Communist Nostalgia in Romania* (12 December 2010), available at: http://laviniastan.wordpress.com/2010/12/12/communist-nostalgia-in-romania/ (accessed on 1 October 2011).

[57] Only 24.1 percent of the students heard about the two commissions. By contrast, 69 percent knew of the Presidential Commission for Analysis and Policy-Making in Education and Research in Romania, 31 percent of the Presidential Commission for Analysis and Policy-Making in Health Care in Romania, and 13.8 percent of the Presidential Commission for the Analysis of the Romanian Political and Constitutional Regime. The percentages might overestimate reality because as many as 37.9 percent of the students reportedly heard about the fictitious Presidential Commission for Promoting

The Commission led to no reforms meant to strengthen the legal system, although the evidence it amassed did not represent "inconsequential truth," to use Wiebelhaus-Brahm's term that refers to facts not used in the court of law.[58] According to Commission Secretary Cristian Vasile, the report was successfully invoked by initial owners seeking the return of their abusively confiscated property in northern Transylvania and by former political prisoners to annul their former sentences.[59] It failed to deprive perpetrators of domestic and international support by exposing their crimes, as many of those named in the report as tainted by association with the dictatorship continued their post-communist political careers unabated (Iliescu included). In addition, the Commission was unable to instill the practice of protecting human rights and to promote the accountability of human rights perpetrators, as the evidence it gathered was not used to indict former perpetrators and no trials that assign responsibility for communist crimes have been organized since 2006. Arguably, the Commission's almost uniform failure to fulfill these harder conditions for success stems from the fact that it was set up as an academic, historical commission with limited powers more than as a genuine truth and reconciliation commission. The Association of Former Political Prisoners underscored the failure of the Tismaneanu Commission to qualify as a truth commission by declaring it "an atypical or partial truth commission" and by calling for the establishment of another "genuine truth commission" that would help Romania end impunity.[60]

Civil Liberties in Romania (Comisia Prezidenţială pentru Promovarea Libertăţilor Cetăţeneşti în România). I thank Prof. Răzvan Zaharia of the Academy of Economic Studies for conducting the survey on my behalf. Personal email communication with Răzvan Zaharia, 11 March 2010.

58 Wiebelhaus-Brahm, *Truth Commissions and Transitional Societies*, 15–16.

59 Vasile claimed that was the case when a court annulled the condemnation to death or lengthy prison terms in 1958 of Aladár Szoboszlay and his friends. Cristian Vasile, "Cinci ani de la Raportul final. Despre o condamnare – nu doar simbolică – a regimului communist," Contributors.ro (17 December 2011), available at: http://www.contributors.ro/cultura/cinci-ani-de-la-raportul-final-despre-o-condamnare-%E2%80%93-nu-doar-simbolica-%E2%80%93-a-regimului-comunist/ (accessed on 15 January 2011). Evidence for other kind of political or social impact is extremely scarce. In a book review, Tismaneanu claimed that Băsescu's suspension as president in 2007 can be directly attributed to his decision to endorse the commission's conclusions, but the impeachment call rested on a wide range of complaints of which only one remotely evoked the report, and Băsescu's removal was supported by the National Liberal Party, which demonstrated a clear commitment to transitional justice. Just one year later, in 2008, the Social Democrats' communist past was no longer an issue for Băsescu and his Democrat-Liberals, who accepted their erstwhile partners in the Salvation Front into the government and offered them several ministerial portfolios. See Vladimir Tismaneanu, "Suspended," *Times Literary Supplement* (12 August 2011), available at: http://www.the-tls.co.uk/tls/public/tlssearch.do?querystring=suspended&sectionId=1797&p=tls (accessed on 28 January 2012), and "Romanian Parliament Suspends President," Radio Free Europe/Radio Liberty (19 April 2007), available at: http://www.rferl.org/content/article/1075960.html (accessed on 28 January 2012).

60 *Contribution to the UPR 2008 by ICAR Foundation and the Association of Former Political Prisoners – Romania*, 3.

As the earlier criteria suggest, a commission's success partly relates to its impact on the victims, victimizers, and the society at large, on the political system (including the functioning of government agencies and the makeup of the political elites), and on the country's political culture, including human rights practices and civic spirit (or social capital, in Robert Putnam's terminology[61]). For Wiebelhaus-Brahm, a way to assess impact is to catalog the recommendations and to examine whether the reforms resulted from them actually changed behavior at the individual and the social level.[62] Unfortunately, very few of the Commission's recommendations have been implemented at the time of this writing.

The Tismaneanu Commission divided its forty-three recommendations into five broad categories. First, measures condemning the communist regime included the president's condemnation of communist crimes in front of parliament, an analysis of the December 1989 events and their connection to the communist regime, and the adoption by parliament of a declaration condemning the dictatorship and apologizing to victims. Second, memorialization consisted of declaring a national day for victims and erecting a monument dedicated to them, creating a Museum of Communist Dictatorship and an information center, presenting communist crimes in history museums across the country, organizing conferences to condemn the regime and to explain the report, continuing the television program *The Memorial of Pain* (see Chapter 9),[63] as well as widely publishing the report, a list of archives consulted by commissioners, a school history textbook, together with an encyclopedia on the communist regime. Although Tismaneanu later drew attention to the fact that "historians are not prosecutors" and "the report is not a call for revenge,"[64] the third group of recommendations related to law and justice: suspending the statute of limitations for communist crimes, adopting radical lustration, rehabilitating former victims, annulling Ceauşescu's amnesty Decree 11/1988, bringing former communist perpetrators to court, granting Romanian citizenship to dissidents exiled abroad by the communist regime, diminishing the pensions of former secret agents and providing compensation packages to political prisoners, banning all forms of denying the criminal character of the communist regime, and opening all communist-era archives, including the collections of the Communist Party and its leadership in view of fully documenting the party's crimes. The fourth category talked about research and archives: the complete transfer of secret archives from the intelligence services to the National Council and the National Archives; analyzing the way in which the archives have been

[61] Robert Putnam, *Making Democracy Work: Civic Traditions in Modern Italy* (Princeton: Princeton University Press, 1993).

[62] Wiebelhaus-Brahm, *Truth Commissions and Transitional Societies*, 10–11.

[63] Lucia Hossu-Longin, Director, *Memorialul Durerii* (1991–2007), 36 episodes.

[64] Tismaneanu, "Confronting Romania's Past," 727.

altered, destroyed, or misplaced after 1989; making all communist-era archives available to researchers; returning abusively confiscated church archives to their rightful owners; and prosecuting those who destroyed or hid documents. Last, education-related recommendations included rewriting history textbooks at all pre-university levels, supporting historical research, and awarding annual bursaries to researchers who want to study the communist regime.[65]

A major stumbling block in fulfilling these recommendations was represented by President Băsescu's decision to endorse only those related to memorialization, rehabilitation, access to secret files, and education in his official condemnation of the communist regime. Not even once did the presidential speech mention what the civil society considered to be the most urgent and important of all recommendations, that is, those related to lustration and court trials. While this decision to focus on nonjudicial methods of working through the communist past might have sought to placate the opposition's animosity, it also sent the message that recommendations could be embraced selectively and proved that the president anticipated lack of support for the more radical recommendations from within his own political camp.[66] To facilitate the implementation of recommendations, in July 2007 President Băsescu announced that the activity of the Tismaneanu Commission will be continued by the Presidential Advisory Commission for the Analysis of the Communist Dictatorship in Romania. Although it worked until late 2009 and included some key members of the Tismaneanu Commission, the new body, which was also chaired by Tismaneanu, proved largely ineffectual and produced few tangible results.[67] Not surprisingly, five years after the publication of the final report, only a handful of these recommendations have been transposed in reality, although not all directly as a result of the Commission's activity: the president condemned the communist regime, the report and a school history textbook were published, and an unprecedented number of archival documents (but not all) were opened to researchers.[68] There are few signs, if any, that these recommendations actually changed behavior at the individual or social level or that the Commission's work helped the civil society overcome the tensions that divided it, Băsescu to "totally and categorically" join

[65] Comisia Prezidenţială pentru Analiza Dictaturii Comuniste din România, *Raport Final*, 637–644.

[66] "Şedinţa comună a Camerei Deputaţilor şi Senatului din 18 decembrie 2006," *Monitorul Oficial al României, partea II-a* (28 December 2006).

[67] The second commission was announced on the same day when Tismăneanu launched a book that took issue with the polemic debates surrounding the formation and activity of the first commission. Vladimir Tismăneanu, *Refuzul de a uita* (Bucharest: Curtea Veche, 2007), and Tismăneanu, "Confronting Romania's Past," 725.

[68] The history textbook would have been completed even in the absence of the final report. Andrei Muraru, "Primul cincinal de condamnare a comunismului: legenda merge mai departe," *Observatorul Cultural* (10 February 2012).

the anticommunist camp, and the political elite no longer to consider communism as an outdated topic, as Tismaneanu hoped.[69]

CONCLUSION

The Tismaneanu Commission undoubtedly marked a significant milestone in Romanian transitional justice by reviving the public debate on the need to come to terms with a dictatorship whose legacies have deeply divided the Romanian society even after its demise. In the span of only six months, the Commission fulfilled its primary mission by compiling the first comprehensive report on the nature of communist repression, submitting it to the president, publicizing it in both electronic and print format, and facilitating the official condemnation of communist crimes before Romania's accession to the EU. Given the scarcity of inquiry commissions in post-communist Europe, the fact that it was set up so late after the collapse of the communist regime, the vicious denigration to which its chairman and members were subjected before, during, and after their mandate, and the Romanian political elite's generally unimpressive record of working through the communist past, the Tismaneanu Commission's very creation constituted an accomplishment in itself.

When judged against criteria of success and impact outlined in the literature, the Commission emerges as a far less remarkable memory exercise that represented no "storming of the Bastille" of public nostalgia and misconceptions about the communist regime. Its ability "to put the past to rest by making it a matter of public record is [as] illusory"[70] as that of many of its Eastern European counterparts that were political top-down "narrative-shaping" institutions, more than investigative bodies.[71] Much of the evidence it unearthed represented what Wiebelhaus-Brahm called "dangerous truth" that generated resentment on the part of victims following the lack of punishment for perpetrators and on the part of perpetrators whose reputation and social standing (if not public office) were threatened by the disclosure of information.[72] Perhaps the Commission's most significant shortcoming was its inability to de-block the vetting process – or this failure could amount to its most significant accomplishment, if President Băsescu created it with the hidden agenda to stall lustration. The inquiry was initially proposed as the prelude for a delayed but much awaited radical, accusation-based lustration program meant to force former communist officials and secret agents out of public office. However, the Commission ultimately

69 Badin, "Nu cred în legenda celor două Securităţi."

70 S. F. Lean, "Is Truth Enough? Reparations and Reconciliation in Latin America," in *Politics and the Past: On Repairing Historical Injustices*, ed. J. C. Torpey (Lanham, MD: Rowman and Littlefield, 2003), 170.

71 Mark, *The Unfinished Revolution*, 38.

72 Wiebelhaus-Brahm, *Truth Commissions and Transitional Societies*, 15–16.

presented itself as the most significant transitional justice measure ever adopted in post-communist Romania and the president's official condemnation as the culmination of state-led efforts to work through the recent past. Designed to placate criticism against its members and President Băsescu, this message also undermined efforts to move the transitional justice project beyond the Commission by implementing its recommendations related to radical lustration. President Băsescu's skillful political instrumentalization of the "politics of memory" meant that he extended support for transitional justice projects only when and to the extent to which they could boost his anticommunist credentials and undermine his political rivals, but he showed little desire to see the vast majority of the recommendations transposed into reality. The Commission's inability to draw support from other political actors meant that neither the Liberals nor the Social Democrats, two other important political formations in the country, embraced its vision about the past or championed the implementation of its recommendations.

6

Restitution of Property

No other transitional justice process demonstrates more clearly the Romanian political elite's unwillingness to work through the communist past promptly, fairly, and judiciously than the restitution of property abusively confiscated by the communist authorities from 1945 to 1989. Apart from the return of farmland, a process completed during the early 1990s, the restitution of other confiscated assets has been seriously delayed, with important consequences for the government, the initial owners, and the individuals, organizations, and institutions that have been using (and often abusing) the property. No other process has been externalized as much as property restitution, which has been brought before the European Court of Human Rights by hundreds of initial owners whose property claims were ignored by Romanian courts and Greek Catholic parishes to which Romanian governments denied the right to petition the courts. No other process has stirred so much hatred and violence as the restitution of property, for which initial owners sometimes had to physically confront the tenants, and both sides staged dramatic street demonstrations aimed to legitimize their position and draw public support behind it. As late as 2011 – that is, over two decades following the collapse of the communist regime – the Greek Catholic owners of some Transylvanian churches and the Orthodox priests and faithful occupying them fought for ownership under the indifferent eyes of the local police, after the courts ordered the property transferred from the Orthodox to the Greek Catholics. No other process has been as costly for the Romanian taxpayers, who have paid damages and compensation to initial owners whose property rights were upheld by the European Court, while tenants have continued to use the confiscated dwellings at rents well below the market level. Last, no other group of victims has been maligned by the general public, the mass media, and even foreign observers more than the owners of confiscated property, whose property right has often been judged not as a constitutional prerogative, but as a privilege that could place them at a comparative advantage over other Romanians.

By 2001, the year when Romania regulated the restitution of nationalized property, Hungary, Bulgaria, Estonia, Lithuania, the Czech and Slovak Republics, and Germany had already adopted relevant legislation in that respect. Bulgaria was the first country to allow individual owners to reclaim their property, but religious minority groups like the Turkish Muslims, the Roman Catholics, and the Jews have been unable to gain back their assets.[1] Two Czechoslovak laws adopted in 1990 and 1991 returned property expropriated before 1955 and some 70,000 small businesses and houses nationalized from 1955 to 1961, offering the property in its original form ("in kind" restitution), financial compensation, or shares in state-owned enterprises slated for privatization.[2] By 2002, Estonia had returned all communal property to religious communities and individual property to all owners who filed claims before the stipulated deadline, irrespective of their citizenship, thus agreeing not to place the Russians, the Russian speakers, and the Jews at a disadvantage.[3] A comprehensive program was adopted in Germany, where the unification treaty solved property claims by East German homeowners under the principle "return instead of compensation" by letting tenants shoulder the compensation cost and exposing them to the threat of eviction as initial owners' rights were reinstated. The social downside of this practice was tragically brought to light in 1992, when two tenants whose homes had been reclaimed hanged themselves in despair. Critics alleged that property return was not uniformly justified because communists seized property from Nazi collaborators who were not morally entitled to restitution, and often claimants were descendants of initial owners and had never lived in those properties.[4] Whereas these countries effected prompt property restitution, Romania's new rulers were unwilling to redress the crimes of the communist system, which many of them had served.

The restitution of property is an important transitional justice process designed to redress and compensate for the harm inflicted by an unjust ancien regime by reinstating the owners of abusively confiscated property to the status quo ante – that is, the position they had prior to the state-led nationalization campaign. Property restitution strengthens the rule of law and upholds the right to property – fundamental for a democratic order. In addition, restitution "restores the confidence of public opinion towards private property" and "allows for the rapid privatization of a large number of public assets."[5] In post-communist countries, when conducted

1 *Summary of Property Restitution in Central and Eastern Europe* (16 July 2002), available at: http://germany.usembassy.gov/germany/img/assets/8497/property.pdf (accessed on 22 July 2011).

2 Lavinia Stan, "The Roof over Our Heads: Property Restitution in Romania," *Journal of Communist Studies and Transition Politics*, 22(2006): 181.

3 See *Summary of Property Restitution in Central and Eastern Europe*.

4 Stan, "The Roof over Our Heads," 182.

5 D. Labaronne, cited in Mariana Karadjova, "Property Restitution in Eastern Europe: Domestic and International Human Rights Law Responses," *Review of Central and East European Law*, 3(2004): 328.

in conjunction with privatization (the transfer of assets from the state to private hands), property restitution "may contribute to new economic development in the direction of a market-type economy and may even help stimulate privatization in those cases where "restitution in kind" is not possible."[6] Concomitantly, restitution may hinder privatization "as a result of difficulties involving the determination of those rightfully entitled to restitution as well as of the length (and complexity) of the procedures involved in administering restitution."[7] The fact that some benefited materially from the suffering of others, by getting access to the victims' former dwellings or places of worship, prompted historian Tony Judt to identify property restoration as "the most telling crisis of memory."[8] The differences between countries and the lack of a unified restitution policy at regional and European levels meant that each post-communist government had the liberty to balance the moral goals of restitution and the means to attain it, sometimes arriving at solutions embroiled in controversy.

This chapter surveys the restitution of dwellings abusively confiscated by the communist authorities from ordinary Romanians from 1945 to 1989 and of places of worship transferred in 1948 by the state from the Greek Catholic to the Orthodox Church. To date, most literature dedicated to property restitution in Eastern Europe has focused on its economic consequences and the way in which various political and social actors have defined property and have understood property guarantees.[9] By contrast, this chapter surveys two distinct property restitution processes as methods of working through the recent past. It asks the following: Was nationalization unjust? Would restitution address one injustice by generating another? What property must be returned? And does procrastination have any moral effect on property restitution?[10] These questions were answered differently by initial owners, tenants, religious denominations, politicians of various ideological persuasions, and Romanian and international courts. As this chapter argues, in the name of the continuity of the

[6] Idem, 326.

[7] Idem.

[8] Tony Judt, "The Past Is Another Country: Myth and Memory in Postwar Europe," *Daedalus*, 21(1992): 104.

[9] Chris Hann, ed., *Property Relations: Renewing the Anthropological Tradition* (Cambridge: Cambridge University Press, 1998); Adam Przeworski, *Democracy and the Market: Political and Economic Reforms in Eastern Europe and Latin America* (New York: Cambridge University Press, 1991); E. Rabinowicz and J. Swinnen, "Political Economy of Privatization and Decollectivization of Central and Eastern European Agriculture: Definitions, Issues and Methodology," in *Political Economy of Agrarian Reform in Central and Eastern Europe*, ed. I. F. M. Swinnen (Brookfield: Ashgate, 1997); Katherine Verdery, *What Was Socialism and What Comes Next?* (Princeton: Princeton University Press, 1996); and Katherine Verdery, *The Vanishing Hectare: Property and Value in Postsocialist Transylvania* (Ithaca: Cornell University Press, 2003).

[10] The framework is borrowed from Emanuel Mihail Socaciu, "Problema dreptăţii şi restituirea proprietăţilor în România post-comunistă," PhD Dissertation, University of Bucharest, 2008.

Romanian state and the separation of church and state, the restitution of dwellings and churches was drastically delayed and limited.

After 1945, Romania confiscated property belonging to individuals, organizations, and communities to ensure the preeminence of state-controlled property in the centrally planned command economy (see Chapter 1). Nationalized residences became state property. Those who used them, including initial owners, became tenants renting from the state. The most attractive residences were handed out to nomenklatura members, party apparatchiks, and secret agents, while the rest were allotted to workers and uprooted peasants who arrived in towns with the industrialization drive. Location and architectural details made confiscated residential units highly desirable, especially those in historic city centers and tranquil residential areas, close to governmental offices and well-stocked shops, better schools, parks, playgrounds, and more considerate neighbors. Such location translated into a higher social status, much sought after even under a regime that ostensibly promoted social homogeneity and equality among classes. Compared to the small, unfinished, damp, and poorly isolated communist-era apartments in the grey blocks that handcuffed historical city centers, nationalized residences included houses with small courtyards and parking spaces or larger apartments with nice architectural details.

Nationalizations also affected persecuted religious denominations. To obliterate religious sentiment and destroy religious institutions, the communist state confiscated land belonging to the majority Orthodox Church, together with icons and chalices belonging to Christian, Muslim, and Jewish denominations. In 1948, the minority Greek Catholic Church was dismantled, and its 1,800 Transylvanian churches, chapels, and cemeteries were transferred to the Orthodox Church, which welcomed the Greek Catholics' return to its fold. The Greek Catholic Church was created around 1700, when Jesuits convinced some Orthodox Transylvanian Romanians to adopt Roman Catholic dogma and retain the Orthodox rite in exchange for political recognition.[11] After 1948, the church continued to exist clandestinely under the patronage of the Roman Catholic Church, from which it was receiving some moral and financial assistance.

THE POLITICS OF RESTITUTION OF DWELLINGS

Calls for the return of confiscated dwellings were heard immediately after the 1989 revolution, when the reconstituted Christian Democrat Peasant and Liberal Parties asked the new rulers to uphold the inviolability of property, a principle observed by the Western democracies that the country hoped to emulate. The new rulers were

[11] Lavinia Stan and Lucian Turcescu, *Religion and Politics in Post-Communist Romania* (New York: Oxford University Press, 2007), especially Chapter 5.

called to move the country away from communism by redressing the injustices of the old regime, withdrawing the privileges of the nomenklatura, and recognizing the victims' rights. In this context, justice meant eviction of tenants and home restitution to initial owners.

The new rulers, drawn primarily from the Communist Party's second echelon leadership, disregarded a demand that directly affected nomenklatura members who still rented nationalized dwellings. After forty-five years of communist rule, the number of tenants exceeded that of initial owners, and thus it was electorally riskier to effect property restitution than to oppose it.[12] In addition, a populist policy introduced in 1990 tipped public support in favor of tenants and away from owners. Decree-Law 61/1990 allowed 3 million tenants to buy, at very advantageous prices, state-owned apartments built by the communist state, and not subject to restitution claims.[13] The decree benefited the new government, because granting Romanians ownership rights over the apartments they had rented from the state for so many years attracted popular support before the first free elections of May 1990 and secured the loyalty of the working class and civil servants renting those dwellings. In turn, Romanians gained ownership rights on homes they could not afford to purchase, if offered on the open market, because the regime change had seriously affected their living standards. The transfer of ownership rights into private hands further allowed the cash-strapped, post-communist state to renege on its responsibility to upgrade the decades-old apartments, which were in need of urgent repair.

Tenants of nationalized residential units capitalized on the Romanians' newly found pride of being home owners and lobbied the government for the chance to acquire ownership rights for the units they occupied. They argued that Decree-Law 61/1990 discriminated against them because they too had rented from the communist state and had no say in the kind of dwelling they were offered. It was not their fault, they said, that the communist state offered nationalized dwellings to them, a mistake for which they should not be punished. In the ensuing public debate, the focus changed from redressing the injustices that the owners suffered at the hands of the communists to avoiding placing the tenants at a comparative disadvantage. The 1991 Constitution echoed this change of heart by ostensibly "protecting" – but not "guaranteeing" – private property.[14] While Prime Minister Petre Roman rejected

12 Many tenants were granted only parts of nationalized dwellings. This is why, for some nationalized dwellings, the number of tenants exceeded the number of initial owners. See, for example, Emanuel Mihail Socaciu, "Restituţia imobilelor naţionalizate: Preliminarii ale unei evaluări morale," *Sfera politicii*, 128(2007), available at: http://www.sferapoliticii.ro/sfera/128/art01-socaciu.html (accessed on 25 July 2011).

13 "Decret-lege nr. 61 din 7 februarie 1990 privind vânzarea de locuinţe construite din fondurile statului către populaţie," *Monitorul Oficial al României, partea I* (8 February 1990).

14 *Constituţia României din 1991*, available at: http://www.cdep.ro/pls/dic/act_show?ida=1&idl=1 (accessed on 26 July 2011).

restitution on the grounds that the country had to effect more urgent economic programs, and President Iliescu suggested that restitution would reconstitute the pre-communist social inequalities that the communist state worked hard to bridge, National Salvation Front Senator Ştefan Glăvan argued that

> after 1945 through expropriation, nationalization and forced donation, many citizens were brutally and illegally thrown out of their homes, which the state then rented out or used as public institutions. The rightful owners want back these properties, abusively and unjustly taken away, and around one million tenants, who for four decades used, maintained and improved these houses, cannot vacate them for lack of alternative dwelling space. The situation needs a clear and fair solution, and calls for identifying residences that can be returned to the owners, those for which owners could receive compensation, and those that tenants could buy out.[15]

It soon emerged that such calls for an in-depth analysis of the subject aimed to postpone indefinitely the adoption of relevant legislation.

A report presented to the Senate in May 1992 unveiled the fate of some Bucharest "protocol residences" that the Communist Party rented to the nomenklatura in virtue of Decree 263/1979, which allowed state dignitaries and party leaders to use those residences during their term of office; many such residences were nationalized houses that constituted prized possessions in terms of both their location and their footage. In early 1990, the government evicted communist officials and rented these residences for low fees to the new post-communist elite, their relatives, friends, and supporters. Communist officials were evicted because they had overstayed their political mandates, but not all those who moved in were entitled to such residences. Tenants included tennis player Ion Ţiriac, anticommunist dissident and poet Mircea Dinescu, actors Ioana Pavelescu and Horaţiu Mălăiele, and academics Lazăr Vlăsceanu, Cătălin Zamfir, and Vasile Secăreş. Roman was criticized for disregarding his cabinet's unpublished Decision 115/1990, which transferred all Communist Party assets to the state and allowed embassies to rent protocol residences from among nationalized dwellings, for personally allocating protocol residences to his friends and supporters, and for transferring 276 such residences to the Bucharest mayor's office, thereby ending their protocol status in view of making them available for sale to selected buyers. The new tenants, private firms or individuals, were offered renewable five-year rental contracts at very advantageous prices.[16]

15 "Stenograma şedinţei Senatului din 14 februarie 1992," *Monitorul Oficial al României, partea II-a* (17 February 1992), 17.

16 "Raportul Comisiei de anchetă pentru stabilirea adevărului şi eliminarea suspiciunii, neîncrederii şi prezentării false a unor fapte de corupţie cu character grav, pretins săvârşite în perioada ianuarie 1990–decembrie 1991," *Monitorul Oficial al României, partea II-a* (15 May 1992), 2–5.

The report unmasked the unwritten pact linking civil society leaders, academics, and artistic luminaries to the government and revealed that the political opposition and the civil society "publicly preached austerity, but practiced shameless gluttony."[17] This collusion of interests explains why property restitution was seriously delayed throughout the 1990s, under governments representing both the center-left Social Democrat Party and the center-right Democratic Convention. Law 85/1992, which expanded the number of state-owned dwellings offered for sale, prompted deputies and senators to reopen the discussion on the interests of initial owners and tenants living in nationalized homes.[18] Debates heated up when the government asked parliament to "freeze" the legal situation of nationalized homes until the adoption of a law. As the parliament refused to decide the legal position of such dwellings, some owners asked the courts to recognize their rights. After lengthy hearings, many judges sided with the owners, recognized their ownership claims, and ordered the eviction of the tenants.[19] The government's position was that property should not change hands in the absence of a law because parliament, not the courts, should settle the issue of nationalized property, as "those homes have been transferred into the hands of the state by legislative acts, and therefore their restitution should be operated by legislation."[20] This position ignored the fact that citizens' rights to approach the court was recognized as fundamental by the Constitution of 1991, which stipulated not only that "every person is entitled to bring cases before the courts for the defense of his legitimate rights, liberties and interests" but also that "the exercise of this right may not be restricted by any law" (Article 21).[21] The Romanian Constitutional Court was too weak at the time to make full note of the unconstitutionality of the government's call.

In the absence of reliable and complete statistics, the report fueled a heated debate on the social background of owners and tenants. For National Liberal Party Deputy Constantin Andreescu, tenants were "communist criminals," "party activists who became ministers, Central Committee members, [county] First Secretaries, and members of the damned nomenklatura which we claim we want to replace! Let's not be Pharisees asking whether it is moral and let's just throw the tenants out

[17] I borrow this phrase from Robert Austin and Jonathan Ellis, "Albania," in *Transitional Justice in Post-Communist Eastern Europe and the Former Soviet Union*, ed. Lavinia Stan (London: Routledge, 2009), 176–199.

[18] "Legea nr.85 din 22 iulie 1992 privind vânzarea de locuinţe şi spaţii cu altă destinaţie construite din fondurile statului şi din fondurile unităţilor economice sau bugetare de stat," *Monitorul Oficial al României, partea I* (29 July 1992).

[19] Socaciu, "Restituţia imobilelor naţionalizate: Preliminarii ale unei evaluări morale."

[20] "Stenograma şedinţei Camerei Deputaţilor din 15 iulie 1992," *Monitorul Oficial al României, partea II-a* (16 July 1992), 12.

[21] *Constituţia României din 1991.*

[of those nationalized dwellings]!"[22] In response to such claims, National Salvation Front Deputy Alexandru Albu insisted that most of the 1.2 million tenants were ordinary Romanians who lived from paycheck to paycheck and should not be denied the right to buy out the homes they legally rented from the state. By ignoring the earlier parliamentary report that disclosed the names of communist and post-communist officials who were using nationalized residences and by painting tenants as ordinary Romanians, Albu tried to legitimize the tenants' demands for ownership rights and made them more acceptable to the wider public.

The single most important development that affected the pace and scope of the property restitution program was neither a parliamentary law nor a government decision, but the president's personal position on the matter. In May 1994, during a visit to the Transylvanian town of Satu Mare, President Ion Iliescu publicly opposed restitution in kind and argued that the courts infringed the law by reconstituting the owners' property rights and ordering the tenants' eviction. Iliescu chided judges who admitted cases lodged by owners before parliament could adopt a law and urged for the non-implementation of court decisions that favored the owners, even when these decisions were irrevocable. His call was not left unanswered. Prosecutor General Vasile Manea Drăgulin (and later his successor, Nicolae Cochinescu) overturned many definitive court verdicts by taking advantage of *recurs în anulare* (appeal to the court of last resort), a procedure that allowed the prosecutor general, a political figure appointed by the executive, to overturn definitive court orders, and of the highly contested Supreme Court Decision 1/1995, which banned lower courts from hearing cases in the absence of a property restitution law. Thousands of homes that owners won in court were therefore nationalized again, this time by a purportedly democratic state that upheld fundamental human rights. Iliescu reacted to the increased number of court decisions that ordered the restitution in kind of nationalized property and complaints from tenants that "the new landlords, distant relatives of the initial owners, behave like tyrants" to make them move out.[23] While criticizing owners for taking advantage of the lack of legislation, Iliescu remained silent on the

[22] "Stenograma şedinţelor comune ale Camerei Deputaţilor şi Senatului din 15 iulie 1992," *Monitorul Oficial al României, partea II-a* (16 July 1992), 2.

[23] "Stenograma şedinţei Camerei Deputaţilor din 15 martie 1994," *Monitorul Oficial al României, partea II-a* (16 March 1994), 2–3. The Romanian procedure differs from the Russian supervisory review (*peresmotr dela v poryadke nadzora*) by allowing the prosecutor general to overturn court decisions without cases being reviewed again. In Russia, the prosecutor general cannot overturn definitive court decisions, but may ask the courts to review cases he considers problematic. I thank Peter Solomon and Alexei Trochev for pointing this difference out to me. For a legal analysis of Iliescu's statement, see Corneliu-Liviu Popescu, "Influenţa politică în soluţionarea proceselor privind dreptul de proprietate asupra imobilelor naţionalizate în perioada comunistă şi consecinţele acestora în cauzele împotriva României aflate pe rolul Curţii Europene a Drepturilor Omului," *Revista Română de Drepturile Omului*, 23(2002): 20–40.

cases in which state agencies overseeing nationalized property unlawfully allowed tenants to buy them.

In June 1994, parliament discussed alternative laws on the return of nationalized homes introduced separately by the government and the opposition. The government deplored the conflict between the owners, "seniors fearful they won't live the day to receive their property, inherited or obtained through hard work," and the tenants, "who face legislative solutions to the problem with fear and uncertainty."[24] In drafting the proposal, the Social Democrat cabinet claimed that it recognized the owners' property rights and the tenants' rights to protection and equitable dwelling, contrasted several alternative solutions, including restitution in kind and financial compensation, and estimated the associated costs and the number of dwellings it could offer to evicted tenants. It announced that the authorities had received 180,000 claims from tenants and owners. Because the state needed 1.3 times the 1994 national budget and eight to ten years to build so many apartments, it was unfeasible to move tenants out of nationalized homes. The government agreed that owners had rights to their property, but restitution had to reflect the "juridical, social, temporal, and material changes these properties suffered" under communism. The owners' demands could be met with "just compensation" instead of restitution in kind, which failed to compensate tenants for improving and maintaining the property, disregarded the tenants' ownership claim to the property, and ignored their good faith when buying out the title to the units. Restitution in kind was also rejected because tenants invested in those properties both financially and emotionally, while the effects of abusive confiscation "attenuated in time," as most owners already found other dwellings. Hence, the government proposed the return of only the dwellings already occupied by initial owners and compensation for all other properties. The Ministry of Finance was to compensate owners, recovering the funds by selling the property to tenants. The law applied to confiscated homes in the possession of the state in December 1989 and for which owners had received no compensation under communism. This political solution, it was hoped, "resulted in the least social strife and change, and the fewest lawsuits."[25]

By contrast, opposition legislators claimed that restitution in kind could not be discarded as an option as it was upheld by the 1991 Romanian Constitution and international law, and compensation could be offered only for demolished residences. Tenants should be allowed to continue to rent the confiscated homes for a further five years, and government should assist them in acquiring or building new houses so that at the end of the contract they will be able to move out. By adopting the

[24] "Stenograma şedinţei Senatului din 2 iunie 1994," *Monitorul Oficial al României, partea II-a* (11 June 1994), 7–16.

[25] Idem.

government's proposal, the opposition argued, parliament would invalidate some 2,000 court decisions favoring the owners and introduce a double standard allowing "the state, through two of its most important institutions [the legislature and the judiciary], to be a friend to some citizens and an enemy to others."[26] Legislators were urged to separate the right to own a property, which had to be reconstituted in favor of the owners, from the right to use the property, and to reject the government's proposal, which unfairly denied initial owners the right to own their property, while granting tenants the right both to own and to use the property. Tenants should remain tenants, renting from the owners, not from the state, and public funds should be used not to compensate owners, but to build new homes for tenants.

The two proposals revealed different interpretations of the right to property in general and the rights of initial owners expropriated by the communist regime in particular. For the Social Democrat government, residential property restitution boiled down to a housing problem in which its responsibility was to ensure that both tenants and owners had roofs over their heads. The most inexpensive and least disruptive solution was to limit to a minimum the number of cases entitled to reparation, by excluding owners with dwellings and declaring them unreasonable claimants and granting tenants the right to use and own those properties. Rather than being inviolable and recognized to all citizens, the right to property depended on the claimants' condition, because owners whose housing problem was unsolved had more claims to their nationalized property than owners who already had somewhere to live. While usually the right to use a property is derived from the right to own it, for the Social Democrats the opposite was true, as tenants were recognized the right to own *because* they used the homes. The government favored the tenants, sparing them the chagrin of moving and finding alternative lodgings, and offering them ownership rights at affordable prices. It subsidized tenants wishing to buy out the dwellings they used, instead of making the funds available to owners as compensation. By contrast, the opposition saw the return of property confiscated under communism as a problem distinct from the housing problem and recognized the right to use as being derived from the right to own.[27]

President Iliescu's intervention was bitterly criticized. In July 1994, 167 opposition legislators called for the president's impeachment on grounds that his Satu Mare statements infringed Articles 41 and 42 of the 1991 Constitution protecting the right to property and inheritance, Article 21 guaranteeing access to the courts, Articles 16 and 21 stipulating that legislation could not limit the citizen's right to petition

[26] Idem.

[27] Karin Dawidson, "Conflict of Interest in the Restitution and Privatization of Housing since the Fall of Socialism: The Case of Central Timisoara City – a Problem of Democracy?," *Europe–Asia Studies*, 56(2004): 119–141.

the courts, and Article 123 upholding a judiciary independent from the executive branch of the government.[28] Iliescu rejected the accusations and blamed owners for approaching the courts, charging tenants exorbitant rents, and evicting them before the five-year rental contracts expired. Iliescu suggested that most, if not all, owners had behaved despicably towards tenants, although in reality very few had acted that way. The Constitutional Court sided with Iliescu, arguing that the initial owners' property rights had ceased with nationalization, but admitted that "the situation is different if owners were denied their property as a result of abusive legislation, as in that case the property right did not legally cease."[29] For the Social Democrats, the impeachment proposal aimed first and foremost "to devalue the presidency and the republic and prepare the ground for reinstating the monarchy" and amounted to a cruel attack against tenant families "thrown in the street by corrupt judges" and driven into despair by "continuous court hearings and wrongful, hasty verdicts."[30] The proposal, which "mimicked democracy," they lamented, was advanced by an opposition that maintained a permanent state of conflict, "demolished but proposed nothing constructive," wanted "chaos instead of normalcy," and "created a negative international image [for Romania] as a country that cannot be governed, a country of handicapped and thieves, where everybody is corrupt and everyone pursues only personal interests."[31]

The opposition voiced regret for the judiciary's continued dependence on the executive and the judges' unwillingness to shake off the communist behavior of "seeking the [government's] approval before handing down verdicts" and condemned the president for saying that "all decisions handed down by the judges were illegal" and calling against their implementation. It insisted that the courts should be allowed to redress communist injustices, if the parliament was unable or unwilling to do so. Christian Democrat leader Gavril Dejeu maintained that, under communism, the homes of ordinary Romanians had been illegally nationalized and then offered to "communist and post-communist elites that, after taking advantage of a regime of cruel exploitation and humiliation of the Romanian people, benefit today of pensions several times larger than the workers', pay meager rents and want to become owners of the houses they and their family abusively took away from workers, civil servants, small artisans, intellectuals, and pensioners."[32] For the opposition forces, the Constitutional Court's decision to exonerate Iliescu proved its obedience to a

[28] "Stenograma şedinţelor comune ale Camerei Deputaţilor şi Senatului din 4 iulie 1994," *Monitorul Oficial al României, partea II-a* (11 July 1994), 1–8.

[29] Idem.

[30] Idem.

[31] Idem.

[32] "Stenograma şedinţelor comune ale Camerei Deputaţilor şi Senatului din 7 iulie 1994," *Monitorul Oficial al României, partea II-a* (16 July 1994), 1–41.

president who defended "the communist nomenklatura members who still occupy the houses of former political prisoners, war veterans, the national heroes."[33] In the end, parliament turned down the impeachment proposal.

Law 112/1995 incorporated the government's earlier proposal and limited restitution in kind to the few cases in which residential units were vacant or occupied by initial owners, allowing tenants to buy the dwellings they inhabited.[34] Although criticized by the civil society and the international community, the law remained unchanged even after the Democratic Convention formed the government in late 1996. The reasons for the politicians' unwillingness to see the merits of the claims of the initial owners became apparent in 1997, when the head of the Prime Minister's Control Office Valerian Stan revealed that well-connected Christian Democrat, Democrat, and Liberal legislators, ministers, and ambassadors had bought nationalized homes in virtue of Law 112/1995. These included communist prime ministers Manea Mănescu (1974–1979) and Ilie Verdeţ (1979–1982), communist Minister of Interior Tudor Postelnicu (1987–1989), communist Minister of Finance Paul Niculescu-Mizil (1978–1981), communist ambassadors to Italy, Malta, and Morocco Cornel Burtică, former head of the Foreign Intelligence Service of the Securitate Nicolae Pleşiţă (1980–1984), and former head of the Securitate Iulian Vlad (1987–1989).[35] Even Iliescu bought for a fraction of its market value the nationalized Bucharest apartment he had rented, showing that his Satu Mare calls had been self-interested more than driven by preoccupation with the tenants' fate. The revelations placed the Democratic Convention government in such an unflattering position that Stan lost his position for failure to obtain clearance from Prime Minister Victor Ciorbea before disclosing them.

Stan's report explained why so many Democratic Convention leaders sided with tenants against owners. A draft law introduced in parliament in 1997 gave initial owners no satisfaction, making a condition of restitution in kind written notification submitted by owners before tenants bought the dwellings, and upholding the tenants' newly acquired ownership rights over such residences in all cases where they acted "in good faith" without knowing that the units had been nationalized. Social Democrat legislators saw the proposal as bringing restitution in kind through the back door, but initial owners insisted on restitution in kind whenever possible and compensation offered in cash at the market value by tenants, not the state. Maria Teodoru, the leader of the Association of Owners of Property Abusively

33 Idem.

34 "Legea nr. 112/1995, privind reglementarea situaţiei juridice a unor imobile cu destinaţia de locuinţe, trecute în proprietatea statului Legea caselor naţionalizate," *Monitorul Oficial al României, partea I* (29 November 1995).

35 Gabriela Palade, "Despăgubirile pentru casele naţionalizate, amânate," *Evenimentul Zilei* (29 December 2002).

Confiscated by the State, declared that the Democratic Convention government prepared the draft not because it wanted to guarantee property rights in Romania – one of the lofty ideals it preached – but because of European Union pressure and in an effort to deter Romanians from petitioning the European Court of Human Rights.[36] The unstable Convention did not pursue the matter further, as it was too preoccupied with sharing the spoils that came with controlling vast state-owned resources and forging alliances with unlikely partners to maintain a fragile parliamentary majority.

After Ion Iliescu returned to the presidency and Adrian Năstase formed a Social Democrat government in 2000, Eugen Pleşa, leader of the Association of Tenants Living in Nationalized Houses, which championed the interests of the tenants, entered parliament as a Greater Romania Party member (and renewed his mandate four years later on the Social Democrat list). As Iliescu and Năstase were already known for their public commitment to the tenants, the initial owners expected no improvement of the situation during their term in office. Nevertheless, the Social Democrat government was determined to bring Romania into the EU. The international community repeatedly asked Romania to respect the right to property and consider seriously the demands of the owners who the communist state robbed of their assets. Resolution 1123 of the Council of Europe Parliamentary Assembly (24 April 1997) encouraged Romania to settle the problem of confiscated property and to amend Laws 18/1991 and 12/1995 to include restitution in kind and just compensation. Resolution A4–0428 (3 December 1998) asked for a "correct and definitive solution guaranteeing 'natural' restitution or, if not possible, due compensation."[37] Resolution 562 (13 October 1998) of the U.S. House of Representatives on the property abusively expropriated by former totalitarian regimes called for restitution in kind whenever possible and "prompt, just, and effective" compensation.[38] The nearer the prospect of integration drew, the more sensitive Bucharest became to EU demands. In this context, parliament adopted Law 10/2001.[39]

36 "Stenograma şedinţei Camerei Deputaţilor din 10 iunie 1997," *Monitorul Oficial al României, partea II-a* (11 June 1997), and Camera Deputaţilor, *Raport asupra propunerii legislative pentru anularea Legii nr. 112/1995 şi restitutirea unor imobile cu destinaţia de locuinţe, trecute în proprietatea statului* (Bucharest: Romanian Parliament, 11 March 1998).

37 European Parliament, "Resolution of 3 December 1998 on Romania's application for membership of the European Union, with a view to the European Council to be held in Vienna (11–12 December 1998). (A4–0428/98)" (3 December 1998), available at: http://www.europarl.europa.eu/enlargement/positionep/resolutions/031298b_en.htm (accessed on 7 July 2012).

38 U.S. House of Representatives, Resolution 562 (13 October 1998), p. 3, available at: "http://www.gpo.gov/fdsys/pkg/BILLS-105hres562eh/pdf/BILLS-105hres562eh.pdf (accessed on 7 July 2012).

39 "Legea nr.10 din 8 februarie 2001 privind regimul juridic al unor imobile preluate în mod abuziv în perioada 6 martie 1945–22 decembrie 1989," *Monitorul Oficial al României, partea I* (14 February 2001).

The law allowed for the return in kind of private property requisitioned by the communist state and cooperative associations and for compensation whenever physical, in kind restitution was not possible. It applied to all property that was abusively confiscated by communist authorities, except for property belonging to religious denominations. The owners' property rights could be exercised only after the courts ordered the property return. Owners who had received compensation by virtue of international accords could not claim restitution in kind. For nonresidential, destroyed, or not returnable property, owners received vouchers for privatized companies, stock market shares, goods, and services. Tenants living in returned properties were protected by the state, legally binding lease and rental contracts had to be observed, and institutional tenants (such as embassies and consulates) were allowed to rent for a further five years. Tenants had to vacate the returned dwellings if offered alternative residential space, and rents were capped at a quarter of the tenant's income. Owners of buildings used by schools, medical clinics and hospitals, state agencies, and political parties were denied restitution in kind, receiving instead equivalent buildings, company shares, goods, and services. Institutional tenants could buy the property they used, even when the owner refused to relinquish the dwelling. Equivalent residential units were offered only when the initial building had been destroyed, had suffered significant transformations, or had been sold to tenants in virtue of Law 112/1995. To qualify for restitution in kind, owners had to lodge restitution claims within six months of the law's adoption. The state agency or organization using the property had sixty days to respond, specifying the level of compensation it could offer, in case it refused to vacate the building or pledged to buy it. In those cases, the initial owner could challenge the decision in court. Owners of buildings used by state-owned companies listed for privatization were offered shares in those companies. For the first ten years after buying the residences through Law 112/1995, tenants were allowed to sell them only to initial owners for prices equal to the buying price. Initial owners had ninety days to announce to tenants they wanted to buy out the property and had to compensate tenants for any improvements they had done to the property.

While it was the first to regulate the situation of nationalized property and it represented a step toward restitution in kind, the law fell short of guaranteeing equitable reparation for the abuses initial homeowners suffered during communism. The legislation recognized the transfer of property rights to tenants who bought nationalized homes through Law 112/1995 or took them "in good faith" without registering the deed. Initial owners insisted that the good faith clause could not be invoked because tenants knew that the residences they occupied had been taken over by the communist state, but tenants claimed that in fact few of them had the knowledge that the requisition was abusive. Owners had to compensate tenants for improvements to the property, even though they did not pre-approve those improvements, but were not compensated for being deprived of their property for decades. In addition, restitution in kind was not provided for buildings used by institutional tenants, except in the unlikely case in which the latter agreed to it, allowed those tenants to set whatever level of compensation they saw fit, and included no sanctions for mayors who refused to answer claims for buildings used by their office. Homeowners were permitted to take institutional tenants to court, but the prosecutor general could still resort to *recurs în anulare* discretionarily.

While supportive of the law in the face of EU pressure, the Social Democrat government quietly undermined its implementation. Ordinance 59/2001 extended by a year the period in which the prosecutor general could overturn court decisions, instead of scrapping an undemocratic procedure with no equivalent in other European countries. Minister of Justice Rodica Stănoiu drew the courts' attention to "the social problems generated by court decisions that evicted tenants."[40] President Iliescu dismissed property as "a trifle," and Prime Minister Năstase remarked that the European Court of Human Rights, which many Romanian homeowners had approached, "was not a real estate agent" and should not be called to meddle in Romanian affairs.[41] Promises of financial compensation remained unfulfilled, as the national budget included no compensation funds and other compensation means were riskier and less attractive to initial owners. Owners did not opt for vouchers in state-owned companies listed for privatization, because the more profitable companies had been privatized long before 2001. In 2002, the cabinet's plan to compensate 60,000 homeowners over the 2005–2015 decade was seen as detrimental to elderly owners, and the proposal to use budget funds was deemed immoral.[42]

At the local level, Law 10/2001 was implemented erratically and slowly. The government's representative in Bucharest, the prefect, challenged the mayor's decisions that favored restitution in kind. Mayors' offices opened special bureaus where homeowners could lodge property restitution claims, but the law complicated the process and seemed to deter homeowners from claiming back their properties. The bureaus were denounced for "imposing impossible conditions," asking initial owners to submit "expensive documents that are time-consuming to obtain" and information they "could not provide, since the property had been in state care for the past fifty years."[43] By mid-2001, local authorities had registered 210,000 claims, 128,000 of which were for restitution in kind and 82,000 for financial compensation, but resolved only 2 percent of all requests. Most claimants received no reply, although local authorities were supposed to respond within sixty days. By 2002, it

[40] "Ministrul justiţiei sugerează judecătorilor să ţină cu chiriaşii," *Evenimentul Zilei* (3 April 2001).

[41] Ioana Câmpean and Mirela Luca, "Iliescu şi Năstase, de aceeaşi parte a baricadei în privinţa securiştilor şi caselor naţionalizate," *Ziarul Financiar* (4 December 2002).

[42] "Cel mai mare miting al opoziţiei extraparlamentare din acest an," *Cotidianul* (16 September 2002).

[43] "Foştii proprietari fac miting de ziua crucii," *Evenimentul Zilei* (5 August 2002).

was estimated that the Bucharest bureau needed another forty years to resolve all outstanding claims. A year later, the bureau had accepted 50,000 claims for financial compensation, but it had resolved only 3,475 petitions.[44] The accepted claims represented only a fraction of all possible claims, as many initial owners had died, emigrated, or simply renounced to fight for their rights.

The opposition criticized the slow pace of resolving restitution requests and charged that the government was refusing to return properties used by organizations, state agencies, and private firms.[45] In 2004, President Iliescu suggested that "few homeowners really need to resort to evacuation" and asked for rental contracts to be extended for another year in the name of "a civic sense of solidarity with these people with problems, most of them retired elderly unable to pay the rent."[46] The government announced plans to protect 1,200 old and poor tenants whose contracts expired in 2004 and asked local authorities to provide tenants with alternative dwellings within a year.[47] Overlooked by authorities, homeowners took to the streets of Bucharest, protesting against the slow pace of property restitution and claiming that only a fraction of all nationalized homes had been returned. Law 112/1995 banned tenants who bought nationalized homes from selling them to parties other than the initial owners for the first ten years after they acquired ownership rights, but tenants and prospective buyers drafted ante-contracts that allowed for earlier exchanges, with the deed being transferred at the end of the ten years.[48]

After the 2004 elections, the ruling Justice and Truth Alliance promised to speed up restitution, replace financial compensation with voucher and share offerings, and assume responsibility before parliament for restitution. Soon afterward, President Traian Băsescu came under fire for buying a nationalized home, a decision that made his criticism of Iliescu sound disingenuous and delegitimized his crusade for strengthened rule of law.[49] After this setback, the government proposed Law 247/2005, which upheld restitution in kind, whenever possible, and set up the Property Fund to compensate initial owners whose property rights were recognized by the courts.[50] The Fund offers shares only to owners of abusively confiscated

44 Gabriela Adameşteanu, "Legile proprietăţii – principala acţiune politică a Alianţei," 22 (12 May 2005).
45 "Stenograma şedinţei Camerei Deputaţilor din 27 mai 2003," *Monitorul Oficial al României, partea II-a* (28 May 2003).
46 "Iliescu, iar de partea chiriaşilor," *Evenimentul Zilei* (19 December 2003).
47 Maria Manoliu, "Chiriaşii din casele naţionalizate trebuie să ceară în scris proprietarilor prelungirea contractelor cu încă cinci ani," *Adevărul* (13 March 2004).
48 An ante-contract is a specific legal device in Romania applied to the sale of property and has prospective effect.
49 Oana Stancu, "Băsescu şi-a luat ilegal casă de la Primărie," *Jurnalul Naţional* (13 February 2005).
50 "Legea nr.247 din 19 iulie 2005 privind reforma în domeniile proprietăţii şi justiţiei, precum şi unele măsuri adiacente," *Monitorul Oficial al României, partea I* (27 October 2005).

property who had received no just compensation for their loss and whose property could not be returned in kind (because it was destroyed or sold). Although bitterly condemning Social Democrat corruption and self-interest, the new government did not annul the Law 112/1995 provisions allowing tenants to acquire nationalized homes. To the chagrin of initial owners and the satisfaction of many post-communist luminaries, Law 247/2005 recognized all those transactions as legally valid.[51] Since its creation, the Fund has been affected by public scandal and mismanagement, being contested by the owners, who must wait between ten and thirty-one months to have their ownership right recognized by four different governmental agencies before the Fund can disburse compensation. Given these lengthy procedures, the Fund has been in no position to compensate anyone to date.[52]

THE ORTHODOX-GREEK CATHOLIC PROPERTY CONFLICT

Decree Law 126/1990, which officially recognized the Greek Catholic Church, created a committee of state and church representatives to oversee the return of Greek Catholic Church assets in state hands at the time.[53] A different committee of Greek Catholic and Orthodox representatives had to discuss the possible return of former Greek Catholic churches used or owned by the Orthodox Church, not without taking into account "the wishes of the faithful in communities with such churches."[54] That was an important caveat, as decades of underground existence had drastically reduced the Greek Catholic Church membership, from a majority church in the province of Transylvania during pre-communist times to a religious denomination that barely represented 1 percent of Romania's population (191,000) in 2002, the year of the first post-communist national census.[55] In addition, the state pledged to subsidize construction in localities with an insufficient number of worship places.

[51] Cited in Damiana Oţoiu, "La (re)construction de la propriete privee en Roumanie post-communiste. 'Anciens' vs. 'nouveaux' proprietaires?," paper delivered at the At the Frontier of Land Issues: Social Embeddedness of Rights and Public Policy international workshop, 17–19 May 2006, Montpellier, France, p. 6, available at: http://www.mpl.ird.fr/colloque_foncier/Communications/PDF/Otoiu.pdf (accessed on 26 July 2011).

[52] "APDAS: Foştii proprietari sunt neîncrezători în corectitudinea evaluării imobilelor," *Ziarul Financiar* (3 October 2006); Roxana Pricop, "Fondul Proprietatea vede profit la jumătate, dar creşte salariile," *Ziarul Financiar* (29 March 2009); and Dan Straut, "Fondul Proprietatea: raiul speculatorilor, iadul proprietarilor," *Adevărul* (29 August 2010).

[53] This section draws on Stan and Turcescu, *Religion and Politics in Post-Communist Romania*, and Lavinia Stan and Lucian Turcescu, ""The Romanian Orthodox Church and Post-Communist Democratization," *Europe-Asia Studies*, 52(2000): 1467–1488.

[54] "Decret-Lege 126 din 24 aprilie 1990," *Monitorul Oficial al României, partea I* (25 April 1990). Several months earlier, Decree Law 9 annulled the 1948 decision to dismantle the Greek Catholic Church. "Decret-Lege 9 din 31 decembrie 1989," *Monitorul Oficial al României, partea I* (31 December 1989).

[55] Centrul de Resurse pentru Diversitate Etnoculturală, *Structura etno-demografică a României*, (2002), available at: http://www.edrc.ro/recensamant.jsp (accessed on 25 November 2011).

The 1990 decree thus separated the return of ecclesiastical property from the return of all other assets. For the government, the two restitution processes (from the state and from the Orthodox Church to the Greek Catholic Church) had two different solutions: the settlement agreed to by the state in its relationship to the Greek Catholics was not binding for the Orthodox, and church restitution was a strictly religious problem that had to be solved by religious actors as a result of religious dialogue. Church restitution was not legislated because post-communist authorities believed they were breaking up with communist practice and upholding separation of church and state. The centrality of Orthodoxy for Romanian national identity and the Orthodox Church's privileged position in the post-1989 ideological void further persuaded authorities not to participate in the property claims settlement. Politically, the position benefited the rulers of the day, who could blame lack of progress on church leaders and ignore their own responsibility for the conflict. Morally, state noninterference in a conflict heavily skewed in favor of the majority church was untenable.

The government prescribed church dialogue not in view of blocking the property restitution process, as it had no indication of how the interchurch dialogue will unfold, but in the desire to exonerate itself of responsibility for settling a dispute whose resolution could make it unpopular. If it sided with the Greek Catholics, it alienated the Orthodox, which accounted for as much as 87 percent of the population. If it sided with the Orthodox, it alienated foreign governments critical of Romania's treatment of its minorities. The government also saw restitution of Greek Catholic property as part of a larger transitional justice drive it wished to stall, because it directly affected its interests. Besides the Greek Catholics, political prisoners, anticommunist dissidents, peasants, intellectuals, and other civil society groups demanded redress for communist injustices, but revisiting the past would have exposed the new rulers' involvement in communist human rights abuses.

To fend off these demands, the government claimed that the new Romanian state was not the successor of its communist predecessor and, as such, was not compelled to redress the latter's injustices, but could do so selectively, if it wished to show benevolence. The country needed consensus, the government argued, as though solving restitution claims would divide the country and leaving them unaddressed would not. It is a matter of contention whether the government really believed in these arguments or was simply intimidated by the Orthodox Church, which denounced parliament's interference in religious affairs and decried Romania's inability to separate church from state as guaranteed by the 1991 Constitution. State non-interference gave the upper hand to the Orthodox, who had access to and the property right over the churches, and left the Greek Catholics with practically no means of appeal. Whenever the Greek Catholics insisted on the urgency of being allowed to organize mass inside their former churches rather than on the street, in public parks, or in ad hoc worship places, state representatives prescribed more dialogue, although concrete results were never in sight.

Post-communist authorities returned some Greek Catholic property kept in the state's hands, but the Supreme Court of Justice Decision 901/1996 and the Constitutional Court Decision 23/1993 recognized the mixed church commission as the only entity entitled to decide the fate of the worship places confiscated by the communists and church dialogue as a binding extrajudicial procedure to settle church restitution.[56] The Orthodox Church mounted resistance and used every conceivable argument to delay the loss of property on its part. By 1997, 160 churches had been returned to the Greek Catholic Church, and alternate masses were organized in thirty other churches, mostly located in the Banat region.[57] Deprived of the right to approach the courts, in 2001 the Greek Catholics appealed to the EU for the return of confiscated property as a precondition for Romania's accession. When Prime Minister Năstase suggested that the government could legislate restitution, the State Secretary for Religious Affairs retorted that the problem was already solved, as most Greek Catholics have remained Orthodox and refused to convert back to Catholicism, 160 churches had been returned, and the restitution of the remaining Greek Catholic churches would block Orthodox faithful "from exercising their own freedom of religion."[58] When asked to convince the government not to limit restitution of Greek Catholic property, President Iliescu replied that justice must be done to the extent that it does not lead to other injustices and reiterated the view that the state could not and should not interfere in the religious conflict.[59]

The property restitution conflict was fueled by the state-led property transfer of Orthodox churches to the Greek Catholic Church in 1700, the Orthodox understanding of church ownership, and the different principles that, according to the two denominations, should guide property restitution. First, the churches have had different readings of key historical events. Greek Catholic restitution claims refer to the 1948 communist legislation that transferred their property to the Orthodox Church and disbanded the Greek Catholic Church. The Greek Catholics have seen the 1948 transfer as an unlawful infringement of basic human rights, but the Orthodox supported the Greek Catholics' return to the church to which their ancestors once belonged as long-overdue reparation of a grave historical injustice.

[56] Curtea Constituţională, "Decizia nr. 23 din 27 aprilie 1993 privind obiectul Dosarului 7967/1992 al Judecătoriei Cluj Napoca," *Monitorul Oficial al României* (11 April 1995). The decision sided with the Orthodox against the Greek Catholics in the case of the Transfiguration Cathedral (Catedrala Schimbarea la Faţă) of Cluj-Napoca.

[57] According to Ştefan Ioniţă of the State Secretariat for Religious Denominations, quoted in *Monitorul Oficial al României, partea II-a* (4 November 1997).

[58] Franz Hoppenbrouwers, "The Greek Catholic Church in Romania," *Journal of Eastern Christian Studies*, 58 (2006): 136.

[59] "Retrocedarea nu trebuie să sacrifice instituţiile de cultură," *Monitorul* (17 June 2002).

The Greek Catholic Church was constituted in 1700, when the Hapsburg regime promised equal status with the Catholic and Protestant clergy to local Orthodox clergy who accepted Catholic dogma and papal authority. The conversion was accompanied by state-enforced transfer of Orthodox property to the new church. While the Orthodox saw Greek Catholicism as the result of political pressure, the Greek Catholics argued that the Transylvanian Orthodox Romanians freely accepted Catholic dogma and refused to acknowledge that the Orthodox were entitled to an apology for their conversion in 1700 or to compensation for the property they lost at the time. As the Orthodox have refused to reexamine the 1948 takeover, the Greek Catholics have refused to reassess the 1700 events, although historical claims are not more legitimate just because they are presented by larger denominations or because they are more recent.

Second, the two churches uphold different understandings of ownership. The Greek Catholics regard their church-related assets as the property of the church as an institution, thus allowing church leaders to determine the use of the property. By contrast, the Orthodox parish – not the Orthodox Patriarch or the Holy Synod – is the owner of the local church, parish house, and cemetery. Thus, only the local Orthodox parishes are entitled, from a legal and religious viewpoint, to decide whether Transylvanian churches could be returned to the Greek Catholics. This position has left the Greek Catholics at the mercy of Orthodox priests who resent them for breaking away from the local parish and of faithful eager to avoid losing the church and thus organizing mass outside.

Third, the two churches have argued that strikingly different principles should drive the restitution process. For the Greek Catholics, restitution was called by Romania's desire to establish democracy. Successful democratization meant respect for fundamental human rights, including the right to own property. By allowing the restitution of Greek Catholic property, the Romanian state and the Orthodox Church would signal their desire to break with the communist past, uphold the rule of law, and guarantee freedom of religion that, in the Greek Catholic case, meant little if parishes were deprived of their right to property restitution. As such, only full restitution of all assets confiscated in 1948 could prove that Romania was a genuine democracy. The Orthodox response was two-pronged. First, they argued that constitutional guarantees of the right to own property protected not only the Greek Catholics, but also the Orthodox Church, which had lost property in 1700 under circumstances that were as unlawful and undemocratic as the 1948 takeover. Redressing past injustice meant revisiting both 1948 and 1700. Second, they underscored that in villages where Greek Catholics were few, restitution would unfairly deprive the Orthodox majority of the only local church by transferring it to the smaller Greek Catholic parish. The relative strength of the two parishes had to be factored in when deciding the transfer, as at least in some localities it was wiser for the Orthodox to use the village church and for the Greek Catholics to build another place of worship. The problem was that not even in localities where they represented a majority did the Greek Catholic receive their former church.

In 2002, a Greek Catholic memorandum asked the Romanian government for an end to the discrimination against their religious group, the restitution of Greek Catholic property confiscated in 1948, and the right to approach the courts, as negotiations with the Orthodox Church had proved inefficient. The document demanded an end to the illegal demolishing and dismantling of their former churches by Orthodox congregations, legal protection for Greek Catholic churches listed as historical monuments, and the unconditional restitution of all Greek Catholic goods nationalized by the state (land and forests). The appeal failed to convince the government to replace interchurch dialogue with a legislative solution to the restitution conflict. The Orthodox Church rejected the memorandum and its demands for full restitution. By that time the Greek Catholic property restitution was no longer a strictly domestic case, because the European Court of Human Rights had accepted to hear cases lodged by Greek Catholic parishes.

EUROPEAN COURT OF HUMAN RIGHTS CASES INVOLVING ROMANIAN OWNERS

In 1994, soon after President Iliescu called on the prosecutor general to overturn definitive and irrevocable court decisions that recognized initial homeowners' rights to their property, Romanians approached the European Court of Human Rights, claiming that the decision of the Romanian Supreme Court of Justice that denied lower courts the competency to hear property restitution cases contradicted the right of access to justice, protected by Article 21 of the Romanian constitution and Article 3 of the Civil Code, and the right to fair trial, stipulated by Article 6.1 of the Human Rights Convention. Homeowners also insisted that Laws 112/1995 and 10/2001 contradicted the Romanian Civil Code. Romanian politicians claimed that, by seeking justice in Strasbourg, the owners exposed the country to the criticism of the international community during EU accession negotiations, which could be threatened as a result. In reply, the owners reiterated their resolve to fight for their property and criticized the courts for dragging out property restitution cases for years and the political class for its "lack of resolve to adopt just legislation."[60]

In the debate that ensued, the public and the press focused primarily on *recurs în anulare*. Until 1996, obedient prosecutors honored President Iliescu's demands to annul hundreds of court decisions without explanation. The Democratic Convention claimed that it appointed to the Supreme Court judges more sympathetic to owners

[60] "Un million de dolari despăgubiri," *Evenimentul Zilei* (6 January 2003).

and recalled that judges sided with the owners in almost 80 percent of all restitution cases lodged after 1998, when the lower courts were allowed to hear property restitution cases. Owners were skeptical of the Convention's political will to solve the problem because the prosecutor general could still initiate *recurs în anulare*, and a number of politicians, judges, prosecutors, and lawyers representing the Democratic Convention and other political formations had bought nationalized homes in virtue of Law 112/1995. This fact, they claimed, explained the judiciary's ambivalence on the issue. Teodoru supported the owners' decision to approach the European Court, because she believed that the slow pace of restitution was simply unacceptable. Even when the owners won their homes in court, tenants refused to vacate them, and the police was unwilling to enforce court orders. By 2004, only 5 percent of all abusively nationalized homes had returned to their initial owners, the rest being bought by tenants, mostly drawn from among the post-communist elite.[61]

Cases involving homes nationalized by Romanian communists were lodged with the European Court starting in 1995. Four years later, the European Court heard the first such case, and in 2001 awarded owner Dan Brumărescu compensation to the tune of US$198,000. The case gave Romanian owners hope, and encouraged them to petition the European Court in ever greater numbers. In the vast majority of the fifty-eight cases it heard from 2002 to 2004, the European Court ruled against the Romanian state and the *recursuri în anulare* handed down on President Iliescu's command. The European Court recognized that the Romanian Supreme Court infringed the claimants' rights to a fair trial by overturning definitive courts decisions and that the lower courts denied citizens access to justice by refusing to hear restitution cases. In most cases, the Romanian state was asked to return the property if wishing to avoid paying compensation that far exceeded the amount the tenants paid to gain ownership of the nationalized property. Over the same period, the European Court ordered the Romanian government to pay damages totaling 4.6 million Euros.[62]

Romania was subject to penalties if it delayed payment of the compensation established by the European Court, but the Social Democrat government was in no rush to comply with the verdicts. It agreed to restitution in kind only in the case of a building that housed a National Art Museum collection for which compensation reached US$900,000, a considerable sum for the cash-poor state. By not returning the homes to their owners before the three-month deadline, the government appeared to opt for financial compensation. Nevertheless, the initial owners

[61] "Demnitari abili şi-au procurat case naţionalizate în ultimii ani," *Evenimentul Zilei* (22 February 2003), and "Statul roman nu respectă întotdeauna hotărârile CEDO," *Evenimentul Zilei* (30 April 2003).

[62] Stan, "The Roof over Our Heads," p. 201.

received no penny, although some of them paid taxes for returned buildings they could not enter and use. A year after the European Court gave him satisfaction, Brumărescu was unable to use his former home because the Bucharest mayor's office had sold part of it, and Romanian authorities regarded the transaction as valid legally. To add insult to injury, in 2002 the Năstase cabinet announced plans to incorporate compensations ordered by the European Court into the compensations provided by Law 10/2001 and to cover all of them by granting initial owners small installments over the 2005–2015 period.[63]

In 2010, the European Court launched a pilot-judgment procedure in response to Romania's lack of progress in resolving the property restitution issue and the 1,500 nearly identical cases that Romanian owners had lodged with the Court.[64] The pilot-judgment procedure signaled that the European Court judges had identified structural legal problems that gave rise to repeated violations by Romania of the European Convention of Human Rights. In October 2010, the European Court further decided to adjourn examining cases lodged by Romanian owners for the following eighteen months, pending adoption by Bucharest of measures streamlining and simplifying property restitution procedures and providing adequate redress to all those affected by the reparation legislation. The procrastination has worked against the individual homeowners, many of whom are old persons lacking the financial means to continue the legal fight. At the same time, noncompliance on the part of the government could lead to Romania's exclusion from the Council of Europe, a prospect that the government seems keen to avoid. By late 2010, however, only 4,000 of the 63,000 property return claims lodged with the National Agency for Property Restitution, the central governmental agency mandated to recognize restitution demands, had been solved.[65]

In 2009, shortly before introducing the pilot-judgment procedure, the European Court also heard the Sâmbăta (Bihor County) and St. Vasile (Bucharest) Greek Catholic parishes, which sought the return of their churches and recognition of the fact that their constitutional right to approach the Romanian courts had been infringed for so many years. To preempt defeat in the European Court, the government asked parliament to permit the Greek Catholics to approach the courts.

[63] Palade, "Despăgubirile pentru casele naţionalizate, amânate."

[64] European Court of Human Rights, *Press Release: In a Pilot Judgment, the Court Adjourns the Cases Concerning Properties Nationalised during the Communist Era in Romania Pending General Measures at National Level* (12 October 2010), available at: http://www.codex-online.com/codex/contents.nsf/WPrintArticles/D89852AF742DB305C22577BB0061B0D6/$file/Chamber_judgment_Maria_Atanasiu_and_Others_v__Romania_12_10_2010.pdf (accessed on 28 March 2011), and Andrei Udişteanu, "Judecătorul român la CEDO: În multe cazuri, Curtea a constatat nefuncţionalitatea Fondului Proprietatea," *Evenimentul zilei* (14 October 2010).

[65] P. Ciocoiu, "European Court Corners Romania on Property Restitution," SETimes.com (20 October 2010).

In 2008, the Constitutional Court recognized the Greek Catholics' right to go to court, upheld by the constitution but unlawfully infringed by the government and the mixed church commission[66] After this ruling, and with an eye to the European Court of Human Rights decisions in the cases mentioned earlier, no Romanian court has declined to hear restitution cases related to Greek Catholic ecclesiastical property. In July 2009 and April 2010 the European Court recognized the right of the two Greek Catholic parishes to receive their churches and criticized the Romanian courts for denying a fair hearing to the minority church.[67]

CONCLUSION

As other Eastern European post-communist states, Romania faced claims of ownership from a variety of individuals and groups wronged by the communist regime. Its choices regarding property restitution were choices about its national culture, as they emphasized national homogeneity and discriminated against religious minorities, by "recognizing and sanctioning the rights of one set of victims while denying other victims theirs."[68] Comparable to other settings, the political voice victims were able to mount determined whether the state admitted responsibility and guilt for historical injustices that took the form of confiscation of property.[69] Unexpectedly, former perpetrators who benefited from wrongful communist policies – the privileged tenants living in confiscated dwellings and the Orthodox parishes using Greek Catholic places of worship – claimed victim status for themselves and successfully counteracted the demands of initial owners, those in whose property the contested houses and churches had been at the time of the confiscation. By recognizing the tenants (presented as hardworking workers and peasants) and the Orthodox Church as being more deserving to protection than the initial homeowners (assimilated to landowners and industrialists) and the Greek Catholic Church, Romanian governments favored the majority (the people and the Orthodox) over the minority (the better off and the Greek Catholics). Besides this specific understanding of the nation, the personal interests of a political elite with strong communist roots and the

66 Curtea Constituţională, "Decizia nr. 1201 din 11 noiembrie 2008 privind excepţia de neconstituţionalitate a dispoziţiilor art.3 din Decretul-lege nr.126/1990 privind unele măsuri referitoare la Biserica Română Unită cu Roma (greco-catolică), astfel cum au fost modificate prin Ordonanţa Guvernului nr.64/2004, aprobată cu modificări şi completări prin Legea nr.182/2005," *Monitorul Oficial al României* (23 December 2008).

67 European Court of Human Rights, *Affaire Paroisse Greco-Catholique Sfantul Vasile Polona c. Roumanie* (7 July 2009), and *Affaire Paroisse Greco-Catholique Sambata Bihor c. Roumanie*, Strasbourg (12 April 2010).

68 Elazar Barkan, *The Guilt of Nations. Restitution and Negotiating Historical Injustices* (Baltimore: The Johns Hopkins University Press, 2000), xxvi.

69 Idem, xxix.

unwillingness of the many to hand over property to the few have caused the delay with which Romanian governments have answered property restitution demands.

The two property restitution cases presented here reveal that successive governments, constituted by both center-left and center-right political formations, have pursued self-serving strategies under the eyes of a weak judiciary unable to resist pressures from the executive. In the case of both dwellings and places of worship, the government had no hesitation to deny plaintiffs the fundamental human right to approach the courts. However, whereas in the case of dwellings parliament insisted on having the final say in solving the matter and on sidelining the courts, in the case of churches it refused to get involved and delegated all its authority to the mixed church commission in the hope of finding an extrajudicial solution to the conflict. Both strategies, although completely opposite, had the same results – prevarication and delay – that could not be curbed even after the European Court of Human Rights handed down final decisions related to the confiscated dwellings. The end results of this stubborn opposition to right past wrongs is that only a very tiny fraction of confiscated dwellings and Greek Catholic churches have returned to their rightful owners, and very few initial owners received financial compensation for their loss. In the case of property restitution at least, justice delayed has amounted to justice denied.

7

Compensation and Rehabilitation

A couple of transitional justice methods representing two of the most pressing demands put forth by communist-era victims in Romania, and Eastern Europe more generally, are the legal rehabilitation and financial compensation of former political prisoners. To mitigate the suffering they endured in prisons, psychiatric wards, labor camps, forced domicile, deportation centers, or secret surveillance programs, former victims have demanded reparation packages that recognize the injustices they faced and cover the cost of their medical treatments, loss of job, and inability to pursue education. Under communism, the imprisonment regime was particularly harsh. During the rule of Stalinist leader Gheorghe Gheorghiu-Dej (1944–1965), political prisoners were badly beaten, forced to work and live in inhumane conditions, prohibited to lie down during the day, regularly transferred from one prison to another, "so as to prevent any type of contact among the detainees, make them lose contact with the outside world, or for administrative reasons [like the] need of working force in certain labor camps,"[1] and more generally subjected to extermination practices such as torture and starvation. This brutality was carried over in the prison system after Nicolae Ceauşescu instituted his megalomaniac regime. True, the number of individuals who were imprisoned for their political opinions decreased significantly after 1965, as most political dissidents and opponents were confined to psychiatric wards or subjected to administrative sentences. But the few who spent time in prison in the 1970s and the 1980s were treated roughly. Priest Gheorghe Calciu-Dumitreasa singled out his imprisonment in 1978 as the harshest of all, although he had spent time in jail during the early decades of communist rule. Tales of similar brutality were narrated

[1] Dana Bichescu, Maggie Schauer, Evangelia Saleptsi, Adrian Neculau, Thomas Elbert, and Frank Neuner, "Long-term Consequences of Traumatic Experiences: An Assessment of Former Political Detainees in Romania," *Clinical Practice and Epidemiology in Mental Health*, 1(2005), available at: http://www.ncbi.nlm.nih.gov/pmc/articles/PMC1266057/ (accessed on 12 October 2011).

by writer Paul Goma, arrested in 1977 for drafting a public letter that called for respect for human rights in Romania. Probably the most poignant testimonials about lingering terror tactics in Ceauşescu's prisons have come from the victims of Tudor Stănică, a brutish officer who before 1989 was one of the most feared criminal investigators working for the Bucharest Militia, nicknamed the Butcher of Rahova. (Rahova was the street where the Militia headquarters, including their feared dungeons, were located.) Stănică gained notoriety for savagely beating the inmates on the head, face, and groin and subjecting them to torture and humiliation (see Chapters 1 and 2).[2]

Rehabilitation has been advocated as a way for Eastern European states to recognize symbolically that the politically motivated convictions handed down by the communist courts infringed basic human rights and the rule of law and to help former political prisoners avoid facing some very practical difficulties after their release from prison. Indeed, until 1989 political prisoners were still viewed as criminals even after their release and therefore were unable to fully reintegrate into society. Their un-expunged criminal record meant that even an offense as a driver could turn them into recidivists and send them to prison once again.[3] After their release, political prisoners had to promise not to disclose the state's investigation methods or prison conditions to anyone, not even their close relatives. They were ostracized by former friends and family members who were afraid to associate with them and were discriminated by the party-state by not being allowed to work in jobs for which they were qualified and by being prohibited from performing public functions because of their past criminal record. The political police placed many of them under constant surveillance, because it was thought that they could engage in conspiracy against the state and the regime both because of their anticommunist beliefs and in revenge for the hardship they endured. Sometimes the Securitate forced them into accepting recruitment as secret informers and signing pledges of cooperation. According to data obtained in 1993 by Senator Constantin Ticu Dumitrescu, between 1948 and 1989 some 2,753 of the 507,003 Securitate informers were former political prisoners.[4] The final Report of the Tismaneanu Commission mentioned a total of 681,000 political prisoners: 600,000 for 1948–1964 and 81,000 for 1945–1948 and 1965–1989

[2] For repression techniques, see Marius Oprea, "The Securitate Legacy – Terror in Romania," in *European Public Hearing on Crimes Committed by Totalitarian Regimes. Crimes Committed by Totalitarian Regimes: Reports and Proceedings of the 8 April European Public Hearing on Crimes Committed by Totalitarian Regimes*, ed. Peter Jambrek (Ljubljana: Slovenian Presidency of the Council of the European Union, 2008), 105–109.

[3] Former political prisoner Josef Stejskal, cited in Klára Pinerová, *The Fate of Czechoslovak Political Prisoners after Release* (25 August 2011), available at: http://www.politicalprisoners.eu/the-fate-of-czechoslovak-political-prisoners-after-release.html (accessed on 12 October 2011).

[4] Lavinia Stan, "Moral Cleansing Romanian Style," *Problems of Post-Communism*, 49(2002): 55.

(see Chapters 1 and 5).[5] Taken together, these numbers suggest that extremely few political prisoners agreed to serve as informers (0.4 percent), and they accounted for only a very small fraction of all communist-era secret informers (0.5 percent).

Most post-communist countries offered reparations and rehabilitation in the early 1990s, both because they wanted to reward the group of victims who had suffered the most under the previous regime and because these victims were already old and frail and needed immediate assistance. Czechoslovakia and Bulgaria were the first to erase the criminal record of former political prisoners through Act 119/1990 on Legal Rehabilitation, Law on Political and Civil Rehabilitation of Oppressed Persons of 15 June 1991, and Law 167/1990 on Amnesty and Restoration of Confiscated Property and Implementing Regulations. The Bulgarian laws amnestied all those convicted on political grounds under communism, ordered the return of their confiscated property, and offered financial reparation packages for past suffering. Also in 1990, after the collapse of the communist regime in the satellite countries of Eastern Europe but before the disintegration of the Soviet Union, Moscow annulled all politically motivated court orders of 1948–1990. Law 119 on Rehabilitation by Court declared null and void the court decisions that punished people who had offended against communist laws, while Law 87 rehabilitated individuals who had been dismissed from their jobs by the communist authorities.[6] Law on the Rehabilitation of Victims of Political Repression of 1991 recognized that during Soviet times "millions of people became victims of the arbitrary actions of the totalitarian state and were subjected to repressive measures because of their political and religious convictions."[7] It rehabilitated individuals who, for political reasons, had been convicted of a state crime, subjected to criminal repression, exile, deportation, or forced labor, committed to psychiatric institutions, or found guilty of anti-Soviet propaganda, maligning the Soviet state through rumors, or performing religious rites. However, those convicted of "betraying the homeland" or of committing war crimes and crimes against order were not rehabilitated. Rehabilitated victims received indemnity, priority in obtaining passes for sanatorium-health resort treatment, free medical treatment in state-owned clinics and hospitals, discounted medication, free travel on urban passenger transportation systems, priority in installing a telephone line (which at the time were strictly controlled by the government), and preferential provision of food

5 Comisia Prezidenţială pentru Analiza Dictaturii Comuniste din România, *Raport Final* (Bucharest, 2006), available at: http://www.presidency.ro/static/ordine/RAPORT_FINAL_CPADCR.pdf (accessed on 24 August 2011).

6 Patricia Goletz, "The Transformation Process and Current Problems of the National Memory Institute of Slovakia (Bratislava)," *Phantasma* 19(2010), available at: http://lett.ubbcluj.ro/~phantasma/caiete/caiete/caiete19/29.html (accessed on 4 October 2011).

7 Neil Kritz, ed., *Transitional Justice: How Emerging Democracies Reckon with Former Regimes* (Washington, DC: US Institute for Peace, 1995), vol. 3, p. 797.

and consumer goods. By 2001, Russia rehabilitated as many as 4.5 million political prisoners, but former victims believed that the program sought "to end discussion of the past, to pacify the victims by throwing them a few extra rubles and free bus tickets, and to avoid any deeper examination of the causes of Stalinism or of its legacy."[8] As to prove these accusations, the limited transitional justice program that the Russian Federation pursued after 1991 has been systematically blocked by the country's post-communist authorities.[9]

The German First Act for Rectification of SED Injustice of 1992 annulled politically based court verdicts and verdicts that imposed legal sanctions grossly disproportionate to the offense. The annulment also benefited victims committed to psychiatric wards or subjected to forced labor. Former victims were entitled to compensation equal to 300 German Marks (equivalent to some US$210) for each month of imprisonment.[10] Victims living in poverty were entitled to "support payments," those whose health was damaged in prison received pensions, and those who could not practice their profession were offered compensation for professional harm. The Hungarian Law 11/1992 Voiding Certain Convictions of 1963–1989 annulled communist-era convictions handed down for acts of conspiracy, insurrection, incitement, abuse of the right to associate with others, illegal border crossing, refusal to return to Hungary after traveling abroad, and crimes against people's freedom.

A series of laws progressively expanded the rehabilitation program in Albania. In 1991, the government rehabilitated former prisoners who had been sentenced under Articles 53, 55, and 57 of the communist Penal Code for "agitation and propaganda," illegal border crossing, or anti-government activity. The law returned confiscated property, compensated victims for damages suffered while in prison, and restored titles, honors, jobs, the right to seek higher education, and pensions, including time served in prison as working time. As part of this program, the government provided jobs in central and local government for former political prisoners and waived the university entrance exams for 2,500 former prisoners and exiles.[11] Two years later, Law 7516/1993 on the Innocence and Amnesty of Those Formerly Convicted and Politically Persecuted and Law 7748/1993 on Former Victims of Persecution offered victims of political persecution – but not former communist officials and secret agents – cash awards, retirement packages, and salary compensations proportional

8 Anne Applebaum, "The Gulag: Lest We Forget," *Hoover Digest* (30 January 2005), available at: http://www.hoover.org/publications/hoover-digest/article/6762 (accessed on 4 October 2011).

9 Lavinia Stan, ed., *Transitional Justice in Eastern Europe and the Former Soviet Union: Reckoning with the Communist Past* (London: Routledge, 2009), 222–246.

10 Kritz, ed., *Transitional* Justice, p. 724.

11 Human Rights Watch, *Human Rights Watch World Report* 1993 – *Albania* (1 January 1993), available at: http://www.unhcr.org/refworld/country,,HRW,,ALB,,467fca6d35,0.html (accessed on 4 October 2011).

to the length of the conviction and the highest salary for work in mines at the 1945 to 1990 levels. In Kazakstan, the Bill on Rehabilitation of the Victims of Political Repressions of 1993 provided similar benefits to victims of communist repression who were nationals of that former Soviet republic.[12]

Reparations took the form of monthly installments or lump sums. In Bulgaria, those who spent time in labor or prison camps received 1,500 Lev per month (equal to US$1,060), up to a total of 50,000 Lev, those deported or assigned forced domicile were entitled to 800 Lev per month up to 25,000 Lev, while students forced to abandon their studies were offered a total of 10,000 Lev. In the Czech Republic, former political prisoners who spent at least one year in prison received a lump sum of 120,000 Koruna (around US$6,660) and an additional 1,000 Koruna for each month of imprisonment. Their living relatives could qualify to receive half that sum. In Lithuania, lump sums of 20,000 Litas (equivalent to some US$8,000) were offered to the surviving relatives of the resistance members who died in the fight, in prison, or during interrogations.[13]

Post-communist Romania has offered reparations (*despăgubiri*) and rehabilitation (*anularea condamnărilor* or *dezincriminarea penală*) to political prisoners with considerable delay.[14] The two victim organizations that called for these forms of redress were the ICAR Foundation, which provides medical, psychological, legal, and social rehabilitation services to survivors of communist-era political persecution and gross human rights abuses, and the Association of Former Political Prisoners, which represents former political prisoners who were repressed until 1989 as "enemies of the people" (see Chapter 1). By contrast, almost no Romanian political party made reparations or rehabilitation an intrinsic part of its political platform, and none saw these transitional justice methods as a policy priority while they were part of the government. True, many former political prisoners joined the "historical" Christian Democrat and Liberal Parties, and in those positions they stressed the need for restoration programs that benefited former communist-era victims.

12 "Monument Erected in Memory of Azerbaijani Victims of Stalin Repression," *Trend* (2 June 2008), available at: http://en.trend.az/regions/casia/kazakhstan/1213254.html (accessed on 4 October 2011).

13 Curtea Constituţională, "Decizia nr. 1360 din 21 octombrie 2010 referitoare la excepţia de neconstituţionalitate a prevederilor art.5 alin.(1) lit.a) teza întâi din Legea nr.221/2009 privind condamnările cu caracter politic şi măsurile administrative asimilate acestora, pronunţate în perioada 6 martie 1945–22 decembrie 1989," *Monitorul Oficial al României, partea I* (15 November 2010).

14 The first to draft a rehabilitation bill was anticommunist opponent Cicerone Ioniţoiu, who after 1946 was interrogated and tortured by the Securitate, sentenced six times by the courts, and freed from prison in 1964. In 1977, he sent a draft bill to Ceauşescu, without receiving any response. In 1979, he obtained permission to emigrate after French President Giscard d'Estaing visited Romania and a street protest in Paris asked the Romanian authorities to allow twenty people to emigrate. See Romulus Rusan, ed., *Cei care au spus NU. Oponenţi şi dizidenţi în anii '70 şi '80* (Bucharest: Fundaţia Academia Civică, 2005).

However, these personal concerns never translated into concerted political action or top policy priorities for these parties, even when they formed the government in 1996–2000 and 2004–2008.

Two general patterns have characterized the Romanian reparations program. First, compensation was offered as early as 1990, two full decades before rehabilitation was adopted in 2009. The Social Democrats' refusal to acknowledge communist crimes explains why in 1990–1996 and 2000–2004 their government blocked efforts to come to terms with the past. Small indemnities were granted in 1990 because at the time the victims of the 1989 revolution were also compensated for their suffering. Acknowledging one set of victims (the so-called revolutionaries) while ignoring another set (communist-era political prisoners) might have led to public outcry at a time of high political volatility. Further explaining the different timing of the two transitional justice policies is the fact that rehabilitation was introduced on the parliamentary agenda with considerable delay in 1997, shortly after the historical parties won the elections, but almost a decade after the collapse of the communist regime. By then, transitional justice had lost its urgency for the entire political establishment, and even the ruling Democratic Convention believed that the alternation in power, the first since Romania plunged into dictatorship during World War II, represented the best form of redress for past injustice that eclipsed other methods of working through the communist past and rendered many of them superfluous (see Chapter 4). Another reason is grounded in semantics, and the different understandings of the term "rehabilitation" among victims and civil society representatives, which impede them to reach common ground and devise unified advocacy platforms. While some understand rehabilitation as the restoration of rights, authority, and abilities to the former political prisoner, others see it as a process that involves the legal annulment of the crime of the accused and insist that the proper term that should be used in connection to communist-era victims is "legal de-incrimination" (*dezincriminare penală*), which acknowledges that those persons were abusively condemned by the communist regime for invented crimes.[15]

Second, the compensation packages offered in 1990 were meager by Eastern European standards and less generous compared to the benefits received by the participants in the 1989 revolution. Romanian indemnities were far below the German, Lithuanian and even Bulgarian levels, although those states, like Romania, underwent a painful transformation program that placed considerable burdens on their cash-strapped governments. Lack of financial resources afflicted both Romania and Bulgaria, but the latter was far more generous toward its former political prisoners. However, these other Eastern European countries did not experience the clear elite reproduction that affected Romania in the early 1990s, when former communist

[15] Personal interview with historian Mircea Stănescu, Bucharest, 29 June 2011.

officials retained their political clout, and this is another reason for the discrepancy. As with other transitional justice demands, the Democratic Convention proved all talk, no action after it won the 1996 elections. Because of its lack of political will, the Convention failed to adopt the rehabilitation law and expanded the reparations program only by adding symbolic benefits, not the financial ones on which former prisoners insisted. The difference in the compensation levels awarded to communist-era political prisoners and those granted to the 1989 revolutionaries hinged on the benefits that the new post-communist leaders, drawn mainly from among former communist officials turned into important revolutionaries, could derive from the latter. Even more disconcerting is the wide gap between the rewards granted by the Romanian government to victims for their past suffering and the pensions offered to their former torturers. The average monthly pension of a former Securitate officer is seven times larger than the compensation received by a former political prisoner for each year of imprisonment.[16]

THE LEGISLATION ON COMPENSATION AND REHABILITATION

In 1990, Romania adopted, at the pressure of the Association of Former Political Prisoners, Decree-Law 118 on Some Rights for People Persecuted for Political Reasons during the Dictatorship Installed in Romania on 6 March 1945, which covered those who were displaced, deported, imprisoned, abused in psychiatric institutions, or confined to a particular place of residence by the communist courts or the Securitate, if these measures were taken as a means of political persecution. Most of the persons covered by that piece of legislation had suffered some form of ill treatment or torture at the hand of the dictatorial regime. The decree-law provided symbolic financial compensation for each year of imprisonment or displacement endured, free medical assistance and medication, free use of public transportation means, and income tax exemptions. The time spent in prison, labor camp, or obligatory residence was recognized as working time for pension purposes. Those who spent time in prison or psychiatric wards could count toward their state pension both that time period and the time they could not work because of some invalidity resulted from imprisonment. When calculating pension rights, each year of persecution counted as eighteen months. The persons who had been assigned forced domicile or had been deported could count that time period toward pension rights, if they had been unable to find work according to their professional qualifications. These

16 Marius Oprea, "About Ideologies, Institutions and Death," in *European Public Hearing on Crimes Committed by Totalitarian Regimes. Crimes Committed by Totalitarian Regimes: Reports and Proceedings of the 8 April European Public Hearing on Crimes Committed by Totalitarian Regimes*, ed. Peter Jambrek (Ljubljana: Slovenian Presidency of the Council of the European Union, 2008), 216.

rights extended to persons who could not work because the Securitate monitored them for some political reason. The victims' living relatives could claim small pension rights as successors. In addition, communist-era victims received a monthly indemnity of 200 Lei (some US$50) for each year of detention, internment, forced domicile, or deportation, free medical checkups and medicine from state-owned clinics and hospitals, and priority to rent state-owned dwellings. These benefits were not extended to former victims who were responsible for crimes against humanity or fascist activities as sympathizers of the interwar Iron Guard. Local commissions consisting of representatives of the Ministry of Labor and the Association of Former Political Prisoners decided which former victims could qualify for these rights. Their decisions could be appealed in the court of law within fifteen days after being communicated to the claimants.[17]

The decree-law was seen as proof that the Romanian state recognized the fact that human rights abuses were committed by the communist state from 1945 to 1989, an important point at a time when the country's new revolutionary leaders insisted that the communist regime was patriotic and lawful, and when they repeatedly harassed the budding pro-democratic opposition by encouraging the Valea Jiului miners to come to the capital to "defend" the new government against peaceful protesters. Several thousand communist-era victims received benefits under the decree-law, but the implementation of this legislative framework was hampered by lack of political will and cooperation on the part of the officials.[18] The decree-law also included one glaring omission because it did not compensate the descendants of the anti-communist fighters who had been punished the worst by communist authorities by being executed, an oversight that left the children of some of the best known communist-era opponents like Toma Arnăuţoiu outside the compensation scheme.[19] As post-communist Romania embarked on transforming its socialist economy by adopting liberalization and macro-stabilization reforms that led to hyperinflation and record prices for basic necessities, the monthly indemnities were soon rendered meaningless. In addition, the decree-law did not meet the former political prisoners' need for specialized medical services that addressed the consequences of their imprisonment. For this reason, the ICAR Foundation was set up shortly after the passing of the decree-law.

Until 1996, the ruling Social Democrats, drawn primarily from the ranks of the former Communist Party, saw this symbolic reparation as sufficient proof of their

[17] "Decretul-Lege 118 din 30 martie 1990 privind acordarea unor drepturi persoanelor persecutate din motive politice de dictatura instaurată cu începere de la 6 martie 1945, precum şi celor deportate în străinătate ori constituite în prizonieri," *Monitorul Oficial al României, partea I* (9 April 1990).

[18] Redress, *Romania Country Report* (May 2003), available at: http://www.redress.org/downloads/country-reports/Romania.pdf (accessed on 3 October 2011).

[19] Alina Mungiu-Pippidi, "Anticomunismul ca politică publică," *România Liberă* (4 August 2011).

goodwill to redress the communist past. While continuing to deny the criminal character of the communist regime and to underscore the merits of national communism, their government refused to raise compensation to more meaningful levels, expand the list of benefits, and adopt a rehabilitation law. It was only after the Christian Democrat and Liberal Parties formed the government in 1996 that parliament started to discuss legislation more advantageous to communist-era victims. However, the internal divisions of the ruling Democratic Convention meant that the government did not have the majority to adopt this new legislation promptly.

In 1999, one year before new elections were to be organized, Emergency Government Ordinance 214 bestowed the title of "fighter in the anticommunist resistance" on persons sentenced during communist times for political reasons such as "protesting against the dictatorship, the cult of personality, communist terror and abuse of power on the part of the communist rulers; promoting democracy and political pluralism; engaging in propaganda in order to oust the communist regime; manifesting resistance to the regime; observing human rights; and fighting [the communist regime's] ethnic, religious, linguistic, social, or political discrimination."[20] Political sentences included imprisonment, placement in a psychiatric ward, forced domicile, deportation, or exile. The title was not granted to Iron Guard members, many of whom had been arrested and imprisoned by the communist regime during the late 1940s and the 1950s. County commissions formed of representatives of the Association of Former Political Prisoners and the Ministries of Justice and Interior decided which persons qualified for the title. Those who did were entitled to the return of their abusively confiscated property, to receive a number of medals and decorations, and to give their names to streets, parks, and other public places, in addition to qualifying for the benefits granted by Decree-Law 118/1990. Law 568/2001 extended these benefits to persons who engaged in armed fighting against the regime during the 1945–1964 period or who were expelled by the communist regime from schools and universities on political grounds.[21] These new laws covered a relatively small number of additional cases.

While the 1999 governmental ordinance represented a decisive step toward redressing communist injustice, its consequences were generally minor, as it granted mostly symbolic benefits. In addition, its property restitution provisions did not mean

20 "Ordonanţă de urgenţă nr. 214/1999 privind acordarea calităţii de luptător în rezistenţa anticomunistă persoanelor condamnate pentru infracţiuni săvârşite din motive politice, precum şi persoanelor împotriva cărora au fost dispuse, din motive politice, măsuri administrative abuzive," *Monitorul Oficial al României, partea I* (30 December 1999).

21 "Legea 568 din 19 octombrie 2001 pentru aprobarea Ordonanţei de urgenţă a Guvernului nr. 214/1999 privind acordarea calităţii de luptător în rezistenţa anticomunistă persoanelor condamnate pentru infracţiuni săvârşite din motive politice, precum şi persoanelor împotriva cărora au fost dispuse, din motive politice, măsuri administrative abuzive," *Monitorul Oficial al României, partea I* (30 October 2001).

much, as by that time many dwellings could not be returned to their rightful owners because the state had sold them to the tenants by disregarding the property rights of the initial owners, and the cash-strapped government was unable to offer financial compensation in lieu of the original property (see Chapter 6). To add insult to the injury, the ordinance was applied differently across the country, generating a series of discrepancies between former victims who had similar cases but resided in different localities. In the Transylvanian county of Cluj, for example, former victims were reportedly unable to receive their rights promptly because the local commission in charge of bestowing the title of fighter in the anticommunist resistance unilaterally decided to reverify all applications after their initial vetting, a decision that unnecessarily postponed the granting of titles.[22]

By awarding honorary titles to former communist-era victims, Government Ordinance 214/1999 echoed Law 42 on Honoring Heroes-Martyrs and Compensating Their Descendants, Those Wounded and the Fighters for the Victory of the Romanian Revolution of 18 December 1990, which recognized as hero-martyrs (*eroi-martiri*) the persons who died in the December 1989 events while fighting against the communist authorities or for Romania's transformation into a democratic country; as fighters in the revolution (*luptători în revoluţie*), the persons who took to the streets during those days to protest against the Ceauşescu regime; and as participants in the revolution (*participanţi în revoluţie*), all other persons who participated in the December 1989 events.[23] The hero-martyr title, awarded posthumously, allowed the parents of the deceased (but not their children) to wear a distinctive honorific insignia and the surviving family to qualify for compensation to the tune of 60,000 Lei (equivalent to US$57,200). The fighters were entitled to receive lump sums of 40,000 Lei (around US$38,200). These victims or their relatives were entitled to reparations for their suffering in the form of monthly payments of up to 1.6 times the monthly average wage, together with assistance by specialized medical staff, priority to rent an apartment from the state, bank credits, free cemetery plot, free access to the clinics, hospitals, and sanatoriums of the Ministries of Health, Defense or Interior, free medicine, free public transportation, and tax exemptions. In their scope, diversity, and level, these benefits exceeded the compensations offered at the time to communist-era victims.

Although in April 1997 Christian Democrat Deputy Silviu Petrescu introduced a bill in parliament, the Democratic Convention was unable to satisfy the demands for rehabilitation of former political prisoners, choosing instead to continue the

[22] Ligia Popa, "Potrivit Avocatul Poporului, legile lacunare lovesc în dizidenţii clujeni," *Gazeta de Cluj* (4 February 2008).

[23] "Legea nr. 42 din 18 decembrie 1990 pentru cinstirea eroilor-martiri şi acordarea unor drepturi urmaşilor acestora, răniţilor, precum şi luptătorilor pentru victoria Revoluţiei din decembrie 1989," *Monitorul Oficial al României, partea I* (19 December 1990).

practice instituted by the National Salvation Front in 1991 and upheld by successive Social Democrat governments until 1996.[24] Throughout the 1990s rehabilitations were operated on an individual basis at the discretion of the prosecutor general, who could invoke the controversial *recurs în anulare* (appeal to the court of last resort), a procedure that allowed a political figure appointed by the executive to overturn definitive court orders (see also Chapter 6). The prosecutor general used the procedure not only to block the return of dwellings awarded by the courts to their initial owners as a result of definitive and irrevocable decisions, but also to challenge the legality of the criminal and administrative court verdicts handed down until 1989, which the former victims wanted to have annulled through rehabilitation. The other way to be rehabilitated was to convince the courts to reopen the case, but former victims did not use that time-consuming method because the reopening of the case placed additional financial burdens on them and they considered it unfair for the state not to recognize its past mistakes and grant rehabilitation automatically.[25] In 2000, in a widely publicized case, the prosecutor general asked the Supreme Court to rehabilitate sixteen political prisoners condemned to forced labor by the communist courts in 1951 through 1954 and to annul the jail sentences which had been handed down in those cases, although the evidence did not point to the high treason specified in the indictment. On 29 October 1954, the military courts sentenced fourteen persons for high treason to forced labor for periods ranging from ten years to lifetime and to the complete confiscation of their property. Among those sentenced was Arlette Coposu, the wife of Corneliu Coposu, leader of the Christian Democrat Peasant Party that in 1996 became the senior partner in the Democratic Convention government. Two other persons indicted in the same case received shorter prison sentences of up to four years.[26] The annulment was granted, but the procedure remained discretionary, denying the state's responsibility for acknowledging the fact that, before 1989, politically based convictions had infringed the rule of law and implying that some cases of communist injustice and some victims, in particular those related to influential post-communist politicians, were more deserving for redress than others.

This discretionary character was underscored by the cases of Mircea Răceanu and Ion-Mihai Pacepa, who both sought legal rehabilitation. While stationed at the Romanian Embassy in Washington, DC, from 1969 to 1979, Răceanu became an American secret agent who reportedly leaked no real secrets, but provided personal

[24] Legislative proposal 97 of 17 April 1997 was rejected by the Chamber of Deputies on 8 June 1998. Petrescu was a former political prisoner during communist times.

[25] George Rădulescu, "Marius Oprea: 'Suntem conduşi de circa 10.000 de ticăloşi'," *Adevărul* (21 January 2010).

[26] "Propunere de reabilitare a soţiei lui Corneliu Coposu şi a altor 15 deţinuţi politici," *Ziarul de Iaşi* (3 November 2000).

insight into the way in which the Ceauşescu regime infringed human rights and religious freedoms. The Romanian Securitate closed down on Răceanu, who was arrested on 31 January 1989. His situation was compounded by the decision of his step-father Gheorghe Răceanu, a long-term communist, to sign a protest letter against Ceauşescu that was broadcasted by Radio Free Europe/Radio Liberty on 11 March. In July, Răceanu was sentenced to death for invented ties to the Soviet Union, but two months later Ceauşescu commuted the sentence to imprisonment for twenty years, at the request of the American President George Bush. On 23 December, Răceanu was freed and soon afterward he was granted permission to emigrate to the United States.[27] Both in 1993, during the presidency of Iliescu, and in 1999, during the presidency of Constantinescu, Răceanu's sentence was upheld, on grounds that his 1989 release was illegal. Years after his rehabilitation in 2000, at the request of intellectuals who portrayed him as an "anticommunist fighter," Răceanu revealed that well-known post-communist luminaries had served as deep-cover Securitate agents. These included former Minister of Foreign Affairs Teodor Meleşcanu, Minister for Reform Mişu Negriţoiu, Ministers of Interior Ioan Mircea Pascu and Gheorghe Tinca, Ambassador to London Dan Ghibernea, Ambassador to Austria Traian Chebeleu, and President of the Romanian Bank for Development Bogdan Baltazar.[28]

After he fled to the United States in July 1978, Pacepa was the highest-ranking intelligence official to ever defect from the communist bloc. At the time, he was both the head of the Securitate's Foreign Intelligence Service and a personal advisor to Ceauşescu, who Pacepa accompanied on each foreign visit. Rewards of US$1 million were offered not only by Ceauşescu, but also by Palestinian leader Yasser Arafat and Libyan dictator Muammar Gaddafi for his death, but Pacepa managed to evade that fate and paint an unflattering portrait of the dictatorial couple in his best seller, *Red Horizons: The True Story of Nicolae and Elena Ceausescu's Crimes, Lifestyle and Corruption*.[29] In 1999, the Romanian Supreme Court canceled Pacepa's death sentence and ordered the return of his property, confiscated after his defection by the communist authorities. However, the Democratic Convention government refused to comply under pressure from members of the intelligence community who saw Pacepa as a traitor of national interests and responsible for thwarting many a promising career. His military rank (general) was restored to him in December 2004.[30]

[27] Mariana Bechir, "Mircea Răceanu, 'Grava acţiune de trădare'," *Adevărul* (14 March 2009).

[28] According to Liviu Avram, "Răceanu îşi lansează lista cu 'securişti acoperiţi'," *9AM News* (30 September 2005).

[29] Ion Mihai Pacepa, *Red Horizons. The True Story of Nicolae and Elena Ceausescu's Crimes, Lifestyle and Corruption* (Washington, DC: Regnery Gateway, 1990).

[30] Lucia Hossu-Longin, *Faţă în faţă cu generalul Ion Mihai Pacepa* (Bucharest: Humanitas, 2009).

During the next two electoral cycles, reparations and rehabilitation were not on the parliamentary agenda, first because the Social Democrat government of 2000–2004 undermined all efforts to work through the communist past and then because the Justice and Truth Alliance government of 2004–2008 was too divided to agree on any substantial policy agenda. By 2006, Romania's accession to the EU became the top government priority, overshadowing all transitional justice concerns. Neither the Parliamentary Assembly of the Council of Europe Resolution 1481 of 26 January 2006 on the Need for International Condemnation of Crimes of Totalitarian Communist Regimes nor the final report of the Tismăneanu Commission and President Traian Băsescu's official condemnation of communist crimes on 18 December 2006 convinced the Romanian parliament of the need to adopt rehabilitation and to expand the scope of reparations (see Chapter 5).[31] In 2006 and 2008, the Hungarian President Solyom Laszlo asked President Băsescu to support the rehabilitation law, which would have benefited many ethnic Hungarians living in Transylvania who had been sentenced for daring to support the 1956 Hungarian Revolution, but these private calls were left unanswered.[32]

Two decades after the collapse of the communist regime, when victims already lost the hope that Romania will ever follow the rest of the region to provide legal redress, the Romanian Parliament passed Law 221/2009 on the Politically Motivated Convictions and Administrative Measures Handed Down from 6 March 1945 to 22 December 1989. The brainchild of historian Marius Oprea, director of the Institute for the Investigation of Communist Crimes, former Senator Constantin Ticu Dumitrescu, head of the Association of Former Political Prisoners, and Minister of Justice Monica Macovei, the proposal was initiated in 2007, but encountered staunch opposition from the Social Democrat Party on grounds that the compensations would have totaled as much as 15 percent of the gross domestic product. In response, Oprea argued that the total was the equivalent of building only two kilometers of highway, suggesting thus the relatively low cost of the reparations program, but in fact his computations took into account only the material, but not the moral, damages that victims could possibly qualify for.[33] The law rehabilitated all persons sentenced for political reasons by communist courts to jail, forced labor,

[31] *Contribution to the UPR 2008 by ICAR Foundation and the Association of Former Political Prisoners – Romania* (2008), available at: http://lib.ohchr.org/HRBodies/UPR/Documents/Session2/RO/ICAR_ROM_UPR_S2_2008_FoundationandtheAssociationofFormerPoliticalPrisoners_uprsubmission.pdf (accessed on 3 October 2011).

[32] "Preşedintele Ungariei cere reabilitarea foştilor deţinuţi politici," *Agerpress* (24 October 2008).

[33] Alina Sabou, "Neaplicarea unei legi, la instanţele din Timişoara, aminteşte de tribunalele staliniste din anii '50," *Opinia Timişoarei* (10 March 2011), and *Letter from the Ministry of Finance, Cabinet of the Deputy Ministry to the Romanian Institute for Recent History* (14 September 2010), available at: http://www.irir.ro/files/pages/Raspuns%20Ministerul%20Finantelor.pdf (accessed on 26 November 2011).

or forced domicile on the basis of criminal code stipulations, communist laws, and administrative measures that condemned acts of dissidence and opposition, armed or unarmed. The law extended to persons who had already benefited from Decree-Law 118/1990 and Government Ordinance 214/1999. All abusive court sentences were annulled and erased from all records, a move that amounted to the full legal rehabilitation of those victims.

In addition, within three years of the law's adoption, politically persecuted persons, or their direct descendants, could apply to the Romanian state for compensation of moral damages for time spent in prison and for property lost in abusive confiscations that accompanied the court sentences to jail, forced labor, or forced domicile. Persons who had been demoted to an inferior army rank could also ask for the reversal of that decision. As in the case of previous legislation on rehabilitation, these advantages did not extend to "persons condemned for crimes against humanity and those who had promoted racist and xenophobic ideas and doctrines that encouraged hate or violence toward ethnic, racial or religious groups"[34] – that is, members of the Ion Antonescu regime and of the fascist Iron Guard. According to the law, convictions for crimes set forth in the communist criminal code were considered political in nature, if the person expressed opposition to the totalitarian regime or affiliation to democratic principles by protesting against the communist dictatorship, the communist ideology, or the abuse of power by those who held the reigns of the country; supported principles of democracy and political pluralism; participated in propaganda that was aimed to revert the social order to democracy; used weapons to eliminate the representatives of the communist regime by force; respected human rights and liberties; and eradicated communist discriminatory measures grounded in religion, political opinion, wealth, or social origin. The political nature of these convictions had to be assessed by the court, because in most cases the communist prosecutor's arraignment had carefully avoided any reference to the political opinions of the accused or the country's political situation. Most of the documents needed to establish the rights to compensation and rehabilitation were housed with the National Council for the Study of Securitate Archive, which was quickly overwhelmed by petitions coming from both the former victims who were seeking redress and the courts asked to recognize those rights. In 2009 through 2010, the council received 1,890 such requests from courts and 6,119 from victims.[35]

[34] "Legea 221 din 2 iunie 2009 privind condamnările cu character politic şi măsurile administrative asimilate acestora, pronunţate în perioada 6 martie 1945–22 decembrie 1989," *Monitorul Oficial al României, partea I* (11 June 2006).

[35] *Letter from the National Council for the Study of Securitate Archives to the Romanian Institute of Recent History* (3 September 2010), available at: http://www.irir.ro/files/pages/Raspuns%20CNSAS.pdf (accessed on 26 May 2011).

By March 2012, the total number of such requests reached 11,000.[36] Former political prisoners could start compiling the documentation by consulting the online archive of some 50,000 detention forms made available by the Institute for the Investigation of Communist Crimes and the Memory of Romanian Exile in Bucharest.[37]

According to Dumitrescu, as many as 1 million Romanians could have benefited from the provisions of Law 221/2009. These included 700,000 former political prisoners sentenced to prison terms in 136,000 different trials and 300,000 others condemned to forced workplace or forced residence.[38] However, only 17,000 of them were still alive by 2007, when parliament started to discuss the law.[39] Data released by the Ministry of Finance, responsible for disbursing the money to the victims, showed that by September 2010 there were 174 cases in which the courts handed down definitive decisions awarding compensations in virtue of Law 221/2009. The courts awarded compensation packages ranging between 1,200 Lei and 1 million Euros (the equivalent between US$354 and US$1.3 million), but the Ministry paid compensations totaling only 134,600 Lei (less than US$41,000).[40]

Rehabilitation was needed because former political prisoners had difficulty obtaining bank loans and travel visas as a result of their prison records. For the former prisoners, the law represented a "delayed victory" in the sense that it granted, albeit with considerable delay, "moral and legal reparation for all those victimized by the communist judiciary and repressive apparatus."[41] While recognizing that this piece of legislation was the first to provide meaningful reparations to communist-era victims for the suffering they endured, former political prisoners denounced its stipulations that called "old people to go to court to find justice" as "incredibly cynical."[42] That was because the law recognized as political in nature only the convictions expressly included among communist laws and criminal code provisions

[36] Germina Nagât and Andreea Pora, "Criteriul pentru numirea în Colegiul CNSAS: şira spinării," 22 (27 March 2012). I thank Cosmin Budeanca for drawing my attention to this interview.

[37] *Letter of the Institute for the Investigation of Communist Crimes and the Memory of Romanian Exile to the Romanian Institute of Recent History* (31 August 2010), available at: http://www.irir.ro/files/pages/Raspuns%20IICCMER.pdf (accessed on 26 November 2011).

[38] Liliana Năstase and Ionel Stoica, "Deţinuţii politici vor fi despăgubiţi, iar condamnările lor, şterse prin lege," *Adevărul* (24 August 2007).

[39] "17.000 de deţinuţi politici vor primi despăgubiri," StiriROL.ro (24 August 2007), available at: http://stiri.rol.ro/17–000-de-detinuti-politici-vor-primi-despagubiri-75185.html (accessed on 3 October 2011).

[40] *Letter from the Ministry of Finance, Cabinet of the Deputy Ministry to the Romanian Institute for Recent History.*

[41] Dumitru Leahu, cited in Rodica Perianu, "Victorie tardivă a foştilor condamnaţi politic," *Obiectiv Vocea Brăilei* (14 May 2009).

[42] Andrea Varga, cited in Andrei Luca Popescu, "Condamnaţii politic, reabilitaţi cu 20 de ani întârziere," *România Liberă* (13 May 2009).

that were listed in its Article 1.2 and asked the courts to demonstrate the political character of all other convictions.[43] The law thus obliged political prisoners who received nonpolitical sentences after 1964, when political dissidents and opponents were charged primarily with petty crimes, to petition the courts to have their rehabilitation rights recognized. Because after 1964 some of those guilty of political crimes were charged with endangering national security, there was no easy way to set them apart from those who had engaged in genuine cases of national treason, espionage, or fascist propaganda.

As the honorific titles mentioned earlier, reparations for political imprisonment during communist times came several years after similar benefits were offered to the victims of and participants in the December 1989 revolution. Law 341/2004 granted monthly compensation to the tune of 3,672 Lei (equivalent to US$1,180) for those disabled during the revolution and 2,200 Lei (US$680) for participants in those events or their surviving relatives, alongside other benefits, including support with medical equipment, housing, and public transportation, free access to public cemetery plots, and free access to public crèches and kindergartens for their children.[44] The beneficiaries of these reparation packages also included persons persecuted for their participation in the 1987 workers' strikes in Braşov, who were assigned forced residences, were relocated to other towns, or were deported. Notably, according to that piece of legislation no other group of communist-era victims qualified for that series of advantages, not even the miners who participated in the Valea Jiului protests of 1977, which were similar in nature to the Braşov strikes of 1987 (see Chapter 1). It is unclear why the victims of the Braşov strikes were singled out by the Social Democrat parliamentary majority, which until 2004 had adamantly opposed any recognition of communist crimes.

After Law 221/2009 came into force, several former political prisoners asked the Romanian government for reparations proportional to the time they spent in communist prison and the suffering they endured. While most claims were rather small and all of them were fully justified, a handful of them reached hundreds of thousands of Euros because they reflected decades-long prison terms followed by years-long persecution and deprivation of civil and political rights. In addition, the law compensated all former political prisoners, even those who eventually turned into informers or torturers, as was the case of Metropolitan of Transylvania Bartolomeu Anania, who asked for compensation to the tune of 800,000 Euros (amounting to

[43] I thank lawyer Carmen Lascu for drawing my attention to this legal distinction and for her constructive comments on several drafts of this chapter.

[44] "Legea 341/2004 a recunoştinţei faţă de eroii-martiri şi luptătorii care au contribuit la victoria Revoluţiei române din decembrie 1989, şi faţă de persoanele care şi-au jertfit viaţa sau au avut de suferit în urma revoltei muncitoreşti anticomuniste de la Braşov din noiembrie 1987," *Monitorul Oficial al României, partea I* (20 July 2004).

over US$1 million).[45] It soon became evident that, if all surviving former political prisoners asked for reparations, the total sum of their claims could seriously burden the national budget, already threatened by a shrinking tax base. Reparations became even more unpopular after journalists disproportionately focused their attention on the few very large claims that, while generally perceived as being fair reparation for extended periods of past duress, were also lodged at a time when the country was seriously affected by the global financial crisis that drove many Romanians out of their jobs and into dire poverty. In this context, the Democrat-Liberal government of Prime Minister Emil Boc decided to cap the amount of compensation to levels that it could afford, without consulting the victims' groups and without making an effort to justify the decision publicly. These new levels were unfortunately well below what the few surviving former prisoners considered to be just and fair retribution.

As a result, Emergency Government Ordinance 62/2010 limited moral damages for political imprisonment to a total of 10,000 Euros (equivalent to US$13,875) for victims, 5,000 Euros for their spouses and children, and 2,500 Euros for their grandchildren. The caps were introduced because of the potential "significant impact on the national state budget" of Law 221/2009, as the government declared.[46] According to the ordinance, to determine the individual reparation levels, the Romanian courts had to take into account the length of the imprisonment, the time when the imprisonment took place, the negative consequences of imprisonment on the victims' physical, psychological, and social well-being, and the reparations the victims might have received in virtue of Decree-law 118/1990, Emergency Ordinance 214/1999, and Law 568/2001. No further details were offered to clarify the way in which these factors and legislative pieces influenced levels of individual compensation packages, but it was assumed that victims who received reparations through Decree-law 118/1990, Emergency Ordinance 214/1999, and Law 568/2001 qualified for lower compensation levels than victims who had received no support from the government before 2010, whereas victims who had suffered for longer periods of time and from more serious human rights violations were entitled to higher compensation levels.

45 "Bartolomeu Anania, în proces cu statul român. Succesorii continuă acţiunea şi cer 800 000 de euro despăgubiri," *Opinia Timişoarei* (4 February 2011). Anania was never officially branded a Securitate collaborator, but there are strong suspicions that he was one, otherwise the Securitate would have not allowed the patriarch of the Romanian Orthodox Church to send Anania to the United States. Some press reports claim that in fact Anania's brother served as a Securitate informer, and Anania did not want to clarify his collaboration for fear of incriminating his brother. Anania's Securitate file, if it exists, remains housed with the External Information Service.

46 "Ordonanţa de Urgenţă nr. 62/2010 pentru modificarea şi completarea Legii nr. 221/2009 privind condamnările cu caracter politic şi măsurile administrative asimilate acestora, pronunţate în perioada 6 martie 1945–22 decembrie 1989 şi pentru suspendarea aplicării unor dispoziţii din titlul VII al Legii nr. 247/2005 privind reforma în domeniile proprietăţii şi justiţiei, precum şi unele măsuri adiacente," *Monitorul Oficial al României, partea I* (1 July 2010).

The ordinance was criticized for severely limiting the amount of compensation allowed for damages incurred as a result of serious levels of harm and suffering, for not providing other means for compensation besides cash payments (e.g., in the form of long-term bonds or grants of title to the state's land holdings), and for asking claimants wishing the court to determine the political nature of their conviction and/or of the administrative measure to produce documents attesting to the measures taken against them (documents that might not be in their possession). Lawyers sympathetic to former victims faulted the ordinance for "turning the hope for justice initially found in Law 221 into an illusion for these hapless victims," for demonstrating that parliament unjustly decided that the persons who suffered the most under the communist regime by losing their liberty for years on end, enduring unspeakable humiliations, and losing their health and property were to receive only meager compensation, and for "transforming a noble endeavor" – that is, the law that finally recognized the tragedies and horrors that the communist regime inflicted upon its victims – into "an unjustified transgression."[47]

In November 2010, the reparations program received a deadly blow when the Romanian Constitutional Court invalidated Emergency Ordinance 62/2010 and Law 221/2009 in response to two petitions lodged by the Ombudsman and the Constanţa County Tribunal, which took issue with some of the compensation provisions.[48] According to Constitutional Court Decision 1354/2010, which responded to the Ombudsman's petition, the capping of reparation packages through Ordinance 62/2010 was unconstitutional because some communist-era victims received generous compensation packages awarded by the courts before the ordinance came into force, while others received only up to 10,000 Euros awarded after the ordinance was enacted. This different treatment of victims amounted to an infringement of their fundamental rights, as it was generated by a factor – the timing of court decisions – that was outside the victims' influence. The hope that this court decision would lift the cap of compensation packages vanished two weeks later, when the

[47] "Romania Offers Piddling Compensation to Former Political Prisoners," *Romanian Digest* (October 2010), available at: http://www.hr.ro/digest/201010/digest.htm (accessed on 3 October 2011).

[48] Curtea Constituţională, "Decizia nr. 1.354 din 20 octombrie 2010 referitoare la excepţia de neconstituţionalitate a dispoziţiilor art.I pct.1 şi art.II din Ordonanţa de urgenţă a Guvernului nr.62/2010 pentru modificarea şi completarea Legii nr.221/2009 privind condamnările cu caracter politic şi măsurile administrative asimilate acestora, pronunţate în perioada 6 martie 1945–22 decembrie 1989, şi pentru suspendarea aplicării unor dispoziţii din titlul VII al Legii nr.247/2005 privind reforma în domeniile proprietăţii şi justiţiei, precum şi unele măsuri adiacente," *Monitorul Oficial al României, partea I* (15 November 2010), and Curtea Constituţională, "Decizia Nr. 1.358 din 21 octombrie 2010 referitoare la excepţia de neconstituţionalitate a prevederilor art.5 alin.(1) lit.a) teza întâi din Legea nr.221/2009 privind condamnările cu caracter politic şi măsurile administrative asimilate acestora, pronunţate în perioada 6 martie 1945–22 decembrie 1989," *Monitorul Oficial al României, partea I* (15 November 2010).

Constitutional Court responded to the Constanţa County Tribunal petition by declaring unconstitutional Article 5 of Law 221/2009, which granted compensation for moral damage. In the court's opinion, the law did not undergo judicial review before its adoption, as the constitution required; the legislation offered compensation that was not "just, equitable, and reasonable"; the post-communist state had only a moral, but not the financial, obligation to redress communist injustice; and financial reparations had already been granted by other decrees and laws that had remained in force after the law's adoption.[49] In short, the court faulted the government for not doing its job of according the new law with the legislation already in force and for disregarding the judicial review procedure. Even afterward, the government found no time and had no interest to reformulate the unconstitutional provisions so that a modified version of the law could be applied to future cases.[50] This disinterest stemmed as much from the desire to save funds during times of economic crisis as from lack of will to support legislation initiated by Oprea, a vocal critic of the Democrat-Liberal government.

These controversial Constitutional Court decisions were based on contradictory justifications and ungrounded opinions, because the first decision acknowledged that Law 221/2009 granted compensation rights to former victims, while the second claimed that victims could *not* have a "legitimate hope" of receiving those rights, and the court deemed reparations offered by the law as *not* being "just, equitable, and reasonable" without explaining why it adopted such a position. Some lawyers pointed out that many former victims might be inclined to turn to the European Court of Human Rights, because not only the Romanian state, but also the victims have to agree on what "reasonable" redress means. However, the requirement to consult the former victims was infringed when the Governmental Ordinance 62/2010 unilaterally instituted the caps. Constanţa Lawyer Carmen Lascu noted the inconsistency of governmental action, as the law was challenged as unconstitutional by the Constanţa Tribunal at the request of the Ministry of Finance, which represented the same government that introduced and supported the law. This Kafka-like inconsistency demonstrated the government's willingness to talk the talk, but not walk the walk, as cabinet members publicly capitalized on a piece of legislation whose inherent flaws made it unconstitutional.[51]

49 Nicoleta Ristea, "Motivarea Deciziei nr.1358/21.10.2010 a Curţii Constituţionale, referitoare la excepţia de neconstituţionalitate a prevederilor art.5 alin.(1) lit.a) teza întâi din Legea nr.221/2009," inLege.ro (10 November 2010), available at: http://www.inlege.ro/2010/11/10/motivarea-deciziei-nr-135821–10–2010-a-curtii-constitutionale-referitoare-la-exceptia-de-neconstitutionalitate-a-exceptia-de-neconstitutionalitate-a-prevederilor-art-5-alin-1-lit-a-teza-intai-din/ (accessed on 18 October 2011).

50 Virgil Burlă, *Marius Oprea: Voiculescu a fost mai mult decât un simplu informator*, Alianţa pentru o Românie Curată (14 March 2011), available at: http://www.romaniacurata.ro/marius-oprea-voiculescu-a-fost-mai-mult-decat-un-simplu-informator-1251.htm (accessed on 26 November 2011).

51 Personal email communication to the author of Constanţa Lawyer Carmen Lascu, 22 October 2012.

The Constitutional Court decision effectively blocked the reparations program and reversed compensations to the meager levels in force prior to the adoption of Law 221/2009.

Such prolonged legal wrangling generated confusion among the potential beneficiaries of the reparations program, who were deterred from seeking redress, and unfairly divided former communist-era victims into three arbitrary categories: 1) those to whom court decisions handed down between the adoption of Law 221/2009 and Emergency Ordinance 62/2010 awarded unlimited reparations; 2) those to whom court decisions handed down between the adoption of the Emergency Ordinance 62/2010 and the Constitutional Court decisions of 2010 granted reparations not exceeding the equivalent of 10,000 Euros; and 3) all the other victims who either did not lodge compensation claims or in whose cases the courts were unable to reach a decision by late 2010.[52] Only the former victims in whose case the Court of Appeal upheld the restitution decision in a pronouncement delivered before 15 November 2010 can receive the compensation levels specified by the court.[53] Besides the division operated by the Constitutional Court decisions, another one emerged when the so-called Small Judicial Reform of November 2010 scrapped the possibility to contest restitution verdicts at the Supreme Court with a second appeal, as had been previously the case. Since then, restitution verdicts could be contested solely at the county appeal courts.[54] The decision sped up the administration of justice, but also halted the cases that were at the time under discussion in the appeal courts without changing the appeal court decisions that had already been handed down. As different appeal courts embraced widely different standards, they gave different solutions to similar restitution cases, a fact that added to the frustration of the former victims and the confusion of their legal representatives. Despite the obstacles mounted by the Constitutional Court, some court decisions have adopted a bold approach of these litigations, which considered that victims had a "legitimate hope" for compensation.

It is difficult to estimate the total number of communist-era victims who have asked for reparations and rehabilitation by the time of this writing. In the Constanţa

[52] An example is the Bucharest Court of Appeal decision of 7 June 2011, which upheld a lower court's verdict granting moral damages to the tune of 10,000 Lei (some US$3,211) to a former ethnic German who was forcefully relocated together with his family and assigned forced residence in Bărăgan from 1951 to 1955. See Curtea de Apel Bucureşti, Secţia a VII-a Civilă şi pentru Cauze privind Conflictele de Muncă şi Asigurări Sociale, *Decizia nr.96/07.06.2011* (7 June 2011), available at: http://portal.just.ro/JurisprudentaVizualizare.aspx?id_speta=28445&idInstitutie=2 (accessed on 18 October 2011).

[53] According to lawyer Carmen Lascu, personal communication to the author, 22 October 2012.

[54] I thank lawyer Carmen Lascu for these details. See "Legea 202/2010 privind unele măsuri pentru accelerarea soluţionării proceselor. Mica reformă a Justiţiei," *Monitorul Oficial al României, partea I* (26 October 2010).

county alone, from June 2009 to October 2011, as many as 756 restitution requests were lodged in court, but it is unclear how many of them were solved definitively. The vast majority of these requests are for restitution, which implies rehabilitation as a first step. Lawyer Lascu, who estimated that very few of these requests asked for rehabilitation alone, also pointed out that all these litigations were emotionally taxing for former victims, their relatives, the lawyers who presented the restitution requests, and the audience present in the courtroom, as the hearings often included vivid description of persecution and torture.[55]

CONCLUSION

By Eastern European standards, post-communist Romania has remained a regional laggard in terms of rehabilitating and compensating former political prisoners, who had suffered the most under the communist dictatorship. The rehabilitation program was launched two decades after other neighboring countries chose to declare communist-era, politically based judicial and administrative verdicts null and void. This deliberate procrastination meant that few former political prisoners were still alive by the time rehabilitation was available as a form of redress. In the Sibiu county, for example, by 2007 only 70 of the 600 political prisoners registered locally in 1990 were still alive,[56] an attrition rate that characterizes other counties as well. Although launched only months after the collapse of the Ceauşescu regime, the compensation program provided for mostly symbolic benefits and very little financial support. The government's attempt of 2009 to expand the compensation scheme and raise the level of individual packages was short-lived, as the legislative stipulations providing for reparations were deemed unconstitutional and disingenuous, because key governmental agencies with restitution responsibilities sought to declare the law unconstitutional and thus block, rather than implement, it.

Therefore, it is fair to say that the Romanian reparations program has suffered from chronic "tokenism," to use Juan Mendez's term, resulted from the adoption of compensation systems that are meager in comparison to the harm done to individuals, even if a justification based on limited resources is offered, and from seriously procrastinated rehabilitation programs launched so late as to benefit only a fraction of all former victims. The Romanian post-communist governments have neglected their obligation to provide reparation, as delayed rehabilitation and meager monetary awards were not accompanied by "apologies, valued information, and other nonmaterial benefits that, in the aggregate, convey the sense that society recognizes

55 Personal email communication to the author of Constanţa Lawyer Carmen Lascu, 23 October 2011.

56 Alin Bratu, "Torţionarii au murit. Mor şi victimele," *Ziarul de Sibiu* (31 May 2007).

the worth and dignity of the human person behind each victim."[57] This is exactly why the monetary awards offered during the first two decades of post-communism were criticized as mere attempts to buy the silence of the communist-era victims, whose numbers are rapidly decreased by the veritable "biological guillotine" of time.[58]

[57] Juan Mendez, "In Defense of Transitional Justice," in *Transitional Justice and the Rule of Law in New Democracies*, ed. A. James McAdams (Notre Dame: University of Notre Dame Press, 1997), p. 15 [1–26].

[58] Personal interview with historian Mircea Stănescu, Bucharest, 29 November 2011.

8

Rewriting History Textbooks

In communist Eastern Europe, a region where historical narratives privileged the rulers, the nation, or the ideology, ignored the contribution of ethnic and religious minorities, provided few alternative views on state-society relationships, offered misleading or no information on the victims of state-sponsored repression, and negatively depicted anticommunist opponents and the democratic world, history textbooks were highly politically charged. Since 1989, the process of rewriting history textbooks has sought to acknowledge the communist past, reflect memory, historical consciousness, and identity in the school curricula, and more simply stop textbook authors from lying about the past. Determining the content of history textbooks, Huma Haider suggested, "requires coming to grips with 1) what can be considered historical fact; 2) which facts should be included in textbooks as legitimate forms of knowledge; and 3) how to portray groups considered historical enemies."[1] In Romania, persistently divergent narratives and the difficulty of reaching broad consensus over historical truths have rendered the revision of history textbooks a challenging, divisive, and largely protracted transitional justice process. At the same time, in 2008 the country introduced in high schools an alternative history textbook exclusively dedicated to presenting the communist-era institutional framework, repression, dissent, and daily life – an accomplishment that at the time of this writing has no correspondent in other corners of Eastern Europe.

In post-dictatorial settings, the importance of history textbooks – a nation's "memory pills," to use a phrase coined by historian Mirela Luminiţa Murgescu[2] – hinges on their content, meaning, and role. As means of socialization, history textbooks are "unparalleled in their capacity to convey a uniform and immovable worldview, lay

[1] Huma Haider, "Rewiting History Textbooks," in *Encyclopedia of Transitional Justice*, eds. Lavinia Stan and Nadya Nedelsky (New York: Cambridge University Press, 2012), vol. 1, 94.

[2] Mirela Luminiţa Murgescu, *Istoria din ghiozdan. Memorie şi manuale şcolare în România anilor 1990* (Bucharest: Do Minor, 2004), 11.

the foundations of belonging to the nation, and instill loyalty towards the state and its institutions, as a state of and for that nation,"[3] because "children have a special rapport with the knowledge they receive at a young age in school, from teachers or textbooks."[4] As such, history can play "a civic education role by teaching students about democracy, state institutions and civil society, and turning them into citizens apt to avoid [political] apathy, intolerance and manipulation."[5] When not just transmitting information and when free from interference on the part of politicians and bureaucrats, history lessons can promote freedom of thought, critical thinking, and respect for the other, can create and recreate collective memory, and can "help successive generations to learn a common social language that can protect them against pernicious influences and political manipulations."[6] Compared to memoires, diaries, and biographies of individual victims or victimizers, history textbooks allow the act of memorialization to enter the domain of collective memory and to go beyond that of personal memory. At the same time, it has been shown that "history can be easily manipulated on ideological grounds and used to legitimate various political interests," and as such, it must be zealously protected from the influence of political factors.[7] State involvement in the revision of history textbooks amounts to an official acknowledgement of past harm by crafting a state-sanctioned narrative of the past that assumes an official character and is usually disseminated much more widely than any other history book. The adequate reflection of communist crimes and repression in textbooks has acquired added relevance as new generations born after 1989 have entered the school, because for them the history textbooks are among the few available sources of information about a regime they had not experienced directly. Hence, the passage of time has placed an additional burden on individual and institutional actors to capture the communist past in material and symbolic acts of remembrance such as textbook rewriting.[8]

After a brief overview of historiography under communist rule and of the changes brought by 1989, this chapter presents the Romanian historians' efforts to expand their analytical tools, rescue their field of study from the influence of ideology, move away from the nationalist historical canon characteristic of Nicolae Ceauşescu's rule, and more importantly reflect the repressive nature of the communist regime in pre-university history textbooks. The following discussion is concerned primarily with

3 Irina Culic, "Re-Writing the History of Romania after the Fall of Communism," *History Compass*, 3(2005): 13–14.

4 Daniela Zaharia, cited in Florin Turcanu and Armand Gosu, "Manualele opţionale de istorie," 22 (28 June 2005).

5 Gabriela Odobariu, cited in Turcanu and Gosu, "Manualele opţionale de istorie."

6 Daniela Zaharia, cited in Turcanu and Gosu, "Manualele opţionale de istorie."

7 Sorin Mitu, cited in Turcanu and Gosu, "Manualele opţionale de istorie."

8 Monica Ciobanu, "Rewriting and Remembering Romanian Communism: Some Controversial Issues," *Nationalities Papers*, 39(2011): 207.

the interplay between the positions on the recent history of historians, politicians, civil society groups, and the society at large, as well as their impact on education policy. The focus is on the textbooks for grades 4, 8, 11, and 12, which after 1989 have been dedicated to the history of Romania and of the Romanians. My goal is not to describe each and every textbook, as other authors have already done so, but to explain how Romania's reckoning with its communist past benefited from the rewriting of history narratives used in the classroom.[9]

During the 1990s, pre-university history textbooks reflected the methods and approaches that were inherited from communist-era historiography and were centered on the national-communism that had played such a pivotal role under Ceauşescu's rule. The rewriting of history textbooks concerned both terms of the national-communism binomial. The first rewriting, completed as early as 1991, revised the presentation of the communist regime, but stirred little public interest, although some intellectuals, historians, parents, and teachers quickly pointed out its limitations. By contrast, the changes operated in 1999, after Romania introduced the so-called alternative textbooks, provoked a "textbook scandal" in which supporters of the older nationalist understanding of historical markers locked horns with younger historians looking for new conceptual approaches and updated pedagogical methods. Once the scandal watered down, the main concern left on the table referred to the still inadequate presentation of Ceauşescu's late communist regime and its many human rights violations. After many failed attempts to convince textbook authors to dedicate more space to the communist repression mechanisms, in 2008 a new alternative high school history textbook dedicated exclusively to communist times was published.

The fact that the revisions dealing with nationalist feelings, but not those referring to communist crimes, provoked a bitter public scandal speaks volumes about the strength of nationalist sentiment in Romania throughout the 1990s, and well after 1996, the year that marked an alternation of power from the Social Democrat Party, heir to the Communist Party, to the Democratic Convention, which gathered anti-communist forces together with the "historical" Christian Democrat and Liberal Parties. One explanation lies in the fact that during the early 1990s "what prevailed was the need to recapture national historical values considered perverted or shadowed by the communist regime."[10] A nation battered by decades of neglect and humiliation at the hands of both Romanian and Soviet dictators needed to find again its core values by mobilizing nationalist feeling which, unfortunately, rapidly distanced itself from civic nationalism to assume strident chauvinistic overtones. Another explanation rests with the decision of the opposition Social Democrats and Greater Romania Party,

[9] For a comprehensive analysis, see Murgescu, *Istoria din ghiozdan*, especially 109–167.

[10] Idem, 16.

which included many former nationalist communists, to seize the reform program that permitted the use of alternative textbooks as an opportunity to attack the legitimacy and credibility of the Democratic Convention government and boost their own popularity in the months preceding the local, parliamentary, and presidential elections of 2000. As explained later in this chapter, several historians and politicians have confirmed that the scandal was primarily political in nature, hinging on the textbook's scientific and pedagogical approach less than on its instrumentalization by certain political actors against their electoral rivals.

The rewriting of history textbooks has progressed unevenly in post-communist Europe. In Russia, for example, by 1993 the textbooks for grades 10 and 11 presented in detail the Soviet institutions and policy making. However, although teachers were encouraged to stimulate class debates on potentially controversial topics such as "The Soviets – People Power or Totalitarianism?," "October 1917 – Revolution or Counter-revolution?," "The Collapse of the USSR – A Necessity or Accident?, and "The Causes and Outcomes of the Collapse of the USSR," textbooks retained a rather uncritical view of Soviet leaders and tended to justify or downplay their crimes.[11] Alternative history textbooks have been used in the Czech Republic as early as 1995, when one such book came under fire for containing a number of anti-Semitic statements, which were later revised. In that country, as in Romania, the Ministry of Education approves alternative textbooks from among those published by local presses, primarily based on how closely they cover a set of topics pre-approved by the Ministry. The textbook authors need not be trained historians.[12] Since the Velvet Revolution, Czech history textbooks have been rewritten to teach children about the communist era, report facts and details that were omitted during the previous decades, and correct some blatant historical misinterpretations. For example, textbooks no longer argue that at the end of World War II Czechoslovakia was freed from Nazi oppression by the valiant efforts of the Soviet Red Army. Similar developments occurred in Slovakia, where after 2006 the process of rewriting history textbooks was complicated by a rift with the government of Hungary, which has championed the interests of the 500,000 Hungarians living in the southern districts of Slovakia. Hungarians both in Hungary and Slovakia were enraged by Slovak history textbooks that included disparaging comments toward minorities. It was only in mid-2011 that the Slovak Ministry of Education approved a new textbook written by Hungarian historians for Slovakia's Hungarian schools.[13]

[11] Joseph Zajda and Rea Zajda, "The Politics of Rewriting History: New History Textbooks and Curriculum Materials in Russia," *International Review of Education*, 49(2003): 375 and 382 [363–384].

[12] Anti-Defamation League, *Press release* (New York, 10 April 1995), available at: http://www.adl.org/PresRele/ASInt_13/2402_13.asp (accessed on 27 November 2011).

[13] *Hungarian History Textbooks Approved in Slovakia* (29 July 2011), available at: http://www.politics.hu/20110729/hungarian-history-textbooks-approved-in-slovakia/ (accessed on 27 November 2011).

By contrast, Bulgaria was unable to effect change during the first two decades of post-communism. As late as October 2010, legislators rejected amendments to the Public Education Act meant to change the content of high school textbooks "in order to inform the young people about the crimes of the communist regimes in Bulgaria and around the world."[14] Sponsored by the right-wing Blue Coalition, the changes were rejected by the ruling Citizens for European Development of Bulgaria, a center-right formation, on grounds that they must first be discussed publicly with the parents and the society at large. Another case is represented by the Balkan countries, where the new post-1989 history textbooks have adopted a mostly anticommunist and pro-Western stance, while at the same time they have presented "the nation as larger than the state," identifying "as 'ours' territories that are not included within state borders," and have promoted the "future's past" by reinterpreting historical events "according to the planning of the future."[15] Until now, few post-communist countries have completely broken with what historian William McNeill called "mythistory," which involves the blurring of distinction between, on the one hand, history based on scholarly research (which is taken to be true) and, on the other hand, imagined or distorted myths (which are understood to be false).[16]

HISTORIOGRAPHY AND HISTORY TEXTBOOKS BEFORE AND AFTER 1989

The Romanian communist regime displayed great interest in historiography, both because its doctrine of "philosophical and historical materialism" postulated that history culminated with the triumph of communism worldwide and because of the "need to acquire internal historic legitimacy, to integrate the Romanian Communist Party, by means of historiography, into the national tradition."[17] After 1945, the pre-communist historical research, inspired by national ideology and European trends, gave way to a historiography that followed "the guidelines of the power which it served, and adapted itself to each and every one of the power's metamorphoses," in the process "evolving from an uncompromising Stalinism to a virulent nationalism."[18] The regime claimed the existence of a unique historical truth that had to be reflected in a single historical narrative. As historian Şerban

14 "Bulgaria MPs Vote Communism out of High School History Textbooks," *Defeat Communism* (29 October 2009), available at: http://www.novinite.com/view_news.php?id=109411 (accessed on 22 October 2011).

15 Christina Koulouri, *Teaching the History of Southeastern Europe* (Thessaloniki: Center for Democracy and Reconciliation in Southeastern Europe, 2001), 19, cited in Murgescu, *Istoria din ghiozdan*, 57.

16 William McNeill, *Mythistory and Other Essays* (Chicago: University of Chicago Press, 1986).

17 Şerban Papacostea, "Captive Clio: Romanian Historiography under Communist Rule," *European History Quarterly*, 26(1996): 181.

18 Idem, 182.

Papacostea explained, the Communist Party subordinated historical interpretation to communist philosophy and policy, revised attitudes toward historical truth, and radically changed the practice of historical research and teaching.[19] Following guidelines derived from the official approach to history, historians focused on phenomena pertaining to economic, social, and cultural history, neglecting the study of political history. These themes were supplemented vigorously by presentations of the benefits of communist internationalism and of the positive role played by the Soviet Union, whose model was to be emulated in all respects. Topics of interest related to the correlation between the economic foundations of society and its social relations, the social aspects of rural history, the land reforms of the nineteenth and twentieth centuries, the peasant revolts and the class struggle, the working class movement, and the resistance of the proletariat to capitalist exploitation. In the process, the state Marxist dogma "generated historical myths, while totalitarian Leninism produced a long trail of outright historical forgeries."[20] In the Orwellian world of Romanian communism, the historian's role was not so much to research the past, ask pertinent questions, and critically assess information obtained from a multiplicity of sources, because this way the historian risked stumbling upon the heretic conclusion that the communist regime was far from representing the apotheosis of national history and the desires of the people. Rather the historian's role was to reconstruct the past in light of the regime's ideological priorities of the moment.[21] Unsurprisingly, history became a matter of faith.

The party's desperate efforts to assign itself a historical role it had never played prompted communist authorities to militarize public archives and to keep the main collections dealing with the interwar period closed even for historians loyal to the communist cause. In 1948, a long list of publications were indexed and removed from libraries. Afterward Romanian libraries and universities no longer acquired books signed by Western scholars. Following a brief post-Stalinist thaw, historiography rapidly degenerated in radical and aggressive nationalism and the preposterous personality cult that underpinned the rule of Ceauşescu. By the late 1970s, historiography had turned into a purely ideological activity subservient to the ruling party and infused with *protochronism*, the notion that "through the years Romanian civilization had preceded the general evolution of European civilization."[22]

By 1989, generations of Romanian pre-university and university students had been exposed to a version of history carefully censored by the Communist Party. National

[19] Idem.

[20] Idem, 187.

[21] Gabriel Marin, "La leçon d'histoire. Les nostalgies du communisme et les manuels scolaires d'histoire des Roumains" (unpublished manuscript), 105. I thank Gabriel for making an electronic copy of this manuscript available to me.

[22] Idem, 197.

communism, the continuity of the Romanian people on their territory across two millennia, the people's unflinching "unity" around communist leaders, the continuous class struggle quenched by the advent of the communist regime, and *protochronism* prevailed as topics of discussion, as did presentations that praised communism and the social classes it promoted and criticized capitalism, democracy, and the individuals and groups who supported them. History textbooks presented minor communist figures as major national heroes, portrayed the Communist Party as having a much larger social basis than its small pre-1945 membership, and kept silent on the thousands of opponents and dissidents subjected to state repression (see Chapter 1). Invariably, the history class exuded conformity, memorization, ideology, and propaganda, more than lively debates and critical thinking about different historical moments and processes. As one historian poignantly sketched the stifled pedagogical approach to teaching history that was embraced under Ceauşescu's sultanist-cum-totalitarian rule, until 1989:

> the history textbook had an absolute authority: the teacher was obliged to follow its pace, steps, itinerary, the material was the same for all [schools and students], not even the words could be changed. Students learnt the Textbook, they reproduced the Textbook in exams, teachers evaluated them against the Textbook, and entry into university depended on the student's loyalty to the Textbook.[23]

With the collapse of the communist regime, censorship ceased and historians had access to a widely liberalized publishing market that consisted of both old communist-era presses and new publishing houses created after 1989. However, during the 1990s historiography retained the strong nationalist tendencies characteristic of late communist times, and most archival collections remained closed to researchers unsympathetic to the country's new political leaders, who retained control over the Communist Party archives and the secret Securitate documents. After surveying the new works published during the first decade of post-communism, historian Bogdan Murgescu remarked that texts examining the period after 1918 prevailed; most new titles dealt with Romanian history or the Romanians' international relations with other countries and groups, whereas theoretical and methodological discussions were almost completely absent. According to him, "methodological backwardness combines with a heavily Romanian-centered approach, which takes into consideration only Romania's relations with the 'great powers,' avoiding any comparison with other small/peripheral countries."[24] Historian Constantin Iordachi

[23] Daniela Zaharia, cited in Turcanu and Gosu, "Manualele opţionale de istorie."

[24] Bodgan Murgescu, "The Romanian Historiography in the 1990s," *Romanian Journal of Political Science*, 2(2003): 37. Murgescu also listed some of the most sensitive topics of Romanian history, reflective of the central role by the nation in the Romanian historiography. See Bogdan Murgescu, *A fi istoric în anul 2000* (Bucharest: All, 2000).

further detected "the absence of deep theoretical debates and of interdisciplinary dialogue, a primordialist perception of ethnicity, and a close relationship between historiography and the political power."[25]

This situation was partly a result of the fact that, throughout the 1990s, historians were unable to access key archives and thus had to employ alternative data collection methods to document communist repression, the activity and structure of the Securitate, the collectivization of land and the nationalization of dwellings, and the comprehensive surveillance program instituted under the Ceauşescu regime. Oral history unearthed new information through interviews with former Communist Party officials, Securitate secret agents, and victims and led to the publication of numerous volumes of interviews, memoirs, and analyses. However, as testimonials of former victims and victimizers could misrepresent the past, they had to be assessed against official documents. Gradually, archives began to open, and collections of original documents produced by various agencies of the communist party-state started to appear. Nevertheless, only part of this new material made its way in history textbooks until 2008.

REFLECTING COMMUNIST CRIMES IN HISTORY TEXTBOOKS

The December 1989 revolution took place three months after the beginning of the school year on September 15. The unprecedented political changes that rocked the country at the time placed teachers between the Scylla of wide post-communist reforms called for by the civil society or historical parties representing the pro-democratic opposition and the Charybdis of political stagnation imposed by the ruling National Salvation Front (later transmogrified in the Social Democrat Party) – an umbrella organization under whose banner scores of national and local Communist Party apparatchiks got a new lease on their political lives. At first, teachers kept silent on the communist regime. As other Romanians, they were divided between supporters and critics of the former regime, and thus they risked facing criticism in class when voicing their personal views. Confusion also played a role, because the boundaries of what was acceptable and what was not in terms of behavior and thought were tested on a daily basis. For want of a better solution, in September 1990 the first post-communist Minister of Education Mihai Şora, an early communist devotee who parted ways with the communist leadership by the 1980s and remained independent from political parties throughout his post-communist mandate, republished *The History of the Romanians*, a textbook that had gained some popularity in schools

[25] Constantin Iordachi, "'Entangled Histories': Re-thinking the History of Central and Eastern Europe," *Regio Yearbook* (2004): 121.

during pre-communist times.[26] Written in 1942 by historian P. P. Panaitescu, the volume completely ignored the communist regime and, thus, signified the desire of some prominent intellectuals in the Group for Social Dialogue, which Şora represented, to simply delete the 1945–1989 period from the school curriculum and recover the country's "authentic national memory,"[27] which in their view preceded the arrival of the communist regime. That decision did not sit well with large segments of the population, unnerved by the thought of having their own lives and personal experiences thrown into the dustbin of history. The attempt to obliterate communism was also debatable because, as Romania hardly had a democratic past to refer to, pre-communist times coincided with the right-wing fascist regimes of Marshal Ion Antonescu and the Iron Guard that Panaitescu reportedly supported. As such, after Şora's replacement with a National Salvation Front member, the ministry published new textbooks that had special chapters dedicated to a revisionist presentation of the 1945–1989 period. These textbooks continued to present the history of the Romanians as an ethnic group, not the history of Romania as a collection of territories inhabited by a plurality of ethnicities and nationalities. Those volumes, which were invariably long, dense, and packed with myriad useless details, aimed to present a comprehensive view of historical events that gained its neutrality through a veritable "cascade of information," which their authors hoped would protect them from charges of ideological bias, pedagogical ineffectiveness, and lack of patriotic sentiment.[28]

In 1994, the year before parliament passed a new education law, the Romanian Social Democrat government negotiated with the World Bank the introduction of alternative textbooks at all pre-university levels to break with the communist practice of allowing teachers to use only one textbook approved by the Ministry of Education. To align Romania to European standards, alternative textbooks were introduced first at the primary (grades 1–4) and secondary levels (grades 5–8), and then in high schools (grades 9–12). Two years later, a newly published history textbook for grade 12 covered the 1821–1989 period (the modern Romanian state), allotting space to the Gheorghe Gheorghiu-Dej and Ceauşescu regimes of 1945–1965 and 1965–1989, respectively, as well as to the December 1989 revolution.[29] While the textbook mentioned the communist prisons of the 1950s, together with the names of the most important communist leaders and best-known political prisoners and anti-communist dissidents, the communist past was presented very briefly compared to other periods of national history. Indeed, the volume covered the entire 1945–1989

[26] P. P. Panaitescu, *Istoria Românilor* (Bucharest: Editura Didactică şi Pedagogică, 1990).

[27] Murgescu, *Istoria din ghiozdane*, 12.

[28] Ibidem, 13.

[29] Mihai Manea and Bogdan Teodorescu, *Istoria Românilor de la 1821 până în 1989. Manual pentru clasa a XII-a* (Bucharest: Editura Didactică şi Pedagogică, 1996), 379–388.

period in only 10 of its 388 pages (amounting to barely 2.5 percent of the textbook's total length). This deliberate choice to downplay the most recent repressive regime set the tone for a pattern that continues to affect history textbooks even at the time of this writing. By contrast, 100 pages were devoted to the twenty-five years of the interwar period, which in many respects represented the new benchmark against which post-communist Romania was assessed from a political, economic, and cultural viewpoint.[30] For anticommunist groups, the textbook did not go far enough in presenting the full blown terror and the overpowering surveillance that characterized the communist ancien regime. The press faulted the Social Democrat Minister of Education Liviu Maior, a historian who before 1989 had collaborated with one of Ceauşescu's brothers while working at the Institute for Military History, for thwarting the reform drive.[31]

THE TEXTBOOK SCANDAL

As Culic noted, by the late 1990s the sensitive process of rewriting history textbooks divided both historians and politicians. Some embraced "a primordialist understanding" of the nation, "a triumphalist interpretation" of the formation of the Romanian nation–state and a "glorious discourse about the past, meant to inculcate in young generations admiration toward their ancestors."[32] Others were experimenting with new approaches and updated methodologies, wished to abandon old stereotypes, but adopted "a defensive position after being accused of iconoclasm while moving away from 'the nation's heroes'."[33] The ensuing battle, known as the textbook scandal, revolved around the introduction in 1999 in high schools of alternative textbooks from which teachers could select one to use in class.[34] Historians were called to propose alternative manuscripts that covered a list of curricula topics designed and approved by the Ministry of Education. Authors could decide how their textbook reflected those topics in detail, how much space they devoted to each theme, how they balanced facts and interpretation, and which theoretical and pedagogical approaches to embrace. On 1 September, the Ministry approved five history textbooks for grade 12, the only high school grade in which Romanian history was taught. One particular manuscript, written by a team of young historians from Cluj,

30 Lucian Boia, *History and Myth in the Romanian Consciousness* (Budapest: Central European University Press, 2001), 233.

31 Nicoleta Nap, "Dinastia Maior," *Bună ziua, Ardeal* (11 November 2005).

32 Culic, "Re-Writing the History of Romania," 13, and Ovidiu Cristea, cited in Turcanu and Gosu, "Manualele opţionale de istorie."

33 Cristea, cited in Turcanu and Gosu, "Manualele opţionale de istorie."

34 Andrei Marga, "Asupra manualelor alternative," *Curentul* (26 October 1999): 12, and Ana-Maria Vieru, "Începând din 2000, piaţă liberă pentru producţia de manual," *Curentul* (1 October 1999): 12.

Transylvania's largest city, challenged core myths of Romanian historiography by presenting the Romanian nation as an "imagined community," instead of a palpable, objective, and immanent historical reality.[35] The perspective, which echoed Benedict Anderson's well-known theory of ethnic identity construction, came as a shock to Romanian readers, unnerved by the new perspective. The book received the most attention from the press, intellectuals, politicians, teachers, and parents, although only 8,000 of Romania's 150,000 grade 12 students reportedly used it.[36]

Reactions to the textbook were swift, radical, and often choleric. As expected, the most virulent attacks were mounted by the Greater Romania Party, the country's most rabid nationalist formation, which at the time was part of the opposition, with the Social Democrats coming in second. Independent Senator Sergiu Nicolaescu, a film director whose career flourished under Ceauşescu with the production of scores of period movies that obliquely supported national-communist tenets, asked for the new textbook, which was "insulting to the Romanian people," to be publicly burned in a dithyrambic speech that evoked the destruction of indexed volumes by an imagined totalitarian regime in the *Fahrenheit 451* movie of 1966.[37] It was unfortunate, Nicolaescu believed, that the textbook described the collectivization process in detail on as many as twelve pages but allocated only three short paragraphs to Michael the Brave, who for a brief period in 1600 de facto ruled the three provinces of modern Romania. Collectivization made thousands of victims, but that human suffering could never eclipse Michael's unification of the Romanian nation avant la lettre (since the term "nation" started to be used only centuries after Michael's death), a moment seen as pivotal to Romanian national identity. Echoing the trepidation, in an open letter disclosed to the press, the Cluj County councilors pleaded with President Emil Constantinescu to sanction the authors of such an "aberrant and insulting" textbook that amounted to a "genuine aggression against our ethnic nation, our country, and all those who feel Romanian,"[38] although presidential prerogatives did not include censure of any kind. Seven deputies representing the nationalist camp and the Social Democrats criticized the "abominable," "anti-national," "idiotic," and "unpatriotic" textbook for "annihilating the historical, cultural and geographic markers of the Romanian people."[39] The Parliamentary

35 Sorin Mitu, Lucia Copoeru, Ovidiu Pecican, Virgiliu Târau, and Liviu Târau, *Istoria Românilor. Manual pentru clasa a XII-a* (Bucharest: Sigma, 1999).

36 Cornel Nistorescu, "Cine îl lucrează pe Vlad Ţepeş?," *Evenimentul zilei* (9 October 1999). I thank Bogdan Murgescu for drawing my attention to this article during his personal interview with me, Bucharest, 3 July 2011.

37 "Şedinţa Senatului din ziua de 5 octombrie 1999," *Monitorul Oficial al României, partea II-a* (18 October 1999), 8–9, and François Truffaut, Director, *Fahrenheit 451* (1966).

38 "Consilierii clujeni sunt indignaţi de conţinutul cărţii de istorie," *Libertatea* (2 October 1999).

39 Greater Romania Party Deputy Mitzura Arghezi, cited in "Şedinţa Camerei Deputaţilor din 26 octombrie 1999," *Monitorul Oficial al României, partea II-a* (4 November 1999).

Education Committees discussed the textbook in two joint special meetings during which both the government and the opposition representatives crossed fire. To ban the volume, the opposition challenged the Democrat Convention government by introducing a no-confidence motion centered on education policies and by asking for the dismissal of Christian Democrat Minister of Education Andrei Marga, a Romanian philosopher of some repute. None of these two proposals was successful, but they occasioned renewed attacks on the entire education reform program introduced at the request of the EU. In a declaration read in front of the house, for example, Greater Romania Party Deputy Nicolae Leonăchescu took issue with the larger education reform program and claimed that the alternative textbooks presented an alternative history that was "delivered in the poisonous package of a cruel reform drive."[40]

Politicians were not the only ones to vituperate. High school teachers from the southern country of Dolj voiced "profound consternation and indignation" at the Ministry's decision to back up a textbook that highlighted "insignificant topics" such as the Jews in Romania, the integration of minority groups in Greater Romania (1918–1940), and the secret monitoring of anticommunist dissidents under Ceauşescu's rule, but "scandalously" divided the three Romanian provinces between the Hungarian Kingdom and the Ottoman Empire, the larger political formations to which they belonged historically.[41] Even respected historian Dinu Giurescu was of the opinion that "we cannot integrate national history in European history if we dilute the first, we cannot dilute national identity in the name of demystifying history and promoting European integration, as the French, English and Germans never forgot that they are French, English and Germans."[42]

The textbook authors were denounced Inquisition-style in a virulent mass media campaign whose occasional melodramatic tones gave the impression that the very survival of the Romanian nation–state rested on concerted efforts to reject the textbook and uphold the historiographic canon. Newspaper *România Liberă* warned that "not everyone should be involved in writing history, otherwise we risk to have no country, and no past!,"[43] as though the journalist who wrote this statement was more competent than the trained historians who authored the textbook. For the *Jurnalul naţional* daily, the authors had "ridiculed our national history" and "turned the Bible of the Romanian people – History – into a telenovela" – that is, a Latin American soap opera that weaved together a series of improbable characters and

[40] "Şedinţa Camerei Deputaţilor din 3 octombrie 2000," *Monitorul Oficial al României, partea II-a* (11 October 1999).

[41] Oana Vasilescu and Marina Dohi, "În manualele de istorie Ţara Românească este denumită 'Ungro-Vlahia'," *Libertatea* (28 September 1999).

[42] Cited in Ovidiu Pecican, "Cronica unei conflagraţii anunţate," *Observatorul cultural* (January 2002).

[43] Adrian Bucurescu, cited in Pecican, "Cronica unei conflagraţii anunţate."

plot lines. "Without illustrious dead leaders, without myths, traditions, legends, a country will break up even in the absence of an external threat,"[44] the editor-in-chief of newspaper *Adevărul*, Cristian Tudor Popescu, lamented in one of his editorials, before suggesting that the textbook was "the fruit of political correctness and multiculturalism, [which are] ways to control majorities by turning the minorities against them."[45] Pointing a denunciatory finger to the alternative textbooks, which had been dismissed as a "national disgrace" by professors at the Craiova Faculty of Law, the daily criticized the import of foreign ideas that "trample on our traditions" and expose Romanian history books to "Western kitsch"[46] – that is, novel interpretative approaches that challenge the traditional historical canon. Journalists prone to give credit to conspiracy theories noted that unnamed linguists who carefully studied the syntax of the controversial textbook arrived at the conclusion that the entire volume had been translated directly from the Hungarian language, a charge implying that it reflected anti-Romanian sentiment more than new theoretical and pedagogical approaches.[47] Surprisingly, the vast majority of these criticisms were raised by persons with no training in historical research and pedagogy, as though scores of ordinary Romanians suddenly metamorphosed into amateur historians enunciating the immovable historical truths that were abandoned or mocked by those who made history their profession.

By contrast, a handful of voices openly defended the textbook, its new historical perspective, and the changes it brought to the Romanian education system. On 10 October 1999, Minister Marga denounced the ignorance of those who expected the history textbooks to instill national pride and boost the students' patriotic feelings and suggested that the members of the Parliamentary Education Committees had no business debating the ministry's decision to adopt the textbooks, although by constitution the executive was responsible to the legislative.[48] Two days later, Christian Democrat Deputy Ioan Vida-Simiti reminded legislators that the textbooks used before 1999 suffered from "serious conceptual and analytical shortcomings," including an "ideological affiliation to Ceauşescu's national-communism," a xenophobia-generating myth of the Romanian peasant exploited by other ethnic groups, and discreet but laudatory allusions to dictatorial regimes. This is why, Vida-Simiti concluded, Romanian schools needed new history textbooks "rescued

44 Cristian Tudor Popescu, "Câte istorii are România?," *Adevărul* (6 October 1999).

45 Cristian Tudor Popescu, "Manualul de Istorie Antinaţională – Crima cu premeditare a Ministerului Educaţiei Naţionale," *Adevărul* (8 October 1999). For an informed response, see Dan Pavel, "The Textbooks Scandal and Rewriting History in Romania. Letter from Bucharest," *East European Politics and Societies*, 15(2000): 179–189.

46 Ştefania Enache and Gabriela Vlăsceanu, cited in Pecican, "Cronica unei conflagraţii anunţate."

47 Pecican, "Cronica unei conflagraţii anunţate."

48 "Şedinţa Camerei Deputaţilor din 19 octombrie 1999," *Monitorul Oficial al României, partea a II-a* (28 October 1999).

from the ideological restraints of the [national-communist] past, anchored in current realities, and aiming decisively at the future goals of the Romanian society."[49] Presidential Councilor Zoe Petre, a professor of ancient history, praised the textbook for "promoting critical thinking, helping students to understand the living experience of humanity, and using new ways to reconstruct the past (daily life, gender relations, cultural creativity), thus going beyond the traditional slogan of 'class struggle as motor of history'."[50] President Constantinescu reminded legislators that "history is not soccer, [a field where] everybody is an expert," while Marko Bela, leader of the Democratic Union of Magyars that represented the Transylvanian ethnic Hungarian community, said that the meeting of the parliamentary committees was "shameful" because it turned back the clock to communist times, when politicians imposed specific interpretations of history on experts.[51] Romanian Academy member Pompiliu Teodor, journalist Cornel Nistorescu, the Group for Social Dialogue, and the Association of Publishers in Romania criticized the reintroduction of censorship and the authors' "crucifixion." From Teodor's perspective, the scandal was "purely political" in nature, because the textbook was sound from a scientific viewpoint, while for historian Alexandru Zub the scandal was about "the manipulation of electoral segments" by the opposition in view of the general elections of 2000.[52]

The textbook also deeply divided the community of historians in Romania. On the one hand, it was praised for its innovative approach by historians teaching in the history departments of the University of Bucharest and the University Babes-Bolyai of Cluj, the country's best higher education establishments. On the other hand, it was vilified by the more conservative History Section of the Romanian Academy, where historians who made careers under communism by accepting compromise and self-censoring still formed a comfortable majority, and history departments of lesser known universities. In their view, the textbook fostered doubt about key moments of Romanian history, attacked national identity, and diluted it by recognizing the country's ethnic diversity.[53] For these critics, there was no room for critical thinking and debates of alternative viewpoints in class, which instead should present history as an unchallenged and unqualified truth, if wishing to avoid historical relativism and confusion on the part of the students. In the face of unrelenting public outcry, criticism from teachers unwilling to adopt what were considered to be highly controversial and untested positions, and reports that students would refuse to read their new books even if their teachers adopted them, the head of the National Council

[49] "Şedinţa Camerei Deputaţilor din 12 octombrie 1999," *Monitorul Oficial al României, partea a II-a* (21 October 1999).

[50] Zoe Petre, cited in Turcanu and Gosu, "Manualele opţionale de istorie."

[51] Adrian Cioflânca, "Scandalul manualelor face primele victime," *Jurnalul de Iaşi* (23 October 1999).

[52] Cited in Pecican, "Cronica unei conflagraţii anunţate."

[53] Culic, "Re-Writing the History of Romania," 14, and Murgescu, *Istoria din ghiozdan*, 130–131.

for Textbook Approval, Iancu Fischer, resigned, and Minister Marga appointed a special commission formed of ten history professors and members of the Romanian Academy to gather suggestions coming from historians and to draft recommendations for improving the textbook.[54] After the 2000 elections, the new Social Democrat Minister of Education Ecaterina Andronescu gave in to her party rank and file and canceled the new textbook's authorization, although the manuscript had been substantially revised by its authors in light of the criticism raised during the "textbook scandal."[55] For historian Victor Neumann, Andronescu's decision was highly debatable not only because it was motivated on solely political grounds, but also because it eliminated an alternative way of thinking about Romanian history.[56] Within weeks, the book completely vanished from bookshops and schools.

This defeat was only momentary, as several alternative history textbooks were introduced in schools after 2000. These new authors remembered the public supplications endured by the writers of the controversial textbook, and often self-censored, preferring to tone down the material and not stray away from widely accepted interpretations, in hope of avoiding criticism and censure. Almost none of the subsequent textbooks were as daring as the grade 12 volume discussed. As late as 2005, observers noted that the textbooks of Romanian history followed the "national conservative canon and even expose[d] nationalist positions," and included "few innovative perspectives informed by recent historiographic trends."[57] While accepting that textbooks are "a possible itinerary that the teacher can embrace, reject or improve on, an average of the situations anticipated by the authors" that need to be supplemented with additional teaching materials and class discussions, teachers noted that the textbooks continued to present historical facts and ideas "as though they possess absolute truth."[58] By doing so, they were failing to admit that "history is a hypothesis," which includes historiographic debates or doubts, and that the textbooks are nothing more than a subjective take on the school curriculum, which retains old clichés and stereotypes, and addresses itself to teachers more than to students.[59] As one author noted, textbooks "teach us that throughout history Romanians were right, whereas

[54] Cioflânca, "Scandalul manualelor face primele victime."

[55] Murgescu, *Istoria din ghiozdan*, 166–167. When she returned to the helm of the ministry in 2008, Andronescu again showed her resolve to quash all initiatives of working through the communist past by quietly removing a question in the baccalaureate oral exam for Romanian language and literature that required candidates to comment on the section of the Tismaneanu Report discussing censorship and the status of literature under communism. See Ciobanu, "Rewriting and Remembering Romanian Communism," 212.

[56] Victor Neumann, "Manualele alternative de istorie: o dezbatere istoriografică sau o imixtiune politică," *Observatorul cultural* (22 January 2002).

[57] Daniela Zaharia, cited in Turcanu and Gosu, "Manualele opţionale de istorie."

[58] L. Capita, cited in Turcanu and Gosu, "Manualele opţionale de istorie."

[59] Turcanu and Gosu, "Manualele opţionale de istorie."

the Russians, Hungarians and Americans were wrong" – a perspective that breeds intolerance toward the other ethnic minorities residing on the territory of Romania and toward other countries that, during the course of the history, influenced the politics of the Balkans.[60] Since the Romanian society has remained unwilling to renounce long-cherished stereotypes, history textbooks are unable to fulfill the goals of a pluralistic society.

The scandal represented a rare instance when discussion of the past was no longer strictly confined to academic and political circles. It engaged large segments of the public that almost overnight, without even bothering to read the textbook, decided to do away with trained historians, offer pronouncements on what history really is and how it should be taught in class, give lessons to young historians, and forget that whatever people knew about history had been handed down by other historians under a dictatorial regime that had reconstructed history for its immediate political purposes. While presented as authoritative, those pronouncements reflected the very stereotypes and clichés the textbook authors had questioned and avoided. Encouraged by the vicious criticisms raised by historians associated with the Romanian Academy, which was discredited in the eyes of the local academia by its long-standing collaboration with the communist regime but which carried considerable weight with the general public, the journalists, teachers, parents, and politicians outraged by the new textbook simply forgot that "critical questioning of the other's interpretation involves being critical of oneself."[61] Given this concerted assault, the textbook scandal constituted a veritable challenge to the public credibility of young historians, who took a step back as a result, renounced their desire to replace historical absolute truth with historical debates and uncertainties, and partly readopted the very canon they wished to dismantle.

More importantly, the textbook scandal addressed only part of the national-communist straitjacket that the Ceauşescu regime once imposed on history textbooks. Besides breaking the long-perpetuated nationalist canon, it was important to continue to open textbooks to narratives of communist repression and its victims, as the Christian Democrat and Liberal Parties, the associations representing the communist-era political prisoners and victims, and numerous civil society organizations insisted. This exercise has been challenging for historians, whose work was constantly interfered with by leftist politicians and communist diehards extolling the accomplishments of the communist regime while downplaying its Stalinist traits.

60 Sorin Mitu, cited in Turcanu and Gosu, "Manualele opţionale de istorie."

61 Falk Pingel, "Can Truth Be Negotiated? History Textbook Revision as a Means to Reconciliation," *Annals of the American Academy of Political and Social Science*, 617(2008): 190.

A History of Communism in Romania Textbook

By 2003, pre-university textbooks on the history of modern Romania "overly remembered" the Gheorghiu-Dej regime at the expense of Ceauşescu's rule, to use Paul Ricoeur's phrase.[62] The three available textbooks designed for grade 8 presented terror under Gheorghiu-Dej and offered examples of repression sites such as the Sighet and Gherla prisons, the Piteşti reeducation program, or the Danube-Black Sea Canal. They included no information on the activity of Ceauşescu's secret political police, its leaders and victims, or the Braşov workers' strikes of 1987.[63] The paucity of information on repression during late communism was carried over in high school textbooks. One textbook briefly presented the topic in a short sentence, stating that "after 1964, the prison system and physical extermination were replaced by more subtle methods of surveillance of the entire society: a strong network of informers, encouraging denunciations, eavesdropping on phone conversations, forced residences, and criminal indictment."[64] Another textbook devoted more space to the topic, named General Iulian Vlad as the last Securitate director, presented the substantial material and financial advantages enjoyed by the secret agents, and described the Securitate victims as isolated individuals convicted for petty crime or confined to psychiatric wards.[65] Only one textbook included a separate chapter on repression under the Ceauşescu regime, a curriculum theme approved by the Ministry of Education.[66] All textbooks only cautiously approached the recent past, which was still seen as politically charged and controversial. As the Romanian society remained divided into supporters and opponents of communism, "authors avoided definitive pronouncements on that period, taking refuge in providing general statements"[67] that seemed callous to former communist-era victims.

Thus, history textbooks treated the two communist regimes differently, and communism received little attention in comparison to other historical periods. For Marius Oprea, a historian known for his incisive studies on the Securitate, the textbooks "say nothing much about the activity of the former Securitate agents because they [the agents] are still living and occupying public office" and "there is a false belief that

62 Paul Ricoeur, *La mémoire, l'histoire, l'oubli* (Paris: Seuil, 2000).

63 Ana-Maria Vieru, "Securitatea a fentat manualul de istorie," *Evenimentul Zilei* (19 November 2003).

64 Nicoleta Dumitrescu, Mihai Manea, Cristian Nita, Adrian Pascu, and Madalina Trandafir, *Istoria Românilor. Manual pentru clasa a XII-a* (Bucharest: Humanitas, 1999).

65 Liviu Lazăr, Bogdan Teodorescu, Mihai Stamatescu, and Ovidiu Bozgan, *Istorie. Manual pentru clasa a XII-a* (Bucharest: 2000).

66 Doru Dumitrescu, cited in Vieru, "Securitatea a fentat manualul de istorie." Also Stelian Brezeanu, Adrian Cioroianu, Florin Muller, Mihai Sorin Radulecu, and Mihai Retegan, *Istorie. Manual pentru clasa a XII-a* (Bucharest: Rao, 2002).

67 Murgescu, *Istoria din ghiozdan*, 34–35.

Ceauşescu's Securitate was benevolent and paternalist."[68] Other historians believed that the textbooks provided all necessary information but "fail to describe the general terror," an important oversight because "one cannot explain history without referring to daily life and mentalities."[69] More than the content of the lessons on communist times, history teachers underscored the practical difficulties encountered when discussing these topics in class. Some teachers did not cover the communist period for fear of being accused of personal bias and lack of neutrality. Others believed that the few classes dedicated to communism cannot present the Securitate as a repressive agency, as long as state institutions responsible for transitional justice do not clarify their position, as though the truth handed down by these institutions could ever settle once and for all the debate on the nature of the communist regime. Still others noted that the history of Romania was included in grades 8 and 12, toward the end of the second semester, when students were already preparing for the qualifying entrance exams for high school or university and therefore had little incentive to study topics not covered in the exam.

Importantly, very few teachers showed interest in examining communism in more detail. The didactic.ro Web site has provided support materials for Romanian teachers, including course notes and PowerPoint slides prepared and uploaded voluntarily by teachers across the country. An analysis conducted in October 2011 revealed teachers' relative disinterest in communism as a topic of history classes. Only 5 percent of course notes for grade 8 (11 of 218) and grade 12 (7 of 146) dealt with the Romanian communist regime. Of the twenty-two notes on communism, half explained the Gheorghiu-Dej regime, three (13 percent) the Ceauşescu regime, two (9 percent) the 1989 revolution, and another two (9 percent) the entire 1945–1989 period. Of the notes for grade 8, one dealt with the 1989 revolution, three with Ceauşescu as the country's leader, and seven with repression under Gheorghiu-Dej. Of the notes for grade 12, one talked about the 1989 revolution, four about the Gheorghiu-Dej regime, its leaders, and terror campaign, one about a panoply of communist leaders (including Ceauşescu and Gheorghiu-Dej), and one about Romania during the Cold War.[70] Teachers' disinterest has translated in students' unfamiliarity with the recent past. According to an opinion poll conducted in 2010, 25 percent of respondents under 20 years of age had no opinion on whether the communist regime was good or bad, and as many as 42 percent had no opinion on its instauration in Romania at the end of World War II. Tellingly, a staggering 85 percent of young respondents considered that they had poor or no knowledge about

[68] Marius Oprea, cited in Vieru, "Securitatea a fentat manualul de istorie."

[69] Alexandru Barnea, cited in Vieru, "Securitatea a fentat manualul de istorie."

[70] *Resurse educaţionale*, didactic.ro (2010), available at: http://www.didactic.ro/resurse-educationale (accessed on 21 October 2011).

the history of communism in Romania, and none of them said that they knew that period very well.[71]

Responding to the paucity of teaching materials dedicated to communism, in 2007 the Institute for the Investigation of Communist Crimes took upon itself the responsibility to compile the alternative history textbook for high schools. The previous year, the textbook had featured the recommendations of the Presidential Commission for the Analysis of Communist Dictatorship in Romania, which compiled a report on the criminality of the communist regime and proposed a series of additional steps designed to push transitional justice further (see Chapter 5). That effort was crowned by the publication in September 2008 of *A History of Communism in Romania* (O Istorie a Comunismului în România), a textbook coordinated by historian Raluca Grosescu and accompanied by a DVD titled *A Day at the Romanian Television in 1988*, an invaluable teaching aid that presented the two-hour television program broadcast daily at the time.[72] The textbook includes twelve chapters surveying such topics as the destruction of civil society, resistance against the regime, the importance of the Marxist-Leninist ideology, the Romanian Communist Party, the command economy, daily life, the instauration of the communist regime (1944–1947), the significance of the 1989 events, and the "other" under the communist regime. It states that communism made between 500,000 and 2 million victims, thus acknowledging both the lower estimate put forward by scrupulous historians and the high number proposed by the Association of Former Political Prisoners. Historians praised this neutrality, adding that "the textbook is well written, includes impressive documentation, is well structured, and reflects pedagogical skill."[73] Whereas other history textbooks present communism very briefly and only from the point of view of its political institutions, the new textbook considers the regime in-depth, incorporates a variety of viewpoints, and encourages critical thinking in class. Without burdening students with unnecessary information but including a variety of photographs, official documents, testimonials from victims, and excerpts from studies signed by reputed analysts, the volume represents an educational tool that "provides a bridge between those who, because of their age, had no possibility to know the horrors of communism and those who lived during those times" and "gives students

[71] The poll was conducted under the aegis of the Institute for the Investigation of Communist Crimes on a sample representative for the entire population of Romania. *Atitudini şi opinii despre regimul comunist din România. Sondaj de opinie public* (23 May 2011), available at: http://www.crimelecomunismului.ro/pdf/ro/raport_sondaj_opinie_publica_iiccmer_mai_2011.pdf (accessed on 27 October 2011).

[72] Dorin Dobrincu, Mihai Stamatescu, Raluca Grosescu, Liviu Plesa, Sorin Andreescu, and Andrei Muraru, *O istorie a comunismului din România. Manual pentru liceu* (Bucharest: Polirom, 2008), and *O Zi la Televiziunea Română în 1988*, DVD movie, Bucharest: Institute for the Investigation of Communist Crimes, Romanian Television and TVR Media, 2008.

[73] Adrian Cioflânca, "O istorie a comunismului," *Ziarul de Iaşi* (11 September 2008).

the possibility to understand the past of their parents and grandparents, a past that is linked to our present."[74]

Because the textbook was introduced only in 2008, it is yet to be adopted by a large number of high schools throughout the country. In fact, half of all Romanian high schools, which include those with so-called technical specializations, cannot adopt the textbook because history is not among the electives students can choose from. The other high schools, those with a theoretical concentration that prepares students for entering the university, streamline students in either hard sciences or humanities/social sciences. Only students interested in the latter elect the optional textbook on communism, because students in hard science streams prefer mathematics, physics, and chemistry as electives. Students in humanities/social science streams can choose from a number of elective subjects, including history, geography, or foreign languages. Those who take history classes can further select from among a number of subject matters and textbooks (the history of communism, of minority groups, of the Holocaust, etc.). Occasionally, the choice for an elective or a textbook is made by the school principal, not the students, who might hire a French over a history teacher, ensuring thus that foreign languages but not history are among the electives. This is another reason why relatively few students have used the textbook on communism at the time of this writing: 1,543 students from 120 high schools in 2008; 3,400 students from 165 high schools in 2009; 3,224 students from 164 high schools in 2010; and 3,570 students from 170 high schools in 2011.[75] To entice teachers, the Institute has offered training programs designed to explain the textbook's narrative, provide course plans, and detail pedagogical methods best suited to explain the institutional and social bases of communism. During the first four years following the textbook's introduction in schools (2008–2011), the Institute trained 365 teachers across the country. Of those, 265 were history teachers and 100 were social science and humanities teachers. Many trained teachers were recruited from Bucharest and Brăila, Braşov, Constanţa, Cluj, Galaţi, Mureş, Olt, Tulcea, and Zalău counties.[76]

With the publication of the textbook, Romania became the first post-communist country to introduce in schools a book dedicated to the communist past. Given the specific Romanian context, the need for publishing the new volume stemmed primarily from dissatisfaction with the briefness and superficiality of the way in which communism was treated in the history textbooks available to children before 2007.

74 Dorin Dobrincu, cited in Armand Gosu, "Procesul comunismului cu manualul pe masă," 22 (17 September 2008).

75 "Raluca Grosescu a adus studiul comunismului în şcoli," *Adevărul* (18 August 2010). Also personal interview with Raluca Grosescu, Bucharest, 28 June 2011, and email communication from Raluca Grosescu to the author, 3 February 2012.

76 Personal email communication from Raluca Grosescu to the author, 3 February 2012.

International actors such as the Embassies of the Netherlands and Germany and the German Konrad Adenauer Foundation financed the project, once it took off, but seemingly played no role in spearheading it. Grosescu proposed an additional explanation for why the textbook was published first in Romania by suggesting that in other countries memory has been recovered through extensive museum projects, part of what transitional justice calls memorialization (see Chapter 9).[77] In Hungary, for example, students can learn a lot about life during communist times in their school-organized visits to the House of Terror in Budapest, a powerful exhibition housed in the former headquarters of the communist secret political police. Romania's only museum dedicated to communist repression is located in Sighetul Marmaţiei, a small town situated in northern Romania close to the border with Ukraine and some 350 miles from Bucharest. As trips to Sighet are prohibitive because of the time, cost, and effort they require for schools in most Romanian counties, Grosescu argued, a textbook was an alternative method of recreating memory and reaching the new generations.

CONCLUSION

In Romania, the rewriting of history textbooks has provided an opportunity to correct the most strident national-communist tenets to which children were exposed in schools before 1989. While started in 1990, the process registered both progress and retreat, thus unfolding over two decades and extending well after the country joined the EU. Since 2008, teachers and students can choose between a number of history textbooks that report on communist crimes in more or less detail and can adopt either the textbook that discusses solely the 1945–1989 period or one of the alternative textbooks that cover the entire history of modern Romania and ponder over the communist regime in several paragraphs. True, a host of practical problems that teachers encounter in class affect the students' knowledge of communism, but the fact remains that Romania was the first in the region to introduce a textbook on communism in its schools.

The rewriting of history textbooks departs from other methods of working through the recent past. First, it has entailed efforts to address both the nationalist and the communist features of the regime of 1945–1989, whereas other methods (especially court trials, lustration, and property restitution) have aimed to undo only the legacies of communism. That nationalism was an important pillar of Romanian national-communism was proven by the divisive textbook scandal that gripped the country in 1999, a decade after Ceauşescu was removed from power and three years after the heirs to the Communist Party, the Social Democrat and the Greater

77 Raluca Grosescu, cited in Gosu, "Procesul comunismului cu manualul pe masă."

Romania Parties, were driven into the opposition. Second, whereas it delayed the adoption of lustration, property restitution, and access to secret files, post-communist Romania turned its attention to history textbooks within days after the 1989 revolution. The need to rewrite history books has been kept in the public's eye and on the government's agenda by reformist politicians like Andrei Marga, governmental agencies like the Institute for the Investigation of Communist Crimes, civil society organizations, historians, and teachers. Early launching did not translate in more efficient results, because alternative textbooks remain a work in progress and the textbook dedicated exclusively to the history of communism was published only two decades after history textbooks started to be rewritten. Third, the rewriting of history became a matter of public concern to a greater extent than any other transitional justice method discussed in this volume. As explained earlier, the textbook scandal managed to rally the successors to the Communist Party and the national segments of the general public against a textbook that proposed a novel interpretation of Romanian history. The ensuing debate involved a wide range of groups, institutions, and organizations that took very little interest, if any, in other methods of reckoning with the communist past, on which they have remained silent.

There are also notable similarities with other transitional justice methods. The most important is that the rewriting of history books has been heavily instrumentalized by post-communist political parties for their own electoral gains. With some exceptions, the center-left and nationalist parties that inherited their membership from the Communist Party and the Securitate have upheld the historical cannon and criticized the overhaul of the education system, even though their government agreed to introduce such reforms as early as 1994. By contrast, the pro-democratic opposition, including the historical parties, has advocated change and renewal, although some of their members openly departed from this position by supporting the no-confidence motion presented earlier.

9

Unofficial Projects

All methods of working through the past discussed in Chapters 2 through 8 represent state-led processes, in which governments have played important roles by launching initiatives, funding institutions and projects, designing the legislative framework that governs the activity of such institutions, establishing which crimes from which time periods should be redressed, defining the categories of victims entitled to compensation, rehabilitation, restitution, and recognition, identifying the communist-era perpetrators targeted for court trials and lustration, selecting from among different versions of "truth" about the past, and endorsing some of them as official by including them in school textbooks or accepting them as basis for official condemnations. True, civil society actors have made significant contributions to all these stages of post-communist transitional justice, but, in terms of importance and scope, their input has remained secondary to that of state actors, as the success of reckoning with the communist past through those processes and practices depend on the cooperation of state actors.

However, the civil society can act as an important facilitator of transitional justice, as David Baker underscored.[1] Non-state actors have been instrumental in pushing forward forensic investigations, an area generally ignored by post-communist governments, and unofficial truth projects, which by definition are the locus of civil society activity. Whether by taking down the portraits of Nicolae Ceauşescu that adorned classrooms or the slogans that defaced factories and train stations, removing the statue of Vladimir Lenin from Piaţa Scînteii in Bucharest, changing the names of public squares to reflect non-communist events and personalities, erecting monuments to mark communist labor camps, exhuming the remains of those executed by the Securitate troops in the 1950s, delivering "justice" through a citizens' opinion tribunal, or publicly disseminating the names of former Securitate agents, the civil

[1] David Baker, "Civil Society and Transitional Justice: Possibilities, Patterns and Prospects," *Journal of Human Rights*, 2(2003): 297–313.

society has engaged in acts of remembrance that, as Jay Winter suggested, search for "meaning in the past."[2] This relentless search has been evident even in the case of "massive, terrifying phenomena" characterized by "unadorned nihilism,"[3] such as the crimes perpetrated at the Sighet prison. All these methods of reckoning with the past demonstrate that memory is "subjective, warm, and emotional,"[4] not cold, objective, and dispassionate, and the past has different meanings to different people, depending on their relation to the dictatorship. The search for meaning can no longer reflect solely the viewpoint of the victors or the political elite. This search must respect the victims, acknowledge their suffering, and educate new generations about the horrors of dictatorship and the value of human rights. Annette Wieviorka's suggestion, that "the age of the witness" has imprinted the way history is written, applies to the way in which meaning has been acquired through memorialization, exhumations, and unofficial truth projects.[5]

This chapter discusses methods to which non-state actors have contributed significantly. Memorialization encompasses symbolic gestures that recognize, remember, and commemorate the past: renaming localities, public squares, streets, schools, institutions, and organizations by removing names that evoke communist leaders, events, and ideological principles and replacing them with names that conjure the new ideals of democracy, freedom, and human rights. It extends to the replacement of communist statues and monuments with new ones dedicated to the fight against communism and for democracy, which "speak about the present through the past," and the opening of museums and exhibitions that "put on cultural trial" the repression sites, the identity of former perpetrators, and their crimes.[6] Such memory projects are closely tied to the commemoration rituals that mark anniversaries of the struggle against dictatorship and to the recognition of national days dedicated to historical milestones important for remembering communist victims. Ideologically laden histories, Maoz Azaryahu reminded us, are spread as everyday political symbols in street names, statues, and memorials that make up the "city-text,"[7] and show that "physical objects play a significant role in

[2] Jay Winter, "Foreword: Historical Remembrance in the Twenty-First Century," *Annals of the American Academy of Political and Social Science*, 617(2008): 7.

[3] Idem.

[4] Carles Maier, "A Surfeit of Memory? Reflections on History, Melancholy and Denial," *History & Memory*, 5(1993): 136–151, and Charles Maier, "Hot Memory … Cold Memory: On the Political Half-life of Fascist and Communist Memory," paper delivered at the conference on "The Memory of the Century," Institut für die Wissenschaften vom Menschen, Vienna, Austria, 9–11 March 2001.

[5] Annette Wieviorka, *L'ère du témoin* (Paris: Plon, 1998).

[6] Anca Benera, *Bucureşti. Materie şi Istorie – Monumentul Public şi Distopiile Lui* (Bucharest: Institutul Cultural Român, 2010).

[7] Maoz Azaryahu, "The Purge of Bismark and Saladin: The Renaming of Streets in East Berlin and Haifa, A Comparative Study in Culture-Planning," *Poetics Today*, 13(1992): 351–367.

the relationship to the recent past."[8] Street names confer meaning to the urban space, allowing people "to affirm, or to contest, control" of the city because they "socialize space and celebrate cultural identity" and "perpetuate tradition even as they register change."[9] New regimes "must decide which, if any, of the heroes of the old regime deserve to continue occupying public space" and must consider "if these heroes might serve as potential symbols of resistance for adherents among the population who must, at least from the perspective of the newcomers, ultimately acquiesce to the new order."[10] Besides bringing legitimacy to the new political order, street names should also represent the country's ethnic and religious diversity that was suppressed by the communist authorities until 1989.[11]

An important method employed in many post-dictatorial settings, forensic investigations identify, locate, and exhume the remains of victims of extrajudicial killings that the state never acknowledged as such. Because these crimes were perpetrated in secret, outside localities, in secluded areas (such as forests or inaccessible mountainous areas), during the night, and without witnesses, exhumations provide much needed closure to families that never recovered the victims' bodies or found out what happened to their loved ones. When carefully conducted, exhumations can offer valuable information on the method of killing and the cause and time of death, together with additional clues on the identity of the perpetrators (e.g., through the ammunition they left behind). Exhumations are commissioned to collect narrative and physical evidence necessary to identify those responsible and bring them to justice, to locate the victims and return the remains to their family, to create a legally and historically valid document that will overwhelm historical revisionist efforts, to provide a rhetorically powerful scientific account of the illegality and criminality of the dictatorship, to prevent future mass human rights violations, and to express a basic dignity for the victims and for human life by not allowing the circumstances surrounding their murder to go undisclosed. Forensic investigations treat historical mass graves as crime scenes and conceptualize remains as evidence through which criminal responsibility could be attributed.[12] In most cases, exhumations are followed by inhumations during which the remains are buried

[8] Peter Apor, "Eurocommunism. Commemorating Communism in Contemporary Eastern Europe," *Eurhistxx* (no date), 3, available at: http://eurhistxx.net/Portals/_eurhistxx/documents/APOR,%20 Eurocommunism.rtf (accessed on 10 November 2011). Also Mia Swart, "Name Changes as Symbolic Reparation after Transition: the Examples of Germany and South Africa," *German Law Journal*, 9(2008): 105–121.

[9] Priscilla Parkhurst Ferguson, "Reading City Streets," *The French Review*, 61(1988): 387.

[10] S. Levinson, *Written in Stone: Public Monuments in Changing Societies* (Place: Duke University Press, 1998).

[11] George Schöpflin, *Nations, Identity, Power: The New Politics of Europe* (London: Hurst, 2000), 130.

[12] Pedro Funari, Andres Zarankin, and Melisa Salerno, eds., *Memories from Darkness: Archeology of Repression and Resistance in Latin America* (New York: Springer, 2009).

with religious rites in the presence of family relatives and community members in properly marked sites.[13]

Unofficial truth projects encompass a range of projects launched, led, funded, or implemented by non-state actors when official attempts to reckon with the past are nonexistent, incomplete, nontransparent, or unsuccessful. As Louis Bickford wrote, in countries where official truth programs "are not feasible because of political constraints, are ineffective or politically compromised, or human rights activists and their allies in government choose not to create them," unofficial truth projects "may represent viable alternative strategies and can be seen as more legitimate interlocutors for the task of confronting the past."[14] These projects sometimes complement state efforts to search for truth and provide redress and other times allow civil society actors to carry out truth and justice programs when governments fail to do so. The most significant Romanian unofficial truth projects include the unauthorized release of secret information (what I called elsewhere "vigilante justice"), a citizens' opinion tribunal, and numerous art, theater, movie, and literature projects focused on the communist past.

In Romania, the civil society has pursued these methods and practices in response to the failure of successive governments to engage with determination and promptness in truth seeking and truth telling. As in the case of other memory programs examined in this volume, the main successors to the Communist Party – the Social Democrat Party and the Greater Romania Party – have generally opposed attempts to reckon with the past through unofficial projects on grounds that the communist regime had a commendable legacy that would be shadowed or even obliterated by close examinations of its repressive nature. Despite repeated promises, the center-right cabinets of the Democratic Convention (1996–2000), the Liberal Party (2004–2008), and the Democratic-Liberal Party (after 2008) have not endorsed the civil society's most important memorialization project: the Museum of Victims of Communism. Until such a museum opens its doors and welcomes its visitors, Romania's main memory projects remain the Sighet Museum, the exhibit on communism displayed at the Peasant Museum in Bucharest, and the small memorials erected across the country by the Association of Former Political Prisoners. Similarly, a citizens' opinion tribunal was enacted in Cluj in 2006 in direct response to the regular courts' refusal to hear the generic Trial of Communism that would expose notorious communist crimes and convict their perpetrators (Chapter 2). Since 2009, forensic investigations have received

[13] William Haglund, "Recent Mass Graves: An Introduction," in *Advances in Forensic Taphonomy: Method, Theory and Archaeological Perspectives*, eds. William Haglund and Marcella Sorg (Boca Raton: CRC Press, 2002), 243–261.

[14] Louis Bickford, "Unofficial Truth Projects," *Human Rights Quarterly*, 29(2007): 995.

no funding from the government, and some local authorities even obstructed exhumations and questioned their need so many decades after the crimes took place, fearing the opening of old wounds. In 2002, secret information was released as part of the "Armageddon" (Armaghedon) in direct response to the failure of the National Council for the Study of Securitate Archives to speed up efforts to name the Securitate agents (see Chapters 3 and 4).

Although all these civil society-driven projects have responded to perceived government failure to work through the past, they are set apart by some important differences. The range of memory gestures encompassed under the heading of memorialization has received far greater public attention than forensic investigations or unofficial truth projects, both because they debuted earlier, during the 1989 revolution, and because they have outnumbered exhumations and unofficial projects. Although civil society groups have engaged in memorialization for over two decades, the vigilante disclosure of information presented in this chapter as an example of unofficial truth projects was launched thirteen years after the regime change, in 2002, and exhumations have been pursued only since 2006, also the year when the citizen's tribunal was organized. Given the time lag, it is unsurprising that hundreds of memory sites (*lieux de memoire*) have been designated throughout Romania, but fewer than thirty exhumation campaigns and only a handful of unofficial truth projects have been conducted to date.

The methods discussed in this chapter have been implemented throughout Eastern Europe, but the Romanian citizens' tribunal remains unique in the region. On the basis of the Hungarian case, Géza Boros identified three positions in the debate on communist statues: some Hungarians wanted to get rid of them, others wanted to do nothing, while still others wanted to preserve those statues in museums.[15] Opinions on street names, Emilia Palonen wrote, followed the same pattern: "removing all the communist-era street names, supporting minimal, if any, removals, or saving some of them by way of a layer of memory in the city."[16] In addition, there has been confusion as to which names belonged to the communist canon and which did not. Many streets in East Berlin still bear their communist names, as testimony of that regime, but few fragments of the Berlin Wall are still standing across the city. In Albania's capital, 3,000 communist street names were scrapped without being replaced with

[15] Géza Boros, "Budapest's Sculptures and Commemorative Plaques in Public Spaces 1985–1998," in *Budapest köztéri szobrai és emléktáblai* 1985–1998, eds. Ágnes Szöllôsy and Géza Boros (Budapest: Budapest Galeria, 1998), 199–212.

[16] Emilia Palonen, "Creating Communities: The Postcommunist City-Text of Budapest," Institut fur die Wissenschaften vom Menschen, *Tr@nsit online* (2006), available at: http://www.iwm.at/index.php?option=com_content&task=view&id=327&Itemid=334#_ednref24 (accessed on 10 November 2011). See also Emilia Palonen, "The City-Text in Post-Communist Budapest: Street Names, Memorials, and the Politics of Commemoration," *Geojournal*, 73(2008): 219–230.

new names, thus leaving citizens and postal workers to find their way in a maze of nameless roads.[17] Generally speaking, Eastern European towns no longer evoke the names of notorious communist leaders. The Czech town of Gottwaldov, bearing the name of the Czechoslovak Stalinist leader Klement Gottwald, became Zlin, the Bulgarian town Tolbukhin, named after a Soviet Marshal, became Dobrich, and the German Karl-Marx-Stadt became Chemnitz. In Hungary, Sztálinváros and Leninváros, dedicated to Soviet leaders Joseph Stalin and Vladimir Lenin, changed names, as did Bierutowice, Poland, named after communist strongman Bolesław Bierut.

After 1989, museums displaying the achievements of state socialism were overhauled. Old communist exhibits disappeared, while new museums were opened. In Germany, the Stasi headquarters, the DDR Museum, and the Checkpoint Charlie museum are visited by thousands of travelers and school children annually. Stasi surveillance devices, the organizational chart of the secret political police, communist identity cards, insignia and uniforms, bulletproof cars used to force the border to democratic West Germany, communist propaganda posters and books, and written presentations detailing the tribulations of East Germans who sought to illegally leave the country are used to recreate the totalitarian regime. The Museum of Communism in Prague, built around the theme of "Dream, Reality, and Nightmare" and focused on the Czechoslovak communist regime, includes an interrogation room, a classroom, a shop with barren shelves, and a workshop adorned with propaganda posters and portraits of communist leaders. Poland boasts a Museum of Communism and an exhibit on the Solidarity movement. In Budapest, the renaming of streets expunged the names of discredited communists, making room for pre-communist symbols. Forty of the most representative communist statues, including all Lenins and "comrades in bronze and stone,"[18] have been on display in the Statue Park in Hungary, the Grutas Park in Lithuania, and the Museum of Socialist Art in Bulgaria. The reconstructed execution chamber in the Museum of Genocide Victims in Vilnius dominates the building of former KGB and Gestapo prisons. In Budapest, the House of Terror recounts the activity of the repressive political police and even allows visitors to deck the uniform of a secret agent, and the Imre Nagy memorial commemorates the leader of the 1956 revolution, Hungary's most important anticommunist event. While the House of Terror received substantial government funding, the Bulgarian museums of communism were founded through private initiatives, because the political elite failed to decide what sort of memorialization projects should deal with the communist past. Throughout the region exhibitions of

[17] Rob Cameron, "Tirana: Where the Streets Have No Name," BBC News (3 December 2004).
[18] Palonen, "Creating Communities."

communism have stirred controversy and raised difficult questions on the choice of artifacts and political narratives.[19]

MEMORIALIZATION

Under communism, historical monuments were targets of selective destruction. Statues were removed and street names changed, as symbols of the old regime. New public symbols celebrated the people's dictatorship, multilateral progress, and scientific socialism, the international pantheon of communist leaders (Marx, Engels, Stalin, Mao Zhe Dong, but also Russian military chiefs like A. Suvorov and R. Malinovsky), revolutionary dates (1 May and 23 August), abstract concepts (the Republic, the Popular Army), and even the tools of the working class (the Plough, the Tractor or the Sowing Machine). The city of Braşov became Stalin. Oneşti took the name of Stalinist dictator Gheorghe Gheorghiu-Dej, and Stei was baptized Dr. Petru Groza, in remembrance of a politician who collaborated with the communists. The erasing of the past was furthered by Ceauşescu's rebuilding of Bucharest and the destruction of its historic center. Old residential districts made way to the Victory of Socialism Boulevard, which opened in front of the gigantic House of the People, a monument to the absurdity of unchecked dictatorial rule. The second largest building in the world, the House was Ceauşescu's personal office more than a space for the use of his subjects, collectively seen as the "people."[20] A bulky granite mausoleum perpetuated the memory of the founding fathers of Romanian communism, entombed together in its vast halls. The monument was erected where the Unknown Soldier once stood, in the Carol Park, a leafy spot named after King Carol I and located not far from the see of the Orthodox Patriarch. The communists renamed that green oasis as the Liberty Park.

During the 1950s and the 1960s new villages were created in the Bărăgan plain, considered one of the most inauspicious areas of the country because of its harsh living conditions. These were colonies of families who were deported from Banat, Oltenia, and other regions before 1956 and of political prisoners who were assigned forced domiciles once they were liberated after 1964. Placed in the proximity of existing villages, these new settlements took the name of those villages but added "new" to it (Mărculeştii Noi or Feteştii Noi). In the new village of Lăteşti the small

[19] Egle Rindzeviciute, *Discussing Communism in the Museums of East Central Europe*, European National Museums EUNAMUS (23 May 2011), available at: http://unfoldingeunamus.wordpress.com/2011/05/23/discussing-communism-in-the-museums-of-east-central-europe/ (accessed on 10 November 2011).

[20] Andrei Pippidi, "Historical Memory and Legislative Changes in Romania," in *Totalitarian and Authoritarian Regimes in Europe. Legacies and Lessons from the Twentieth Century*, eds. Jerzy W. Borejsza and Klaus Ziemer (Warsaw: Berghahn Books, 2006), 466.

houses were located along dirty roads so that the colony was shaped as the hammer and sickle, the preeminent communist symbol. The political prisoners living in the colony – writers Paul Goma and Adrian Marino – became aware of this fact only later. After their inhabitants were allowed to return to their homes after years of internal exile, the colonies, which included small houses of clay, were razed and their names erased from the maps.[21]

After 1965, Ceauşescu replaced Stalinist symbols with new ones reflective of his megalomaniac national-communism. Regardless of the time period or region they dealt with, history museums needed to include the full circuit (*circuitul complet*) and present the complete history of the Romanian nation from prehistory to the communist days. As such, all museums had rooms dedicated to communist achievements, whereas regional museums were forced to abandon regional history and present the national history narrative.[22] Once Ceauşescu was removed from office, post-communist changes to the city-text sought to erase the memory of the communist regime and celebrate the victory of the 1989 revolution. These modifications took the form of destruction and construction, sometimes pursued simultaneously, other times separately or in quick succession. It started with the smallest change of all: the addition of one word.

No foreign visitor who reached Bucharest in December 1989, when Ceauşescu desperately clung to power, could ignore the haste with which communist institutions and organizations proclaimed themselves to be "free," as though that very announcement liberated them from dictatorial legacies and guaranteed their democratic performance. The national Romanian Television station, which for decades had been the party's obedient mouthpiece, exulted Ceauşescu's "monumental accomplishments," justified his most irrational policies such as village systematization, and denounced Western-style democracy and the Romanians who defected abroad, suddenly became the Free Television station and sided with the revolution. Even after declaring itself free, the Television station remained a propaganda tool in the hands of the government, its sole source of funding. The Radio Station suffered a similar transmogrification. When it was clear that Ceauşescu no longer controlled the country, the official newspaper of the Communist Party, *Scînteia*, declared itself free of communism, well before it was freed from communists. Its headquarters were rebaptized the Free Press House, although the building was one of Bucharest's most recognizable communist symbols. Constructed in 1950 through 1956 in the

[21] I. Nicolae, "Changes of Romanian Place Names during the Communist Era," in *Post-Communist Romania: Geographical Perspectives*, eds. D. Light and D. Phinnemore (Liverpool: Liverpool Hope Press, 2000), 3. I thank Paul Goma for describing Lăteşti to me and for showing me photographs of the colony.

[22] Simina Bădică, "The Black Hole Paradigm. Exhibiting Communism in Post-Communist Romania," *History of Communism in Europe*, 1(2010): 85 [81–99].

style of Soviet socialist realism, the complex resembled, at a smaller scale, the main building of the Moscow State University Lomonosov and included bas-reliefs symbolizing the people's alphabetization, the country's rapid industrialization, the hammer and sickle, and the bright socialist star.[23] The rush to include the word "free" in the name of government agencies, institutions, organizations, factories, schools, and enterprises engulfed the country, prompting observers to ask where have all the communists gone and to complain that soon even the barber shops will declare themselves free, although the communist propaganda and ideology never reached the combs and dyes. Once it became clear that the regime change was irreversible and the country was heading toward democracy, the word was dropped.

Toponymic changes sought to erase discredited communist symbols and resurrect the memory of the pre-communist "golden age," regarded as the true Romanian history with which the country had to reconnect.[24] The towns of Drs. Petru Groza and Gheorghe Gheorghiu-Dej resumed the names Stei and Oneşti. Bucharest boulevards assumed names connected to the royal family, pre-communist politicians, or new political ideals.[25] Alexandru Moghioroş and Ho Chi Min are no longer on the Bucharest map, which includes streets named after King Carol I and his wife Elisabeta, King Ferdinand, pre-communist politicians Iuliu Maniu, Ion Mihalache, Corneliu Coposu, and Nicolae Titulescu, and writer Eugen Lovinescu, whose daughter mounted a tireless anticommunist campaign from Paris. Compared to Berlin and other Balkan capitals, Bucharest has more streets named after religious and military leaders, reflecting strong veneration of historical figures connected to popular institutions like the Orthodox Church and the army. At the same time, one-fifth of its street names refer to flowers and animals, which denotes the residents' desire for political neutrality, as the naming of streets is a prerogative of local communities.[26] The collective amnesia promoted by the drive to rename public spaces has affected the country's other towns. Piteşti has a square and Sibiu a street named after General Vasile Milea, who lost his life in the 1989 events in circumstances not

[23] "Casa Presei Libere," *Rezistenţa Urbană* (5 August 2008), available at: http://www.rezistenta.net/2008/08/casa-presei-libere.html (accessed on 10 November 2011).

[24] Nicolae, "Changes of Romanian Place Names," 1–6.

[25] According to Duncan Light, the local Bucharest authorities asked the public to submit new street names. Over 10,000 suggestions were made, but only 7 percent of streets were renamed, mostly in 1990. Over time, the state usurped the process and started to control it again. Duncan Light, "Street Names in Bucharest, 1990–1997: Exploring the Modern Historical Geographies of Post-Socialist Change," *Journal of Historical Geography*, 30(2004): 160.

[26] Marius Cosmeanu, "Numele străzilor deseneazǎ portretul-robot al poporului," *Evenimentul Zilei* (29 October 2009). In the early 1990s, hundreds of street names in Bucharest were changed. Since 1996, only forty name changes occurred. "Schimbarea numelor de străzi în Bucureşti," Romania News (23 January 2007), available at: http://www.mail-archive.com/bucuresti@yahoogroups.com/msg02965.html (accessed on 5 April 2012).

yet completely elucidated, Constanţa has Iuliu Maniu and Ferdinand streets, in Braşov the 15 November Boulevard commemorates the 1987 workers' strikes, and in Timişoara the 16 December 1989 and Martyrs Way streets evoke the 1989 revolution, which started in the city.

Smaller towns or towns where the 1989 revolution had no presence were unaffected by the regime change. Some localities have streets named 1 May, the workers' day, or Constantin Dobrogeanu-Gherea, the socialist theorist, and some new streets are named after various Orthodox feasts and saints of local importance. Even in larger towns, lesser known communist names and symbols have survived. A Bucharest street is named after Eremia Popescu, a Securitate officer who deported 40,000 people in the 1950s.[27] A street in Piteşti is still named Mitrea Cocor, after the protagonist of the first socialist-realist novel published by Mihail Sadoveanu in 1949, when he placed his pen in the service of the communists.[28] A street in Cluj evokes the name of Emil Petrovici, an academic who denounced his colleagues, including philosopher Lucian Blaga, for refusing to support the Communist Party's efforts to assert control over the country.[29] In October 2011, eight small towns as well as the city of Constanţa had streets named 23 August, the communist national day, four towns had streets named Work, five had Worker's streets, three had Peasants' streets, and one had a Miners' street.[30]

Conflict mounted when the new names were those of members of the fascist Iron Guard and when Hungarian names replaced Romanian ones. Street naming is the prerogative of the elected local councils, as representatives of the residents. The most controversial case referred to Marshal Ion Antonescu, the pro-Nazi leader of 1940–1944, whose name was preferred in towns where he was revered as a national hero. During the 1990s, several statues of Antonescu also appeared. After the Presidential Commission for the Study of Holocaust concluded its work in 2004 and parliament banned fascist symbols in public places, the streets were renamed, and the statues were removed or made unavailable for public viewing.[31] Other controversial cases hinged on ethnic identity. In 2011, for example, the Senate criticized the town council of Miercurea Ciuc, located in the predominantly Hungarian county of Harghita,

[27] Idem.

[28] Mircea Crăciun, "Relicve din perioada dictaturii comuniste în judeţul Argeş," *Memoria. Revista Gândirii Arestate* (no date), 44–45, available at: http://revista.memoria.ro/?location=view_article&id=644 (accessed on 10 May 2011).

[29] Claudiu Pădurean, "Torţionarul lui Lucian Blaga, omagiat la Cluj," *RomâniaLiberă* (7 January 2011).

[30] Cf. an examination of the names of streets, boulevards, squares, and markets conducted with Google maps.

[31] "Serialul Ion Antonescu şi asumarea istoriei," BBC Romanian.com (1 August 2008), available at: http://www.bbc.co.uk/romanian/news/story/2008/08/080801_serial_antonescu_episod1.shtml (accessed on 7 July 2012).

for changing a street name from Liviu Rebreanu, a Romanian writer (1885–1944) critical of Hungarian rule in Transylvania, to Vorosmarty Mihaly, a Hungarian poet (1800–1855) who never visited Harghita.[32]

The pattern of demolishing the old and constructing anew was also noticeable with respect to statues and memorials. In March 1990, the statue of Lenin that had dominated the Press House Square in Bucharest for thirty years was removed amid the applause of the crowds. Bronze taken from older statues of pre-communist political luminaries removed from public places in the late 1940s was used to make Lenin's statue. Also in 1990, citizens demolished the bust of Dobrogeanu-Gherea, whom they mistook for Groza.[33] The statues of communist leaders parked outside Bucharest, in Mogoşoaia, lay horizontally on the grass and are not arranged for public viewing, but they are easily reached by any visitor who takes the trouble to look for them. Their power is deadened and their political irrelevance confirmed with every child picking Lenin's nose, riding him like a horse, or pressing his shoe on his face. Communist statues in other towns have met the same fate, and the spots where many of them once stood remain empty.

At the same time, new works of art have been placed on display to celebrate anticommunist heroes. In Bucharest, the Revolution Square has been transformed into a site with symbolic importance for the anticommunist resistance, a place where "memory crystallizes and secretes itself," as Pierre Nora wrote.[34] The square is guarded on one side by the former headquarters of the Romanian Communist Party, the building from where Ceauşescu delivered his last speech and fled Bucharest on board a helicopter on 22 December 1989, and on the other side by the former Royal Palace and the much older Kretzulescu church. The University Library, an imposing building that once housed the Carol Foundation, and a series of multilevel buildings rumored to have served as Securitate stations guard the other sides of the square. The square's centerpiece is represented by the statue of Coposu, from where tourists can gaze upon bullet-scarred buildings that bear the signs of the 1989 revolution. Together with the House of the People, the square is often included among "communist heritage" tourist destinations and is popular with foreign visitors interested to find out more about Ceauşescu's times.[35]

Regarding the way in which Romanian museums present communism, Simina Bădică noted that after 1989 the insistence of the new leaders, represented by the

[32] "UDMR, înfrânt la Senat – primăriile nu mai pot pune nume maghiare străzilor," Ziare.com (1 June 2011), available at: http://www.ziare.com/politica/maghiari/udmr-infrant-la-senat-primariile-nu-mai-pot-pune-nume-maghiare-strazilor-1098509 (accessed on 10 November 2011).

[33] Domniţa Ştefănescu, *Cinci ani din istoria României. O cronologie a evenimentelor Decembrie 1989-Decembrie 1994* (Bucharest: Editura Maşina de Scris, 1995).

[34] Pierre Nora, "Between Memory and History: *Les Lieux de Memoire*," *Representations*, 26(1989):7.

[35] Duncan Light, "An Unwanted Past: Contemporary Tourism and the Heritage of Communism in Romania," *International Journal of Heritage Studies*, 6(2000): 149.

Salvation Front and its successor, the Social Democrat Party, to impose the "politics of amnesia"[36] and their refusal to open the debate on the recent past radicalized the position of their political rivals, who felt the need for such investigation, and made them describe the entire communist regime as criminal, although most crimes occurred before 1964 (see Chapter 1). As such, since the collapse of the Ceauşescu regime anticommunist groups have tended to treat the communist period as a "black hole" from which Romania was "miraculously delivered" in 1989.[37] After the regime change, the national and local history museums have opted to eradicate communist exhibits and artifacts from their public collections. In the National History Museum in Bucharest, which glorified Ceauşescu before 1989, the presentation of history stops abruptly in the 1920s and covers neither the right-wing nor the left-wing dictatorial regimes of 1940–1989. When they were asked to explain their policy of prevarication vis-a-vis the legacy of communism, museum officials pointed out that the time is not yet right for the museum to interpret the very recent past. Only after professional historians produce a balanced narrative of the period, they said, could the museum interpret communist times.[38] Interestingly, this position did not change after the release of the final report of the Presidential Commission for the Analysis of Communist Dictatorship in Romania in 2006 (see Chapter 5). This museum, and its smaller local counterparts, continues to treat the communist period as Romania's "black hole."

The best-known site of encounter with the history of Romanian communism is the former prison of Sighetul Marmaţiei, located close to the border with Ukraine, in the northern region of Maramureş, over 350 kilometers from Bucharest. Erected in 1897 as an army barracks, the building became the "Prison of Ministers" in 1950, when over 100 pre-communist luminaries were brought there. Some had been condemned to lengthy prison terms, others had never been indicted. Fifty died in captivity. The prison ceased to accept political convicts in 1955 and was closed in the 1970s. In 1995, the Memorial of Victims of Communism and of the Resistance was launched by the Civic Academy first in a torture chamber called the Black Room. Other prison cells were opened as they were reconstructed. The museum is affiliated to an International Centre for the Study of Communism, whose executive scientific board is all-European. Sighet was deemed a "site of national importance" in 1997, when it started to receive minimal government funding. That year, the Council of Europe recognized it among the most significant European monuments, on par with the Auschwitz Museum and the Peace Memorial in Normandy. Until 2000, the

[36] Vladimir Tismaneanu, "Democracy and Memory: Romania Confronts Its Communist Past," *Annals of the American Academy of Political and Social Science*, 617(2008): 168.

[37] Bădică, "The Black Hole Paradigm," 82.

[38] Light, "An Unwanted Past," 156.

museum was a memorial to the victims of communism who lost their lives at Sighet. While preserving the original prison structure and atmosphere and representing the most repressive aspects of communism (including the forced collectivization and the labor camps), the museum is a site where visitors encounter irrefutable evidence of the criminality of the ancien regime, because, as Civic Academy leader Ana Blandiana eloquently wrote, "When justice does not succeed in being a form of memory, memory itself can be a form of justice."[39]

In 2000, the permanent exhibition was expanded to propose a global discourse on Romanian communism that also touched on Ceauşescu's personality cult, everyday life under communism, and communist regimes in other countries. By turning away from the prison theme, Sighet became "the black hole of Romanian history to be looked at through prison bars,"[40] a place that forges communism into an "abstract, ahistorical period of violent clashes between oppression and resistance."[41] In this site of terror that acts as a "cultural courtroom," "politicized condemnatory accounts could be made historically credible" so that the entire nation can be portrayed as having been victimized, in spite of the widespread collaboration that bound the majority of the Romanian people to the communist dictatorship. The ethnic character of suffering is underscored by a vegetal border that marks the perimeter of the former paupers' cemetery, located in the proximity of the Sighet prison, and carefully draws the contours of the Romanian state, thus symbolizing the nation's eternal embrace of its martyrs. In addition, the Civic Academy has "failed to notice obvious ways in which Sighet was not the site of one single type of oppression," as the town's large Jewish population, which included the Nobel Prize laureate Elie Wiesel, had suffered tremendously before the site became a communist prison.[42]

Besides ongoing oral history programs, Sighet organizes a yearly summer school for pre-university students, publishes a monumental scholarly journal, and commemorates each year on the day of the Ascension a Day of Memory, dedicated to those who suffered in communist prisons.[43] By far, the summer school attracts the most attention, because leaders of the Civic Academy come from Bucharest to meet the students and foreign researchers are invited to lecture. During those meetings, the prison becomes a nontraditional classroom that provides teenagers between 14 and 18 years old with a unique possibility to learn about communist times. The

39 Ana Blandiana, "Memoria ca formă de justiţie," *Dilema*, 518(2003): 10.

40 Bădică, "The Black Hole Paradigm," 94.

41 Apor, "Eurocommunism," 4.

42 Maria Bucur, *Heroes and Victims. Remembering War in Twentieth-Century Romania* (Bloomington: Indiana University Press, 2009), 241.

43 Fundaţia Academia Civică, *Memorialul Victimelor Comunismului şi al Rezistenţei* (2009), available at: http://www.memorialsighet.ro/index.php?option=com_content&view=frontpage&Itemid=1&lang=ro (accessed on 20 July 2011).

school, which includes workshops, conferences, roundtables, documentaries, and music concerts, has attracted reputable foreign scholars, including Stephane Courtois, the editor of the *Black Book of Communism*, Russian dissident Vladimir Bukovsky, British academics Dennis Deletant and Tom Gallagher, or Solidarity leaders Bogdan Lis and Tadeusz Fiszbach.[44]

The only other permanent exhibitions on communism are housed with the County Museum in Alexandria and the Peasant Museum in Bucharest. The small display in Alexandria, which surveys collectivization in the Teleorman county, is seldom visited. The Peasant Museum opened in 1990 in a building formerly occupied by the History Museum of the Romanian Communist Party. Since 1997 The Plague exhibition can be visited in the basement. Its display of communism was meant to counterbalance the serenity and balance of the permanent exhibit on peasant life, which hid the fact that peasants were deprived of their possessions and lifestyle during the collectivization drive of the 1940s. The small and ugly room, which is "a memorial of the pain and suffering collectivization caused to the peasant world,"[45] includes issues of *Scînteia* that name peasants who resisted collectivization and poems children had to learn and write about the benefits of the collective. The display's radical position transpired in the claim that it represented the entire communist regime, not just the Stalinist period. As museum director Horia Bernea wrote in the booklet accompanying the display, communism was "a disease of society and soul," an "ideal stupidity, totally oriented against life," a "destructive atheistic sect," the "exultation of shameful evil," "absolute hatred," and a "sinister utopia."[46] To convey a dictatorial reality that no longer exists, the museum had to be an antidote to amnesia.

Sighet is the country's best organized and most visible museum of communism, but the largest memory project enacted to date has been overseen by the Association of Former Political Prisoners, which, after 1989, erected seventy-five monuments dedicated to the victims of communism and posted tens of explanatory marble plaques on former communist prisons and labor camps throughout Romania.[47] Most of these memorials and plaques also name those killed by the communist authorities. In addition, Romanians can visit the memorial houses dedicated to Christian Democrat leader Coposu, who spent seventeen years in communist prisons and labor

[44] Monica Ciobanu, "Teaching History and Building a Democratic Future: Reflections from Post-Communist Romania," *Democracy & Education*, 17(2008): 58–62, and Stephane Courtois, ed., *The Black Book of Communism: Crimes, Terror, Repression* (Cambridge, MA: Harvard University Press, 1999).

[45] Bădică, "The Black Hole Paradigm," 91.

[46] Idem, 92–93.

[47] A complete list is included in Asociaţia Foştilor Deţinuţi Politici din România, *Album Memorial. Monumente închinate jertfei, suferinţei şi luptei împotriva comunismului* (Bucharest: AFDPR, 2004).

camps, including Sighet, former political prisoner Constantin Ticu Dumitrescu, a Christian Democrat senator and a tireless champion of transitional justice, and Monica Lovinescu, a Paris correspondent of Radio Free Europe and a vocal anticommunist campaigner. Most of these memory projects have received no financial support from the government.[48]

The fate of the former communist prisons merits some attention. Besides Sighet, which is open to the public as a memorial and a museum, other former communist-era prisons of ill repute have served as sites of memory. Since the mid-2000s, small exhibits or education programs geared on the communist past have been organized in the former prisons of Râmnicul Sărat and Gherla, often with the help of the Institute for the Investigation of Communist Crimes and the Memory of Romanian Exile. The Făgăraşi Fortress, built in 1310 by Ladislau Apor, was transformed into a museum that remains silent on 1949–1960, when the fortress served as a political prison that received pre-communist police, gendarmerie, and intelligence officers. In 2004, the Negru Vodă Foundation set to transform the fortress into a memorial and incorporate information about the 1950s into a new Memorial Museum of Anticommunist Resistance Făgăraşi opened in the fortress.[49] The buildings that once held other communist-era prisons remain silent on that dark past. The notorious Piteşti prison was transformed into an office space, while a motel is to be built on the land where once stood the Periprava forced labor camp in the Brăila Big Island. The Aiud, Gherla, and part of the Jilava prisons remain in use.[50]

Several broad patterns characterize memorialization in Romania. First, memorials, statues, and museums representing the communist past build extensively on Christian symbols, especially the cross, which symbolizes both the death of the victims of communism and their religiosity, a mark of anticommunism under a self-avowed atheistic regime. The unveiling of these monuments was accompanied by elaborate and well-attended religious services. Orthodox priests were called to exorcise the Peasant Museum of its communist ghosts, a ritual that showed religion as a vehicle of catharsis, purification, and remembrance. Second, these representations articulate quasi-religious interpretations of the martyrdom of the nation. The Sighet memorial, which presents the fallen as fighters for national dignity, is

[48] Lavinia Stan, "National Report on Romania," part of the How the Memory of Crimes Committed by Totalitarian Regimes is Dealt with in the Member States project, commissioned by the Direction D: Fundamental Rights and Citizenship of the Directorate-General for Justice, Freedom and Security of the European Commission, 2009.

[49] Fundaţia Culturală Negru Vodă, *Muzeul Memorial Rezistenţa Anticomunistă Făgărăşeană* (2011), available at: http://negruvoda.ro/muzeu2.html (accessed on 29 November 2011). I thank Cosmin Budeanca for drawing my attention to this project.

[50] Personal interview with Cosmin Budeanca, Bucharest, 28 June 2011.

constructed as "a holy place of the Romanian nation."[51] The victims are part of the historical continuity of the struggle for the state of all Romanians, and thus the monuments define the nation in connection to the Orthodox Church and the Romanian nation–state. National virtues become eternal entities when the Peasant Museum shows the peasantry as permanent and profoundly Christian and portrays communism as "a brutal rupture in the harmonious history of the nation, its state and Church,"[52] although the Church engaged in a long-term profitable collaboration with the communists. Memory projects thus contribute to the commemoration of national pride by presenting the nation as an eternal entity and the communist rule as a historical accident caused by external forces and maintained by violence.[53] As such, they delegate responsibility for communist horrors to the Soviets or the generic "communists," who are always treated as alien "others," and allow the Romanian visitor to identify only with the victims, offering no option between victim and villain.[54] Third, although museums create historical authenticity and render communist terror tangible and credible, their reconstruction of communism as an "icon of violence" is part of a political agenda that seeks to legitimize communism as "the twin of the ultimate horrors of Nazism and as the Eastern double of the ultimate catastrophe of European civilization," a regime that was as destructive and merciless as the Third Reich.[55]

A permanent exhibition that departs from these traits opened in 2004 in Bucharest under the title Domestic Red. Created by Gabriela Cristea, it combines museum anthropology and art installations to display private life under communism by showing old objects and colors, background music, and a list of the problems caused by communist legislation in everyday life (e.g., illegal abortion). According to the artist, this exhibit of private space seeks to complement Sighet's "nationalist and victim-centered" display of public space by focusing on the life of the ordinary person and recreating the family space, that is, "how we ate, what we saw, what we heard" during communist times.[56] An abortion kit, a number of communist consumer goods no longer produced, the *Scînteia* newspaper, and a pioneer tie are also on display.

[51] Gabriela Cristea and Simina Radu-Bucurenci, "Raising the Cross: Exorcising Romania's Communist Past in Museums, Memorials and Monuments," in *Past for the Eyes: Cinema and Museums in Representing Communism in Eastern Europe after 1989*, eds. Oksana Sarkisova and Péter Apor (Budapest: Central University Press, 2007), 301.

[52] Cristea and Radu-Bucurenci, "Raising the Cross," 279–295.

[53] Apor, "Eurocommunism," 10–11.

[54] Bădică, "The Black Hole Paradigm," 96.

[55] Apor, "Eurocommunism," 12–13.

[56] Bogdan Iancu, "Muzeu despre viaţa privată în communism," *Evenimentul Zilei* (10 November 2004).

THE CITIZEN'S OPINION TRIBUNAL

Frustrated with the judiciary's incapacity and unwillingness to organize a Nuremberg-type trial to condemn the crimes of the communist regime, on 7 September 2006 in Cluj-Napoca civil society groups decided to create an opinion tribunal composed of nine former victims of communist repression representing different counties, one counselor each for the prosecution and defense, and 150 audience members who acted as jurors. Charged with genocide and crimes against humanity (including premeditated murder, extermination, forced deportation, arrests, torture, disappearances, and ethnic and religious persecution), crimes not protected from prosecution by the statute of limitations, the communist regime was found guilty of all charges after the opinion tribunal discussed a summary of its human rights abuses.[57]

Although it had no correspondent in Eastern Europe, the Romanian tribunal resembled opinion tribunals organized in other parts of the world in that it lacked legal standing and was unable to apply punishment.[58] Given these limitations, "the public relations impact through media attention" determined the tribunal's ability to further its legal and moral case."[59] The poorly advertised tribunal had little public echo inside and outside Romania, being disregarded by the population, the political elite, the local press, and the associations representing victims and intellectuals. Not only have Romanians been reluctant to support a generic Trial of Communism indirectly implicating the four million former ordinary party members who consider themselves untainted by collaboration, but former communist-era victims have argued that the post-communist state (as legal successor to the communist state that perpetrated the atrocities) should acknowledge responsibility for communist crimes through its regular courts. Romanian courts have ignored such demands, pointing to the statute of limitations applicable to those cases and refusing to recognize communist crimes as crimes against humanity (see Chapter 2). The tribunal's poor reception further stemmed from the elitist manner in which it was assembled, its predetermined outcome, and failure to question the premises of its condemnation of the communist regime and to adhere to legal procedures to enhance its legitimacy. In particular, the Romanian tribunal made no effort to include a defense, although "fairness is important in terms of the public and media images, a point

57 Curtea Penală de Condamnare Juridico-Morală a Crimelor Regimurilor Comuniste, *Procesul Comunismului* (October 2006), available at: http://redholocaust.org/procesul.html (accessed on 29 March 2011).

58 Arthur Klinghoffer and Judith Klinghoffer, *International Citizens' Tribunals: Mobilizing Public Opinion to Advance Human Rights* (London: Palgrave Macmillan, 2002).

59 Idem, 7.

not adequately taken into account by many tribunals that don't place a premium on impartiality."[60]

Victims' and intellectual groups have challenged the legitimacy of the opinion tribunal, calling instead for a Trial of Communism in the courts of law. In March 2003, for example, the ICAR Foundation filed with the Bucharest Court a complaint asking the government to acknowledge the "communist Holocaust" of 1945 to 1989, to officially apologize to the victims for the abuses they suffered, and to admit that the Securitate was a political police that infringed human rights. According to the Foundation, the Trial of Communism is "a duty to the victims who died with the hope that justice would be done and to those who survived and are still waiting for this justice to be done," as well as "a necessary and expected acknowledgement of the state abuses of the past, and a sign of maturity for the Romanian democracy."[61] President Ion Iliescu and his Social Democrat government ignored the request. After the 2004 elections, Democrat-Liberal President Traian Băsescu received the ICAR representatives, who convinced him of the power of an official apology from the head of state for communist crimes addressed to the victims and the society at large. Băsescu agreed to deliver the apology, after the Tismaneanu Commission documented the communist crimes (see Chapter 5). The apology never came, but the work of the Presidential Commission became a substitute for the Trial of Communism for which the civil society so passionately advocated.

FORENSIC INVESTIGATIONS

Forensic investigations were first conducted by the Association of Former Political Prisoners at the request of the victims' relatives. The press reported two cases. In 1995, the remains of seven members of an anticommunist armed resistance group led by Major Dabija, who were killed by the Securitate and placed in an unmarked tomb in 1949, were exhumed and moved to the Sibiu municipal cemetery. Two years later, the remains of Ioan Andraş, a student from Târgu Mureş who joined the resistance Yellow Shirts group before being killed and buried in the Ibăneşti village in 1951, were transferred to the village cemetery.[62] These forensic investigations were conducted by volunteers with little expertise in the domain. The victims, members of the anticommunist resistance, were executed by Securitate during the first decade of communism in secret extrajudicial executions perpetrated in remote mountainous areas.

[60] Idem, *International Citizens' Tribunals*, 190.

[61] ICAR Foundation, *Communism Trial* (2010), available at: http://www.icarfoundation.ro/index.php?option=com_content&task=view&id=29&Itemid=44 (accessed on 1 September 2011).

[62] Lavinia Stan, "National Report on Romania," 86.

After 2006, historian Marius Oprea has conducted exhumations in collaboration with the Military Section of the Supreme Court first under the aegis of the Institute for the Investigation of Communist Crimes and since 2009 as part of the Center for the Investigation of Communist Crimes (see Chapter 1). Whereas the Institute is funded by the government, through the Prime Minister's Office, the Center is a nongovernmental organization financed by the Konrad Adenauer Foundation, a German think-tank.[63] After the relatives of the deceased notify it, the forensic team looks for information on the date and place of the crime in the Securitate files housed with the National Council for the Study of Securitate Archives, searching for clues about the crime's exact location. Then they visit the site, which is usually indicated by the relatives, and launch archeological investigations.[64]

In 2006 through 2007, Oprea worked in the paupers' cemetery at the Sighet prison, located the forced labor colonies on the Big Island of Brăila, exhumed the remains of six people shot in 1950 in Bistriţa-Năsăud for refusing to be drafted in the army, and established that the Securitate killed Iosif Orsa in 1950.[65] In 2009 through 2010, his team uncovered the remains of ten anticommunist resistance members killed by the Securitate in the counties of Bistriţa-Năsăud, Hunedoara, Cluj, and Sălaj in 1949 to 1952.[66] In one case, the local police cooperated only after receiving an order from the Ministry of Interior, as a former Securitate officer who perpetrated the killings was a powerful local leader.[67] In another case, the team exhumed the remains of two young peasants from Băieşi village who refused to join the collective and instead hid in the mountains for two years before their location was disclosed to the Securitate by their most trusted friend.[68] In 2011, Oprea was praised for locating the remains of celebrated writer Mircea Vulcănescu, killed in 1952, near the Aiud prison.[69] These efforts to identify and relocate the victims' remains were detailed in a volume, a movie, and a traveling exhibition titled "Common Denominator: Death," which displays photos of the victims and

63 Marius Oprea, cited in "Comunismul s-a bazat pe teroare şi ceea ce descoperim noi demonstrează acest lucru," *BN Observator* (17 July 2010).

64 Laura Oana Iancu and Ciprian Iancu, "Numitor comun: moartea," *Replica Hunedoara* (8 June 2011).

65 Mirela Corlăţan, "O crimă a Securităţii este scoasă azi la iveală prin deshumare," *Ediţie Specială* (3 July 2007), and Violeta Fotache, "Procesul comunismului – Exhumări în Munţii Tibleşului," *9AM News* (24 April 2007).

66 Centrul de Investigare a Crimelor Comunismului, *Cazuri* (2010), available at: http://www.condamnareacomunismului.ro/Proiecte/Programuldearheologiecontemporan%C4%83/Cazuri.aspx (accessed 3 April 2011).

67 Mihai Soica, "Luptători anticomunişti, exhumaţi din groapa comună," *Evenimentul Zilei* (29 April 2009).

68 Ianuc and Iancu, "Numitor comun: moartea."

69 C. Padurean, "Mormântul lui Mircea Vulcănescu, identificat la Râpa Robilor," *România Liberă* (1 April 2011).

the exhumations and personal objects found next to the deceased: boots, bullets, crosses, and even wood spoons.[70]

Such efforts to set the historical record straight and provide closure to the surviving relatives have received little financial and logistical support from state authorities, which show no interest in taking the lead and devising a comprehensive plan for exhumations, although the number of victims of extrajudicial killings buried in unmarked graves might reach 10,000.[71] Some village mayors and police officers have helped the archeologists, but there has been very little coordinated effort on the part of the authorities to facilitate and expand the forensic program. As such, investigations are still conducted by small teams of volunteers with limited funds at their disposal and on a largely ad hoc basis – characteristics that have prevented the courts from hearing legal cases built on grave excavations.[72] The victims' relatives participate in these campaigns, often insisting on inhumations accompanied by Orthodox religious ceremonies.

Exhumations reflect the problematic tension of integrating "autobiographical memory" into "collective memory," as Monica Ciobanu argued, because they open old wounds and re-divide local communities along old lines. Indeed, resistance members were supported by some villagers, relatives, and neighbors who provided aid or refuge, but were loathed by other local residents who believed that the victims' anticommunist fight placed the village into the hands of the Securitate and exposed residents to unnecessary suffering. Division lines reflect the existence of competing memories, "current ideological conflicts connected to issues of social identity and competition over status and resources."[73] In one such case, exhumations split the community of the Teregova village in the Caraş-Severin county between those who supported the effort to reveal communist crimes and those who opposed it. The two opposing camps were led by the town mayor, critical of the exhumation because one of his relatives had worked for the Securitate at the time of the executions, and the local priest, who favored the investigations because his family had supported the victims. At the same time, villagers who had been monitored by the Securitate because of their ties to the resistance members resented the fact that, in contrast to the relatives of the partisans, they received no material compensation and public recognition.

[70] Centrul de Investigare a Crimelor Comunismului, "Common Denominator: Death," 2011, exhibition, M. Bran, *La Roumanie vingt ans après – Le chasseur de la Securitate* (Paris: Cygne, 2009), and M. Bran and J. Mercier, Directors, *Le chasseur de la Securitate*, DVD movie, 2009.

[71] Marius Oprea, cited in "Comunismul s-a bazat pe teroare."

[72] James Mark, "What Remains? Anti-Communism, Forensic Archaeology, and the Retelling of the National Past in Lithuania and Romania," *Past and Present*, Supplement 5 (2010): 276–300.

[73] Monica Ciobanu, "Rewriting and Remembering Romanian Communism: Some Controversial Issues," *Nationalities Papers*, 39(2011): 214.

THE ROMANIAN ARMAGEDDON

From 2001 to 2007, a series of anonymous and controversial emails were distributed to the Romanian press for publication under the general title "Armageddon" (Armaghedon). The first to receive attention was "Armageddon 2," which accused the Social Democrat Prime Minister Adrian Năstase of corruption. The government's reaction was swift, although the allegations had appeared in the press before being summarized and expanded in the "Armageddon." In 2002, the prosecutor general ordered the arrest of journalist Ovidiu Cristian Iane and the search of former government official Mugur Ciuvică's home, claiming that the two suspected authors of the document had damaged national security and violated article 168 of the Criminal Code on disseminating false information (a provision intended to cover acts that posed a threat to the public, not to limit freedom of the press). Năstase later acknowledged that he had overreacted, but failed to repeal the Criminal Code provisions. The allegations of corruption followed Năstase long after he ceased his mandate, and at the time of this writing he has already been indicted in a number of cases by the National Anticorruption Department.

Two months later, on 28 March 2002, "Armageddon 7" created another scandal by publicly listing former Securitate officers who continued to hold key posts in post-communist intelligence services. The email reached the press when the country was about to join NATO, which, journalists argued, had asked for the vetting of former Securitate "dinosaurs" from intelligence services as a precondition for accepting Romania as a member. The author of "Armageddon 7" remained unknown, but rumors had it that the list originated with Oprea. The press suggested that the Interior Ministry or the Romanian Information Service might know something and hoped that, by printing the text, the government will confirm the list's accuracy. Although daily *Ziua*, which published "Armageddon 7," believed that only part of the information was true, as the list included blatant mistakes that could be spotted even by non-experts, it noted that "the names on this list are not names of ghosts. These persons have acquaintances, neighbors, who can deny or confirm the facts.... We are inviting them to the debate."[74]

"Armageddon 7" alleged that since 1990, when the Romanian Information Service was established as heir to the Securitate, the public was "systematically and shamelessly lied about its composition." Instead of becoming a modern intelligence service with increasingly fewer Securitate officers on its payroll, the Service was controlled by the Securitate, whose officers prevailed in its

74 "Romanian Daily Publishes List of Securitate Agents Working in Intelligence," Foreign Broadcast Information Service (28 March 2002), FBIS-EEU-2002–0405, available at: http://cryptome.org/ro-spy-list.htm (accessed on 20 February 2011).

leadership. Responding to claims that the Service hired Securitate officers as experts, "Armageddon 7" asked for the disclosure of information about the expertise of Securitate officers and Service leaders involved in political scandals and claimed that the Service had kept Securitate officers "who shamelessly made every possible move to get ahead, polishing the shoes of figurehead politicians, hanging around talking and pretending they were good at something, or putting up for bid documents that could be used for blackmail." As such, the Service included "people who pull strings behind the scenes, engage in intrigues, or are good for nothing," that is, the active and retired Securitate officers who "troubled our society."[75]

The influence of retired Securitate officers allegedly extended to financial institutions, as they were "managing public and private money" and private security and protection firms "in permanent conflict with the law" and leeched numerous banks "under the pretext of assuring these banks' internal and external protection, but the banks they protected have collapsed, one by one." It further tied former Securitate officers to "great robber" Sorin Ovidiu Vântu, the owner of the Financial Investment Fund, whose collapse made many ordinary Romanians lose their life savings. The relationship was allegedly proved by the fact that "320 Securitate and Intelligence Service reservists worked, shoulder to shoulder, for this profoundly dubious man, cashing in their shares" when ordinary people went bankrupt and by the fact that "our vigilant domestic intelligence service pretended not to notice anything when Vântu's clay empire was riding on top of the wave." Even more disconcerting, according to "Armageddon 7," was the Securitate officers' penetration of the legislature after Law 187/1999 asked members of parliament and government to disclose their past collaboration with the Securitate. The authors of "Armageddon 7" had allegedly identified six or seven former Securitate agents close to Prime Minister Năstase and wondered why the "highly educated" Năstase put up with agents who were "poor in spirit" or were "nobody in their profession," unless "there is a dictatorship in store for us" that satisfied both the prime minister and the secret agents.[76]

The anonymous authors claimed to have compiled a list of over 1,600 names of former Securitate officers connected to the Romanian Information Service and the External Information Service from 1990 to 2002. They offered for publication only 287 individuals, of which 25 were identified solely by their family names. Each name was followed by a short paragraph detailing that person's association with the Securitate, the post-communist intelligence services, political parties, state agencies, or public utilities. Except for the most recognizable names, the identity of

[75] Idem.
[76] Idem.

the persons was difficult to make out, because many names were common and not accompanied by further details (such as the place of birth or residence). In a handful of cases in which only the family name was listed, it was impossible to make out the person's gender. "Armageddon 7" was followed by no lists disclosing the identity of other secret agents.

"Armageddon 7" hoped to lead to the removal of former Securitate officers from post-communist intelligence services. By the time it reached the press, the identification of former secret agents was seriously stalled, although the civil society had repeatedly underscored the need to make a clear break with the past and had emphasized that former Securitate agents were engaged in notorious corruption scandals. Law 187/1999 launched the public identification of Securitate agents, regardless of whether or not they occupied post-communist public positions, and created the governmental agency responsible for the identification process. During its first years of activity, the National Council for the Study of Securitate Archives was obstructed by the Romanian Information Service, which housed 60 percent of Securitate files, and Năstase's Social Democrat government, which kept under lock the vast majority of the secret files under the pretext that they were touching on national security. By the time "Armageddon 7" was released, the Council had publicly unveiled only 29 of the 486,000 to 700,000 secret informers who had worked for the Securitate before 1989 and none of its 13,275 officers.[77] Months after the release, the Council identified the first Securitate officers and accelerated the identification of informers.

"Armageddon 7" was part of a wave of post-communist unofficial disclosures of the identity and activity of former communist-era secret agents that took place in the Czech Republic, Poland, and Slovenia and were initiated to prevent those named from continuing their political careers and to harm their chances of being elected or nominated to public positions as much as to uncover the truth about the past. Given their propensity for revenge, these disclosures represent instances of "vigilante justice," meted out by self-appointed inquisitors who believed they furthered the common good by publicly releasing information and thus compelling state institutions to de-block lustration, provide access to the secret files, and reform the intelligence services. For them, the need to disclose the names was more urgent and imperative than the need to offer accurate information. The danger of discrediting the list by including incomplete or very common names was apparently of little concern for these lonely crusaders.[78]

77 Lavinia Stan, "Spies, Files and Lies: Explaining the Failure of Access to Securitate Files," *Communist and Post-Communist Studies*, 37(2004): 348.

78 Lavinia Stan, "Vigilante Justice in Post-Communist Europe," *Communist and Post-Communist Studies*, 44(2011): 307–315.

ART AND MOVIE PROJECTS FOCUSED ON THE COMMUNIST PAST

After 1989, the literature and the arts were no longer understood as either "a protest discourse or as cheering the Ceauşescu regime."[79] While writers and artists continued to feel the pressure to opt for a "pure" artistic career dissociated from civic activism, the opening of the public discourse allowed previously unheard voices to be heard and encouraged established authors and artists to reaffirm their commitment to the new democratic ideals, without critically evaluating their collaboration with the ancien regime. With a handful of notable exceptions, literary, artistic, and intellectual circles avoided the question of moral responsibility by concluding that their communist-era works served the role of a quiet resistance, and most artists, writers, and philosophers had refused compromise. This position was unequivocally promoted during the first weeks after the ousting of the communist regime by the weekly *Romania literară*, which described communist Romania not as a country where resistance and opposition were minimal but as one where the literati had fearlessly engaged in resistance tactics. A handful of subliminal innuendos and expressions between the lines were seen as mounting to a "long and tiring" opposition campaign to which "the real representatives of Romanian literature have taken part ... for an equally artistic and moral ideal."[80] Because the literati were beacons of morality, the reexamination of the communist past revolved around the memory of the writers killed and persecuted from 1945 to 1989 and the need to save their work, largely avoiding public identifications of the former Securitate agents from among writers. That information became public in 2001, when journalists accessed the secret files housed with the National Council. These public unveilings have covered the front pages of newspapers ever since.

The most daring productions on communist times have come from a talented young generation of movie makers, who carved a niche for themselves despite the ubiquitous presence of Sergiu Nicolaescu, a communist-era film director who retained popularity by assuming a string of political roles. A participant in the 1989 revolution, Nicolaescu headed a Senate inquiry commission that uncovered neither why peaceful demonstrators were shot nor why most killings occurred after Ceauşescu was apprehended, at a time when the Salvation Front ruled the country. Some new movies have a clear political focus, others make no mention of the old regime, although they depict life during those times. Some comment on the brutality of early communist rule, others on the inescapable surveillance instituted by

[79] M. Răduţă, "The Day Before, the Day After: Canonic and Self-Legitimation Changes in the Romanian Literature before and after the Fall of the Communist Regime," in *The Canonical Debate Today: Crossing Disciplinary and Cultural Boundaries*, eds. Liviu Papadima, David Damrosch, and Theo D'haen (Amsterdam: Rodopi, 2011), 151.

[80] Gheorghe Grigurcu, cited in Răduţă, "The Day Before, the Day After," 158–159.

Ceauşescu. These films' international success prompted critics to talk about a new Romanian cinema, characterized by "long takes, controlled camera and an astonishing ear for natural dialogue."[81] Although these productions are of high quality, for now they are simply too few to entitle the movie studios in Buftea, the Bucharest suburb where the Romanian film industry is based, to name themselves Rollywood and claim status on par with the American Hollywood, the Indian Bollywood, or the Nigerian Nollywood.

The Red Rats (*Şobolanii roşii*) was the first post-communist movie to reflect on the communist regime and the political changes of 1989. The story focused on Ştefan, who was monitored by the Securitate for criticizing the regime at a party. After spending some time abroad, he returned to Romania after 1989 to see that the Securitate agents who once beat and interrogated him still occupy high-ranking positions. *Somewhere in the East* (*UndevaînEst*) presented the resistance to collectivization of peasants living in a non-descript Transylvanian village in the late 1940s. *The Oak* (*Balanţa*) narrated the adventures of the daughter of a disgraced Securitate officer, who decided, after her father's death, to relocate to a small, polluted town far from Bucharest. The story depicted the last days of Ceauşescu's regime and the first days of directionless political change experienced by the town folks. *E pericoloso sporgersi* followed the adventures of three residents of a provincial town – a high school student, an actor, and a soldier – in the days leading to the 1989 revolution, juxtaposing the protagonists' desire to escape to freedom to the dictatorship's inhumanity. Released in 1993, *The Most Loved Human Being* (*Cel mai iubit dintre pământeni*), based on the book of writer Marin Preda, presented the difficult reinsertion into society of liberated political prisoners, the humiliations and brutality they endured in prison, the absurdity of communist arrests, and the compromises needed for survival under an aberrant dictatorship.[82]

In 2001, *The Afternoon of a Torturer* (*După-amiaza unui torţionar*) depicted the interview a member of the Association of Former Political Prisoners carried out with sadistic communist torturer Franţ Ţandăra, who once brutalized political prisoners. This dense movie, which was loosely based on the interview book, touched on the complicity between victims and victimizers, the humanity and inhumanity of the torturer, his role in perpetuating the dictatorship, and his post-1989 fate. *Bless You, Prison* (*Binecuvântată fii, închisoare*) recounted the four-year prison experience of Nicole Valéry-Grossu, who became an ardent Christian after being subjected to torture. The movie was directed by Nicolae Mărgineanu, whose own father

81 Jay Weissberg, "4 Months, 3 Weeks & 2 Days," *Variety* (6 June 2007).

82 Florin Codre, Director, *Şobolanii roşii* (1990); Nicolae Mărgineanu, Director, *Undeva în Est* (1991); Lucian Pintilie, Director, *Balanţa* (1992); Nicolae Caranfil, Director, *E pericoloso sporgersi* (1993); and Şerban Marinescu, Director, *Cel mai iubit dintre pământeni* (1993).

spent sixteen years in communist prisons, and was based on the heroine's real-life experience. *12:08 East of Bucharest* (*A fost sau nu a fost*), which won a prize at the Cannes festival, has been widely regarded as one of the best movies commenting on the failure of the 1989 revolution to touch smaller towns, where the post-communist and communist political arrangements shared more similarities than differences. *How I Spent the End of the World* (*Cum mi-am petrecut sfârşitul lumii*) presented a Bucharest suburb during late communism through the eyes of a seven-year-old boy who, together with his friends, hatched a plan to kill Ceauşescu and leave the country for the free world. The movie's most poignant scene showed a girl refraining from denouncing the boy who called for her transfer to another school as punishment for destroying a bust of Ceauşescu that in fact he had knocked down. *The Silent Wedding* narrated an incident that happened in a small village in 1953 on the day when Stalin died. Instead of observing the seven-day mourning imposed by the authorities, a family decided to go ahead with wedding plans and invite neighbors and friends to the festivities on condition that the party make no noise that would alert the local law enforcement agents. When the silent wedding turned boisterous, the authorities arrested and deported all male participants, including the groom, who returned to his wife eleven years later. A 2009 production, *The Movie Caravan* (*Caravana cinematografică*) depicted the tribulations of a desolate Transylvanian locality where in 1959 an official caravan arrived to broadcast Soviet propaganda movies designed to educate the villagers on the benefits of communism. Little by little, the villagers made compromises and started to fear the new communist regime and its presence in their lives.[83]

The Romanian artistic film best known internationally is *4 Months, 3 Weeks and 2 Days* (*4 luni, 3 săptămâni şi 2 zile*), which received a Palme d'Or at Cannes for rendering the dilemmas and travail of a university student who underwent an illegal abortion in gloomy Bucharest in the late 1980s with the help of her roommate. Without direct reference to the political conditions that framed the story, the movie depicted an "era of bad luck and unhappiness,"[84] and the consequences of the draconic pro-natal program imposed by Ceauşescu from 1967 to 1989, which drove abortion underground by prohibiting it in most circumstances, even when the life of the mother was endangered. *Tales from the Golden Age* (*Amintiri din Epoca de Aur*), an anthology film that recounted the 1980s, consecrated as the Golden Age by Ceauşescu's propaganda machine. Notwithstanding the film's comical accents,

[83] Lucian Pintilie, Director, *După-amiaza unui torţionar* (2001); Nicolae Mărgineanu, Director, *Binecuvântată fii, închisoare* (2002); and Corneliu Porumboiu, *12:08 East of Bucharest* (2006).

[84] *4 luni, 3 săptămâni şi 2 zile (2007)* (2011), available at: http://www.cinemarx.ro/filme/4-luni-3-saptamani-si-2-zile-4-luni-3-saptamani-si-2-zile-385029.html (accessed on 12 November 2011).

the situations it depicted revealed the deprivations ordinary Romanians faced on a daily basis.[85]

These artistic movies were complemented by the *Autobiography of Nicolae Ceauşescu* (*Autobiografia lui Nicolae Ceauşescu*), which included original footage of the dictator, his wife, and children, travels across Romania and abroad, most significant political speeches, and personal hobbies arranged chronologically. As the movie offered no explanations of the events in which Ceauşescu participated, the meetings he attended, the names of the people he met, or the dates when the shots were taken, the director hoped that the original footage alone will convey Ceauşescu's political career, personality, and daily life even to viewers unfamiliar with Romanian communist realities. Although suggestive, many details presented in the footage are lost to foreign audiences or younger Romanian generations, who have difficulty deciphering them.[86]

By far, the most influential movie production to dwell on communism has been the *The Memorial of Pain* (*Memorialul Durerii*) television series, broadcast by the National Television since 1991.[87] With its focus on the broad victimization of Romanians under the Gheorghiu-Dej and Ceauşescu regimes, the series presents the heroism of anticommunist resistance fighters, the terror and abuse they endured in prisons, the persecution of their families, and their difficult reinsertion in society after the release from prison, occasionally glossing over these fighters' ties to interwar right-wing organizations. The series "greatly impacted a whole generation of young people coming of age in the mid-1990s, through rendering vivid images of suffering and injustice associated with men and women who could have been their own grandparents."[88] It is by far the best-known description of communism among younger generations.

CONCLUSION

Given the relative weakness of non-state actors in Romania, the variety of civil society contributions to transitional justice is astonishing, ranging from the only citizens' opinion tribunal in Eastern Europe and the unofficial but public disclosure of the names of active Securitate agents to forensic investigations, reconfigurations of the city text, and a variety of art projects. These efforts would have been commendable

85 Cristian Mungiu, Director, *4 luni, 3 săptămâni şi 2 zile* (2007) and *Amintiri din Epoca de Aur* (2009).

86 Adrian Ujică, Director, *Autobiografia lui Nicolae Ceauşescu* (2010).

87 Lucia Hossu-Longin, Director, *Memorialul Durerii* (1991–2007), 36 episodes. It is accompanied by Lucia Hossu-Longin, *Memorialul Durerii. O istorie care nu se învaţă la şcoală* (Bucharest: Humanitas and Institutul de Investigare a Crimelor Comunismului din România, 2007).

88 Bucur, *Heroes and Victims*, 243.

even if seeking to remove only the most ostensible symbolical markers of communism, but they went well beyond that by contributing to the official truth-telling process and seeking justice through nonjudicial channels such as an opinion tribunal. Slowly but surely, these mostly small but often bold unofficial projects have changed the way communism is represented in the public space, thus counterpoising powerful narratives to those upheld by communist diehards. The variety of these methods and projects attests to the continued preoccupation of the civil society, especially groups connected to the former victims, to hold communism accountable for its crimes.

As in other post-communist countries, the reconstruction of memory has proved to be a highly contested territory, where the descendants of the former victims, the victims groups, and the anticommunist parties have locked horns with the former perpetrators, their descendants, and the successors to the Communist Party. Contestation also ensued when communist symbols have been replaced by symbols related to Romania's pre-communist fascist past and when the changes tried to reflect the country's ethnic diversity by replacing Romanian with Hungarian symbols.

When contrasted to general rules identified in the recent literature, memorialization in post-communist Romania presents a relative paradox. By analyzing the construction and reconstruction of memory in twenty-five post-communist countries, Forest and Johnson concluded that "the more democratic the state, the more private as opposed to official activity takes place" and therefore "the higher the ratio of private to official material – but not discursive – action."[89] In Romania, most of the memory projects have been initiated, funded, and maintained by the civil society, without this over-involvement of non-state actors being able to strengthen in any significant way the quality of the local democracy. In fact, there are signs that the retreat of the Romanian state from memorialization, concretized by the refusal or reluctance of successive governments largely unresponsive to societal demands, to shoulder the costs of key monuments and museums, made way for the civil society to take responsibility for public goods (memory sites) created through private actions.

[89] Benjamin Forest and Juliet Johnson, "Monumental Politics: Regime Type and Public Memory in Post-Communist States," *Post-Soviet Affairs*, 27(2011): 270.

10

Conclusion: Memory, Timing, and Democracy

This volume's close investigation of truth-telling and justice-seeking efforts reveals that post-communist Romania has engaged in a multitude of processes and programs aimed at reevaluating the communist past of 1945–1989. The complexity of human right violations perpetrated under the rule of Gheorghe Gheorghiu-Dej and Nicolae Ceauşescu – gruesome human rights abuses in the 1940s through the 1960s, widespread surveillance programs in the 1970s and 1980s, persecution effected in response to perceived individual and collective guilt, and state crimes ranging from abusive confiscation of personal and church property to imprisonment, torture, and even murder – has called for a wide variety of transitional justice methods. Some of these efforts were conducted by state institutions, others were championed by civil society groups, and a handful enjoyed the support of the European Court of Human Rights or the EU. Overall, the repertoire of transitional justice mechanisms Romanian state and non-state actors submitted to public attention has been very large, and more extensive than in neighboring countries (Bulgaria, Moldova, Ukraine, Yugoslavia, and even Hungary). Indeed, only a handful of Eastern European states constituted history commissions and initiated forensic investigations, and no other country in the region organized a citizens' opinion tribunal.

At the same time, Romanian transitional justice actors have failed to translate quantity into quality. Key programs were never fully implemented (lustration), were enacted only if advancing the interests of the political establishment (access to the secret files, the restitution of dwellings, the public identification of former Securitate agents, or 'wild' executive lustrations), or were blocked until the passing of time ensured that alternative solutions could be designed (the restitution of Greek Catholic Church assets) or that the number of victims and perpetrators dwindled so significantly as to render those programs meaningless (compensation, lustration, and court trials). Most programs implemented in Romania have scored low in terms of efficiency and efficacy. Of the thousands of army, police, secret police, and party agents engaged in human rights violations between 1945 and 1989, only a handful were brought to court, and even fewer were found guilty for their crimes, a failure that raised public accusations of gross miscarriage of justice. For the first five years of its activity, the National Council for the Study of Securitate Archives was unable to fulfill its main functions – to grant citizens access to the secret files and unveil the identity of former Securitate agents – because it could not reach the bulk of the secret archives, kept under lock by self-interested political leaders. Compensation has trailed behind Eastern European levels, and rehabilitation came two full decades after the collapse of the communist regime. While providing a platform for the official condemnation of communist crimes, the history commission did not significantly change the way in which Romanian state institutions and ordinary citizens relate to human rights, the rule of law, the communist past, and national reconciliation. Lingering nationalist and communist sympathies among historians and teachers, as well as within research and education institutions (such as the Romanian Academy and the Ministry of Education) procrastinated the rewriting of history textbooks and perpetuated popular nostalgia about a regime that many Romanians consider more just, safe, equitable, and predictable than the post-communist democracy.

The elite reproduction that followed the Stalinist dictatorship of Ceauşescu and the bloody revolution of 1989 represented the most significant stumbling block the post-communist transitional justice program had to overcome. Former Communist Party officials and Securitate agents filled the vast majority of positions in the three branches of government, being present in large numbers at both central and local levels. Their adversity to any attempt to reconsider the legitimacy and legality of a regime under whose protection they launched their careers was matched only by the indifference with which international organizations and foreign governments viewed the perpetuation of communist power networks after 1989. Perhaps no reckoning with the recent past would have taken place in Romania in the absence of a handful of civil society organizations who stubbornly unveiled the new leaders as former second-echelon communist officials whose commitment to democratic principles was not genuine, who vocally criticized the lack of transparency and accountability of successive governments and the corrupt and self-interested judiciary, and who repeatedly called for truth and justice. Most transitional justice initiatives have been initiated by the civil society, and some benefited from the participation of non-state actors (the history commission) or were financed and completed by the civil society with little or no support from the state (forensic investigations and the citizens' tribunal). These significant contributions were made in spite of the general weakness of the Romanian civil society, the opposition to transitional justice of the former communist nomenklatura and secret agents, the inability of non-state groups to accord their positions on the communist past, and the sustained efforts of politicians of all ideological persuasions to render the independence of those non-state actors meaningless.

This concluding chapter seeks to answer the two sets of questions that drive the present case study research and to assess globally the Romanian transitional justice program of the first two decades of post-communist transition. First, it inquires about the role of sequencing transitional justice methods, noting that timing and sequencing were of essence, the use of some approaches informed the application of others, the relationship between state-sponsored and civil society-sponsored *lieux de memoire* was indirect, and the nature of the communist past privileged truth and justice over reconciliation and informed the choice of transitional justice methods. Second, the chapter investigates the correlation between transitional justice and democracy in post-communism, arguing that the forgive-and-forget policy envisioned by the first post-communist governments of Prime Ministers Petre Roman, Teodor Stolojan, and Nicolae Văcăroiu deeply divided the post-dictatorial society and undermined trust in the new democracy because the former victims rejected it. In such cases, post-authoritarian countries must engage in transitional justice immediately after the regime change, as early reckoning with the past can allow state and non-state actors to choose from among a larger and diversified smorgasbord of retributive and reparative methods. The process of working through the past is significantly helped when foreign actors openly support it or at least do not send mixed signals (by condemning and praising it at different times, or by criticizing methods on procedural grounds, while supporting them on moral grounds, without specifying clear guidelines for how to improve the process). While Romania is its starting point, this discussion is relevant for other countries.

As this analysis rests on a case study, not a comparative examination of several countries with similar past, the conclusions formulated here have limited generalizability. Whereas comparisons can allow for variation, including the simultaneous presence and absence of a given transitional justice method, this case study can only guess what the Romanian democracy would have looked like if lustration were implemented immediately after 1989, in such a way as to lead to the removal of numerous former Communist Party officials and Securitate agents from post-communist politics, and how the rule of law would have been strengthened if communist perpetrators were brought before the courts to answer for their crimes. At the same time, even in the absence of a multi-country comparative study, the accumulation of evidence provides valuable insight into possible relationships between the quality of democratic development in Romania and the presence or absence of specific transitional justice programs at different times.

THE ROLE OF TIMING AND SEQUENCING

There is consensus among transitional justice scholars that timing and sequence matter, although there is considerable disagreement regarding the way in which they do so. A report of the United Nations Office for the Coordination of Humanitarian Affairs acknowledged that "timing is of the essence" when countries set out to work through their recent past and argued that the impact of timing is differential and heavily dependent on the context. Justice cannot begin as long as a country cannot withstand the pressure of potentially divisive investigations, as was the case in Argentina and Chile where, as a result of the threat of a new military coup, it took close to twenty years to abolish amnesty laws and confront those responsible for human rights abuses in court. At the same time, the report contended, the experience of post-Taliban Afghanistan suggests that waiting too long to reconsider the past might severely block the democratization process, and as such, "palatable choices may have to be made in the short term for longer term stability."[1] Because of little or no vetting, known warlords have held seats in the post-Taliban Afghan parliament, and this elite reproduction has damaged the credibility of the government and promoted "an image of lawlessness."[2]

Based on seven cases drawn from around the world, Laurel Fletcher and Harvey Weinstein with Jamie Rowen found out that "the ability of a country to address structural aspects of the violence is related to the length of time that a country has had to undertake such reforms."[3] More specifically, they noted that, in countries which experienced at least a decade since the conclusion of the conflict or return to democracy, a shift in transitional justice policies occurred at six to eight years after the onset of the transition when the government offered monetary compensation to the victims of repression for the harm inflicted by the state. Initial national transitional justice responses were modified after a moderate time period possibly to satisfy the victims' needs. It is therefore significant "that we see countries taking modest steps toward fulfilling the spirit, if not the letter, of the commitments originally made to victims at the start of the transition period."[4]

In the post-communist context, Helga Welsh distinguished a "window of opportunity" for transitional justice, which opened during the first years that followed the regime change, when the new leaders who wish the country to come to terms with its recent past enjoy popular support for their actions. Once that window is closed, reckoning is more difficult to enact.[5] The urge to purge was also noted by Monika Nalepa, who compared predictions about timing put forth in eight

1 "In Depth Report," *IRIN Humanitarian News and Analysis* (2012), available at: http://www.irinnews.org/InDepthMain.aspx?InDepthId=7&ReportId=59492 (accesses on 11 February 2012).

2 Idem.

3 Laurel E. Fletcher, Harvey M. Weinstein with Jamie Rowen, "Context, Timing and the Dynamics of Transitional Justice: A Historical Perspective," *Human Rights Quarterly*, 31(2009): 206.

4 Idem.

5 Helga Welsh, "Dealing with the Communist Past: Central and East European Experiences after 1990," *Europe-Asia Studies*, 48(1996): 413–428.

analyses.[6] Jon Elster, Samuel Huntington, Guillermo O'Donnell and Philippe Schmitter, Carlos Nino, and Kathryn Sikkink predicted that countries will engage in lustration (or executive purges) sooner rather than later in the transition aftermath.[7] B. A. Ackerman and Stephen Holmes predicted the absence of lustration, whereas no analysis predicted late reckoning with the recent past.[8] Cynthia Horne, by contrast, discussed the late lustration programs Poland and Romania adopted in 2006, well after the initial window of opportunity had closed, to show that these late initiatives "expanded the scope and transparency measures associated with lustration as a form of transitional justice."[9] In short, transitional justice can represent a delayed political option, without running the risk of being more restrictive in scope than early programs.

Not only the timing but also the sequencing of transitional justice mechanisms constitutes an important but understudied aspect of transitional justice, as Eric Wiebelhaus-Brahm, but also Tricia Olsen, Leigh Payne, and Andrew Reiter, claimed.[10] Elin Skaar argued that the experience accumulated to date demonstrates that sequencing matters for impact assessment. For example, in Chile, Argentina, and Uruguay, where a truth commission preceded trials, the information gathered by the commission was used as evidence in subsequent trials launched against former perpetrators. In those cases, truth commissions facilitated court trials, while in South Africa the amnesty handed down by the Truth and Reconciliation Commission protected offenders from prosecution. Conversely, Skaar argued, when trials are conducted before truth commissions start their truth-finding activities, the information disclosed through trials may prompt public demands for more justice

6 Monika Nalepa, *Skeletons in the Closet. Transitional Justice in Post-Communist Europe* (New York. Cambridge University Press, 2010), 24.

7 Jon Elster, *The Roundtable Talks and the Breakdown of Communism: Constitutionalism in Eastern Europe* (Chicago: University of Chicago Press, 1996); Jon Elster, "Coming to Terms with the Past," *European Journal of Sociology*, 39(1998): 7–48; Jon Elster, *Closing the Books: Transitional Justice in Historical Perspective* (New York: Cambridge University Press, 2004); Samuel Huntington, *The Third Wave: Democratization in the Late Twentieth Century* (Norman: University of Oklahoma Press, 1991); Guillermo O'Donnell and Philippe Schmitter, *Tentative Conclusions about Uncertain Democracies* (Baltimore: Johns Hopkins University Press, 1986); Carlos Nino, *Radical Evil on Trial* (New Haven: Yale University Press, 1996); and Kathryn Sikkink, *Mixed Signals: US Human Rights Policy and Latin America* (Ithaca: Cornell University Press, 2004).

8 B. A. Ackerman, *The Future of Liberal Revolution* (New Haven: Yale University Press, 1992), and Stephen Holmes, "The End of Decommunization," *East European Constitutional Review*, 31(1994): 33–36.

9 Cynthia Horne, "Late Lustration Programmes in Romania and Poland: Supporting or Undermining Democratic Transitions?," *Democratization*, 16(2009): 344.

10 Eric Wiebelhaus-Brahm, *Truth Commissions and Transitional Societies. The Impact on Human Rights and Democracy* (London: Routledge, 2010), and Tricia D. Olsen, Leigh A. Payne, and Andrew Reiter, *Transitional Justice in Balance: Comparing Processes, Weighing Efficacy* (Washington, DC: United States Institute of Peace Press, 2010).

or for truth. When trials and truth commissions run simultaneously, as in Sierra Leone, different dynamics and expectations are created.[11] The literature generally keeps silent on whether the use of some transitional justice mechanisms preempts the use of other methods.

Applying these insights to Romania unveils the importance of timing and sequence. Because of the country's violent exit from communism dislocated the top communist leadership (the Ceauşescu family) but permitted the second-echelon communist officials to further their political careers by advancing to the top state positions with little opposition from the weak local civil society, the Romanian transitional justice program was severely delayed. No meaningful transitional justice process was launched until 1996 – that is, as long as the former communist officials retained firm control over the country (see Table 10.1). The Ceauşescu trial was conducted during highly volatile times to address the security problem of December 1989 (the fact that Ceauşescu's supporters continued to fight in the street in hope of restoring the communist regime) more than the Romanians' need for truth and justice. The compensation scheme was mostly symbolic, the reconstituted Greek Catholic Church and initial homeowners were prevented from claiming back their property, and the government rejected civil society calls for lustration. The reckoning programs adopted at the time were either symbolic (the removal of statues, the renaming of public places) or completed by the civil society despite the state (commemoration projects, the Sighet Memorial, and the vetting programs adopted by opposition parties). Notwithstanding public expectations, the Democratic Convention government was unwilling to turn the tide, the first three years of its rule marking a period of stagnation.

After 2000, Romania's transitional justice fortunes were again tied to the heirs of the Communist Party, the Social Democrats. By then, a new generation of party leaders had gained prominence. Whereas their mentors, who had led the country in the early 1990s, had blocked transitional justice because of their direct personal ties to the communist regime, the new Social Democrat leaders opposed it because they considered it a relic of the past, a misguided attempt to engage in witch-hunts, and a waste of valuable resources needed to integrate Romania into the EU and NATO. Only the family of Gheorghe Ursu managed to capitalize on the government's accession aspirations, convincing foreign politicians to apply pressure to bring Ursu's murderers to trial. This small victory came at a time when the country's main transitional justice agency, the National Council for the Study of Securitate Archives, was severely crippled by a government willing to prevent efforts to open

[11] Elin Skaar, "Understanding the Impact of Transitional Justice on Peace and Democracy," paper presented at the European Consortium of Political Research conference, Reykjavik, Iceland, 25–27 August 2011, pp. 30–31.

TABLE 10.1. *Time line of transitional justice mechanisms and processes*

1989	December 22	Communist dictator Nicolae Ceauşescu and his wife, Elena, flee Bucharest.
		They are apprehended and brought to the Târgovişte military unit.
		The unpublished decree no. 33 of the revolutionary government dismantled the communist secret political police, the Securitate.
		During and after the revolution, scores of public places changed their names.
		Statues of communist leaders were knocked down.
	December 25	The trial and execution of Nicolae and Elena Ceauşescu. That day, their corpses are brought to Bucharest and buried separately in the Ghencea Cemetery.
	December 30	The communist decree that dismantled the Greek Catholic Church is annulled.
		The reconstituted church asked for the return of its assets, including 1,800 churches, chapels, and cemeteries used by the Romanian Orthodox Church.
1990	January 18	Decree-Law 30 transfers the Communist Party assets to the state.
	March 12	Article 8 of the Timişoara Declaration explicitly called for lustration.
	March 30	Decree-law 118 recognizes the period when communist victims were imprisoned, had assigned domicile, suffered forced deportation or were placed in psychiatric wards for political reasons toward their state-sponsored pension plans. They also received other benefits.
	May 20	The first post-communist elections bring to the government the successor to the Communist Party, the Social Democrat Party. Ion Iliescu, former collaborator of Ceauşescu, becomes president of the Republic.
	September	*The History of the Romanians*, written by P. P. Panaitescu in 1942, replaces the communist history textbook at the pre-university level.
1992	September 27	The second general elections are organized. Iliescu and his Social Democrats consolidate their power.
1993	April 23	The Constitutional Court recognized the mixed church commission as entitled to decide the fate of churches confiscated by the communists. The Greek Catholics are thus prevented from petitioning the courts.
1994	May	In Satu-Mare, President Ion Iliescu criticizes courts for reconstituting the property rights of initial homeowners. In response, the prosecutor general invalidates definitive court decisions by making use of *recurs înanulare*.

TABLE 10.1 (*cont.*)

1995		The Memorial of Victims of Communism is opened by the Civic Academy in the communist prison of Sighet.
		First set of forensic investigations launched by the Association of Former Political Prisoners.
	November 29	Law 112 restricts restitution of dwellings to cases when homes are vacant or occupied by initial owners. Tenants can obtain ownership of the abusively confiscated dwellings they occupy.
1996		In anticipation of general elections, the Democratic Convention introduces "wild lustration".
	November 3	The opposition wins the elections. University Professor Emil Constantinescu becomes president, and the Democratic Convention forms the government.
1997		The Plague exhibition, evoking communist times, opens at the Peasant Museum in Bucharest.
1999	September 1	The "textbook scandal" erupts, after the Ministry of Education approves a new high school history textbook. After the late 2000 elections, the new Social Democrat minister canceled the textbook's authorization.
	December 9	Law 187 on access to one's own secret file and the unveiling of the Securitate as a political police comes into effect.
	December 30	Emergency Governmental Ordinance 214 bestows the title of "fighter in the anticommunist resistance" on some communist-era victims.
2000	November 26	Following elections, Iliescu becomes president, and the Social Democrats form the government.
2001	February 8	Law 10 on the juridical situation of buildings confiscated from 6 March 1945 to 22 December 1989 is adopted. It recognizes the tenants' right to dwellings bought "in good faith."
2002	March	In the Bus Trial, Communist Party leader Tudor Postelnicu and eight militia and Securitate officers are sentenced to jail time for the death of three young people who, in 1981, sought to leave the country.
	March 28	"Armageddon 7" hits the press. A list of alleged former Securitate agents is released publicly.
2003	July	Former militia officers Tudor Stănică and MihailCreangă are sentenced to jail time for their involvement in the 1985 death of Gheorghe Ursu.
	October 22	The International Commission for the Study of the Holocaust in Romania is created, at the request of President Ion Iliescu, under the chairmanship of Nobel Prize winner Elie Wiesel.
2004	November 11	The International Commission for the Study of the Holocaust submitted its final report to President Iliescu.

TABLE 10.1 (*cont.*)

2005	February	At President Băsescu's request, the Country's Supreme Defense Council orders the transfer of 1 million secret files from the Romanian Information Service to the National Council for the Study of Securitate Archives.
	October 25	Law 247 upholds restitution in kind, whenever possible, and creates the Property Fund to compensate owners whose ownership rights are recognized in court.
2006	February 22	Governmental Emergency Ordinance 16 introduces mild lustration.
	April 11	The Presidential Commission for the Study of the Communist Dictatorship in Romania (the Tismaneanu Commission) is created.
	September 7	The citizens' opinion tribunal in Cluj condemns the communist regime for its crimes against humanity.
		Historian Marius Oprea launched forensic investigations in several Transylvanian villages. Such investigations continue at the time of this writing.
	November	The Tismaneanu Commission submits its final report to President Băsescu.
	December 18	Speaking to Parliament, President Băsescu condemns the communist regime based on the commission's final report.
	December 29	All Securitate files were transferred from the Romanian Information Service to the Council for the Securitate Archives. Some 102,000 files touching on national security remain with the Information Services.
2007	January 1	Romania joins the EU.
	July	The Presidential Consultative Commission for the Study of the Communist Dictatorship in Romania is mandated to facilitate the implementation of the Tismaneanu Commission recommendations.
2008	February 6	Decision 51 of the Constitutional Court invalidates Governmental Emergency Ordinance 16, thus ending lustration.
	September 10	The Institute for the Investigation of Communist Crimes launches *O Istorie a Comunismului din România*, the first textbook in Eastern Europe dedicated exclusively to discussing the communist regime.
	November 28	After elections, the Democrat-Liberals form the government with the help of the Democratic Union of Magyars in Romania.
2009	June 2	Law 221 on politically motivated criminal and civil sentences and administrative measures handed down from 1945 to 1989 annuls those sentences and offers compensation to victims.
	July 9	The European Court of Human Rights hears the case of St. Basil parish and orders the return of that place of worship to the Greek Catholic Church.

TABLE 10.1 (*cont.*)

2010	April 12	The European Court of Human Rights hears the case of Sâmbăta parish and orders the return of that place of worship to the Greek Catholic Church.
	June 7	The Constitutional Court rejects the Lustration Bill (Pl-x 282/2006).
	July 1	Governmental Emergency Ordinance 62/2010 caps compensation to 10,000 Euros for former victims and 5,000 Euros for direct descendants.
	October	In a pilot judgment, the European Court of Human Rights adjourns cases about nationalized dwellings pending measures at the national level.
2012	February 28	The Chamber of Deputies approved a modified version of the Lustration Law (Pl-x 282/2006).
	March 28	The adopted Lustration Bill (Pl-x 282/2006) is deemed unconstitutional.

the secret files, unmask secret agents, and recognize former victims. Vigilante initiatives such as "Armageddon 7" unsuccessfully aimed to conquer the government's stubborn immobility.

For transitional justice, the busiest period came after the 2004 elections, when large secret file collections were transferred to the National Council, providing that institution with the means to fulfill its mandate for the first time since its creation, the Presidential Commission compiled a new official narrative about 1945–1989, communist crimes were formally condemned by the head of state before parliament, the Institute for the Investigation of Communist Crimes became a new transitional justice institution, the Property Fund was designated to facilitate the compensation of initial homeowners when restitution in kind was not possible, a new textbook dedicated exclusively to the history of communism was introduced in pre-university schools, a rehabilitation law annulled the sentences handed down against communist-era political prisoners, and a mild lustration program gained parliamentary approval. Besides these important government initiatives, the civil society intensified its efforts by launching a citizens' opinion tribunal, several forensic investigations, and numerous commemoration projects. The window of opportunity marked by the political actors' willingness to redress the recent past was short lived. By 2008, lustration was discontinued before producing tangible effects, and the Property Fund became grossly mismanaged. Afterward, the political elite was unwilling to support the recommendations of the history commission, no new court proceedings were launched against communist perpetrators, the Institute discontinued efforts to compile evidence for prosecutors, and compensation levels were capped at points considered meager by former victims.

Thus, in terms of timing, in Romania, as in other democratizing countries, demands for transitional justice have occurred in "bouts and spurts," to quote Roht-Arriaza.[12] Significant transitional justice efforts were made immediately after Ceauşescu's ousting from power (1989–1991) in response to popular demands to distance the new regime from its predecessor, during the months leading to the 2000 elections when the Democratic Convention anticipated defeat at the hands of the Communist Party successors, and after the 2004 elections when civil society groups asked the Democrat president and the Liberal prime minister to fulfill their campaign promises. As such, most, but not all, reckoning with the communist past took place with considerable delay, outside of the window of opportunity that opened in the early 1990s.

In Romania, the sequencing of transitional justice methods has had tangible differential effects. First, the implementation of some methods of reckoning with the past facilitated the use of others. For instance, the final report of the history commission allowed the president to condemn the crimes of communism in December 2006, as its detailed account of communist human rights abuses gave weight to the condemnation. After 2005, unprecedented direct access to over 1 million extant Securitate files allowed the National Council to unveil the identity of former secret collaborators, thus opening the possibility of lustration with job loss, a measure long awaited by victims. Finally, in 2009 the legal rehabilitation of former political prisoners paved the way for financial compensation schemes recognizing suffering at the hands of communist perpetrators. These three examples refer to official measures that opened the way for the adoption of other official measures.

Second, the failure of some mechanisms led to the adoption of others. The civil society organized a citizens' opinion tribunal in 2006 in response to the regular courts' failure to push the Trial of Communism forward, although prosecutors had gathered valuable information implicating a number of former perpetrators. Parliament's unwillingness to adopt lustration convinced some opposition parties of the need to launch limited vetting programs before the 1996 elections to find out the past of leaders seeking election or nomination to public office. Since 1996, failure to enact radical lustration with job loss has been supplemented by repeated executive purge campaigns initiated after each and every general election. In the last decade, the Institute for the Investigation of Communist Crimes and then the Center for the Investigation of Communist Crimes have coordinated forensic investigations

[12] Naomi Roht-Arriaza, "The New Landscape of Transitional Justice," in *Transitional Justice in the Twenty-First Century. Beyond Trust versus Justice*, eds. Naomi Roht-Arriaza and Javier Mariezcurrena (Cambridge: Cambridge University Press, 2006), 13.

because state actors have refused to design a comprehensive program in that area. Last, the author of the "Armageddon 7" and the civil society groups promoting the Coalition for a Clean Parliament took issue with the National Council's inability to identify former political police agents promptly and accurately, given the Council's continuous lack of independence from political parties represented in parliament. These examples show that in Romania, as in Latin America, civil society groups have tried to substitute themselves for reluctant state authorities and to push transitional justice forward by designing and implementing alternative programs of working through the past. Non-state initiatives have partly compensated for "the failure of the state to live up to its obligations."[13]

Third, some methods were intended to block the adoption of other processes and mechanisms. As Chapters 4 and 5 show, the history commission was conceived as an alternative to radical job-loss lustration, a program that would directly hurt the political career of President Traian Băsescu. Despite Băsescu's electoral promises, his Democrat-Liberals introduced no lustration bill in parliament in 2004–2012, when they commanded a legislative majority, stalled the legislative proposals of their Liberal rivals, and adopted a lustration bill in 2012 only after making sure that it did not affect President Băsescu and Prime Minister Mihai Răzvan Ungureanu by excluding from investigations the categories of communist decision makers and secret informers to which the two politicians allegedly belonged. Thus, political actors promoted one official mechanism (history commission) in lieu of another method (lustration) that they saw as potentially more detrimental to their legitimacy and credibility. This calculated choice echoed the situation in Poland, where the successors to the once hegemonic United Workers' Party supported mild lustration in 1997 because they anticipated losing the upcoming elections to anticommunist forces willing to enact harsher legislation. To protect their "skeletons in the closet," as Monika Nalepa called their past association with the repressive regime, and to limit eventual damages to their political careers, the former communists agreed to enact a toned down version of the very screening policy against which they raised against initially.[14] As long as their leaders are tainted, successors to the Romanian Communist Party (the Social Democrats and the Democrat-Liberals) will likely agree only to mild transitional justice. "Former perpetrators have a personal interest in avoiding transitional justice," their long-term interest in continuing to participate in corrupt exchanges further explains their universal solidarity

[13] Juan E. Mendez, "Lessons Learnt," in *Victims Unsilenced: The Inter-American Human Rights System and Transitional Justice in Latin America*, Washington, DC: Due Process of Law Foundation (July 2007), available at: http://www.dplf.org/uploads/1190403828.pdf (accessed on 26 July 2011), 194.

[14] Nalepa, *Skeletons in the Closet*.

against transitional justice, and they know that "they hang together or are hanged separately," as Tucker noted.[15]

TRANSITIONAL JUSTICE AND DEMOCRACY

A widely held assumption holds that transitional justice fosters democracy by strengthening the rule of law, aiding the replacement of elites involved in human rights abuses with new elites committed to democratic values, reforming repressive institutions, demilitarizing them and placing them under democratic oversight, and fostering reconciliation of divided societies and respect for human rights. Although many transitional justice scholars and practitioners endorse this view, to date only a handful of studies have empirically investigated this correlation and even fewer have demonstrated it. Besides the scarcity of large data sets and case studies that often reach contradictory conclusions, the correlation is difficult to examine as a result of the different possible definitions of the two concepts under consideration: democracy and transitional justice. The wide diversity of opinions regarding the meaning of democracy is well documented in political science and parallels the equally vast array of methods, practices, and mechanisms subsumed under the general heading of transitional justice. At a minimum, studies pondering over the correlation must differentiate between electoral and liberal democracies, and between incipient and consolidated democracies. When it comes to transitional justice, some authors reduce it to one single method of reckoning with the past taken in isolation (most often lustration or court trials, when investigating Eastern Europe), while others understand it as a much wider bundle of judicial and nonjudicial, retributive and reparatory mechanisms operating simultaneously. Welsh, in particular, called for "acknowledging the many features of transitional justice that Central and Eastern Europe have in common, despite variety in scope and timing."[16]

At the same time, in spite of the assumption that reckoning with the past is a necessary step toward constructing a democracy, many observers warn that transitional justice is not always positively correlated to democracy, as some processes can prolong social divisions and inhibit reconciliation. To make this point, Tricia Olsen, Leigh Payne, and Andrew Reiter distinguished between a minimalist and a maximalist approach to transitional justice and human rights violations. A minimalist approach stresses that amnesties provide the stability needed to nurture democracy

[15] Avizier Tucker, "Paranoids Must Be Prosecuted. Post-Totalitarian Transitional Justice," in *Retribution and Reparation in the Transition to Democracy*, ed. Jon Elster (New York: Cambridge University Press, 2006), 186.

[16] Helga Welsh, "Beyond Lustration: Transitional Justice in Central and Eastern Europe," paper delivered at the Meeting of the Council for European Studies, Montreal, Canada, 15–17 April 2010, p. 16.

and human rights regimes and argues that "trials potentially perpetuate more, not less, violence and instability."[17] A minimalist approach would also argue that lustration turns the victims against their former victimizers, prolongs instability by depriving the state of knowledgeable professionals, and might possibly lead to violence. A maximalist approach "contends that holding individuals accountable through prosecutions deters future perpetrators from committing violence, establishes and legitimizes the rule of law, and thereby strengthens democracy. The failure to prosecute, in contrast, results in a culture of impunity, erodes the rule of law, and encourages vigilante justice."[18] Similarly, the failure to open the secret files and sideline the former communist decision makers from positions of power and responsibility perpetuates the culture of impunity and the secrecy of the surveillance operations and allows people engaged in actions condemned even by the communist constitutions (such as the opening of the correspondence) to shape the new democracy to their advantage.

A look at the transitional justice literature and practice proves these points. In 1996, a Council of Europe resolution argued that "lustration is meant to create a breathing space for democracy, where it can lay down roots without the danger that the people in high positions of power will try to undermine it."[19] Its aim is "not to punish people presumed guilty – this is the task of prosecutors using criminal law – but to protect the newly-emerged democracy."[20] Examining the propensity of lustration to facilitate elite change, Anđelko Milardović argued that "the change of elite is a presumption of social change" and a sign of democratization. In democracy, elites must be representative and their permanence is expressed in their rotations. In totalitarian regimes, by contrast, "upper social classes are appointed or nominated within the political system" and "members of the military-political-police segments lead and supervise the whole repressive state apparatus."[21] For Mark Arenhover, "only truth and justice can sustain a democratic state,"[22] but other scholars were less enthusiastic of the democratic potential of lustration. In 2007, Dvořáková argued that lustration represents "the main challenge" to the rule of law when premised on collective guilt principles that "blur the difference between the victims and the offenders, between those who were forced to some form of collaboration with secret

[17] Tricia Olsen, Leigh Payne, and Andrew Reiter, "The Justice Balance: When Transitional Justice Improves Human Rights and Democracy," *Human Rights Quarterly*, 32 (2010): 985.

[18] Idem, 983.

[19] Council of Europe, "Measures to Dismantle the Heritage of the Former Communist Totalitarian Systems," Doc. 7568 (3 June 1996), 12.

[20] Idem.

[21] Anđelko Milardović, "Elite Groups in the Waves of Democratization and Lustrations," in *Lustration and Consolidation of Democracy and the Rule of Law in Central and Eastern Europe*, eds. Vladimira Dvořáková and Anđelko Milardović (Zagreb: Political Science Research Centre, 2007), 85.

[22] Mark Arenhövel, "Democratization and Political Justice," *Democratization*, 15(2008): 581.

police … and those who were active, or even paid collaborators and whose activity led to the persecution of their fellow-citizens."[23] Although difficult to operate in Eastern Europe because of the length of communist rule, the large number of people placed under surveillance, and the destruction of valuable secret files in the 1990s, the need to "find individual guilt is very important for any form of justice" and cannot be ignored when ascertaining the impact of lustration.[24] After analyzing the impact of the arrests and judgments handed down by the International Criminal Court of the Former Yugoslavia in cases related to Bosnia-Herzegovina, James Meernik found that they had no impact on whether the different ethnic groups in the country cooperated or became more conflicted, and as such did not influence tolerance toward other ethnic groups – a democratic requirement.[25]

The link between transitional justice and democracy was discussed in relation to other methods and regions as well. Matthew Draper pointed out that in Latin America prosecutions of human rights violators may foster democracy because they "will attract greater popular support for the government and lead to the removal of individuals and institutions undermining democratic reform efforts."[26] Also in reference to Latin America, Juan Mendez argued that "in making efforts to reckon with the legacy of human rights violations left by the dictatorships, our societies have contributed to the stability of democracy," and although not successful in all countries, "the effort itself – to recover the memory of the abuses, to hold individuals and institutions accountable, to recognize the inherent worth of each victim through reparations, and to tell the truth where denial and oblivion have long prevailed – has convinced broad majorities in the region that even the worst democracy is preferable to a de facto regime."[27] Jon Elster suggested that transitional justice is inherently a political process focused on advancing democratization and protecting national unity more than compensating victims and meting out punishments to perpetrators. For him, the success of transitional justice programs rested on their ability to enable and sustain democracy more than on the number of perpetrators executed or imprisoned. For example, post-apartheid South Africa progressed toward reconciliation and democracy without prosecuting many offenders, whereas Argentina brought many senior military officials to justice, but its democratization remains

[23] Idem, 14. Also Vladimira Dvořáková, "Introduction," in *Lustration and Consolidation of Democracy and the Rule of Law in Central and Eastern Europe*, eds. Vladimira Dvořáková and Anđelko Milardović (Zagreb: Political Science Research Centre, 2007), 11.

[24] Idem.

[25] James Meernik, "Justice and Peace? How the International Criminal Tribunal Affects Societal Peace in Bosnia," *Journal of Peace Research*, 42(2005): 271–289.

[26] Matthew Draper, "Justice as a Building Block of Democracy in Transitional Societies: The Case of Indonesia," *Columbia Journal of Transnational Law*, 40(2001–2002): 391–418.

[27] Mendez, "Lessons Learnt," 191–192.

incomplete.[28] He further outlined the differential impact of court trials on the quality of democracy. In Chile, the armed forces resisted attempts to bring human rights violators to justice by adopting amnesty. In Argentina, the new government was lenient toward the military perpetrators, but the existence of an independent judiciary and active political parties and civil society ensured a fairly severe transitional justice process. The quality of democracy differed significantly. In Chile, the army has its own budget and the constitution gives it the right to guarantee law and order, opening the door for continued military interference in politics. In Argentina, by contrast, civilians lead the Ministry of Defense, parliament controls the military budget, and the army is mandated to prevent foreign aggression, not to interfere in domestic politics.[29] Another comparative study showed that "countries utilize truth commissions to ease democratic transitions, regardless of the strength of their legal systems," although "these governments appear more interested in the symbolic value of truth commissions to review the past, rather than as a blueprint for structural or programmatic change," and "the impact of truth commissions was diminished in countries with weak legal traditions."[30]

In 2007, Kathryn Sikkink and Carrie Booth Walling examined the effect of human rights trials in Latin America from 1979 to 2004 with a new database of truth commissions and court trials relevant to transitional justice.[31] They sought to test the pessimistic claims that trials of human rights violators threaten democracy, increase the number of violations, and exacerbate conflict. As such, they explored the impact of court trials on human rights, conflict, democracy, and the rule of law in post-junta Latin America. A close look at the data prompted them to reject all three pessimistic claims: human rights trials neither undermined democracy, nor increased the number of human rights violations, nor exacerbated conflict in the region. The study made no claims related to the positive effects of trials on the establishment of democracy in countries where none previously existed.

In 2011, Sikkink reiterated the connection between transitional justice and democracy by commenting on the new Arab revolutions and noting that the trial of Egyptian dictator Hosni Mubarak "provoked a chorus of trial skeptics, who contend that the threat of prosecution undermines democracy, exacerbates conflict and could lead to

[28] Jon Elster, ed., *Retribution and Reparation in the Transition to Democracy* (New York: Cambridge University Press, 2006).

[29] Carlos H. Acuna, "Transitional Justice in Argentina and Chile: A Never-Ending Story," in *Retribution and Reparation in the Transition to Democracy*, ed. Jon Elster (New York: Cambridge University Press, 2006), 206–238.

[30] Fletcher and Weinstein with Rowen, "Context, Timing and the Dynamics of Transitional Justice," 194.

[31] Kathryn Sikkink and Carrie Booth Walling, "The Impact of Human Rights Trials in Latin America," *Journal of Peace Research*, 44(2007): 427.

greater human rights violations."[32] Those arguments have little merit, because they "rest on proving or disproving a counterfactual," and evidence showed that "transitional countries – those moving from authoritarian governments to democracy or from civil war to peace – where human rights prosecutions have taken place subsequently become less repressive than transitional countries without prosecutions, holding other factors constant."[33] More specifically, "countries that have prosecuted former officials exhibit lower levels of torture, summary execution, forced disappearances and political imprisonment. Although civil war heightens repression, prosecutions in the context of civil war do not make the situation worse," Sikkink wrote, as "the possibility of punishment and disgrace makes violating human rights more costly, and thus deters future leaders from doing so."[34]

By contrast, Omar G. Encarnación argued that the Spanish and Portuguese cases disprove the widely held assumption that "the more comprehensive and vigorous the effort to bring justice to a departed authoritarian regime the better the democratizing outcome will be."[35] After the collapse of the right-wing dictatorial regimes of Antonio Salazar and Francisco Franco, Portugal and Spain have developed into consolidated democracies, but their transitional justice approaches were markedly different. In Portugal, a "sweeping policy of purges" seeking to cleanse the state and society of the authoritarian past "nearly derailed the transition to democracy by descending into a veritable witch-hunt." In Spain, by contrast, "letting bygones be bygones, became a foundation for democratic consolidation,"[36] which evolved in the absence of significant reckoning with the past. These contrasting cases demonstrate that, in fact, transitional justice does not always precede, and explain, successful democratization.

In the most comprehensive study to date, Olsen, Payne, and Reiter used the Transitional Justice Data Base to examine which transitional justice mechanisms and combinations of mechanisms are associated with positive or negative changes in human rights and democracy. The database covered transitional justice efforts undertaken by governments in 161 countries in 1970 through 2007. Their analysis suggested that single transitional justice mechanisms used in isolation do not have statistically significant and positive effects on democracy and human rights. By contrast, specific combinations of mechanisms – trials and amnesties or trials, amnesties, and truth commissions – explained improvements in those two political goals. Surprisingly, they found support for a combination of two incompatible

32 Kathryn Sikkink, "Making Tyrants Do Time," *New York Times* (15 September 2011).
33 Idem.
34 Idem.
35 Omar G. Encarnación, "Justice in Times of Transition: Lessons from the Iberian Experience," *Center for European Studies Working Paper Series*, 173(2009): 1.
36 Idem.

mechanisms (court trials and amnesties) and explained that trials provide accountability and amnesties provide stability, both leading to improvements in democracy and human rights. Equally unexpected was their conclusion that truth commissions operating in isolation have a negative impact on democracy and human rights, but have a positive impact when combined with trials and amnesties. These findings held true across different contexts.[37]

Let me apply these insights to the case of Romania, to ascertain the impact of transitional justice measures on the quality of post-communist democracy. Did those programs facilitate the strengthening of the rule of law, the end of impunity on the part of perpetrators, the abandonment of secret surveillance of political opponents by intelligence services, the observance of human rights by state agencies and their acceptance by political actors, the press, and the larger population, the changing of the balance of power between victims and victimizers, the emergence of a historical narrative facilitating ethnic and religious tolerance, and more generally, the establishment of a political process that places the interests of the electorate above those of individual politicians and powerful social groups? What might have happened if particular methods were enacted more fully with the support of larger segments of the political elite and the public? As this analysis rests on a single country and examines so many transitional justice programs simultaneously, its conclusions are tentative, as causation cannot be established without isolating the effects of specific programs from those of other local, national, and international factors shaping the Romanian post-communist democracy. That holds true even when one compares the situation before and after the introduction of a particular program (i.e., access to the secret files).

Let us divide transitional justice methods championed by Romanian state and non-state actors into three distinct groups according to the degree to which they were implemented, as many programs were adopted but only a handful of them were enacted. The first category includes fully or almost fully implemented programs: access to the secret files, the citizens' opinion tribunal, rehabilitation of former political prisoners, the history commission and the official condemnation of communist crimes, the rewriting of history textbooks, and the removal of public communist symbols. Some of these efforts were conducted in the early 1990s (memorialization), others during the mid-2000s (access to the secret files, the commission, and the condemnation), and still others as late as 2008 to 2009 (the introduction of a history of communism textbook and rehabilitation). The second group consists of partially implemented programs: prosecutions of communist human rights violators, the public identification of former Securitate agents by the National Council for the Study of Securitate Archives and non-state actors like the author of

[37] Olsen, Payne, and Reiter, eds., *Transitional Justice in Balance*.

"Armageddon 7," property restitution, compensation, forensic investigations, and the redesigning of history museum collections. The court trials and museum programs were included in this category, although important individual trials and museums have been completed (e.g., the trials in the Ursu case or the Sighet Memorial Museum), because what was accomplished to date represents a fraction of what victims consider should have been done in these areas. Only a handful of unimportant perpetrators have assumed responsibility for their crimes through trials, and forensic investigations have unearthed few of the victims who lost their lives in extrajudicial killings. In addition, Romania has no Museum of Victims of Communism, and its national and county history museum exhibitions keep silent on the communist past. The third category includes an important program not implemented as a result of the complicity between successive governments and the courts: radical lustration with job loss.

Have the fully or almost fully implemented transitional justice programs helped Romania's democratization? Consider first the programs implemented in the early 1990s that had decades to prove their worth. Communist symbols were removed from the public space, often being replaced with nationalist and chauvinist symbols that discouraged tolerance and civic trust. Some new statues and public names make reference to the pre-communist fascist Iron Guard and Marshal Ion Antonescu or to Romanian personalities in predominantly Hungarian localities. As a result, new generations nostalgic for the communist regime have emerged, either because they believe that the communist regime more efficiently addressed socio-economic problems than the post-communist democracy, or because they identify with Nicolae Ceauşescu's rabid national communism. Nostalgia further stemmed from the inability of the victims, the historians, and the journalists to explain and document the crimes of communism on the basis of the archives, the final commission report, and oral history projects and to propose a hierarchy of guilt more credible than the one advocated by a post-communist political elite heavily populated by former second-echelon communist officials. Because they were introduced recently, the history of communism textbooks, the full public access to Securitate secret files, and the rehabilitation program are yet to demonstrate their capacity to facilitate a more stable and inclusive democracy.

As a result of their heavy instrumentalization at the hand of political actors of all ideological persuasions, who have generally decided which measures were enacted in which order, the partially implemented transitional justice programs have had a mixed impact on Romanian democracy. Court trials and property restitution showed the willingness of the judiciary to disregard the rule of law, treat citizens differently on the basis of their social standing and political clout, hand down decisions that protect the rulers' interests, and perpetuate the legal arbitrariness of communist times. The Constitutional Court's contradictory decisions on lustration legislation, which it first found constitutional and then unconstitutional on the basis of equally unconvincing arguments (see Chapter 4), convinced Romanians that the Court is misinterpreting the law to suit the needs of selected politicians more than to uphold the rule of law. The judiciary's political dependence on and deference to the executive has characterized property restitution. Magistrates arbitrarily denied ordinary citizens and the Greek Catholic Church the right to approach the courts and bowed to President Ion Iliescu's opposition to restitution of dwellings and the Orthodox Church's preference for ecclesiastical negotiations, although by doing so constitutionally guaranteed rights were infringed. The National Council leaders, historians, civil society groups, and isolated vigilante who publicly identified former Securitate agents have yet to explain how the names were selected, why some informers were unveiled but others were not, and why the process remained open to manipulation from powerful parties and government officials. Instead of fostering trust in public institutions, these identifications have bred distrust and suspicion, contributing little to democratization.

It is harder to ascertain the impact on democracy of transitional justice methods that were adopted but never implemented. It is a matter of contention whether lustration with job loss would have strengthened the Romanian post-communist democracy. Its few supporters remain convinced that radical lustration applied immediately after 1989 could renew the political elite, as in Germany and the Czech Republic. Elite renewal would have allowed new politicians, untainted by involvement in communist repression and thus not open to blackmail threats coming from individuals familiar with their past, to enact pro-democratic reforms promptly. Elite renewal could have also stifled the patron–client networks binding former communist decision makers and Securitate agents engaged in corruption, who kept the state a prisoner, syphoning off public resources and treating the national budget as their personal wallet. By contrast, for its many critics, radical lustration would have negatively affected democratization by denying the political rights of former communist decision makers and secret agents, because a true democracy should uphold the rights of those who oppose it. However, the assumption that the absence of radical lustration is more democratic than its presence does not seem to hold in the case of Romania. Let me explain why.

In that country, the absence of radical lustration did not mean that governments refrained from seeking the renewal of public officials, as transitional justice scholars and practitioners assumed. After the elections of 1996, 2000, 2004, and 2008, as well as in 2009, following the Social Democrats' withdrawal from the government dominated by the Democrat-Liberals, the executive enacted purges that often affected not only the central and local public administration systems, but also the leadership of the national radio and television stations, the local education boards, public universities and hospitals, and even joint companies with significant, but not overwhelming, state ownership. Lustration laws are debated by parliament in joint sessions attended by both the government and the opposition, allowing legislators with widely different ideological preferences and career paths to voice their position on lustration. By contrast, wild purges were enacted by the executive in the absence of any consultations with the opposition but with an evident desire to end the careers of opposition representatives. These purges have affected many more categories of elected and nominated public officials than those specified in any lustration law ever placed before parliament. As they could not target elected officials, who drew legitimacy from the popular vote directly (in the case of the president and the mayors) or indirectly (in the case of members of parliament and county and local councilors elected on party lists), purges focused exclusively on nominated officials, who were removed because of their suspected sympathy and support for the outgoing cabinet, with little or no consideration for their individual performance in the office. Article 8 of the Timişoara Declaration called for a twelve-year ban on occupying public office, but purges were carried out in the late 2000s with the same intensity as in 1997. All in all, failure to implement lustration did not protect Romania from political vendetta and denial of fundamental human rights, as observers hoped. Instead, it made way for a much more politically instrumentalized elite renewal method. In this respect, Romania was not a regional outlier. Another country that resisted lustration, Albania, saw its political elites divided between successors of the Communist Party and their opponents, each camp trying to sideline the other after each alternation in power.[38] In Bulgaria, where lustration affected only the banking and education sectors, purges were pursued as relentlessly during the first two decades of post-communist transformation.[39]

Note that the principle of collective guilt, the main accusation brought against lustration, also underlined the logic of purges. The quick dismissal of public officials was seldom the result of in-depth analyses of their performance, or predicated on their failure to fulfill the duties assigned to them. Lustration requires the government to demonstrate that targeted individuals were once communist decision makers or secret agents, but purges were conducted in the absence of any clear legislation defining the targeted categories or in-depth investigations of past or present activity. Instead of a strictly controlled one-time lustration program temporarily banning public officials connected to the communist regime, Romania opted for frequent purge campaigns affecting anybody the new government suspected of sympathizing with its predecessor. Purges were carried out even after Law 215/2001

[38] Robert Austin and Jonathan Ellis, "Albania," in *Transitional Justice in Eastern Europe and the Former Soviet Union: Reckoning with the Communist Past*, ed. Lavinia Stan (London: Routledge, 2009), 176–199.

[39] Momchil Metodiev, "Bulgaria," in *Transitional Justice in Eastern Europe and the Former Soviet Union: Reckoning with the Communist Past*, ed. Lavinia Stan (London: Routledge, 2009), 152–175.

on Local Public Administration specifically prohibited them and the EU officials called on Romanian governments to refrain from dismissing public officials on political grounds if wishing to join the Union in 2007. Some observers might argue that these purges, while somewhat excessive, are legally acceptable and morally defensible. The post-communist constitution protects the right to run in elections, but not the right to be nominated to public office. Voters can use the information about the tainted past of candidates when casting the ballot but have no input in nominations of public officials, although some of these officials hold a great deal of power. While these two arguments might suggest that purges are preferable to lustration, the capacity of purges to facilitate Romanian democracy seems illusory at best.

CONCLUSION

A close look at an understudied country like Romania, often considered a non-case by transitional justice scholars, reveals a wealth of state and non-state responses to the communist past. Since 1989, Romania has experimented with court trials, public identifications of former communist officials and secret agents, property restitution, compensation and rehabilitation, access to the secret files, a history commission, and the official condemnation of communist crimes. When state actors blocked, slowed down, or ignored them, other transitional justice processes were often rescued by the civil society. This is how post-communist Romania became the first Eastern European country to organize a citizens' opinion tribunal and introduce a history textbook on the communist regime in schools. Non-state actors also championed forensic investigations related to the whereabouts of victims of communist-era extrajudicial killings, launched a small number of important exhibitions and museums, and developed a wide range of memorialization and art projects. These processes, whose timing and sequencing prove of some importance, have met with various degrees of success in terms of their contribution to truth, justice, and more generally, democratization.

Bibliography

4 luni, 3 săptămâni şi 2 zile (2007) (2011), available at: http://www.cinemarx.ro/filme/4-luni-3-saptamani-si-2-zile-4-luni-3-saptamani-si-2-zile-385029.html (accessed on 12 November 2011).

"17.000 de deţinuţi politici vor primi despăgubiri," StiriROL.ro (24 August 2007), available at: http://stiri.rol.ro/17–000-de-detinuti-politici-vor-primi-despagubiri-75185.html (accessed on 3 October 2011).

Ackerman, B. A. 1992. *The Future of Liberal Revolution*. New Haven: Yale University Press.

Acuna, Carlos H. 2006. "Transitional Justice in Argentina and Chile: A Never-Ending Story," in *Retribution and Reparation in the Transition to Democracy*, ed. Jon Elster. New York: Cambridge University Press, 206–238.

Adameşteanu, Gabriela. 2005. "Legile proprietăţii – principala acţiune politică a Alianţei," 22 (12 May).

Adler, Nanci, Gerard Mueller, and Mohammed Ayat. 1993. "Psychiatry under Tyranny: A Report on the Political Abuse of Romanian Psychiatry during the Ceausescu Years," *Current Psychology: Research & Reviews*, 12:3–17.

"AFDPR cere Guvernului să condamne Holocaustul roşu," *România Liberă* (30 June 2003).

Albu, Mihai. 2008. *Informatorul. Studiu asupra colaborarii cu Securitatea*. Iaşi: Polirom.

Alianţa Civică. 1991. *Declaraţia de Reconciliere Naţională* (13 March), available at: http://www.aliantacivica.ro/documente/Declaratia%20de%20reconciliere%20nationala%20-%2013%20martie%201991.htm (accessed on 14 December 2011).

Ames Cobián, Rolando, and Félix Reátegui. 2009. "Toward Systemic Social Transformation: Truth Commissions and Development," in *Transitional Justice and Development: Making Connections*, eds. Pablo De Greiff and Roger Duthie. New York: Social Science Research Council, 142–169.

Andreescu, Gabriel. 2009. "Necesitatea judecătorilor specializaţi în cazurile de colaborarea cu Securitatea ca poliţie politică," *Noua Revistă de Drepturile Omului*, 5:13–26.

2006. "Raportul privitor la dictatura comunistă: Lumini şi umbre (II)," *Ziua* (28 December).

2006. "Raportul privitor la dictatura comunistă: Lumini şi umbre (I)," *Ziua* (21 December).

2003. "Cazul Grigore Opriţă: a început vânătoarea zăpăciţilor şi a aiuriţilor," *Observator Cultural*, 180 (August), 3.

2003. "Cazul Vasile Vetişanu şi aplicarea Legii 187/1999," *Revista Română de Drepturile Omului*, 25:63–83.

Anisescu, Cristina. No date. *Dinamica de structură şi rol a reţelei informative în perioada 1948–1989*, available at: http://www.comunism.ro/images/anisescuagentura.pdf (accessed on 29 August 2011).

Anti-Defamation League. 1995. *Press release* (10 April), New York, available at: http://www.adl.org/PresRele/ASInt_13/2402_13.asp (accessed on 27 November 2011).

"APDAS: Foştii proprietari sunt neîncrezători în corectitudinea evaluării imobilelor," *Ziarul Financiar* (3 October 2006).

Apor, Peter. No date. "Eurocommunism. Commemorating Communism in Contemporary Eastern Europe," *Eurhistxx*, 3, available at: http://eurhistxx.net/Portals/_eurhistxx/documents/APOR,%20Eurocommunism.rtf (accessed on 10 November 2011).

Applebaum, Anne. 2005. "The Gulag: Lest We Forget," *Hoover Digest* (30 January), available at: http://www.hoover.org/publications/hoover-digest/article/6762 (accessed on 4 October 2011).

Arenhövel, Mark. 2008. "Democratization and Political Justice," *Democratization*, 15(3):570–587.

Artene, Adrian. 2003. "Dreptate pentru Ursu," *Ziua* (15 July).

Ash, Timothy Garton. 2002. "Trials, Purges and History Lessons: Treating a Difficult Past in Post-Communist Europe," in *Memory and Power in Post-War Europe: Studies in the Presence of the Past*, ed. Jan-Werner Muller. Cambridge: Cambridge University Press, 265–282.

Asociaţia Foştilor Deţinuţi Politici din România. 2009. *Memoriul Asociaţiei Foştilor Deţinuti Politici din România*, available at: http://www.bumbacari.net/news.php?extend.3 (accessed on 23 June 2011).

2004. *Album Memorial. Monumente închinate jertfei, suferinţei şi luptei împotriva comunismului*. Bucharest: AFDPR.

Asociaţia Persoanelor Deposedate Abuziv Foştilor Deportaţi Refugiaţi din România. 2009. *Ştiri, Legea 290/2003, Legea 10/2001, Legea 247/2005* (7 August), available at: http://caritas-craiova.piczo.com/stiri,legea2902003,legea102001,legea2472005,?cr=5&linkvar=000044 (accessed on 23 June 2011).

"Aţi auzit de Punctul 8?," *Evenimentul Zilei* (29 July 2004).

"Atitudini şi opinii despre regimul comunist din România. Sondaj de opinie public" (23 May 2011), available at: http://www.crimelecomunismului.ro/pdf/ro/raport_sondaj_opinie_publica_iiccmer_mai_2011.pdf (accessed on 27 October 2011).

Austin, Robert, and Jonathan Ellis. 2009. "Albania," in *Transitional Justice in Eastern Europe and the Former Soviet Union: Reckoning with the Communist Past*, ed. Lavinia Stan. London: Routledge, 176–199.

Avram, Liviu. 2005. "Răceanu îşi lansează lista cu 'securişti acoperiţi'," *9AM News* (30 September).

Azaryahu, Maoz. 1992. "The Purge of Bismark and Saladin: The Renaming of Streets in East Berlin and Haifa, A Comparative Study in Culture-Planning," *Poetics Today*, 13:351–367.

Bacu, Dumitru. 1989. *Piteşti. Centru de reeducare studenţească*. Hamilton: Cuvântul Românesc.

Bădică, Simina. 2010. "The Black Hole Paradigm. Exhibiting Communism in Post-Communist Romania," *History of Communism in Europe*, 1:81–99.

Bădin, Andrei. 2006. "Mai mulţi ofiţeri de informaţii pe cap de locuitor decât în perioada comunistă," *Adevărul* (4 April).
2006. "Nu cred în legenda celor două Securităţi, una bună şi alta rea," *Adevărul* (10 April).
Baias, Ionuţ. 2007. "Mircea Dinescu: Bălăceanu-Stolnici s-a autopropus pentru colaborare cu Securitatea," *Hotnews* (3 December).
Baker, David. 2003. "Civil Society and Transitional Justice: Possibilities, Patterns and Prospects," *Journal of Human Rights*, 2:297–313.
Bancheş, Ovidiu. 2006. "Nomenclaturiştii, mai vinovaţi decât securiştii," *Ziua* (9 May).
2006. "Sorin Ilieşiu cere Preşedintelui înfierarea regimului criminal la 11 martie," *Ziua* (26 January).
2006. "Ticu Dumitrescu: FSN conduce CNSAS," *Ziua* (12 May).
Banu, Florian. No date. *Adevăr şi ficţiune în documentele Securităţii*, available at: http://www.cnsas.ro/documente/istoria_comunism/studii_articole/arhiva_securitatii/Adevar%20si%20fictiune.pdf (accessed on 22 September 2011).
Bara, George. 2009. "Este Emil Boc lustrabil? Istoria politică a premierului României," *Napoca News* (20 May).
Barkan, Elazar. 2000. *The Guilt of Nations. Restitution and Negotiating Historical Injustices*. Baltimore: The Johns Hopkins University Press.
"Bartolomeu Anania, în proces cu statul român. Succesorii continuă acţiunea şi cer 800 000 de euro despăgubiri," *Opinia Timişoarei* (4 February 2011).
"Băsescu a furat ideea anticomunismului şi i-a prostit pe intelectuali," Ziare.com (20 December 2010), available at: http://www.ziare.com/basescu/presedinte/marius-oprea-basescu-a-furat-ideea-anticomunismului-si-i-a-prostit-pe-intelectuali-1063547 (accessed on 7 July 2012).
"Băsescu: Ceauşescu rămânea un mare preşedinte în istorie, dacă stătea doar zece ani," *România Liberă* (5 November 2010), available at: http://www.romanialibera.ro/actualitate/politica/basescu-ceausescu-ramanea-un-mare-presedinte-in-istorie-daca-statea-doar-zece-ani-204863.html (accessed on 11 February 2012).
Bechir, Mariana. 2009. "Mircea Răceanu, 'Grava acţiune de trădare'," *Adevărul* (14 March).
Benea, Daniela. 2008. "Musceleni, la şedinţa pentru modificarea Legii Chiriaşilor," *Evenimentul Muscelean* (28 October).
Benera, Anca. 2010. *Bucureşti. Materie şi Istorie – Monumentul Public şi Distopiile Lui* (Bucharest: Institutul Cultural Român).
Betea, Lavinia. 2010. *Poveşti din Cartierul Primăverii*. Bucharest: Curtea Veche.
2006. *Lucreţiu Pătrăşcanu – Moartea unui lider communist*. Bucharest: Curtea Veche.
2001. *Convorbiri neterminate. Corneliu Mănescu în dialog cu Lavinia Betea*. Iaşi: Polirom.
1997. *Alexandru Bârlădeanu despre Dej, Ceauşescu şi Iliescu*. Bucharest: Evenimentul Românesc.
1995. *Maurer şi lumea de ieri. Mărturii despre stalinizarea României*. Arad: Editura Fundaţiei Ioan Slavici.
Bichescu, Dana, Maggie Schauer, Evangelia Saleptsi, Adrian Neculau, Thomas Elbert, and Frank Neuner. 2005. "Long-term Consequences of Traumatic Experiences: An Assessment of Former Political Detainees in Romania," *Clinical Practice and Epidemiology in Mental Health*, 1, available at: http://www.ncbi.nlm.nih.gov/pmc/articles/PMC1266057/ (accessed on 12 October 2011).
Bickford, Louis. 2007. "Unofficial Truth Projects," *Human Rights Quarterly*, 29:994–1035.

Biografie Traian Băsescu (no date), available at: http://www.presidency.ro/?lang=ro (accessed on 26 July 2011).

Blandiana, Ana. 2003. "Memoria ca formă de justiţie," *Dilema*, 518:10.

Boia, Lucian. 2001. *History and Myth in the Romanian Consciousness*. Budapest: Central European University Press.

Boldur-Lăţescu, Gheorghe. 2005. *The Communist Genocide in Romania*. New York: Nova Science Publishers.

Boros, Géza. 1998. "Budapest's Sculptures and Commemorative Plaques in Public Spaces 1985–1998," in *Budapest köztéri szobrai és emléktáblai 1985–1998*, eds. Ágnes Szöllôsy and Géza Boros. Budapest: Budapest Galeria, 199–212.

Bran, M. 2009. *La Roumanie vingt ans après – Le chasseur de la Securitate*. Paris: Cygne.

Bratu, Alin. 2007. "Torţionarii au murit. Mor şi victimele," *Ziarul de Sibiu* (31 May).

Brezeanu, Stelian, Adrian Cioroianu, Florin Muller, Mihai Sorin Radulecu, and Mihai Retegan. 2002. *Istorie. Manual pentru clasa a XII-a*. Bucharest: Rao.

Brucan, Silviu. 1998. *De la capitalism la socialism şi retur. O biografie între două revoluţii*. Bucharest: Nemira.

Bruce, Gary. 2009. "East Germany," in *Transitional Justice in Eastern Europe and the Former Soviet Union: Reckoning with the Communist Past*, ed. Lavinia Stan. London: Routledge, 15–36.

Bucur, Maria. 2009. *Heroes and Victims. Remembering War in Twentieth-Century Romania*. Bloomington, IN: Indiana University Press.

Bucura, Dan. 2006. "La mila securiştilor," *Adevărul* (17 February).

"Bulgaria MPs Vote Communism out of High School History Textbooks," *Defeat Communism* (29 October 2009), available at: http://www.novinite.com/view_news.php?id=109411 (accessed on 22 October 2011).

Burlă, Virgil. 2011. "Marius Oprea: Voiculescu a fost mai mult decât un simplu informator," Alianţa pentru o Românie Curată (14 March), available at: http://www.romaniacurata.ro/marius-oprea-voiculescu-a-fost-mai-mult-decat-un-simplu-informator-1251.htm (accessed on 26 November 2011).

Buzea, Gianina. 2002. "Cazul Gheorghe Ursu, o ruşine pentru justiţia română," 22 (10 June).

Calhoun, Noel. 2004. *Dilemmas of Justice in Eastern Europe's Democratic Transitions*. New York: Palgrave MacMillan.

Camera Deputaţilor. 1998. *Raport asupra propunerii legislative pentru anularea Legii nr. 112/1995 şi restitutirea unor imobile cu destinaţia de locuinţe, trecute în proprietatea statului*. Bucharest: Romanian Parliament (11 March).

Cameron, Rob. 2004. "Tirana: Where the Streets Have No Name," BBC News (3 December).

Câmpean, Ioana, and Mirela Luca. 2002. "Iliescu şi Năstase, de aceeaşi parte a baricadei în privinţa securiştilor şi caselor naţionalizate," *Ziarul Financiar* (4 December).

"Casa Presei Libere," *Rezistenţa Urbană* (5 August 2008), available at: http://www.rezistenta.net/2008/08/casa-presei-libere.html (accessed on 10 November 2011).

Catalan, Gabriel, and Mircea Stănescu. 2004. "Scurtă istorie a Securităţii," *Sfera politicii*, 12:38–53.

Cauza intitulată generic procesul comunismului – Ordonanţă (19 October 2010), available at: http://www.universulromanesc.com/ginta/showthread.php?t=919 (12 January 2012).

Ceauşescu, Mihaela M. 2004. *Nu regret, nu mă jelesc, nu strig*. Bucharest: Editura Meditaţii.

"Cel mai mare miting al opoziţiei extraparlamentare din acest an," *Cotidianul* (16 September 2002).
Centrul de Investigare a Crimelor Comunismului. "Common Denominator: Death," 2011, exhibition.
2010. *Cazuri*, available at: http://www.condamnareacomunismului.ro/Proiecte/Programulde arheologiecontemporan%C4%83/Cazuri.aspx (accessed 3 April 2011).
Centrul de Resurse pentru Diversitate Etnoculturală. 2002. *Structura etno-demografică a României*, available at: http://www.edrc.ro/recensamant.jsp (accessed on 25 November 2011).
Cesereanu, Ruxandra. 2008. "The Final Report on the Holocaust and the Final Report on the Communist Dictatorship in Romania," *East European Politics and Societies*, 22:270–281.
ed. 2006. *Comunism şi represiune în România. Istoria tematică a unui fratricid national.* Iaşi: Polirom.
2005. *Gulagul în conştiinţa românească. Memorialistica şi literatura închisorilor şi lagărelor comuniste.* Iaşi: Polirom.
2004. "Greva minerilor din Valea Jiului, 1977," 22 (3 August).
2003. "Revolta muncitorilor din Braşov, 1987," 22 (2 December).
Chivu, Carmen, and Mihai Albu. 2007. *Dosarele Securităţii. Studii de Caz.* Iaşi: Polirom.
Ciobanu, Monica. 2011. "Rewriting and Remembering Romanian Communism: Some Controversial Issues," *Nationalities Papers*, 39:205–221.
2009. "Criminalizing the Past and Reconstructing Collective Memory: The Romanian Truth Commission," *Europe-Asia Studies*, 61:313–336.
2008. "Teaching History and Building a Democratic Future: Reflections from Post-Communist Romania," *Democracy & Education*, 17:58–62.
Ciocoiu, P. 2010. "European Court Corners Romania on Property Restitution," SETimes.com (20 October), available at: http://setimes.com/cocoon/setimes/xhtml/en_GB/features/setimes/features/2010/10/20/feature-02 (accessed on 7 July 2012).
Cioflânca, Adrian. 2008. "O istorie a comunismului," *Ziarul de Iaşi* (11 September).
1999. "Scandalul manualelor face primele victime," *Jurnalul de Iaşi* (23 October).
Coaliţia pentru o Românie Curată. 2008. *Listele negre realizate de echipa Alianţa pentru o Românie Curată*, available at: http://www.romaniacurata.ro/listelenegre.php (accessed on 22 August 2011).
Combes, Ariadna, Mihnea Berindei, and Anne Planche. 2010. *Mineriada. 13–15 iunie 1990. Realitatea unei puteri neocomuniste.* Bucharest: Humanitas.
Comisia Prezidenţială pentru Analiza Dictaturii Comuniste din România. 2006. *Raport Final*, Bucharest, available at: http://www.presidency.ro/static/ordine/RAPORT_FINAL_CPADCR.pdf (accessed on 24 August 2011).
"Comisie pentru studierea crimelor comunismului," BBC Romanian Service (April 2006), available at: http://www.bbc.co.uk/romanian/news/story/2006/04/060405_comunism_basescu.shtml (accessed on 26 July 2011).
"Comunismul s-a bazat pe teroare şi ceea ce descoperim noi demonstrează acest lucru," *BN Observator* (17 July 2010).
"Consilierii clujeni sunt indignaţi de conţinutul cărţii de istorie," *Libertatea* (2 October 1999).
Constante, Lena. 1995. *The Silent Escape: Three Thousand Days in Romanian Prisons.* Berkeley: University of California Press.
Constantinescu, Emil. 2002. *Timpul dărâmării, timpul zidirii.* Bucharest: Universalia.

Contribution to the UPR 2008 by ICAR Foundation and the Association of Former Political Prisoners – Romania (2008), available at: http://lib.ohchr.org/HRBodies/UPR/Documents/Session2/RO/ICAR_ROM_UPR_S2_2008_FoundationandtheAssociationofFormerPoliticalPrisoners_uprsubmission.pdf (accessed on 3 October 2011).

Coposu, Corneliu. 1998. *Confessions*. Boulder: East European Monographs.

Corbeanu, Nicolae. 2002. *Vara transfugului*. Bucharest: Humanitas.

Corlăţan, Mirela. 2010. "Nota lui Băsescu către Securitate, văzută de Andrei Pleşu," *Evenimentul Zilei* (29 September).

2007. "O crimă a Securităţii este scoasă azi la iveală prin deshumare," *Ediţie Specială* (3 July).

Cornea, Andrei. 2012. "Legea lustraţiei – o eroare," 22 (6 March).

1995. *Directocraţia şi sfârşitul tranziţiei în România*. Bucharest: CSPAC.

"Corneliu Vadim Tudor, următorul pe lista CNSAS," *Evenimentul Zilei* (19 July 2006).

Corpaş, Ioan. 2003. *Secvenţe din fostele închisori politice*. Bucharest: Humanitas.

Cosmeanu, Marius. 2009. "Numele străzilor desenează portretul-robot al poporului," *Evenimentul Zilei* (29 October).

Council of Europe. 1996. "Measures to Dismantle the Heritage of the Former Communist Totalitarian Systems," Doc. 7568 (3 June).

Courtois, Stephane. 1999. *The Black Book of Communism: Crimes, Terror, Repression*. Cambridge: Harvard University Press.

Crăciun, Andrei, and Adrian Grama. 2008. "Vasile Paraschiv – nebunul care a învins Securitatea," *Evenimentul Zilei* (6 February).

Crăciun, Mircea. No date. "Relicve din perioada dictaturii comuniste în judeţul Argeş," *Memoria. Revista Gândirii Arestate*, 44–45, available at: http://revista.memoria.ro/?location=view_article&id=644 (accessed on 10 May 2011).

Cristea, Gabriela, and Simina Radu-Bucurenci. 2007. "Raising the Cross: Exorcising Romania's Communist Past in Museums, Memorials and Monuments," in *Past for the Eyes: Cinema and Museums in Representing Communism in Eastern Europe after 1989*, eds. Oksana Sarkisova and Péter Apor. Budapest: Central University Press, 273–303.

Cristea, Romulus. 2006. "Un dosar incomod pentru cei care au fost la putere," *RomâniaLiberă* (16 June).

"Cronologie," 22 (7 December 2010).

Culic, Irina. 2005. "Re-Writing the History of Romania after the Fall of Communism," *History Compass*, 3:1–21.

Curtea Constituţională. 2010. "Decizia nr. 1360 din 21 octombrie 2010 referitoare la excepţia de neconstituţionalitate a prevederilor art.5 alin.(1) lit.a) teza întâi din Legea nr.221/2009 privind condamnările cu caracter politic şi măsurile administrative asimilate acestora, pronunţate în perioada 6 martie 1945–22 decembrie 1989," *Monitorul Oficial al României, partea I* (15 November).

2010. "Decizia nr. 1.354 din 20 octombrie 2010 referitoare la excepţia de neconstituţionalitate a dispoziţiilor art.I pct.1 şi art.II din Ordonanţa de urgenţă a Guvernului nr.62/2010 pentru modificarea şi completarea Legii nr.221/2009 privind condamnările cu caracter politic şi măsurile administrative asimilate acestora, pronunţate în perioada 6 martie 1945–22 decembrie 1989, şi pentru suspendarea aplicării unor dispoziţii din titlul VII al Legii nr.247/2005 privind reforma în domeniile proprietăţii şi justiţiei, precum şi unele măsuri adiacente," *Monitorul Oficial al României, partea I* (15 November).

2010. "Decizia nr. 820 din 7 iunie 2010 referitoare la obiecţia de neconstituţionalitate a dispoziţiilor Legii lustraţiei, privind limitarea temporară a accesului la unele funcţii şi demnităţi publice pentru persoanele care au făcut parte din structurile de putere şi din aparatul represiv al regimului communist în perioada 6 martie 1945 – 22 decembrie 1989," *Monitorul Oficial al României, partea I* (23 June).

2010. "Decizia rr. 1.358 din 21 octombrie 2010 referitoare la excepţia de neconstituţionalitate a prevederilor art.5 alin.(1) lit.a) teza întâi din Legea nr.221/2009 privind condamnările cu caracter politic şi măsurile administrative asimilate acestora, pronunţate în perioada 6 martie 1945–22 decembrie 1989," *Monitorul Oficial al României, partea I* (15 November).

2008. "Decizia nr. 1201 din 11 noiembrie 2008 privind excepţia de neconstituţionalitate a dispoziţiilor art.3 din Decretul-lege nr.126/1990 privind unele măsuri referitoare la Biserica Română Unită cu Roma (greco-catolică), astfel cum au fost modificate prin Ordonanţa Guvernului nr.64/2004, aprobată cu modificări şi completări prin Legea nr.182/2005," *Monitorul Oficial al României, partea I* (23 December).

2008. "Decizia nr. 51 din 31 ianuarie 2008 referitoare la excepţia de neconstituţionalitate a dispoziţiilor Legii nr. 187/1999 privind accesul la propriul dosar şi deconspirarea poliţiei politice comuniste," *Monitorul Oficial al României, partea I* (6 February).

1995. "Decizia nr. 23 din 27 aprilie 1993 privind obiectul Dosarului nr. 7967/1992 al Judecătoriei Cluj Napoca," *Monitorul Oficial al României, partea I* (11 April).

Curtea de Apel Bucureşti, Secţia a VII-a Civilă şi pentru Cauze privind Conflictele de Muncă şi Asigurări Sociale. 2011. *Decizia nr.96/07.06.2011* (7 June), available at: http://portal.just.ro/JurisprudentaVizualizare.aspx?id_speta=28445&idInstitutie=2 (accessed on 18 October 2011).

Curtea Penală de Condamnare Juridico-Morală a Crimelor Regimurilor Comuniste. 2006. *Procesul Comunismului* (October), available at: http://redholocaust.org/procesul.html (accessed on 29 March 2011).

Damian, Miron. 2006. "Şantajul Român cu Informaţii," *Cotidianul* (7 August).

David, Roman. 2011. *Lustration and Transitional Justice. Personnel Systems in the Czech Republic, Hungary and Poland*. Philadelphia: University of Pennsylvania Press.

2003. "Lustration Laws in Action: The Motives and Evaluation of Lustration Policy in the Czech Republic and Poland (1989–2001)," *Law and Social Inquiry*, 28:387–439.

Dawidson, Karin. 2004. "Conflict of Interest in the Restitution and Privatization of Housing since the Fall of Socialism: The Case of Central Timisoara City – a Problem of Democracy?," *Europe–Asia Studies*, 56:119–141.

"Deconspirarea foştilor securişti, indiferent de 'pierderile colaterale'," *România Liberă* (18 February 2005).

Deletant, Dennis. 2006. "Romania, 1945–89: Resistance, Protest and Dissent," in *Revolution and Resistance. Challenges to Communist Rule*, eds. Kevin McDermott and Matthew Stibbe. Oxford: Berg, 81–100.

1999. *Communist Terror in Romania: Gheorghiu-Dej and the Police State, 1948–1965*. New York: St. Martin's Press.

1995. *Ceausescu and the Securitate: Coercion and Dissent in Romania, 1965–1989*. Armonk: M. E. Sharpe.

"Demnitari abili şi-au procurat case naţionalizate în ultimii ani," *Evenimentul Zilei* (22 February 2003).

Diaconescu, Ion. 2003. *După temniţă*. Bucharest: Nemira.

2003. *Temniţa, destinul generaţiei noastre*. Bucharest: Nemira.
"Din nou despre moştenirea fostei Securităţi," *22*, 36(1998).
Dobre, Florica, Florian Banu, Camelia Duică, Silviu B. Moldovan, and Liviu Ţăranu. 2004. *Trupele de Securitate (1949–1989)*. Bucharest: Nemira.
Dobrincu, Dorin, and Constantin Iordachi, eds. 2005. *Ţărănimea şi puterea. Procesul de colectivizare a agriculturii în România (1949–1962)*. Bucharest: Polirom.
Dobrincu, Dorin, Mihai Stamatescu, Raluca Grosescu, Liviu Plesa, Sorin Andreescu, and Andrei Muraru. 2008. *O istorie a comunismului din România. Manual pentru liceu*. Bucharest: Polirom.
"Dosarul lui 'Felix', secretizat de SRI-ul şi CNSAS-ul lui Constantinescu," *22* (3 March 2011).
Draper, Matthew. 2001–2002. "Justice as a Building Block of Democracy in Transitional Societies: The Case of Indonesia," *Columbia Journal of Transnational Law*, 40:391–418.
Dumitrescu, Nicoleta, Mihai Manea, Cristian Nita, Adrian Pascu, and Madalina Trandafir. 1999. *Istoria Românilor. Manual pentru clasa a XII-a*. Bucharest: Humanitas.
Dvořáková, Vladimíra. 2007. "Introduction," in *Lustration and Consolidation of Democracy and the Rule of Law in Central and Eastern Europe*, eds. Vladimira Dvořáková and Anđelko Milardović. Zagreb: Political Science Research Centre, 11–17.
Elster, Jon. ed. 2006. *Retribution and Reparation in the Transition to Democracy*. New York: Cambridge University Press.
2004. *Closing the Books: Transitional Justice in Historical Perspective*. New York: Cambridge University Press.
1998. "Coming to Terms with the Past," *European Journal of Sociology*, 39(1998):7–48.
1996. *The Roundtable Talks and the Breakdown of Communism: Constitutionalism in Eastern Europe*. Chicago: University of Chicago Press.
Encarnación, Omar G. 2009. "Justice in Times of Transition: Lessons from the Iberian Experience," *Center for European Studies Working Paper Series*, 173:1–46.
Ernu, Vasile, Costi Rogozanu, Ciprian Şiulea, and Ovidiu Ţichindeleanu. 2008. *Iluzia anti-comunismului. Lecturi critice ale Raportului Tismăneanu*. Chisinau: Cartier.
European Court of Human Rights. 2010. *Affaire Paroisse Greco-Catholique Sambata Bihor c. Roumanie*, Strasbourg (12 April).
2010. *Press Release: In a Pilot Judgment, the Court Adjourns the Cases Concerning Properties Nationalised during the Communist Era in Romania Pending General Measures at National Level* (12 October), available at: http://www.codex-online.com/codex/contents.nsf/WPrintArticles/D89852AF742DB305C22577BB0061B0D6/$file/Chamber_judgment_Maria_Atanasiu_and_Others_v__Romania_12_10_2010.pdf (accessed on 28 March 2011).
2009. *Affaire Paroisse Greco-Catholique Sfantul Vasile Polona c. Roumanie* (7 July). Bucharest: Fundatia Societatea Civila.
"Evidenţa reţelei informative a aparatului de securitate," *Sfera politicii*, 52(1997):39.
"Fără un process al comunismului sfidări de genul Pleşiţă sunt oricând posibile," *România Liberă* (9 February 2005).
"Faţă în faţă," Radio Free Europe (30 May 1999).
Fati, Sabina. 2006. "(Anti)comunismul lui Băsescu şi jocurile politice ale PNL," *Observator Cultural* (April).
2003. "Orniss-securişti – siguranţa naţională," *22* (23 June).

Ficeac, Bogdan. 2003. "Căutaţi securistul," *România Liberă* (30 October).

Fiul dizidentului Ursu acuză justiţia română că pactizează cu foştii securişti (no date), available at: http://www.luju.ro/opinii/interviu/exclusiv-fiul-disidentului-ursu-acuza-justitia-romana-ca-pactizeaza-cu-fostii-securisti?pdf (accessed on 31 July 2011).

Fletcher, Laurel E., Harvey M. Weinstein with Jamie Rowen. 2009. "Context, Timing and the Dynamics of Transitional Justice: A Historical Perspective," *Human Rights Quarterly*, 31(1):163–220.

Forest, Benjamin, and Juliet Johnson. "Monumental Politics: Regime Type and Public Memory in Post-Communist States." *Post-Soviet Affairs*, 27(2011): 269–288.

"Foştii proprietari fac miting de ziua crucii," *Evenimentul Zilei* (5 August 2002).

Fotache, Violeta. 2007. "Procesul comunismului – Exhumări în Munţii Tibleşului," *9AM News* (24 April).

Freeman, Mark. 2006. *Truth Commissions and Procedural Fairness*. New York: Cambridge University Press.

Funari, Pedro, Andres Zarankin, and Melisa Salerno, eds. 2009. *Memories from Darkness: Archeology of Repression and Resistance in Latin America*. New York: Springer.

Fundaţia Academia Civică. 2009. *Memorialul Victimelor Comunismului şi al Rezistenţei*, available at: http://www.memorialsighet.ro/index.php?option=com_content&view=frontpage&Itemid=1&lang=ro (accessed on 20 July 2011).

Fundaţia Culturală Negru Vodă. 2011. *Muzeul Memorial Rezistenţa Anticomunistă Făgărăşeană*, available at: http://negruvoda.ro/muzeu2.html (accessed on 29 November 2011).

Gabor, A. 2006. "Note de lectură asupra Raportului Tismăneanu," *Anuarul Facultăţii de Teologie Ortodoxă*, 6:185–208.

Gallagher, Tom. 2005. *Modern Romania. The End of Communism, the Failure of Democratic Reform, and the Theft of a Nation*. New York: New York University Press.

Georgescu, Adriana. 2003. *In the Beginning Was the End*. Bucharest: Memoria Cultural Foundation.

Getty, J. Arch, and Oleg V. Naumov. 1999. *The Road to Terror: Stalin and the Self-Destruction of the Bolsheviks, 1932–1939*. New Haven: Yale University Press.

Giurescu, Constantin C. 1994. *Five Years and Two Months in the Sighet Penitentiary (May 7, 1950-July 5, 1955)*. Boulder: East European Monographs.

Gledhill, John. 2011. "Integrating the Past: Regional Integration and Historical Reckoning in Central and Eastern Europe," *Nationalities Papers*, 39:481–506.

Gluck, Carol. 2008. *Thinking with the Past: Japan and Modern History*. Berkeley: University of California Press.

Golebiewska, D., G. Brycki, and W. Sochacki. 1996. "A Mixed Bag of Communist Trials," *World Press Review*, 43, available at: http://scilib.univ.kiev.ua/doc.php?5779544 (accessed on 28 December 2007).

Goletz, Patricia. 2010. "The Transformation Process and Current Problems of the National Memory Institute of Slovakia (Bratislava)," *Phantasma*, 19, available at: http://lett.ubbcluj.ro/~phantasma/caiete/caiete/caiete19/29.html (accessed on 4 October 2011).

Gosu, Armand. 2008. "Procesul comunismului cu manualul pe masă," 22 (17 September).

Grodsky, Brian. 2011. *The Costs of Justice: How New Leaders Respond to Previous Rights Abuses*. Notre Dame: University of Notre Dame Press.

2008. "Justice without Transition: Truth Commissions in the Context of Repressive Rule," *Human Rights Review*, 9:281–297.

Grosescu, Raluca. 2007. "The Role of the Civil Society and Anticommunist Political Actors in the Romanian Transitional Justice Partial Failure," in *Lustration and Consolidation of Democracy and the Rule of Law in Central and Eastern Europe*, eds. Vladimíra Dvořáková and Anđelko Milardović. Zagreb: Political Science Research Center, 183–196.

2006. "Conversia elitelor comuniste din România în perioada de tranziţie: 1989–2000," in *De ce trebuie condamnat comunismul*. Bucharest: Institutul de Investigare a Crimelor Comunismului din România, 229–254.

Grosescu, Raluca, and Raluca Ursachi. 2009. *Justiţia penală de tranziţie. De la Nurnberg la postcomunismul românesc*. Bucharest: Institutul de Investigare a Crimelor Comunismului din România.

Gross, Peter and Vladimir Tismaneanu. 2005. "The End of Postcommunism in Romania," *Journal of Democracy*, 16:146–162.

Gussi, Alexandru. 2011. *La Roumanie face a son passé communiste. Memoires et cultures politiques*. Paris: L'Harmattan.

Haglund, William. 2002. "Recent Mass Graves: An Introduction," in *Advances in Forensic Taphonomy: Method, Theory and Archaeological Perspectives*, eds. William Haglund and Marcella Sorg. Boca Raton: CRC Press, 77–90.

Haider, Huma. 2012. "Rewiting History Textbooks," in *Encyclopedia of Transitional Justice*, eds. Lavinia Stan and Nadya Nedelsky. New York: Cambridge University Press, pp. 93–98.

Hall, Richard A. 1999. "The Uses of Absurdity: The Staged War Theory and the Romanian Revolution of December 1989," *East European Politics and Societies*, 13:501–542.

Hann, Chris, ed. 1998. *Property Relations: Renewing the Anthropological Tradition*. Cambridge: Cambridge University Press.

Hoandră, Octavian. 2006. "Colaborarea ca memorie," *Ziua* (19 Iunie).

Hoffman, Eva. 1993. *Exit into History. A Journey through the New Eastern Europe*. New York: Penguin Books.

Holmes, Stephen. 1994. "The End of Decommunization," *East European Constitutional Review*, 31:33–36.

Hoppenbrouwers, Franz. 2006. "The Greek Catholic Church in Romania," *Journal of Eastern Christian Studies*, 58:125–136.

Horne, Cynthia. 2009. "Late Lustration Programmes in Romania and Poland: Supporting or Undermining Democratic Transitions?," *Democratization*, 16(2):344–376.

Horne, Cynthia, and Margaret Levi. 2003. *Does Lustration Promote Trustworthy Governance? An Exploration of the Experience of Central and Eastern Europe* (January), available at: http://www.colbud.hu/honesty-trust/horne/LeviHorne.doc (accessed on 18 August 2011).

Hossu-Longin, Lucia. 2009. *Faţă în faţă cu generalul Ion Mihai Pacepa*. Bucharest: Humanitas.

2007. *Memorialul Durerii. O istorie care nu se învaţă la şcoala*. Bucharest: Humanitas and Institutul de Investigare a Crimelor Comunismului din România.

Human Rights Watch. 1993. *Human Rights Watch World Report 1993 – Albania* (1 January), available at: http://www.unhcr.org/refworld/country,,HRW,,ALB,,467fca6d35,0.html (accessed on 4 October 2011).

Hungarian History Textbooks Approved in Slovakia (29 July 2011), available at: http://www.politics.hu/20110729/hungarian-history-textbooks-approved-in-slovakia/ (accessed on 27 November 2011).

Huntington, Samuel. 1991. *The Third Wave: Democratization in the Late Twentieth Century*. Norman: University of Oklahoma Press.

Iancu, Bogdan. 2010. "Post-Accession Constitutionalism with a Human Face: Judicial Reform and Lustration in Romania." *European Constitutional Law Review*, 6:28–58.

2004. "Muzeu despre viaţa privată în communism," *Evenimentul Zilei* (10 November).

Iancu Laura, Oana, and Ciprian Iancu. 2011. "Numitor comun: moartea," *Replica Hunedoara* (8 June).

ICAR Foundation. 2010. *Communism Trial*, available at: http://www.icarfoundation.ro/index.php?option=com_content&task=view&id=29&Itemid=44 (accessed on 1 September 2011).

2010. *Who Is ICAR Foundation*, available at: http://www.icarfoundation.ro/ (accessed on 1 September 2011).

Ierunca, Virgil. 1990. *Fenomenul Piteşti*. Bucharest: Humanitas.

"Iliescu, iar de partea chiriaşilor," *Evenimentul Zilei* (19 December 2003).

Ilieşiu, Sorin, and Alin Rus. 2010. *Raport-rechizitoriu despre fratricidul din 13–15 iunie 1990*, available at: http://www.projects.expertvision.ro/luju/static/attachments/article/303/Raport%20-%20Rechizitoriu%20despre%20Dec%201989.pdf (accessed on 28 July 2011).

Ilonszki, Gabriella, and Michael Edinger. 2007. "MPs in Post-communist and Post-Soviet Nations: A Parliamentary Elite in the Making," *Journal of Legislative Studies*, 13:142–63.

"In Depth Report," IRIN Humanitarian News and Analysis (2012), available at: http://www.irinnews.org/InDepthMain.aspx?InDepthId=7&ReportId=59492 (accesses on 11 February 2012).

Institutul de Investigare a Crimelor Comunismului din România. 2008. *Sesizare penală în cazul inginerului Gheorghe Ursu* (20 June), available at: http://www.valerianstan.ro/files/Sesizare%20penala%20in%20cazul%20inginerului%20Gheorghe%20Ursu%20(iunie%202008).pdf (accessed on 31 July 2011).

International Center for Transitional Justice. 2011. *What Is Transitional Justice?*, New York: International Center for Transitional Justice, available at: http://ictj.org/about/transitional-justice?gclid=CKDu_eem5qoCFQrf4AodZlU49g (accessed on 23 August 2011).

International Commission on the Holocaust in Romania. 2004. *Final Report* (11 November), Bucharest, available at: http://www.inshr-ew.ro/pdf/Final_Report.pdf (accessed on 26 July 2011).

Ioanid, Ioan. 1999. *Închisoarea noastră cea de toate zilele*. Bucharest: Humanitas, 3 volumes.

Ionescu, Dan. 1990. "Old Practices Persist in Romanian Justice," *Report on Eastern Europe*, 1(9 March):44–48.

Iordachi, Constantin. 2004. "'Entangled histories': Re-thinking the History of Central and Eastern Europe," *Regio Yearbook*, 2:113–47.

Jela, Doina. 2007. "Gulagul şi Holocaustul în conştiinţa românească – perspectiva unui editor de carte," *Caietele Echinox*, 13:205–211.

Jela, Doina, Cătălin Strat and Mihai Albu. 2004. *Afacerea Meditaţia Transcedentală*. Bucharest: Humanitas.

Judt, Tony. 1992. "The Past Is Another Country: Myth and Memory in Postwar Europe," *Daedalus*, 21:83–118.

Karadjova, Mariana. 2004. "Property Restitution in Eastern Europe: Domestic and International Human Rights Law Responses," *Review of Central and East European Law*, 3:325–363.

King, Charles. 2007. "Remembering Romanian Communism," *Slavic Review*, 66:718–723.

Kirchheimer, Otto. 1961. *Political Justice: The Use of Legal Procedure for Political Ends*. Westport: Greenwood Press.

Kligman, Gail, and Katherine Verdery. 2011. *Peasants under Siege: The Collectivization of Romanian Agriculture, 1949–1962*. Princeton: Princeton University Press.

Klinghoffer, Arthur, and Judith Klinghoffer. 2002. *International Citizens' Tribunals: Mobilizing Public Opinion to Advance Human Rights*. London: Palgrave Macmillan.

Koehler, John. 1999. "Revenge versus the Rule of Law," *New York Times*, available at: http://www.nytimes.com/books/first/k/koehler-stasi.html (accessed on 29 August 2011).

Kraus, Michael. 1995. "Settling Accounts: Post-Communist Czechoslovakia," in *Transitional Justice: How Emerging Democracies Reckon with Former Regimes*, ed. Neil Kritz. Washington, DC: United States Institute of Peace, **2**, 542–544.

Kritz, Neil, ed. 1995. *Transitional Justice: How Emerging Democracies Reckon with Former Regimes*. Washington, DC: US Institute for Peace, 3 vol.

Kröhnert, Steffen, and Samuel Skipper. 2010. *Demographic Development in Eastern Germany*. Berlin: Berlin-Institut fur Bevolkerung und Entwicklung.

Kundera, Milan. 1981. *The Book of Laughter and Forgetting*. New York: Penguin.

Lazăr, Liviu, Bogdan Teodorescu, Mihai Stamatescu, and Ovidiu Bozgan. 2000. *Istorie. Manual pentru clasa a XII-a*. Bucharest: Sigma.

Lean, S. F. 2003. "Is Truth Enough? Reparations and Reconciliation in Latin America," in *Politics and the Past: On Repairing Historical Injustices*, ed. J. C. Torpey. Lanham, MD: Rowman and Littlefield, 169–181.

Lee, Ching Kwan, and Guobin Yang. 2007. *Re-envisioning the Chinese Revolution: The Politics and Poetics of Collective Memories in Reform China*. Washington, DC: Woodrow Wilson Center Press.

"Legea lustraţiei," 22 (13 July 2005).

Letter from the Ministry of Finance, Cabinet of the Deputy Ministry to the Romanian Institute for Recent History (14 September 2010), available at: http://www.irir.ro/files/pages/Raspuns%20Ministerul%20Finantelor.pdf (accessed on 26 November 2011).

Letter from the National Council for the Study of Securitate Archives to the Romanian Institute of Recent History (3 September 2010), available at: http://www.irir.ro/files/pages/Raspuns%20CNSAS.pdf (accessed on 26 May 2011).

Letter of the Institute for the Investigation of Communist Crimes and the Memory of Romanian Exile to the Romanian Institute of Recent History (31 August 2010), available at: http://www.irir.ro/files/pages/Raspuns%20IICCMER.pdf (accessed on 26 November 2011).

Leustean, Lucian. 2009. *Orthodoxy and the Cold War. Religion and Political Power in Romania, 1947–1965*. London: Palgrave.

Levant, Cristian. 2003. "Surse din Parchetul General dezvăluie: Informaţii clasificate, pe mâna torţionarilor lui Ursu," *Evenimentul Zilei* (10 November).

Levinson, Stanford. 1998. *Written in Stone; Public Monuments in Changing Societies*. Durham, NC: Duke University Press.

Light, Duncan. 2004. "Street Names in Bucharest, 1990–1997: Exploring the Modern Historical Geographies of Post-Socialist Change," *Journal of Historical Geography*, 30:154–72.

2000. "An Unwanted Past: Contemporary Tourism and the Heritage of Communism in Romania," *International Journal of Heritage Studies*, 6:145–160.

Liiceanu, Aurora. 2003. *Rănile memoriei. Nucşoara şi rezistenţa din munţi*. Bucharest: Polirom.

Linz, Juan, and Alfred Stepan. 1996. *Problems of Democratic Transition and Consolidation: Southern Europe, South America, and Post-Communist Europe*. Baltimore: Johns Hopkins University Press.

Lowenthal, David. 1985. *The Past Is a Foreign Country*. Cambridge: Cambridge University Press.

Lucescu, Pavel. 2003. "De ce ne interesează CNSAS?," *Monitorul de Iaşi* (12 March).

Lutz, Ellen, and Kathryn Sikkink. 2001. "The Justice Cascade: The Evolution and Impact of Foreign Human Rights Trials in Latin America," *Chicago Journal of International Law*, 2:1–33.

Magierescu, Eugen. 1994. *Moara Dracilor. Amintiri despre Piteşti*. Alba Iulia: Fronde.

Maier, Charles. 2001. *Hot Memory ... Cold Memory: On the Political Half-life of Fascist and Communist Memory*, paper delivered at the conference on The Memory of the Century, Institut für die Wissenschaften vom Menschen, Vienna, Austria, 9–11 March.

1993. "A Surfeit of Memory? Reflections on History, Melancholy and Denial," *History & Memory*, 5:136–151.

Manea, Mihai, and Bogdan Teodorescu. 1996. *Istoria Românilor de la 1821 până în 1989. Manual pentru clasa a XII-a*. Bucharest: Editura Didactică şi Pedagogică.

Manoliu, Maria. 2004. "Chiriaşii din casele naţionalizate trebuie să ceară în scris proprietarilor prelungirea contractelor cu încă cinci ani," *Adevărul* (13 March).

Marga, Andrei. 1999. "Asupra manualelor alternative," *Curentul* (26 October).

Mărgineanu, Nicolae. 2006. *Un psiholog în temniţele comuniste. Documente preluate din arhiva CNSAS*. Iasi: Polirom.

Marian, Mircea, George Rădulescu, and Bogdan Costache. 2006. "SRI şi CNSAS au secretizat la discreţie dosarele Securităţii," *Adevărul* (31 August).

Marin, Gabriel. No date. "La leçon d'histoire. Les nostalgies du communisme et les manuels scolaires d'histoire des Roumains," unpublished manuscript.

Mark, James. 2010. *The Unfinished Revolution. Making Sense of the Communist Past in Central-European Europe*. New Haven: Yale University Press.

2010. "What Remains? Anti-Communism, Forensic Archaeology, and the Retelling of the National Past in Lithuania and Romania," *Past and Present*, Supplement 5:276–300.

Mârzanca, G. 1997. *Patru ani am fost ... 'bandit.' Confesiuni*. Bucharest: Vasile Carlova Press.

McAdams, A. James. 2001. *Judging the Past in Unified Germany*. Cambridge: Cambridge University Press.

McNeill, William. 1986. *Mythistory and Other Essays*. Chicago: University of Chicago Press.

Meernik, James. 2005. "Justice and Peace? How the International Criminal Tribunal Affects Societal Peace in Bosnia," *Journal of Peace Research*, 42:271–289.

Mendez, Juan. 2007. "Lessons Learnt," in *Victims Unsilenced: The Inter-American Human Rights System and Transitional Justice in Latin America*. Washington, DC: Due Process of Law Foundation (July), available at: http://www.dplf.org/uploads/1190403828.pdf (accessed on 26 July 2011), 191–202.

1997. "In Defense of Transitional Justice," in *Transitional Justice and the Rule of Law in New Democracies*, ed. A. James McAdams. Notre Dame: University of Notre Dame Press, 1–26.

Metodiev, Momchil. 2009. "Bulgaria," in *Transitional Justice in Eastern Europe and the Former Soviet Union: Reckoning with the Communist Past*, ed. Lavinia Stan. London: Routledge, 152–175.

Mica, Adriana. 2009. "Forgiveness and Disclosure Scandals in Romania," in *Forgiveness: Probing the Boundaries*, eds. Stephen Bloch-Schulman and David White. Oxford: Inter-Disciplinary Press, 257–274.

Milardović, Anđelko. 2007. "Elite Groups in the Waves of Democratization and Lustrations," in *Lustration and Consolidation of Democracy and the Rule of Law in Central and Eastern Europe*, eds. Vladimira Dvořáková and Anđelko Milardović. Zagreb: Political Science Research Centre, 85–108.

"Ministrul justiţiei sugerează judecătorilor să ţină cu chiriaşii," *Evenimentul Zilei* (3 April 2001).

Miroiu, Mihaela. 2006. "Delaţiunea ca obligaţie, cruciadă şi voluptate," 22 (29 September).

Mititelu, Christian. 2005. "Securitatea 'nedreptăţită'," *Evenimentul Zilei* (30 November).

Mitu, Sorin, Lucia Copoeru, Ovidiu Pecican, Virgiliu Târau, and Liviu Târau. 1999. *Istoria Românilor. Manual pentru clasa a XII-a*. Bucharest: Sigma.

Mogoş, Adrian. 2011. "Trei oficiali CNSAS au anunţat Ambasada SUA că au fost distruse 1.000 de dosare," *Jurnalul Naţional* (30 March).

Monitorul Oficial al României, partea II-a (4 November 1997).

"Monument Erected in Memory of Azerbaijani Victims of Stalin Repression," *Trend* (2 June 2008), available at: http://en.trend.az/regions/casia/kazakhstan/1213254.html (accessed on 4 October 2011).

Moran, John. 1994. "The Communist Torturers of Eastern Europe: Prosecute and Punish or Forgive and Forget?," *Communist and Post-Communist Studies*, 27:95–109.

Muller, Jan-Werner. 2002. "Introduction: The Power of Memory, the Memory of Power and the Power over Memory," in *Memory and Power in Post-War Europe*, ed. Jan-Werner Muller. Cambridge: Cambridge University Press, 1–35.

Müller-Enbergs, H. 1993. *IM-Statistik 1985–1989*. Berlin: Bundesbeauftragter für die Stasi-Unterlagen.

Mungiu, Alina. 2005. "The Coalition for a Clean Parliament," *Journal of Democracy*, 16:154–155.

Mungiu-Pippidi, Alina. 2012. "Când demilitarizăm România?," *România Liberă* (1 March).

2011. "Anticomunismul ca politică publică," *România Liberă* (4 August).

2002. "Romania: From Procedural to European Integration," in *Democratization in Central and Eastern Europe*, eds. Mary Kaldor and Ivan Vejvoda. London: Continuum, 136–138.

Mungiu-Pippidi, Alina, and G. Althabe. 2002. *Secera şi buldozerul. Scorniceşti şi Nucşoara. Mecanisme de aservire a ţăranului roman*. Bucharest: Polirom.

Muraru, Andrei. 2012. "Primul cincinal de condamnare a comunismului: legenda merge mai departe," *Observatorul Cultural* (10 February).

2011. "Ne mor torţionarii, doamnă Kovesi!," *Observatorul cultural* (28 July).

Murgescu, Bodgan. 2003. "The Romanian Historiography in the 1990s," *Romanian Journal of Political Science*, 2:19–27.

2000. *A fi istoric în anul 2000*. Bucharest: All.

Murgescu, Mirela Luminiţa. 2004. *Istoria din ghiozdan. Memorie şi manuale şcolare în România anilor 1990*. Bucharest: Do Minor.

Nagât, Germina, and Andreea Pora. 2012. "Criteriul pentru numirea în Colegiul CNSAS: şira spinării," 22 (27 March).

Nalepa, Monika. 2012. "Lustration," in *Encyclopedia of Transitional Justice*, eds. Lavinia Stan and Nadya Nedelsky. New York: Cambridge University Press, volume 1, pages 46–51.

2010. *Skeletons in the Closet: Transitional Justice in Post-Communist Europe*. New York: Cambridge University Press.

Nap, Nicoleta. 2005. "Dinastia Maior," *Bună ziua, Ardeal* (11 November).

Năstase, Liliana, and Ionel Stoica. 2007. "Deţinuţii politici vor fi despăgubiţi, iar condamnările lor, şterse prin lege," *Adevărul* (24 August).

National Council for the Study of Securitate Archives. No date. *Lista persoanelor pentru care Consiliul a solicitat instanţei constatarea calităţii de colaborator al Securităţii, în temeiul Art. 3 din Legea 293/2008*, available at: http://www.cnsas.ro/colaboratori.html (accessed on 22 August 2011).

2011. "Adeverinta nr. 748/22.02.2011" (23 March), available at: http://www.cnsas.ro/documente/adeverinte/2011/748%20Plesu%20%28Petrulian%29%20Lacramioara%20Maria%20Catrinel.pdf (accessed on 9 March 2012).

Neumann, Victor. 2002. "Manualele alternative de istorie: o dezbatere istoriografică sau o imixtiune politică," *Observatorul cultural* (22 January).

Nicolae, I. 2000. "Changes of Romanian Place Names during the Communist Era," in *Post-Communist Romania: Geographical Perspectives*, eds. D. Light and D. Phinnemore. Liverpool: Liverpool Hope Press, 49–53.

Nicolaescu, Sergiu. 1995. *Revoluţia, începutul adevărului*. Bucharest: Editura Topaz.

Nino, Carlos. 1996. *Radical Evil on Trial*. New Haven: Yale University Press.

Nistorescu, Cornel. 2003. "Cazul Temeşan, spre final," *Evenimentul Zilei* (15 March).

1999. "Cine îl lucrează pe Vlad Ţepeş?," *Evenimentul zilei* (9 October).

Nora, Pierre. 1989. "Between Memory and History: Les Lieux de Memoire," *Representations*, 26:7–24.

O'Donnell, Guillermo, and Philippe Schmitter. 1986. *Tentative Conclusions about Uncertain Democracies*. Baltimore: Johns Hopkins University Press.

Offe, Claus. 1996. *Varieties of Transition. The East European and East German Experience*. Cambridge: Polity Press.

1993. "Disqualification, Retribution, Restitution: Dilemmas of Justice in Post-Communist Transitions," *Journal of Political Philosophy*, 1:17–44.

Olaru, Stejărel, and Marius Oprea. 2003. *The Day We Won't Forget. 15 November 1987*. Bucharest: Polirom.

Olick, Jeffrey. 1999. "Collective Memory: The Two Cultures," *Sociological Theory*, 17:333–348.

Olsen, Tricia, Leigh Payne and Andrew Reiter. 2010. "The Justice Balance: When Transitional Justice Improves Human Rights and Democracy," *Human Rights Quarterly*, 32:980–1007.

2010. *Transitional Justice in Balance. Comparing Processes, Weighting Efficacy*. Washington, DC: United States Institute of Peace Press.

Onken, Eva-Clarita. 2007. "The Politics of Finding Historical Truth: Reviewing Baltic History Commissions and Their Work," *Journal of Baltic Studies*, 38:109–116.

Oprea, Cornel. 2007. "Pleşiţă, diplomaţii şi terorismul de stat," *România Liberă* (8 November).

Oprea, Cristian, Christian Levant, Lidia Moise, and Alina Mihai. 2003. "Am făcut operaţiuni din ordinul serviciilor secrete," *Evenimentul Zilei* (15 March).

Oprea, Marius. 2008. "About Ideologies, Institutions and Death," in *European Public Hearing on Crimes Committed by Totalitarian Regimes. Crimes Committed by Totalitarian Regimes: Reports and Proceedings of the 8 April European Public Hearing on Crimes Committed by Totalitarian Regimes*, ed. Peter Jambrek. Ljubljana: Slovenian Presidency of the Council of the European Union, 215–216.

2008. *Bastionul cruzimii. O istorie a Securităţii (1948–1964)*. Iaşi: Polirom.

2008. "The Securitate Legacy – Terror in Romania," in *European Public Hearing on Crimes Committed by Totalitarian Regimes. Crimes Committed by Totalitarian Regimes: Reports and Proceedings of the 8 April European Public Hearing on Crimes Committed by Totalitarian Regimes*, ed. Peter Jambrek. Ljubljana: Slovenian Presidency of the Council of the European Union, 105–109.

2005. "Onişoru, vinovat pentru criza CNSAS," 22 (4 October).

2002. *Banalitatea răului. O istorie a Securităţii în documente 1949–1989*. Bucharest: Polirom.

Oţoiu, Damiana. 2009. "Negocier la (re)constitution de la propriete privee en Roumanie postsocialiste. (Nouveaux) acteurs, (anciennes) strategies," *Options Mediterraneennes*, A92:65–75.

2006. *La (re)construction de la propriete privee en Roumanie post-communiste. "Anciens" vs. "nouveaux" proprietaires?*, paper delivered at the At the Frontier of Land Issues: Social Embeddedness of Rights and Public Policy workshop, Montpellier, France, 17–19 May, available at: http://www.mpl.ird.fr/colloque_foncier/Communications/PDF/Otoiu.pdf (accessed on 26 July 2011).

Pacepa, Ion Mihai. 1990. *Red Horizons. The True Story of Nicolae and Elena Ceausescu's Crimes, Lifestyle and Corruption*. Washington, DC: Regnery Gateway.

Padurean, Claudiu. 2011. "Mormântul lui Mircea Vulcănescu, identificat la Râpa Robilor," *România Liberă* (1 April).

2011. "Torţionarul lui Lucian Blaga, omagiat la Cluj," *România Liberă* (7 January).

Palade, Gabriela. 2002. "Despăgubirile pentru casele naţionalizate, amânate," *Evenimentul Zilei* (29 December).

Palade, Rodica. 2006. "Raportul nu e un rechizitoriu," 22 (19–25 December).

Palonen, Emilia. 2008. "The City-Text in Post-Communist Budapest: Street Names, Memorials, and the Politics of Commemoration," *Geojournal*, 73:219–230.

2006. "Creating Communities: The Postcommunist City-Text of Budapest," *Tr@nsit online*, Vienna: Institut fur die Wissenschaften vom Menschen, available at: http://www.iwm.at/index.php?option=com_content&task=view&id=327&Itemid=334#_ednref24 (accessed on 10 November 2011).

Panaitescu, P. P. 1990. *Istoria Românilor*. Bucharest: Editura Didactică şi Pedagogică.

Papacostea, Şerban. 1996. "Captive Clio: Romanian Historiography under Communist Rule," *European History Quarterly*, 26:181–208.

Parkhurst Ferguson, Priscilla. 1988. "Reading City Streets," *The French Review*, 61:386–397.

Parliamentary Assembly of the Council of Europe. 2005. *Report on the Need for International Condemnation of Crimes of Totalitarian Communist Regimes, Doc.* 10765 (16 December), available at: http://assembly.coe.int/Documents/WorkingDocs/Doc05/EDOC10765.htm (accessed on 30 July 2011).

Pătraşcu Buse, E. 2003. *Lumea pierdută*. Bucharest: Humanitas.
Pavel, Dan. 2006. "Lustraţia – tardivă, nedreaptă, ilogică," *Ziua* (17 April).
2000. "The Textbooks Scandal and Rewriting History in Romania. Letter from Bucharest," *East European Politics and Societies*, 15:179–189.
Pavel, Dan, and Iulia Huia. 2003. *Nu putem decât împreună. O istorie analitică a Convenţiei Democratice, 1989–2000*. Iaşi: Polirom.
Pecican, Ovidiu. 2002. "Cronica unei conflagraţii anunţate," *Observatorul cultural* (January).
Perianu, Rodica. 2009. "Victorie tardivă a foştilor condamnaţi politic," *Obiectiv Vocea Brăilei* (14 May).
Petrescu, Dragoş. 2007. "Dilemmas of Transitional Justice in Post-1989 Romania," in *Lustration and Consolidation of Democracy and the Rule of Law in Central and Eastern Europe*, eds. Vladimíra Dvořáková and Anđelko Milardović. Zagreb: Political Science Research Center, 127–151.
Petriceicu, B. 2003. "NUP în 'procesul comunismului'," *România Liberă* (1 August).
Petrişor, Dorin. 2007. "Iliescu scapă de procesele mineriadei şi revoluţiei," *9AM News* (21 June).
Petrovici, Arina. 2006. "Sorin Antohi – între sferturi de adevăr şi jumătăţi de minciună," *Observator Cultural*, 344:3.
Pinerová, Klára. 2011. *The Fate of Czechoslovak Political Prisoners after Release* (25 August), available at: http://www.politicalprisoners.eu/the-fate-of-czechoslovak-political-prisoners-after-release.html (accessed on 12 October 2011).
Pingel, Falk. 2008. "Can Truth Be Negotiated? History Textbook Revision as a Means to Reconciliation," *Annals of the American Academy of Political and Social Science*, 617:181–198.
Pintilie, Florin. 2004. "Constituirea arhivei Securităţii," *Profil*, 2:6–8.
1998. "Păstrare şi acces la documentele Securităţii aflate în arhivele SRI," 22 (17 November).
Pippidi, Andrei. 2006. "Historical Memory and Legislative Changes in Romania," in *Totalitarian and Authoritarian Regimes in Europe. Legacies and Lessons from the Twentieth Century*, eds. Jerzy W. Borejsza and Klaus Ziemer. Warsaw: Berghahn Books, 35–50.
Popa, Ligia. 2008. "Potrivit Avocatul Poporului, legile lacunare lovesc în dizidenţii clujeni," *Gazeta de Cluj* (4 February).
Popescu, Andrei Luca. 2009. "Condamnaţii politic, reabilitaţi cu 20 de ani întârziere," *România Liberă* (13 May).
Popescu, Corneliu-Liviu. 2002. "Influenţa politică în soluţionarea proceselor privind dreptul de proprietate asupra imobilelor naţionalizate în perioada comunistă şi consecinţele acestora în cauzele împotriva României aflate pe rolul Curţii Europene a Drepturilor Omului," *Revista Româna de Drepturile Omului*, 23:20–40.
Popescu, Cristian Tudor. 1999. "Câte istorii are România?," *Adevărul* (6 October).
1999. "Manualul de Istorie Antinaţională – Crima cu premeditare a Ministerului Educaţiei Naţionale," *Adevărul* (8 October).
Portocală, Radu. 2005. "Deconspirarea crimelor comuniste," *Ziua* (3 March).
"Preşedintele Societăţii Timişoara: Legea Lustraţiei e o victorie parţială," *Evenimentul Zilei* (2 March 2012).
"Preşedintele Ungariei cere reabilitarea foştilor deţinuţi politici," *Agerpress* (24 October 2008).

Pricop, Roxana. 2009. "Fondul Proprietatea vede profit la jumătate, dar creşte salariile," *Ziarul Financiar* (29 March).

"Problema CNSAS, un simptom al unei crize mai grave," 22 (2 March 2004).

"Propunere de reabilitare a soţiei lui Corneliu Coposu şi a altor 15 deţinuţi politici," *Ziarul de Iaşi* (3 November 2000).

Przeworski, Adam. 1991. *Democracy and the Market: Political and Economic Reforms in Eastern Europe and Latin America*. New York: Cambridge University Press.

Putnam, Robert. 1993. *Making Democracy Work: Civic Traditions in Modern Italy*. Princeton: Princeton University Press.

Rabinowicz, E., and J. Swinnen. 1997. "Political Economy of Privatization and Decollectivization of Central and Eastern European Agriculture: Definitions, Issues and Methodology," in *Political Economy of Agrarian Reform in Central and Eastern Europe*, ed. I. F. M. Swinnen. Brookfield: Ashgate.

Racinskas, Ronaldas. 2008. "Historical Justice for Europe: Why, When and How?," in *European Public Hearings on Crimes Committed by Totalitarian Regimes. Crimes Committed by Totalitarian Regimes: Reports and Proceedings of the 8 April European Public Hearing on Crimes Committed by Totalitarian Regimes*, ed. Peter Jambrek. Ljubljana: Slovenian Presidency of the Council of the European Union, 13–19.

Rădulescu, George. 2010. "Marius Oprea: 'Suntem conduşi de circa 10.000 de ticăloşi'," *Adevărul* (21 January).

Răduţă, Magda. 2011. "The Day Before, the Day After: Canonic and Self-Legitimation Changes in the Romanian Literature before and after the Fall of the Communist Regime," in *The Canonical Debate Today: Crossing Disciplinary and Cultural Boundaries*, eds. Liviu Papadima, David Damrosch, and Theo D'haen. Amsterdam: Rodopi, 151–166.

"Raluca Grosescu a adus studiul comunismului în şcoli," *Adevărul* (18 August 2010).

"Raportul Comisiei de anchetă pentru stabilirea adevărului şi eliminarea suspiciunii, neîncrederii şi prezentării false a unor fapte de corupţie cu character grav, pretins săvârşite în perioada ianuarie 1990–decembrie 1991," *Monitorul Oficial al României, partea II-a* (15 May 1992), 2–5.

"Reacţii privind un eventual process al comunismului," *Ziua* (3 March 2005).

"Recunoaşterea, asumarea şi condamnarea genocidului communist," 22 (22 March 2006).

"Recursul la discurs," 22, 45(1998):5–8.

Redress. 2003. *Romania Country Report* (May), available at: http://www.redress.org/downloads/country-reports/Romania.pdf (accessed on 3 October 2011).

"Resurse educaţionale," didactic.ro (2010), available at: http://www.didactic.ro/resurse-educationale (accessed on 21 October 2011).

"Retrocedarea nu trebuie să sacrifice instituţiile de cultură," *Monitorul* (17 June 2002).

Ricoeur, Paul. 2000. *La mémoire, l'histoire, l'oubli*. Paris: Seuil.

Rindzeviciute, Egle. 2011. *Discussing Communism in the Museums of East Central Europe* (23 May), European National Museums EUNAMUS, available at: http://unfoldingeunamus.wordpress.com/2011/05/23/discussing-communism-in-the-museums-of-east-central-europe/ (accessed on 10 November 2011).

Ristache, Roxana. 2005. "Traian Băsescu nu e preocupat de condamnarea regimului totalitar," *România Liberă* (7 July).

Ristea, Nicoleta. 2010. "Motivarea Deciziei nr.1358/21.10.2010 a Curţii Constituţionale, referitoare la excepţia de neconstituţionalitate a prevederilor art.5 alin.(1) lit.a) teza întâi din Legea nr.221/2009," in Lege.ro (10 November), available at: http://www.inlege.ro/2010/11/10/

motivarea-deciziei-nr-135821–10–2010-a-curtii-constitutionale-referitoare-la-exceptia-de-neconstitutionalitate-a-exceptia-de-neconstitutionalitate-a-prevederilor-art-5-alin-1-lit-a-teza-intai-din/ (accessed on 18 October 2011).

Roht-Arriaza, Naomi. 2006. "The New Landscape of Transitional Justice," in *Transitional Justice in the Twenty-First Century. Beyond Trust versus Justice*, eds. Roht-Arriaza, and Javier Mariezcurrena. Cambridge: Cambridge University Press, 1–16.

"Romania Offers Piddling Compensation to Former Political Prisoners," *The Romanian Digest* (October 2010), available at: http://www.hr.ro/digest/201010/digest.htm (accessed on 3 October 2011).

"Romanian Daily Publishes List of Securitate Agents Working in Intelligence," Foreign Broadcast Information Service, FBIS-EEU-2002–0405 (28 March 2002), available at: http://cryptome.org/ro-spy-list.htm (accessed on 20 February 2011).

"Romanian Parliament Suspends President," Radio Free Europe/Radio Liberty (19 April 2007), available at: http://www.rferl.org/content/article/1075960.html (accessed on 28 January 2012).

"Romania's Iliescu Says Holocaust Comments Taken out of Context," *Haaretz* (29 July 2003).

Roper, Steve. 1994. "The Romanian Revolution from a Theoretical Viewpoint," *Communist and Post-Communist Studies*, 27:401–410.

Rosenberg, Tina. 1996. *The Haunted Land: Facing Europe's Ghosts after Communism*. New York: Vintage.

Rusan, Romulus, ed. 2005. *Cei care au spus NU. Oponenţi şi dizidenţi în anii '70 şi '80*. Bucharest: Fundaţia Academia Civică.

Ruse, L., and F. Negroj. 2006. "Băsescu a încasat primele huiduieli de când e preşedinte," *Gândul* (5 April).

Rushton, Sharon. 2011. *No Easy Shore*. No place: Rushton Press.

Sabou, Alina. 2011. "Neaplicarea unei legi, la instanţele din Timişoara, aminteşte de tribunalele staliniste din anii '50," *Opinia Timişoarei* (10 March).

Safran Naveh, Gila. 2004. "Violence as Culture: 'Educating' Political Prisoners in Romania," in *Cultural Shaping of Violence. Victimization, Escalation, Response*, ed. Myrdene Anderson. West Laffayete: Purdue University Press, 258–267.

Samuelli, Annie. 1997. *Woman behind Bars in Romania*. London: Frank Cass.

Săraru, Dinu, and Victor Atanasie Stănculescu. 2005. *Generalul Revoluţiei cu piciorul în gips*. Bucharest: Rao.

Savin, Nicoleta. 2010. "25 de ani de la asasinarea lui Gheorghe Ursu," *Realpolitic* (1 December).

"Schimbarea numelor de străzi în Bucureşti," Romania News (23 January 2007), available at: http://www.mail-archive.com/bucuresti@yahoogroups.com/msg02965.html (accessed on 5 April 2012).

Schöpflin, George. 2000. *Nations, Identity, Power: The New Politics of Europe*. London: Hurst.

"Şedinţa Camerei Deputaţilor din 16 noiembrie 1999," *Monitorul Oficial al României, partea II-a* (26 November 1999).

"Şedinţa Camerei Deputaţilor din 26 octombrie 1999," *Monitorul Oficial al României, partea II-a* (4 November 1999).

"Şedinţa Camerei Deputaţilor din 19 octombrie 1999," *Monitorul Oficial al României, partea II-a* (28 October 1999).

"Şedinţa Camerei Deputaţilor din 12 octombrie 1999," *Monitorul Oficial al României, partea II-a* (21 October 1999).
"Şedinţa Camerei Deputaţilor din 3 octombrie 2000," *Monitorul Oficial al României, partea II-a* (11 October 1999).
"Şedinţa Camerei Deputaţilor din 19 martie 2002," *Monitorul Oficial al României, partea II-a* (29 March 2002).
"Sedinţa Camerei Deputaţilor din 28 februarie 2012," *Monitorul Oficial al României, partea II-a* (3 March 2012).
"Şedinţa Camerei Deputaţilor din 29 martie 2005," *Monitorul Oficial al României, partea II-a* (5 April 2005).
"Şedinţa Camerei Deputaţilor din 30 martie 2004," *Monitorul Oficial al României, partea II-a* (8 April 2004).
"Şedinţa comună a Camerei Deputaţilor şi Senatului din 18 decembrie 2006," *Monitorul Oficial al României, partea II-a* (28 December 2006).
"Şedinţa Senatului din 25 martie 1992," *Monitorul Oficial al României, partea II-a* (26 March 1992).
"Şedinţa Senatului din ziua de 5 octombrie 1999," *Monitorul Oficial al României, partea II-a* (18 October 1999).
"Şedinţa solemnă comună a Camerei Deputaţilor şi Senatului din 22 decembrie 1997," *Monitorul Oficial al României, partea II-a* (12 January 1998).
"Serialul Ion Antonescu şi asumarea istoriei," BBC Romanian.com (1 August 2008), available at http://www.bbc.co.uk/romanian/news/story/2008/08/080801_serial_antonescu_episod1.shtml (accessed on 7 July 2012).
Shafir, Michael. 2007. "Raportul Tismăneanu: Note din public şi din culise," *Tribuna* (1–15 March).
1990. "The Isolation of Romania and the Fall of Nicolae Ceausescu," *Report on Eastern Europe*, 1:28–32.
Siani-Davies, Peter. 2006. *The Romanian Revolution of December 1989*. Ithaca: Cornell University Press.
Sikkink, Kathryn. 2011. "Making Tyrants Do Time," *New York Times* (15 September).
2004. *Mixed Signals: US Human Rights Policy and Latin America*. Ithaca: Cornell University Press.
Sikkink, Kathryn, and Carrie Booth Walling. 2007. "The Impact of Human Rights Trials in Latin America," *Journal of Peace Research*, 44:427–445.
Simina, A. 2010. "Cum pregăteşte Boc a treia politizare neconstituţională," *Evenimentul Zilei* (3 February).
Simonca, Ovidiu. 2003. "Sub presiunea societăţii civile. Interviu cu Adrian Ursu," 22 (28 July).
Sislin, John. 1991. "Revolution Betrayed? Romania and the National Salvation Front," *Studies in Comparative Communism*, 29:395–412.
Skaar, Elin. 2011. "Understanding the Impact of Transitional Justice on Peace and Democracy," paper presented at the European Consortium of Political Research conference, Reykjavik, Iceland, 25–27 August.
1999. "Truth Commissions, Trials or Nothing?: Policy Options in Democratic Transitions," *Third World Quarterly*, 20:1109–1128.
Smith, Kathleen. 1996. *Remembering Stalin's Victims. Popular Memory and the End of the USSR*. Ithaca: Cornell University Press.

Snyder, Timothy. 2010. *Bloodlands. Europe between Hitler and Stalin*. New York: Basic Books.

Socaciu, Emanuel Mihail. 2008. "Problema dreptăţii şi restituirea proprietăţilor în România post-comunistă," PhD Dissertation, University of Bucharest.

2007. "Restituţia imobilelor naţionalizate: Preliminarii ale unei evaluări morale," *Sfera politicii*, 128:3–19.

"Societatea civilă cere condamnarea oficială a regimului communist," BBC Romanian Service (10 March 2006), available at: http://www.bbc.co.uk/romanian/news/story/2006/03/060310_condamnare_comunism.shtml (accessed on 26 July 2011).

Soica, Mihai. 2009. "Luptători anticomunişti, exhumaţi din groapa comună," *Evenimentul Zilei* (29 April).

"Sondaj ISS pentru urechile lui Onisoru," *Ziua* (24 April 2003).

"Sorin Antohi a recunoscut colaborarea cu Securitatea," *Ziarul de Iaşi* (5 September 2006).

"Sorin Antohi: Am turnat la Securitate," *Cotidianul* (5 September 2006)

"SRI a fătat o vacă de muls pentru securişti," *Ziarul de Iaşi* (25 July 2003).

Stan, Lavinia. 2012. "Neither Forgiving, Nor Punishing?: Transitional Justice in Romania," in *After Dictatorship: Transitional Justice and Democratic Consolidation: Lessons from Eastern Europe and Latin America*, ed. Vesselin Popovski. Tokyo: United Nations University Press.

2012. "Reckoning with the Communist Past in Romania: A Scorecard," *Europe-Asia Studies*, 64(8):1–20.

2011. "Vigilante Justice in Post-Communist Europe," *Communist and Post-Communist Studies*, 44:307–315.

2011. "Witch-hunt or Moral Rebirth? Romanian Parliamentary Debates on Lustration," *East European Politics and Societies* (6 April), available at: http://eep.sagepub.com/content/early/20.11/04/05/0888325411403922.full.pdf+html (accessed on 21 August 2011).

2010. Communist Nostalgia in Romania (12 December), available at: http://laviniastan.wordpress.com/2010/12/12/communist-nostalgia-in-romania/ (accessed on 25 August 2011).

2010. "Romania: In the Shadow of the Past," in *Central and Southeastern European Politics since 1989*, ed. Sabrina P. Ramet. Cambridge: Cambridge University Press, 379–400.

2009. "National Report on Romania," part of the "How the Memory of Crimes Committed by Totalitarian Regimes is Dealt with in the Member States" project, commissioned by the Direction D: Fundamental Rights and Citizenship of the Directorate-General for Justice, Freedom and Security of the European Commission.

2009. "The Former Soviet Union," in *Transitional Justice in Eastern Europe and the Former Soviet Union: Reckoning with the Communist Past*, ed. Lavinia Stan. London: Routledge, pp. 234–240.

ed. 2009. *Transitional Justice in Eastern Europe and the Former Soviet Union: Reckoning with the Communist Past*. London: Routledge.

2009. "Truth Commissions in Post-Communism: The Overlooked Solution?," *Open Political Science Journal*, 2(2009):1–13, available at: http://www.bentham.org/open/topolisj/openaccess2.html (accessed on 28 January 2012).

2007. "Comisia Tismăneanu între adevăr şi reconciliere," 22 (2–8 March).

2006. "Lustration: The Story of a Failure," *Studia Politica. Romanian Political Science Review*, 6:135–156.

2006. "The Roof over Our Head: Property Restitution in Romania," *Journal of Communist Studies and Transition Politics*, 22:180–205.
2005. *Inside the Securitate Archives* (4 March), Woodrow Wilson Center for International Scholars, Cold War International History Project, available at: http://www.wilsoncenter.org/article/inside-the-securitate-archives (accessed on 17 September 2011).
2004. "Spies, Files and Lies: Explaining the Failure of Access to Securitate Files," *Communist and Post-Communist Studies*, 37:341–359.
2002. "Access to Secret Files: The Trials and Tribulations of a Romanian Law," *East European Politics and Society*, 16:55–90.
2002. "Comparing Post-Communist Governance: A Case Study," *Journal of Communist Studies and Transition Politics*, 18:77–109.
2002. "Moral Cleansing Romanian Style," *Problems of Post-Communism*, 49:52–62.
Stan, Lavinia, and Diane Vancea. 2009. "Old Wine in New Bottles: The Romanian Elections of 2008," *Problems of Post-Communism*, 56:1096–1109.
Stan, Lavinia, and Lucian Turcescu. 2007. *Religion and Politics in Post-Communist Romania*. New York: Oxford University Press.
2000. "The Romanian Orthodox Church and Post-Communist Democratization," *Europe-Asia Studies*, 52:1467–1488.
Stan, Lavinia, and Răzvan Zaharia. 2010. "Romania," *European Journal of Political Research*, 49:1139–1153.
2009. "Romania," *European Journal of Political Research*, 48:1087–1099.
Stan, Liviu. 2011. "Rusaliile Negre. Deportarea în Bărăgan," *Obiectiv Vocea Brăilei* (8 September).
Stan, Valerian. 2009. "Răul communist: amnezie şi amnistie," *New York Magazine* (17 June).
2007. "Tismaneanu Report: Another Delay in the Trial of Communism," *New York Magazine* (6 February).
Stancu, Oana. 2005. "Băsescu şi-a luat ilegal casă de la Primărie," *Jurnalul Naţional* (13 February).
Stănescu, Mircea. 2010. *Reeducarea în România comunistă (1945–1952). Aiud, Suceava, Piteşti, Braşov*. Iaşi: Polirom.
"Statul roman nu respectă întotdeauna hotărârile CEDO," *Evenimentul Zilei* (30 April 2003).
"Statul român trebuie să-şi asume întregul trecut," *România Liberă* (26 March 2005).
Stefănescu, Domniţa. 1995. *Cinci ani din istoria României. O cronologie a evenimentelor decembrie 1989-decembrie 1994*. Bucharest: Maşina de Scris.
"Stenograma Camerei Deputaţilor din 7 February 2006," *Monitorul Oficial al României, partea II-a* (17 February 2006).
"Stenograma Camerei Deputaţilor din 17 octombrie 2005," *Monitorul Oficial al României, partea II-a* (24 October 2005).
"Stenograma şedinţei Camerei Deputaţilor din 10 iunie 1997," *Monitorul Oficial al României, partea II-a* (11 June 1997).
"Stenograma şedinţei Camerei Deputaţilor din 15 iulie 1992," *Monitorul Oficial al României, partea II-a* (16 July 1992).
"Stenograma şedinţei Camerei Deputaţilor din 15 martie 1994," *Monitorul Oficial al României, partea II-a* (16 March 1994), 2–3.

"Stenograma şedinţei Camerei Deputaţilor din 27 mai 2003," *Monitorul Oficial al României, partea II-a* (28 May 2003).
"Stenograma şedinţei Senatului din 2 iunie 1994," *Monitorul Oficial al României, partea II-a* (11 June 1994), 7–16.
"Stenograma şedinţei Senatului din 14 februarie 1992," *Monitorul Oficial al României, partea II-a* (17 February 1992).
"Stenograma şedinţelor comune ale Camerei Deputaţilor şi Senatului din 4 iulie 1994," *Monitorul Oficial al României, partea II-a* (11 July 1994).
"Stenograma şedinţelor comune ale Camerei Deputaţilor şi Senatului din 7 iulie 1994," *Monitorul Oficial al României, partea II-a* (16 July 1994).
"Stenograma şedinţelor comune ale Camerei Deputaţilor şi Senatului din 15 iulie 1992," *Monitorul Oficial al României, partea II-a* (16 July 1992).
Straut, Dan. 2010. "Fondul Proprietatea: raiul speculatorilor, iadul proprietarilor," *Adevărul* (29 August).
Subotic, Jelena. 2009. *Highjacked Justice: Dealing with the Past in the Balkans*. Ithaca: Cornell University Press.
Summary of Property Restitution in Central and Eastern Europe (16 July 2002), available at: http://germany.usembassy.gov/germany/img/assets/8497/property.pdf (accessed on 22 July 2011).
Swart, Mia. 2008. "Name Changes as Symbolic Reparation after Transition: The Examples of Germany and South Africa," *German Law Journal*, 9:105–121.
Tabacu, Horia, and Vlad Teodorescu. 2011. "Generalul Locotenent (r) Nicolae Stan: Elena mai trăia cu trei înalţi activişti. Doi sunt în viaţă," *Evenimentul Zilei* (29 September).
Tănase, Stelian. 2003. *Anatomia mistificării*. Bucharest: Humanitas.
2002. *Acasă se vorbeşte în şoaptă. Dosar & jurnal din anii târzii ai dictaturii*. Bucharest: Compania.
Tănăsoiu, Cosmina. 2007. "The Tismaneanu Report: Romania Revisits Its Past," *Problems of Post-Communism*, 54:60–69.
Tapalagă, Dan. 2007. "Raportul Tismăneanu notat cu şapte. Un interviu cu Michael Shafir," *Ziua de Cluj* (12 January).
Teitel, Ruti. 2001. *Transitional Justice*. Oxford: Oxford University Press.
"The Timişoara Declaration," *Report on Eastern Europe* (6 April 1990): 41–45.
Theissen, Gunnar. 2000. *International Internet Bibliography on Transitional Justice* (27 January), available at: http://userpage.fu-berlin.de/theissen/biblio/ (accessed on 24 August 2011).
Thompson, Janna. 2002. *Taking Responsibility for the Past. Reparation and Historical Justice*. Cambridge: Polity Press.
Tismaneanu, Vladimir. 2011. "Suspended," *The Times Literary Supplement* (12 August), available at: http://www.the-tls.co.uk/tls/public/tlssearch.do?querystring=suspended&sectionId=1797&p=tls (accessed on 28 January 2012).
2008. "Democracy and Memory: Romania Confronts Its Communist Past," *Annals of the American Academy of Political and Social Science*, 617:166–180.
2007. "Confronting Romania's Past: A Response to Charles King," *Slavic Review*, 66:724–727.
2007. *Refuzul de a uita*. Bucharest: Curtea Veche.
2006. "Alexandru Drăghici şi teroarea comunistă în România," *Cotidianul* (27 Aprilie).

2003. *Stalinism for All Seasons: A Political History of Romanian Communism*. Berkeley: University of California Press.

Tismaneanu, Vladimir, and Mircea Mihăeş. 2011. *O tranziţie mai lungă decât veacul. România după Ceauşescu*. Bucharest: Curtea Veche.

Tismăneanu, Vladimir, Dorin Dobrincu, and Cristian Vasile, eds. 2007. *Comisia Prezidenţială pentru Analiza Dictaturii Comuniste din România. Raport Final*. Bucharest: Humanitas.

Transcriptul 'procesului' Nicolae şi Elena Ceauşescu (2008), available at: http://www.ceausescu.org/ceausescu_texts/revolution/trial-ro.htm (accessed on 30 July 2011).

Transparency International. 2010. *Corruption Perception Index 2010 Results*, available at: http://www.transparency.org/policy_research/surveys_indices/cpi/2010/results (accessed on 21 August 2011).

Transitional Justice Data Base (no date), available at: https://sites.google.com/site/transitionaljusticedatabase/transitional-justice-bibliography/europe-and-the-former-soviet-union (accessed on 24 August 2011).

Troncotă, C. 1998. "Securitatea – Începuturile," *Magazin Istoric*, 10(October), available at: http://www.itcnet.ro/history/archive/mi1998/current10/mi24.htm (accessed on 29 May 2008).

Tucker, Avizier. 2006. "Paranoids Must Be Prosecuted. Post-Totalitarian Transitional Justice," in *Retribution and Reparation in the Transition to Democracy*, ed. Jon Elster. New York: Cambridge University Press, 181–205.

"Tudor Postelnicu şi-a executat pedeapsa, a decis instanţa militară," *Mediafax* (29 April 2002).

"Tudor Postelnicu şi alţi opt foşti ofiţeri de Securitate şi Miliţie îşi aşteaptă sentinţa," *Gazeta de Sud* (21 February 2002).

Tudor, Radu. 2002. "Televiziunea Română s-a întrecut pe sine," *Ziua* (25 March).

Turcanu, Florin, and Armand Gosu. 2005. "Manualele opţionale de istorie," 22 (28 June).

"Twenty Years after the Fall, Ghost of Ceausescu's Government still Haunts Romanians," France 24 (25 December 2009).

Udişteanu, Andrei. 2010. "Judecătorul român la CEDO: În multe cazuri, Curtea a constatat nefuncţionalitatea Fondului Proprietatea," *Evenimentul zilei* (14 October).

"UDMR, înfrânt la Senat – primăriile nu mai pot pune nume maghiare străzilor," Ziare.com (1 June 2011), available at: http://www.ziare.com/politica/maghiari/udmr-infrant-la-senat-primariile-nu-mai-pot-pune-nume-maghiare-strazilor-1098509 (accessed on 10 November 2011).

"Un million de dolari despăgubiri," *Evenimentul Zilei* (6 January 2003).

Un parlamentar UE cere monitorizarea 'dosarului Ursu' (no date), Bucharest: Fundaţia Gheorghe Ursu, available at: http://gh-ursu.ong.ro/ziua_spt.htm (accessed on 31 July 2011).

Ursachi, Raluca, and Raluca Grosescu. 2010. "Transitional Criminal Justice in Post-Communist Romania," paper delivered at the Crimes of the Communist Regimes conference, Prague, the Czech Republic, 24–26 February, available at: https://www.ustrcr.cz/data/pdf/konference/zlociny-komunismu/Raluca_Grosescu.pdf (accessed on 10 December 2011).

Valery-Grossu, Nicole. 2002. *Binecuvântată fii, închisoare*. Bucharest: Univers.

van der Merwe, Hugo. 2009. "Delivering Justice during Transition: Research Challenges," in *Assessing the Impact of Transitional Justice: Challenges for Empirical Research*, eds.

Hugo van der Merwe, Victoria Baxter, and Audrey R. Chapman. Washington, DC: United States Institute for Peace, 115–142.
Vasile, Cristian. 2011. "Cinci ani de la Raportul final. Despre o condamnare – nu doar simbolică – a regimului communist," Contributors.ro (17 December), available at: http://www.contributors.ro/cultura/cinci-ani-de-la-raportul-final-despre-o-condamnare-%E2%80%93-nu-doar-simbolica-%E2%80%93-a-regimului-comunist/ (accessed on 15 January 2011).
2005. *Biserica Ortodoxă Română în primul deceniu comunist (1945–1959)*. Bucharest: Curtea Veche.
2004. *Între Vatican şi Kremlin. Biserica Greco-Catolică în timpul regimului communist*. Bucharest: Curtea Veche.
Vasilescu, Oana, and Marina Dohi. 1999. "În manualele de istorie Ţara Românească este denumită 'Ungro-Vlahia'," *Libertatea* (28 September).
Vatulescu, Cristina. 2010. *Police Esthetics. Literature, Film, and the Secret Police in Soviet Times*. Stanford, CA: Stanford University Press.
Verbitsky, Horacio. 2001. "El fin del eufemismo," *Página/12* (6 March), available at: http://members.tripod.com/doska_/democKracia/ElFallo.htm (accessed on 31 July 2011).
Verdery, Katherine. 2003. *The Vanishing Hectare: Property and Value in Postsocialist Transylvania*. Ithaca: Cornell University Press.
1996. *What Was Socialism and What Comes Next?* Princeton: Princeton University Press.
Vieru, Ana-Maria. 2003. "Securitatea a fentat manualul de istorie," *Evenimentul Zilei* (19 November).
1999. "Începând din 2000, piaţă liberă pentru producţia de manual," *Curentul* (1 October).
Vulpe, Marius. 2012. "Antonescu: Lustraţia, demers ratat. PDL, campionul unei cauze care nu i-a aparţinut niciodată," *Evenimentul Zilei* (5 March).
Weissberg, Jay. 2007. "4 Months, 3 Weeks & 2 Days," *Variety* (6 June).
Welsh, Helga. 2010. "Beyond Lustration: Transitional Justice in Central and Eastern Europe," paper delivered at the Meeting of the Council for European Studies, Montreal, Canada, 15–17 April
1996. "Dealing with the Communist Past: Central and East European Experiences after 1990," *Europe-Asia Studies*, 48:413–428.
Wiebelhaus-Brahm, Eric. 2010. *Truth Commissions and Transitional Societies. The Impact on Human Rights and Democracy*. London: Routledge.
Wieviorka, Annette. 1998. *L'ère du témoin*. Paris: Plon.
Winter, Jay. 2008. "Foreword: Historical Remembrance in the Twenty-First Century," *Annals of the American Academy of Political and Social Science*, 617:6–13.
Woolford, Andrew, and R. S. Ratner. 2008. *Informal Reckonings. Conflict Resolution in Mediation, Restorative Justice and Reparations*. New York: Routledge-Cavendish.
Wroe, David. 2009. "East German Victims Lament Lack of Justice," *The Local* (5 November), available at: http://www.nytimes.com/books/first/k/koehler-stasi.html (accessed on 29 August 2011).
Zajda, Joseph, and Rea Zajda. 2003. "The Politics of Rewriting History: New History Textbooks and Curriculum Materials in Russia," *International Review of Education*, 49:363–384.
Zugravu, C. 1995. "Securitatea m-a programat 'turnător'," *Memoria* 10:60.

LEGISLATION

"Codul Penal al României. Lege nr. 15 din 21 iunie 1968," *Monitorul Oficial al României* (16 April 1997).

Constituţia Republicii Populare Române 1948, available at: http://legislatie.resurse-pentru-democratie.org/const_1948.php (accessed on 22 July 2011).

Constituţia României din 1991, available at: http://www.cdep.ro/pls/dic/act_show?ida=1&idl=1 (accessed on 26 July 2011).

Convention on the Non-Applicability of Statutory Limitations to War Crimes and Crimes against Humanity (26 November 1968), available at: http://www2.ohchr.org/english/law/warcrimes.htm (accessed on 10 December 2011).

Decret nr. 11 din 26 ianuarie 1988 privind amnistierea unor infracţiuni şi reducerea unor pedepse (26 January 1988), available at: http://www.legex.ro/Decret-Nr.11-din-26.01.1988–860.aspx (accessed on 24 November 2011).

"Decret-Lege 9 din 31 decembrie 1989," *Monitorul Oficial al României, partea I* (31 December 1989).

"Decret-Lege nr. 3 din 4 ianuarie 1990," *Monitorul Oficial al României, partea I* (5 January 1990).

"Decret-lege nr. 61 din 7 februarie 1990 privind vânzarea de locuinţe construite din fondurile statului către populaţie," *Monitorul Oficial al României, partea I* (8 February 1990).

"Decret-Lege 126 din 24 aprilie 1990," *Monitorul Oficial al României, partea I* (25 April 1990).

"Decretul-Lege 118 din 30 martie 1990 privind acordarea unor drepturi persoanelor persecutate din motive politice de dictatura instaurată cu începere de la 6 martie 1945, precum şi celor deportate în străinătate ori constituite în prizonieri," *Monitorul Oficial al României, partea I* (9 April 1990).

"Legea 187/1999 privind accesul la propriul dosar şi deconspirarea Securităţii ca poliţie politică," *Monitorul Oficial al României, partea I* (9 December 1999).

"Legea nr.10 din 8 februarie 2001 privind regimul juridic al unor imobile preluate în mod abuziv în perioada 6 martie 1945–22 decembrie 1989," *Monitorul Oficial al României, partea I* (14 February 2001).

"Legea nr. 42 din 18 decembrie 1990 pentru cinstirea eroilor-martiri şi acordarea unor drepturi urmaşilor acestora, răniţilor, precum şi luptătorilor pentru victoria Revoluţiei din decembrie 1989," *Monitorul Oficial al României, partea I* (19 December 1990).

"Legea nr. 85 din 22 iulie 1992 privind vânzarea de locuinţe şi spaţii cu altă destinaţie construite din fondurile statului şi din fondurile unităţilor economice sau bugetare de stat," *Monitorul Oficial al României, partea I* (29 July 1992).

"Legea nr. 112/1995, privind reglementarea situaţiei juridice a unor imobile cu destinaţia de locuinţe, trecute în proprietatea statului Legea caselor naţionalizate," *Monitorul Oficial al României, partea I* (29 November 1995).

"Legea nr. 215/2001 a administraţiei publice locale," *Monitorul Oficial al României, partea I* (23 April 2001).

"Legea nr. 247 din 19 iulie 2005 privind reforma în domeniile proprietăţii şi justiţiei, precum şi unele măsuri adiacente," *Monitorul Oficial al României, partea I* (27 October 2005).

"Legea 202/2010 privind unele măsuri pentru accelerarea soluţionării proceselor. Mica reformă a Justiţiei," *Monitorul Oficial al României, partea I* (26 October 2010).

"Legea 221 din 2 iunie 2009 privind condamnările cu character politic şi măsurile administrative asimilate acestora, pronunţate în perioada 6 martie 1945 – 22 decembrie 1989," *Monitorul Oficial al României, partea I* (11 June 2006).

"Legea 341/2004 a recunoştinţei faţă de eroii-martiri şi luptătorii care au contribuit la victoria Revoluţiei române din decembrie 1989, precum şi faţă de persoanele care şi-au jertfit viaţa sau au avut de suferit în urma revoltei muncitoreşti anticomuniste de la Braşov din noiembrie 1987," *Monitorul Oficial al României, partea I* (20 July 2004).

"Legea 568 din 19 octombrie 2001 pentru aprobarea Ordonanţei de urgenţă a Guvernului nr. 214/1999 privind acordarea calităţii de luptător în rezistenţa anticomunistă persoanelor condamnate pentru infracţiuni săvârşite din motive politice, precum şi persoanelor împotriva cărora au fost dispuse, din motive politice, măsuri administrative abuzive," *Monitorul Oficial al României, partea I* (30 October 2001).

"Ordonanţa de Urgenţă nr.16 din 22 februarie 2006 pentru modificarea şi completarea Legii nr. 187/1999 privind accesul la propriul dosar şi deconspirarea Securităţii ca poliţie politică," *Monitorul Oficial al României, partea I* (27 February 2006).

"Ordonanţa de Urgenţă nr.24 din 5 martie 2008 privind accesul la propriul dosar şi deconspirarea Securităţii," *Monitorul Official al României, partea I* (10 March 2008).

"Ordonanţa de Urgenţă nr. 62/2010 pentru modificarea şi completarea Legii nr. 221/2009 privind condamnările cu caracter politic şi măsurile administrative asimilate acestora, pronunţate în perioada 6 martie 1945–22 decembrie 1989 şi pentru suspendarea aplicării unor dispoziţii din titlul VII al Legii nr. 247/2005 privind reforma în domeniile proprietăţii şi justiţiei, precum şi unele măsuri adiacente," *Monitorul Oficial al României, partea I* (1 July 2010).

"Ordonanţă de urgenţă nr. 214/1999 privind acordarea calităţii de luptător în rezistenţa anticomunistă persoanelor condamnate pentru infracţiuni săvârşite din motive politice, precum şi persoanelor împotriva cărora au fost dispuse, din motive politice, măsuri administrative abuzive," *Monitorul Oficial al României, partea I* (30 December 1999).

MOVIES

Bran, M., and J. Mercier, Directors. 2009. *Le chasseur de la Securitate*, DVD movie.

Caranfil, Nicolae, Director. 1993. *E pericoloso sporgersi.*

Codre, Florin, Director. 1990. *Şobolanii roşii.*

Hossu-Longin, Lucia, Director. 1997–2007. *Memorialul Durerii*, 36 episodes.

Mărgineanu, Nicolae, Director. 2002. *Binecuvantată fii, închisoare.*

Director. 1991. *Undeva în Est.*

Marinescu, Şerban, Director. 1993. *Cel mai iubit dintre pământeni.*

Mungiu, Cristian, Director. 2009. *Amintiri din Epoca de Aur.*

Director. 2007. *4 luni, 3 săptămâni şi 2 zile.*

Lucian Pintilie, Director. 2001. *După-amiaza unui torţionar.*

Director. 1992. *Balanţa.*

O Zi la Televiziunea Română în 1988, DVD movie, Bucharest: Institute for the Investigation of Communist Crimes, The Romanian Television and TVR Media, 2008.

Porumboiu, Corneliu, Director. 2006. *12:08 East of Bucharest.*

The Lost World of Communism: Socialism in One Family, documentary (2009), available at: http://www.cosmolearning.com/documentaries/the-lost-world-of-communism-socialism-in-one-family-2009/ (accessed on 24 August 2011).
Truffaut, François, Director. 1966. *Fahrenheit 451*.
Ujică, Adrian, Director. 2010. *Autobiografia lui Nicolae Ceauşescu*.

PERSONAL INTERVIEWS, LETTERS, AND COMMUNICATIONS

Email communication with Claudiu Secaşiu, member of the leadership of the National Council for the Study of Securitate Archives, 7 December 2011.
Email communication with Cosmin Budeanca, 29 March 2012.
Email communication with Raluca Grosescu, 3 February 2012.
Email communication with Răzvan Zaharia, 11 March 2010.
Email communications with Constanţa Lawyer Carmen Lascu, 22 and 23 October 2012.
Email communications with Levente Salat, 27 March 2012 and 1 April 2012.
Letters to the author from Dragoş Petrescu, president of the National Council for the Study of Securitate Archives, 20 December 2011 and 10 January 2012.
Personal interview with Bogdan Murgescu, Bucharest, 3 July 2011.
Personal interview with Cristian Vasile, Bucharest, 30 June 2011.
Personal interview with Cosmin Budeanca, Bucharest, 28 June 2011.
Personal interview with Damiana Oţoiu, Bucharest, 29 June 2011.
Personal interview with Gabriel Andreescu, Bucharest, 29 June 2011.
Personal interview with Mircea Stănescu, Bucharest, 29 June 2011.
Personal interview with Raluca Grosescu, Bucharest, 28 June 2011.

Index